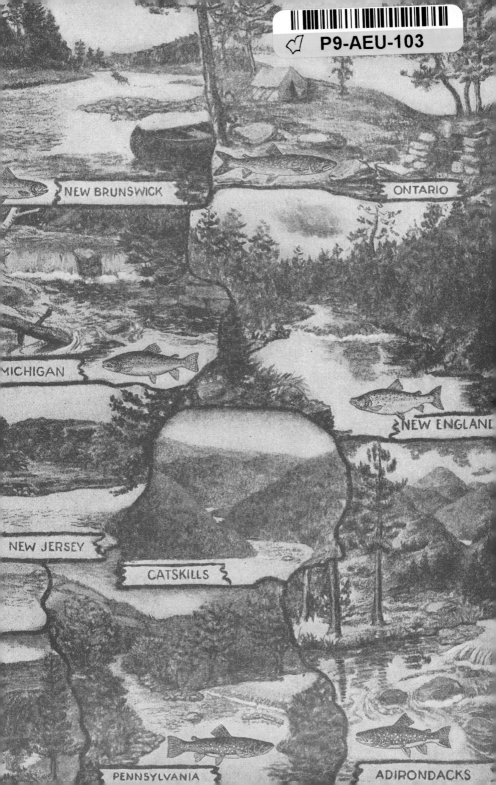

NEW BRUNSWICK

ONTARIO

MICHIGAN

NEW ENGLAND

NEW JERSEY

CATSKILLS

PENNSYLVANIA

ADIRONDACKS

This Book Belongs To

2/11/46

Angelo J. Accurso

DOLLY VARDEN TRUUT
Wildlife Conservation Stamp
© 1946 National Wildlife Federation, Washington, D.C.

PUBLISHED NOVEMBER, 1938
REPRINTED SIX TIMES
EIGHTH PRINTING, OCTOBER, 1944
NINTH PRINTING, JULY, 1945

TROUT

RAY BERGMAN
Author of "Just Fishing"

FLY PLATES IN FULL COLOR PAINTED BY
DR. EDGAR BURKE

PHOTOGRAPHS OF FLY TYING BY
CHARLES S. KRUG

ALSO MANY DIAGRAMS IN LINE BY
IVIN SICKLES

ALFRED A. KNOPF: NEW YORK
1945

To you all

THE MANY GOOD FELLOWS I KNOW AND HAVE
FISHED WITH, AND THOSE WHOSE PATHS MAY
NEVER CROSS MINE EXCEPT THROUGH THE
MEDIUM OF THESE PAGES. THIS IS MY VISIT WITH
YOU, OUR FISHING ADVENTURE TOGETHER. I
TRUST IT WILL BE ENJOYABLE, INSTRUCTIVE AND
MEMORABLE. WHEN I AM GONE; WHEN ALL
WHO NOW READ THESE PAGES HAVE PASSED
BEYOND, I HOPE THAT "TROUT" WILL CON-
TINUE TO LIVE, PERHAPS TO INSTILL IN FUTURE
GENERATIONS A LOVE AND UNDERSTANDING
OF ANGLING

Introduction

PERHAPS *an introduction to a book such as this should be written by someone else, especially someone prominent in the field of fresh water fishing. But because I have always fought my own battles through the business of life I felt that "Trout" also should go out into the world without any outside help from a name which might increase its sale. I felt that it should stand on its own merits; on the strength of its character; on my own efforts in my chosen field of endeavor. Therefore I did not ask anyone to write an introduction.*

But it seems that this type of book must have one. It is customary and expected. So I had to do it myself.

Many hours of hard work, sacrifice and self-denial went into these pages. What has been written is frank and accurate according to my personal experiences. There has been an earnest desire to segregate important facts and to present them graphically. When a problem has been encountered it has been met and overcome even though in some cases it took hours to write a single page. I have relaxed and written from the heart as well as the brain; drawing from thirty-five years of experience gained in waters from coast to coast. I have written it as if it were addressed directly to a dear friend who had stopped in to see me and to ask for information. As the pages were written

INTRODUCTION

I re-lived the experiences described—became transported to the localities where they occurred even though actually they were written at home.

To pick out a title for this volume was a difficult job—or at least I made it so. For days I struggled with ideas. Then one evening Herbert S. Pettit, friend and neighbor, dropped in to see how I was progressing with the manuscript and I told him what a time I was having with this simple problem. Why not call it "Trout" he suggested. Why not indeed? As always, simplicity proved to be the need and so Pettit's suggestion was used.

Because "Trout" is sincere in purpose and thought I know it is genuine and think you will like it. I trust we will become friends because of it.

RAY BERGMAN

Contents

Illustrations

CHAPTER ONE

Early Experiences

As far back as I can remember I have been passionately fond of the outdoors. Memories of childhood are mostly vague and dreamlike but I have some recollections of these early days which have survived the years. Oddly enough they are of rainstorms and in them I am either fishing with a hand line from a long stone dock jutting out into the Hudson River or else I am wandering along the rocky shores of the river in the vicinity of Hook Mountain, that isolated northern rampart of the Palisades.

With startling reality I can still feel the sting of rain on my face, blown against it by the eastern gale. Vividly I can see the angry waters of the river buffeting the dock and the shore, the border of light gray along the eastern horizon and the restless black clouds which seemed to form directly on that border of light and then rush madly across the sky finally to bank in huge masses against the western horizon.

The catching of fish seems insignificant in these memories of the play of the elements and I don't remember much about it but as I see it now I believe that the fishing was simply an excuse to get out in the open, to breathe air that came to me directly over open spaces, to face nature when she bared her soul. I remember plainly that my favorite wind was a howling northeaster, the sort of a wind which usually brought a three-day storm. During such periods even the village streets were deserted and quiet. To me this condition was ideal and I could not be kept indoors. Wild storms appealed to me, transported me back through the ages to primitive days, brought me thrills which made my body quiver with sheer physical delight. I would rather face the storms at the river's edge or from a mountain top than to have many dollars' worth of fireworks on the 4th of July and in the eyes of youth this was a mighty comparison indeed.

Somehow I feel that the elements and all life, whether human or otherwise, are directly related, so much so that anyone who is sincerely enraptured by the wonders of nature stands very close to the great beyond. To such souls fishing is an outlet to the feelings, a surcease from life's trials. Being so closely attuned to nature's whims I drifted naturally into out-of-door pursuits and fishing seemed to be the one sport which best gratified that innate craving for an intimacy with those forces of which I knew so little. Is it any wonder that I made the study of fishing my life's work?

*   *   *   *   *   *

When I was a boy conditions were quite different from to-day. I am old enough to have experienced the old-fashioned ways of the latter part of the 19th century and the rapid-fire progress of the 20th. I saw the horse and carriage give way to the automobile, the dusty roads change rapidly from macadam to tarvia and then to smooth ribbons of concrete. Each advance of progress had its effect on the fishing. I started writing about angling when the outdoor magazines paid little or nothing for stories, when their files were filled with material submitted without any thought of recompense, submitted simply because the contributors wanted to see their names in print. I saw these conditions gradually change as more people became interested in fishing and demanded first class articles in the magazines they read. The leading magazines grew in size and their contents in quality which was as it should be. I received only thirty-five dollars for my first story and it ran through two issues of the magazine in which it was published. This periodical was later absorbed by another and has since lost its identity.

Naturally my early fishing was confined to bait which was well enough because it taught me where the trout were located. As a matter of fact no one in our territory ever used flies nor did they know anything about fly fishing. Even as recently as eighteen years ago I doubt if there were more than six fly fishermen in our community. I had a fairly accurate check-up on this because at the time I happened to own the most popular sporting goods store in the county. I tried my best to get others interested in fly fishing but it was slow work and when I sold out most of the liberal fly stock was left on the shelves. There were fifty buyers of bait hooks to one customer for flies. It is quite different today. There are now more fly than bait fishermen so that flies and fly tying materials find a ready sale.

Considering these things it is somewhat remarkable that I started fly fishing as early in my life as I did. However this was due mostly to chance although my keen desire to find out the hidden secrets of fishing had something to do with it. You see, even after everyone else had quit for the season I kept on trying though I didn't get anything. I felt sure there was a way to catch trout at that time of the year and kept trying to find out how to do it. Because of that I happened to be at the right place at the right time and so met a man who was able to show me that trout could be taken late in the season.

I shall never forget that day. It was early July and I was eating lunch on the bank of a meadow stretch of my favorite stream. I had fished down some two miles and had caught only two six inch trout. When this angler came along he stopped for a chat and showed me one of the prettiest catches of Brook Trout I had ever seen.

Here was a chance to find out just what I wanted and I grasped the opportunity. I told him of the poor luck I had been having since the middle of June and how the other fellows in town said all the fish were caught out during April and May and made fun of me because I felt differently about it. " I just couldn't believe that," I said, " because if it were true we wouldn't get any fish the next spring and we always do. Now you have proved that I was right and they were wrong." *

The man smiled indulgently. " All the trout are never caught out. Sometimes they get very scarce and the fewer there are the wiser they seem to get. Some become too smart to be taken even by the most expert and these fish constitute the seed which keeps the streams stocked. But around here there are always plenty of trout left after the bait fishermen get through. You see, hardly anyone ever fishes these streams with a fly and that is about the only way to take them during the latter part of the season—except after a heavy rain when worms are best. That is why you hear that cry of ' fished out ' so often. Now just watch. See that clump of alders? "

He pointed to a group of bushes at a bend some forty feet downstream. " It is quite deep there," he explained, " and the trout stay well under the brush at this time of day but I think I can stir up some action."

He made a cast of some forty-five feet, dropping the flies lightly at the very bend of the stream and so close to the alders that they almost snagged. He let them sink for a few moments and then with a slight twitch of the rod started them jerking through the water. On the third jerk I saw a flash of pink and the water boiled. His first cast had brought results. He landed the fish and killed it by rapping it on the head with his knife. He then placed it on some green moss near by and we looked at it exultingly. The man dismounted his rod and made preparations to leave. " Well, good-bye," he said. " Take that fish home and show it to those boys who make fun of you."

* At this time restocking streams was very uncertain and legal sized fish were not used for the purpose. The stream in question had not been stocked for several years.

Such generosity overwhelmed me. I stammered my thanks incoherently. After he was gone I was sorry that I had not asked his name and address or perhaps I might have made arrangements to meet him on the stream again. There were so many questions I would have liked to ask him. It seemed to be so hard to find out anything about fly fishing in those days. Nevertheless, the incident had been very enlightening and the knowledge gained was absorbed completely so that the effects were lasting. The man probably forgot the incident within a few days but I never did and I often wonder what he would think if he knew the thought his passing interest had provoked.

I did not have any fly outfit nor enough money to buy one immediately so I spent the next few weeks observing the stream instead of fishing. In the meantime I saved every cent of my allowance and what I made on my paper route against the purchase of an outfit which I hoped that I could get before the close of the season. Incidentally I found the occupation of watching the stream so fascinating that temporarily I forgot the fishing. This was the best thing that could have happened and I learned more during this time than I had in all my previous fishing experience. I spent tedious hours crouched in the alders which sheltered deep holes and from these vantage points I could see how the trout acted. I did not realize that I was building up my fund of fishing lore that would be invaluable to me in the years to come. I did it simply because I was intensely interested and wished to find out how and where the trout did their feeding in the late season. Here are some of the important things I discovered and which later improved my game.

First, that most of the trout, when not feeding, stayed close to the bank in the deepest parts of the deepest holes near their feeding grounds.

Second, that nearly all of the trout in the brook preferred shade and thick cover when not actually engaged in feeding, also that they had certain hours when they fed most. This was in the late afternoon as soon as the direct rays of the sun left the water and in the early morning immediately after daybreak up until the time that the full force of the sun made its presence felt on the water. During these periods they left the deep holes and took strategic locations along the shallow stretches which connected the various holes.

Third, that these particular trout preferred to feed under water rather than on the surface. I couldn't tell what they were taking because whatever it was could not be seen but when I cleaned a trout I caught just before the end of the season I found that it was filled with a solid black mass which looked like scum but which I diagnosed as very small underwater insects. Occasionally when some large juicy looking flies floated down on the surface they would take them but by far most of the action took place under water.

Fourth, that the effects of vibration were very disturbing. The surrounding ground being very boggy it trembled on the slightest provocation and sent the warning vibrations down to the bed of the stream. The instant the trout felt these vibrations they immediately scurried for cover where they stayed for considerable time before venturing forth again. This time varied greatly. Sometimes they would stay under cover for only a half hour. At other times they would not come out again until the next feeding period. It showed clearly how one could easily spoil his chances of taking fish by making a careless approach. Six times while I was watching, a cow caused the vibrations and in each case the trout went for cover. If the cow stayed on the bank for a half hour or longer the trout came out again and did not seem to mind the presence of the animal. They seemed to know that the cow was harmless and associated with the animal the vibrations which frightened them.

I managed to get a nondescript fly outfit together before the end of the season and started fishing again. The results were far from satisfying. I ruined my chances on every stretch at the very first cast. Because I did not know any better I thought my outfit quite swell but in reality the rod was heavy, cumbersome and dead and the line did not fit it. Besides, the guides were spaced so far apart that the line kept wrapping around the bamboo between them. Of course it was a cheap outfit so one could not expect much but it was certainly discouraging to learn to cast with it. This first experience with fly casting was a veritable nightmare. All I had to guide me was that memory of one cast I had seen made by an accomplished fisherman. Half the time the line was tangled around my body and count- less times I had to cut the fly from my clothes or my person. I always frightened the trout at the first cast and then struggled with the outfit for an hour after, fishing water from which the fish had disappeared. On the last day of the season I caught one trout by accident and this saved me from utter rout. With this fish to cheer me I faced the closed season with a peaceful mind filled with dreams of the season to come. For I had caught a trout on a fly and had done it at a time when the other fellows said it couldn't be done. That was glory enough for an unsophisticated fisherman.

It took time and many a heartache to correct the faults of my outfit and my casting. More than a year had passed before I knew that the line I had was entirely too light for the rod, and that the guides had to be spaced much closer than they were on my rod to give best results. I have no vivid memories of this period so can't tell much about it but I must have succeeded in getting things ironed out very well as is shown by the following notes made several years later.

" I find that these trout of the Crumb Creek meadow stretch cannot be taken during July and August unless I use extreme care, not only in the approach but in the cast and the selection of flies. The flies must be of subdued coloration, they must alight on the water softly and sink immediately and the retrieve must be made slowly and with deliberation. It takes from fifteen to twenty-five minutes to work to a suitable casting location and the slightest misstep on the way is fatal to my chances.

"When I started fishing this water the trout weren't so particular. As long as the flies alighted softly and you did not frighten the trout by your approach they would rise no matter how you handled the retrieve. This last season it has been different and for some time I haven't been taking any fish. I felt sure that the way I handled the flies was the cause of the trouble and as I had been retrieving them fast close to the surface I changed today and fished them slow and deep. It seemed to be the solution as I took a good trout from each stretch. Would probably have taken more but they ran so large that I had to go to the water's edge to land them and so spoiled my chances of taking any more from those particular locations."

My notes for the next six years are of scattered experiences and rather incomplete but through them I find a continual striving to perfect my fly fishing. Some of the experiences are worth recounting, especially the early trips to the Catskills. Such trips were real events in those days. They took a lot of time and were quite expensive. We did not have cars to carry our duffel. It had to be carried by hand and our means of transportation were the railroads and the old horse and wagon at the end of our journey. There was something sweetly pleasing about those days which seems to have vanished with the coming of the automobile. Our simple pleasures were most enjoyable and the air did not carry the taint of gasoline or the atmosphere of irreverence which seems to be generated by the numbers of people who now frequent the mountains and who are not in accord with the true spirit of nature. All lovers of the out-of-doors can sense this disturbing influence although they probably do not give much thought to the real cause of the feeling. The streams alone offer relief that is complete. When one feels the rush of cold water against his waders and pits his skill against the natural instincts and wariness of the trout everything else is lost in the sheer joy of the moment.

It must be admitted that our early fishing in the Catskills was crude. There were plenty of fish and no competition to speak of so you did not have to be very skillful to be successful. The notes I made in those days do not offer much in the way of angling knowledge. They are but simple accounts of the fish caught. We fished with worms more than we did with flies and when we used flies it was with a hit or miss careless-ness which did not tend to develop one's fishing technique. I believe that during this period I really went backward rather than forward. It shows how one's progress may be retarded by fishing places where the trout are easy to catch.

But as time went on and automobiles became more plentiful, there began to be a vast difference in these conditions. Here and there we came across skillful anglers who took trout when the rest of us could not do a thing. A few such experiences started me thinking and from then on my notes began to show the influence of constructive thought thus becoming of some value. Consider the following quotation which was taken from the first notes worth mentioning ever since the experiences on Crumb Creek.

" It is becoming increasingly difficult to catch trout. Our last three trips to Sundown have been very poor. Lots of fishermen and no one caught anything except one fly fisherman I met who was far above the average. He did not seem to have the least trouble catching them and thought the fishing exceptionally good. Clearly something is wrong with our methods and our tackle. I didn't want to bother the man but I did find out that he used 9 foot leaders about half as thick as our 3 and 6 foot ones. I also noticed that he did not give the flies any motion, just let them float as they would with the current. It has started me thinking and my thoughts are not very complimentary to us.

PLATE NO. 1
Wet Flies

Abbey	Academy	Adder	Adirondack	Admiral	Alder
Alexandria	Allerton	Apple Green	Arthur Hoyt	Artful Dodger	Babcock
Barrington	Baldwin	Beauty	Beamer	Bee	Beamis Stream
Beatrice	Beeman	Belgrade	Big Meadow	Bishop	Bisset
Black Dose	California Black Gnat	Black Gnat Silver	Black Palmer Red Tag	Black June	Black Moose
Black Prince	Black Quill	Block House	Blue Blow	Blue Bottle	Blue Dun
Blue Jay	Blue Professor	California Blue Quill	Bob Lawrence	Bog Pond	Bostwick

Full descriptions of the flies on this plate will be found on pages 408–409.

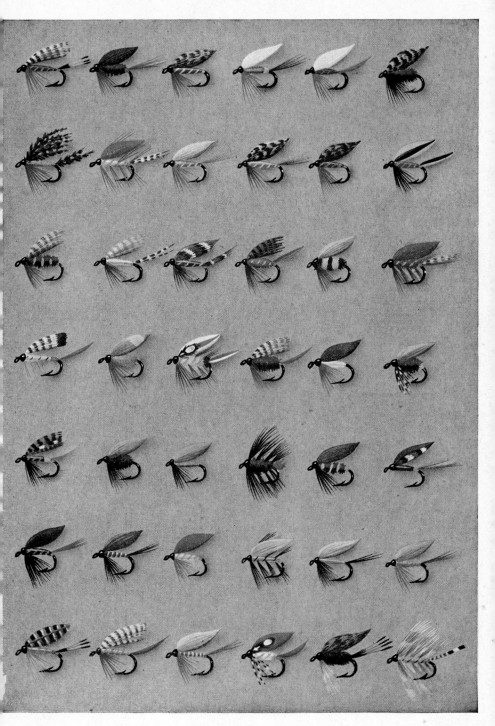

PLATE No. 1

" After seeing this man I found a pond formed by a small spring brook which is filled with trout, some of them as large as 15 inches, as far as I could judge from seeing them under water. Tried my best to get one but my coarse tackle scared them. I finally put on a worm, cast it out and waited. After two hours I got a bite and took a ten incher. Don't feel a bit satisfied with myself. It all shows that I've been standing still for several years—worse than that, I've been sliding backward. Next week I'm coming back with suitable tackle and really try to do some fishing."

That I meant what I wrote is proved by the notes made the following week.

" It was dumb of me to forget my experiences on Crumb Creek. It was all due to the easy fishing we've been having in the Catskills. Here I have been fishing like a novice when I have had experiences which should have taught me better. It all came back today as I stood on the banks of the spring pond. Here were trout in absolutely still water which was clear as crystal. You could not get near the bank by walking in an upright position without causing a lot of excitement among the trout living in it. I found that out as I approached the first time. I sat down and stayed perfectly still for an hour before attempting to fish.

" Made a bungle with my first cast and scared the fish again. This necessitated another wait and I made it more than an hour to be sure that the trout had forgotten about it. Remembering Crumb Creek I wet my flies and leader thoroughly before making the cast. Still influenced by old memories I let the flies sink before starting the retrieve and placed the cast so that they went to one side of the school instead of directly over them. As the retrieve progressed I saw some shadowy forms start after the flies and then the reflections on the surface hid them from my sight. The next instant I felt a tug and connected with a really good fish—about 1½ pounds. Of course

I was elated and proud, in fact I was so excited that I quit fishing and rushed back to camp to show my fish."

Subsequently my experiences at this pond taught me many useful facts. It was there that I discovered you could approach trout with less chance of disturbing them if you did so with the sun at your back. At the time I did not know why this was so but later on I realized it was because the sunlight blinded them and so they did not see you silhouetted against the sky. There are many interesting angles to this which I shall take up exhaustively in another chapter. I think that the most important thing that the spring pond taught me was the necessity for perfect casts, with fine long leaders and proper manipulation. After I learned how to take trout from this place consistently my results in the main stream immediately showed improvement. I was able to get fish from the most difficult still waters, places which we had formerly passed by unless the stream was discolored when we fished them with bait. Of course I was not a master at the game. Usually I was satisfied with one or two fish from each still water. But it was a step in the right direction and as long as I kept thinking constructively I was bound to improve as the years went by.

The medium fast, smooth-topped glides bothered me for a long time. Occasionally the fast skittering method worked but it was very uncertain. When I fished from the side I was invariably too late on the strike, especially when I let the flies float down on a slack line which seemed to be by far the most effective way of fishing them. Finally I overcame the trouble by a very simple thing. Far up on the leader, near the line, I tied on a Coachman or a White Miller so that I could follow the progress of the flies as they floated downstream. On my first attempt with this cast I noted that the light-colored indicator fly made several peculiar motions during the course of its float but because I didn't know any better I thought they were caused by the water currents. Once, however, I felt a slight tug at the moment the motion occurred and then I realized that it was caused by a trout taking one of the lower flies. From then on I struck no matter how slight the motion of the indicator fly was and at once began to catch trout. From that time on I advanced rapidly. It seemed to be the one thing needed to spur me on to greater efforts. I learned to keep my nerves at hair trigger tension so that I reacted instantaneously to anything which was the least bit suggestive of a contrary action on the part of fly, line and leader. Every shadow or flash of light was treated as a striking fish. After a time I found that I could sense things which my eyes did not see but I must admit that sometimes my nerves played me false and I found myself striking to the shadow of a bird flying overhead or to the flash of a leaf or twig twisting and turning in the current. But this all went with the game and more often than not these never-failing reactions produced a fish when the strike was made. Usually I was more surprised than the trout every time this happened, even after the method became an old story as far as I was concerned.

It was subtle fishing and developed intuitive reactions to a remarkable extent. Before long I was doing it all unconsciously and was seeing things which happened under water. That is one of the important educational angles of wet fly fishing. It trains the eye to recognize significant trifles and to pick out both fish and pocket holes from the confusion of rapidly moving water.

At the same time I found that I had to be in the proper mood to have success when fishing a wet fly. If I wasn't I usually failed miserably. It was this fact that started me fishing with a dry fly. I found that I could handle the floating fly easier than wet flies and it did not make as much difference if I felt a bit out of sorts. This is readily understandable. The dry fly is always in plain sight. I could tell just what was going on so it was much easier to do what I wanted to do. Then too it did not require such nerve tension. However I must warn all beginners that the dry fly game is an insidious one. It creeps upon you unawares and unless you fight the tendency you will eventually fish in no other way. And to keep in the pink of wet fly perfection you must follow it consistently. It takes only a few weeks to lose that fine sense of perception which is needed to do it properly but it often takes much longer than that to regain it once you get out of practice.

Sometimes I wonder if it isn't best to have plenty of hard knocks when learning how to fish. There isn't any doubt that the things we learn from our own observations and mistakes stay by us while the things we learn from reading and study are easily forgotten. I know that I never gained any substance from what I read until after I had started to think things out for myself. After that the experiences of others were real and I learned a great deal from them because I could put myself in the place of the writers. Always keep in mind that the way to get the most out of reading and study is to supplement it with actual practice.

Many years have passed since my first experiences at fishing but the memories of them remain to keep me company during many a thoughtful hour. If you would like to preserve your memories, keep a diary of your experiences. In later years it will serve to bring back to you many of the days you would like to live over again. No fish will ever give you the same thrill as your first good trout. One of the penalties of becoming experienced is the fact that you become somewhat blasé and so lose some of the acute sensations which attend first experiences. Not that you like fishing less. Far from it. You find that your love for the sport grows with the years. But you will no longer tremble and throb as you put your net under a large old trout. It will be just another fish. I know I wish I could once again experience the thrill which came with the catching of my first big fish. There was something about it that cannot be compared with any other sensation. But on the other hand there are other interests to absorb the old timer, the greatest of which is to get the best of some knotty angling problem. If this book serves to stimulate your own powers of observation and common sense then I shall feel that it has served its purpose.

CHAPTER TWO

Wet Fly Fishing

I N DISCUSSING the methods and uses of wet flies it is necessary to reduce all explanations to the simplest form so that beginners at wet fly fishing will derive some benefit from them. I trust that the experienced angler will forgive me when I appear too obvious and will realize that it is only by so doing that I can hope to be of some help to those who have not had previous training in the art. It is a common fault for experts at any game to overlook many things which have an acute bearing on it simply because they are so well versed that they cannot conceive of anyone else not knowing the fundamentals.

As a matter of fact, apparently it is the insignificant things which really mark the dividing line between success and failure. That you cast so well that others compliment you for your skill is not so important, but that you handle the flies in some particular and almost indescribable way may be very important indeed. You may gather from this that I am not particularly interested in perfect-form casting and that is very true. The main thing is to have the flies alight correctly on the place where they are most likely to produce results. After that they should be handled in the most efficacious way for the time, location and type of water. If you become a perfect-form caster while achieving the necessary results so much the better but it is best to concentrate on the other points rather than on form and the casting will usually take care of itself. In this connec-

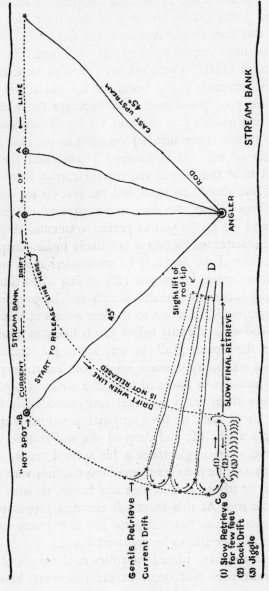

STREAM BANK

LINE

CAST UPSTREAM 45°

ROD

A

OF

A

ANGLER

DRIFT

STREAM BANK

45°

"HOT SPOT" B

CURRENT

START TO RELEASE LINE HERE

DRIFT WHEN LINE IS NOT RELEASED

Slight lift of rod tip

D

SLOW FINAL RETRIEVE

Gentle Retrieve
Current Drift

Slow Retrieve
for few feet

C

(1) Slow Retrieve
for few feet

(2) Back Drift

(3) Jiggle

(1)

(2)

(3)

WET FLY "Natural Drift"

tion let me say that some of the best fishermen I know could not be called pretty casters but they do cast their flies so that they act the way they should and catch the fish.

One of the most important methods of fishing the wet fly is the "Natural Drift." There are several ways to accomplish this, the most generally useful being the up and across stream cast. You take your position directly opposite the water you wish to fish and make a cast at about a forty-five degree angle to the opposite side. (See sketch.) As soon as the cast is completed the tip of the rod is lowered a trifle and then kept pointed directly at the flies as the current carries them downstream. The line should be slack and yet just on the verge of being taut. This allows the flies to be affected naturally by the current and yet leaves you in perfect command if you get a strike. If the water below you is not likely to be occupied by fish then the float of the flies may be terminated at an angle of about forty-five degrees below you (B) or just when they have started to drag across the stream. Watch and be prepared for a rise at this particular position as it often occurs at this point. However, if the water directly below you is likely to hold some trout then let the flies drag all the way across the stream until they come to a stationary position below you. Let them play in this water a moment or two and then if a strike is not forthcoming retrieve them for a few feet and immediately let the current pull them back to their original position. Vary this procedure by a slight lift and drop of the rod instead of the longer retrieve, even jiggle them a bit several times. If this does not bring a strike then start retrieving the flies very slowly until only ten or fifteen feet of line and leader remains below the end of the rod. At this point lift the flies preparatory to another cast. Sometimes you will get a rise at the very moment you start to make the lift so be prepared for it.

As a rule, if you have placed your flies in the right place to start with, most rises will occur at the following locations:

from A to A; at B just at the moment the flies begin to drag; at C when you are working the flies in the small area below you as described, or between C and D when you are retrieving. (See sketch.) Inasmuch as the positions from A to A are the most likely places for the trout to be, provided you have started your flies at the most effective point, most of the rises will occur in this locality or at B which is well known to wet fly anglers as a "hot spot." I have often watched a trout look over the flies between A and A but refuse them for some reason only to follow and rise viciously just when the flies started to drag. I have also noticed many anglers missing this chance to take a trout by lifting their flies too quickly. Many fishermen seem to think that it is absolutely necessary to get in as many casts per hour as possible; that the number of casts made will determine the size of the catch. This does not work out in practice because a desire to make casts rapidly tends to make the angler slight the actual fishing of the flies which, after all, is the thing that catches the trout. Fish out each cast completely. Flies will not catch fish while they are in the air.

As a general rule it is best to have the sun at your back when fishing with this method—first because it allows you to see the flies clearly and second because it decreases the chances of the fish seeing you. Even if the hole under the bank or brush is in deep shade it is to your advantage to have the sun at your back because the glare on the water between you and the fish acts as a cover to your operations. Of course under some conditions rocky cliffs or bright colored light reflecting vegetation will create counter rays of light which changes this condition to a certain extent; also when the sun is near the horizon your shadow may have some effect on the fish, but on the whole you cannot go far wrong by following this hint. Just remember that fish are blinded by direct bright light the same as we are and choose your fishing locations accordingly. The accompanying diagram will serve to illustrate this graphically. Naturally a reversal of this condition would mean that your eyes are disturbed by the sun and that the trout can readily see you unless you are far enough away so that his line of sight does not carry to you.

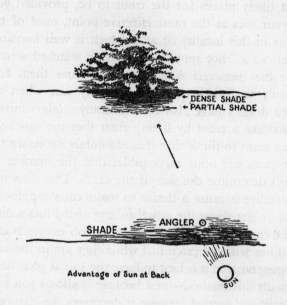

Advantage of Sun at Back

Every rocky stream contains many pocket holes which are a bit difficult to locate. Unless you fish very carefully you are bound to skip many of these pockets. If they are shallow you can see the trout rush away from them as you get close. For this reason, unless you know the water thoroughly, it is best to fish all broken water in a very painstaking manner, being sure not to miss any part of it. Often you will go through most of a pocket stretch without getting a rise so that you get discouraged and start skipping places here and there. As a rule this means that you are passing up opportunities to take fish; the very best chances of all, according to my personal experiences. It was only after I made it a point to fish these places ordinarily neglected that I began to show a decided improvement in my average catch. Of course when you have been over a section of pocket water a great many times you get to know it quite well so that you do not miss these spots but even here you must not be guided too much by past experiences. Every once in a while I find that pockets which have been unproductive for a long while will suddenly start to be very productive. For this reason I do not hesitate to advise a minute covering of all pocket stretches regardless of what may be your personal opinion of them. Only by doing this can you be sure that you have taken advantage of all opportunities.

This type of water requires different technique than fishing bank pockets which have no badly broken water between them and the angler. It is quite imperative to use a short line, not more than twenty feet at the most and in many cases even less than that. Fortunately this is possible in water of this character as long as you proceed cautiously and do not cause too much disturbance with your feet when wading. You really do nothing more than flick the flies to each spot but you do it systematically so that you do not skip any hidden pockets. You should pay especial attention to the sides, back and front of all sizeable rocks, both sunken and those which show above the surface. Let the flies float around the rocks with the line held so that they do it quite naturally even though the line is kept taut. Following the course of the flies with the tip of the rod makes it possible to do this. Let the flies rest in the pocket behind the rocks and occasionally manipulate the cast so that the dropper fly dances on the water above the most likely locations. Probably the best way to fish this type of water is downstream but do not confine your casts to sections below you. Also cover the stream on both sides of you.

On some occasions and in some streams a variation of this method is to be recommended. Fish the water thoroughly as described but use a cast of three large flies, about sixes, and work them over the pockets with fast jerks. To do this do not use any slack line, in fact do not use your retrieving hand at all. Everything is accomplished with the rod and a short line which is kept taut against the reel. The very instant the flies touch the water on the forward cast you start them moving, bringing the rod back and upward with a speedy, jerky movement. The instant the tail fly reaches the surface of the water on the retrieve the rod should be in a position to make a quick lift and a new cast. Avoid fishing the flies after the rod reaches a vertical position because in that case a striking fish may break the tip. I have had many occasions to bless this method of fishing although I must admit that I had neglected it for many years until it was again brought to my attention in the following manner.

We were on the lower stretches of the Neversink River, in New York State, where the fish run large and are exceedingly temperamental. Three of us had been fishing for more than five hours without seeing a trout. We had fished upstream with a dry fly and had worked back with a wet fly, fishing it in the regulation ways. On the way back we caught up with another fellow who was also fishing with wet flies. But instead of using only one small fly his cast was made up of three large flies dangling on a heavy leader. His casts were short and quick. Within one minute he made twelve. He paid particular attention to all the rocks and could certainly make those flies flutter across the little pockets in a teasing manner. Even as we watched he took two Brown Trout which were better than 14 inches in length.

It brought back memories of the old days when I had used this method for Brook Trout. Because I had become interested in more advanced ways I had forgotten this old one, or to be really candid I had come to consider its use out of the question when it came to Brown Trout. But when I saw how it produced for this angler on the Neversink when our fancy methods had failed, my feelings in the matter experienced a sudden reversal.

We could not take advantage of the idea at this time. All our wet flies were small and delicate and our leaders too fine. I did try it a while with large dry flies but somehow they would not work. I have since found that the best combination is a three loop heavy trout leader six to nine feet in length and three bushy wet flies size 6 of various colors. (See Chapter Three for specifications and other wet fly tackle information.) With this combination it is possible to get the right effect and the heavy leader enables you to hook a large fish, on the jump as it were, without breaking the gut. Incidentally the heavy leader is not detrimental in this case because it is above the water practically all the time. In some cases a 6 foot leader is better than a longer one.

But do not get the idea that this method is infallible. As a matter of fact it is worth while only in streams of very fast flow. But for fishing pocket water in rapids and also for fishing the speedy parts of riffles, it is invaluable.

Here is another way useful for almost any type of water ranging from fast to medium slow and particularly for Steelheads. The cast is made quartering downstream. At the completion of the cast the rod is immediately manipulated with a rhythmic up and down motion, the movement being very slight and slow. To be specific the wrist should not move more than 7 inches and there should be about 28 upward movements to the minute. To further aid you in visualizing this method I have attempted to show you in a sketch the action this imparts to the fly. As the fly proceeds downstream you retrieve line slightly, about a total of six inches for the entire float, that is until the fly comes into position directly below you. When this point is reached several different ways of finishing the cast may be used. One is to keep the fly working slowly upstream using the " hand twist " retrieve. Another is to release the small quantity of line which was gathered in and when the line comes taut work the fly up and down in an area of six inches to one foot. If no strike is forthcoming within a couple of minutes it should then be retrieved. Last, you may strip off six to eight feet of line when the fly comes taut and then release this footage of line all at once so that the fly will sink and at the same time go a bit further downstream. When it comes taut again you may either retrieve it by the "hand twist" method or else reel it in slowly. Incidentally this reeling in process is often deadly, so much so that I rarely fail to give it a try when fishing wet.

Sometimes it is advantageous to strip off six or seven feet of line at the moment the cast has been completed—before the fly has floated downstream. This gives the fly a greater depth and if the fish are "using" on bottom, results in better catches. In all these methods it is imperative to have the fly sink as soon as it touches the water. All that is needed to accomplish this is to soak the fly thoroughly before making the cast.

In addition to these various methods of fishing the wet fly there are some others which, while not so well known, are equally important. For instance, there is the count system for still waters which I believe Clyde Post and I originated at Brandy Brook in the Adirondacks. We stumbled on this method by chance. We had been fishing in the late afternoon without success when Clyde suddenly became tired and let his fly sink at the completion of his cast. He came to life just in time to keep it from getting caught in the snags and as he brought the line taut felt a tug. Of course we both started letting our flies sink after this and several times felt fish as well as snags but did not connect with any trout. Because we noted that all the hits came just at the moment we were likely to get snagged we decided to see just how long it took for the fly to reach bottom. To ascertain this we counted. Before long we knew exactly how much to count for the fly to reach a point just above the snags and when we got that we started striking at the very moment the total count was reached. About every fifth cast our blind strike was rewarded with a trout.

In all still water fishing it is usually best to let the flies sink before starting the retrieve. The depth to let them sink depends on the circumstances and it pays to try all depths until the best one is reached. As a rule the " hand twist " retrieve is best for waters of this type. The name of this retrieve is my own and right here I shall describe it. It is really the most important in wet fly fishing and yet I've never seen it described so that anyone not knowing it could tell what it was. At the start of the retrieve take the line between your thumb and forefinger. With them pull the line in as far as your fingers will normally move. Then immediately reach up with the other three fingers and pull the line with them as far as they will move normally. This brings your thumb and forefinger into position again and you simply keep repeating this performance, maintaining a steady and even rhythm until the retrieve is completed. This may be regulated as to speed and this regulation is often necessary.

This is an antique method of retrieving but it has never lost its effectiveness as those who use it will readily testify. I shall no doubt mention this retrieve by name from time to time in subsequent chapters so to those who are not conversant with it I would recommend that you string up a rod at this time so that the principle of it will be impressed on your mind. If you can visualize these things as you read of incidents where the methods are used, what you read will have much more interest and value.

Another method is one which came from watching an angler fish from a high point on the bank from where I could see the flies and the creek bed while he could not. At this time the trout were apparently off feed and I had quit fishing, preferring to wait until they started to rise. I watched this fellow carefully. I felt sure that he wouldn't get any fish but if he did I

PLATE NO. 2

Wet Flies

Bouncer	Bonnie View	Bootes Black	Bottle Imp	Brandreth	Bright Fox
Brown Hen	Brown Mallard	Brown Sedge	Brown Turkey	Brunton's Fancy	Bunting
Butcher	Cahill	Calder	Caldwell	Canada	Captain
Caperer	Cardinal	Carter Harrison	Cassard	Cassin	Catskill
Caughlan	Chamberlain	Chantry	Chateaugay	Cheney	Cinnamon
Claret Gnat	Coachman	Coachman Leadwing	Cobler	Colonel Fuller	Concher
Cooper	Cornell	Cowdung	Critchley Fancy	Critchley Hackle	Cupsuptic
Dark Spinner	Down Looker	Deacon	Deer Fly	Denison	Dolly Varden

Full descriptions of the flies on this plate will be found on pages 410–412

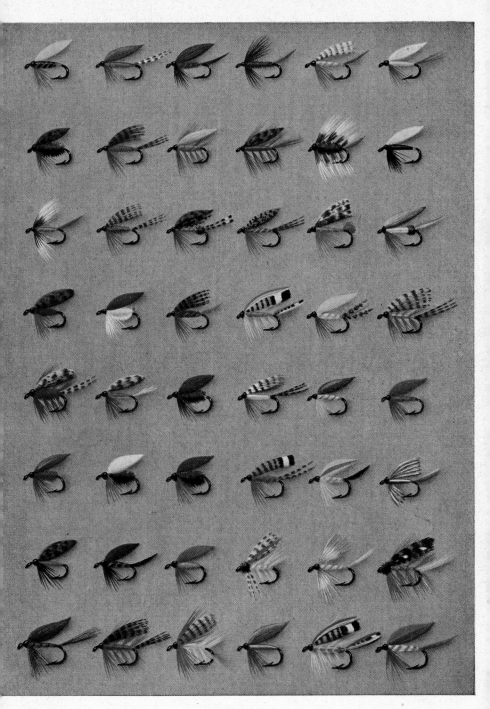

PLATE No. 2

wanted to see how he did it. Then I saw something which made me sit up and take notice. The fisherman had stopped his retrieve shortly after starting it to turn around to speak to his guide. It was only a slight pause and then he started moving the flies again. A second later he again paused as he spoke to the guide a second time. As the fly started sinking on the slack line I saw the flash of a trout as it took the fly and then immediately spit it out. A fraction of a second later the angler resumed the retrieve but by this time the fish was gone. Of course he knew nothing about it. A little while later I tried the stunt a bit further downstream and it produced a limit catch even though others on the stream failed to take a fish. Following is the method which is very useful in spring holes or in the still waters of any stream.

At the completion of the cast start the flies moving rapidly with an upward movement of the rod. Make about three fast jerks and then lower the rod tip and allow the flies to sink for a count of fifteen or longer if the water is more than five feet deep. Then make three more jerks and follow it again by the pause and lowering of the rod tip. Continue this procedure until the retrieve is completed. Whenever the fly is sinking watch it carefully. If you see a flash or see the line twitch strike hard and quickly. If you are too slow or don't strike hard enough to offset the disadvantage of the slack line the fish will spit out the fly before you can set the hook.

When a similar but faster action than that which can be maintained by the " hand twist " retrieve is needed you may use what I call the " line retrieve." In making this you hold the line with the thumb and forefinger of the rod hand. Then with the other hand you strip in the line with jerks. These may be short and deliberate or fast and erratic, in fact you can mix up the speed and the length of the jerks to suit the conditions.

A variation of this retrieve is made by using both the rod and the line at the same time. In this case the rod supplies most of the action during the start of the retrieve while the hand finishes it when the rod has reached a point slightly under vertical. This method is used when you wish the flies to come along rapidly near the surface of the water and is very effective with a bucktail as I discovered while fishing Encampment Brook in Wyoming. A 9 or 9½ foot rod is needed to do it effectively and it is rather exhausting because you must not let the flies rest on the water a second after the cast is completed and the faster you get the next cast back if you miss a fish on the first retrieve the better chance you have of taking him.

Occasionally I use a style of wet fly fishing which I call the " continuous roll." It is really nothing more than one switch or roll cast after another. You start with a regular cast across and downstream. When the fly comes taut below you the rod is lifted slowly to the perpendicular and then given a quick downward movement which is completed with the rod pointing toward a spot several feet further upstream. If done correctly the fly will alight some five or six feet nearer shore and a bit further upstream than it was at the end of the float. As no back cast is needed in making this cast it proves very useful in fishing narrow and brush-lined streams or when you are fishing one side of the stream and your comrade the other and you have the side where you cannot make a regular cast without getting hung up. It is also very useful on a flooded stream when the trout are in the backwaters and eddies under low-hanging trees and brush or under the banks. The fly stays low and so can be put under obstructions and in addition it stays so water logged that it sinks deeper than it would when making an ordinary cast. No motion is given the fly when fishing in this manner. It is allowed to float as it will and the line must be watched carefully for any indications of a strike which is not felt.

When fishing very deep water it is necessary to use a split shot. After the fly reaches bottom bring it in slowly using the

" hand twist " retrieve. As a rule it is best to fish upstream in quiet pools and sometimes in fast water. However if the stream contains irregular shaped boulders in quantity the upstream method of fishing a weighted fly is likely to be very troublesome due to the fly becoming snagged on the rocks frequently. If it is necessary to get a fly very deep under these conditions it is best to use sufficient lead to get it down when dragging against the current. Any fly fishing with lead is similar to bait fishing although much more difficult but if flies will not produce any other way and you want to use them there's nothing else you can do.

Remember that wet flies may represent many different things so that various methods are needed to make them consistently effective. The trout may take them for nymphs, drowned surface flies, minnows or small crustaceans. In subsequent chapters I shall illustrate by actual experiences how these different styles of wet fly fishing brought results and also explain some variations of the different methods which were needed under certain conditions.

Avoid being a slave to one style. It may be all right for the particular stream you fish most and know intimately but it may not be a bit satisfactory for other streams you may fish. The man who is well informed on different methods and has had practice in using them has a decided advantage on one who fishes the same way no matter what the conditions. I know it is easier to follow along the lines of least resistance and keep fishing one way because it does not require any mental effort. You can do the same thing in the business of life but it doesn't get you anywhere. It will pay you to get out of the rut and try different things, to experiment a bit. It is only by doing this that you can expect to overcome a few of the obstacles which prevent you from being successful. No one can possibly hope to overcome them all.

CHAPTER THREE

A Discussion on Wet Fly Tackle

Flies

THE SUBJECT of fly patterns is a complicated and absorbing one. There is hardly an angler who hasn't some pet fly which he considers better than any other. Often it is a well-known standard pattern but sometimes it is a fly which is known very little or which perhaps he may have designed himself. It would be an endless task to try out all these patterns so that one could talk about them intelligently. For this reason I shall take up only those flies which have served me through the years and which I know make a well-balanced assortment. However, in addition I have assembled a large number of patterns which have been successful all over America and from them Dr. Edgar Burke has made accurate color plates. This is probably the largest collection of flies to be reproduced in color in any one book. In most cases the materials used in the tying of each fly are given in detail so that you may have duplicates made if you choose. Needless to say I became enthused with many of the patterns while assembling the collection and will be trying them out by the time this book is published. For the present I give you my impressions of flies which have served me for many years and which are no doubt known by every seasoned angler.

BLACK GNAT. Here is a fly of proven worth. It is especially effective in the north country where the black flies make life miserable in the early season. It also proves very useful in the

Catskills, Pennsylvania, Connecticut, New Jersey and many other waters in the East. It is best in the small size although large sizes have proved effective in the north. My own selection contains only 10's, 12's, 14's and 18's. Sometimes when a midge hatch is on, a wet black gnat in size 18 or 20 will bring results. It is usually necessary to have these smaller flies tied to order as the demand for them is so slight that dealers generally do not stock them. Nevertheless I believe that a few of them in your box will be well worth your trouble and expense.

BLUE DUN and BLUE QUILL. I could never decide whether both of these patterns are necessary. My own tendency is to favor the dun. There is something about the blue-gray fur dubbin body when wet which makes a very juicy looking fly. But others feel that the quill body more nearly imitates nature and will use nothing else, so there you are. I believe personal preference to either one body or the other is the prime reason for the difference in opinion. Ordinarily, either pattern is an early season fly and I've yet to find any section of the country where it will not produce at one time or another. Locations where it has proved unusually effective for me are Wyoming, New York, Vermont and New Brunswick. This does not mean that it is not just as effective in other sections. I simply had better luck with some other patterns when fishing such places. Sizes 10, 12, 14 and 18 are recommended.

CAHILL—Regular or dark. This dull colored brown hackled fly with its blue-gray body and wood duck or dyed mallard wing is a standard fly wherever any fly of a brown cast is needed. I have used it successfully from one coast to the other and on occasion have found it deadly in the north country. Sizes—8, 10, 12 and 14.

CAHILL—Light or ginger. Here is a pattern to conjure with in the Catskills. Also of general use anywhere that trout occupy the water. If I had to confine my assortment of wet flies to two patterns this would be one of them. Sizes—10, 12 and 14.

COACHMAN.

ROYAL COACHMAN. I list these flies together because I hardly think it necessary to carry both. Either one is of inestimable worth to the angler and useful in almost any stream and pond in this country and Canada. While presumably they do not imitate any natural fly they evidently have a decided appeal to the trout. My own preference is for the Coachman in a wet fly and a Royal Coachman in a dry fly although I am at a loss to give a good explanation as to why I have this preference. Of course I have had best results when using them this way but that may have come about because I favor the patterns in this manner and so use one more than the other. At any rate I would never be without a Coachman when wet fly fishing. Sizes—6, 8, 10, 12 and 14.

GOLD RIBBED HARE'S EAR. In my opinion this is one of the best wet fly patterns ever produced. I have used it as a nymph on more than one occasion and often as a fresh water shrimp. Its scraggy body simulates underwater insect life quite successfully and its usefulness is not confined to any one locality. It is well worth an honored place beside the most popular flies ever produced. Sizes—8, 10, 12 and 14.

GREENWELL'S GLORY. A dark brown pattern not very well known but very essential nevertheless as it supplies that need between a black and a regular brown fly. On many occasions it has brought me success when the better known patterns have failed to produce. Best sizes—10, 12 and 14.

GRIZZLY KING. A proven fish-getter in the north and northeast, this fly is rarely used by anglers who fish the streams in the more heavily populated sections. Despite this I use it frequently in the Catskills, Pennsylvania and New Jersey with very good results. As I have never used it in any other states I do not know whether it would be effective in the midwest and west. However, I believe it would. Best sizes—6, 8 and 10.

McGINTY. Not a popular fly by any means and in my estimation best during the summer months only. Several times it has saved the day for me in widely separated parts of the United States. A good Canadian and Maine pattern.

MARCH BROWN. This comes in five designs and they are all good. The female, male and ginger are excellent as nymph imitations and the American pattern has proved a good fly wherever used. It is especially effective in New Jersey. Best sizes—10, 12 and 14.

MONTREAL.

MONTREAL—SILVER BODY. A fancy pattern which is invaluable in all parts of the north where Brook Trout flourish. Mostly used in Maine, Canada and the Adirondacks and also useful when fishing for freshly stocked fish in the thickly settled districts. It sometimes produces under the most unexpected circumstances and I believe would prove a good fly in almost any water if it was given a fair chance. For the north I've found sizes 4, 6 and 8 most satisfactory and in the more settled sections 10's and 12's. Both patterns are good but I think the silver body is best in any place where the water is somewhat discolored.

ORANGE FISH HAWK. A pattern which hasn't so many boosters considering the number of anglers but which is considered excellent by those who do use it. My personal experience with it has been such that I consider it a very necessary addition to my fly assortment. Best sizes—10, 12 and 14.

OLIVE DUN.

OLIVE QUILL. As a rule I do not find much need for these two patterns but when I do I need them very badly indeed. Perhaps I don't use them as much as I should. There are many streams which contain worms and larvæ of this coloration and I believe we are neglecting a good bet by not using them more than we do. Unlike my preferences in the blue flies I prefer the quill to the dun in this fly. Best sizes—10, 12 and 14.

PROFESSOR. Another pattern used extensively in the north

and northeast but rarely used in the other sections of the country. It is especially attractive for Brook Trout, and on the few occasions I have tried, it was taken by the Cutthroat. It has been more or less crowded out of the picture by other patterns but it has its uses and should always be included in the assortment for Brook Trout or for any wilderness fishing. Sizes—6, 8, 10 and 12.

PARMACHENIE BELLE. A bright colored fancy fly which has won an enviable reputation in Maine, Canada and some parts of the Adirondacks. Although principally a Brook Trout fly I have used it with success on Browns and Rainbows. Best sizes—6, 8 and 10.

QUILL GORDON. Here is a fly of extreme usefulness in the Catskills, Pennsylvania and wherever the fish are located in hard fished waters. In a measure it simulates a drowned mosquito, and also imitates quite well any dun-colored, quill body fly which might be on the water. In a large size I have found it very effective in the north country when fishing for Brook Trout. One of the essential flies which should be in every fly box. Best sizes—8, 10, 12 and 14.

QUEEN OF THE WATERS. Once in a while you will find this fly very handy to have with you but of the lot I would consider it the less necessary. It has been most useful to me in the state of New Jersey. Sizes—10, 12 and 14.

SILVER DOCTOR. Here is a fly useful and effective in any water under certain conditions. Although primarily a northern pattern it has proved very satisfactory in Brown Trout streams in the thickly settled sections. It is especially useful at night or in the case of high water and often produces at times when live minnows are being used with good results. Best sizes—6, 8 and 10.

WICKHAM'S FANCY.

CAMPBELL'S FANCY. I have listed these two flies together because they are somewhat of the same type and where one is good the other usually is also. The Campbell's Fancy is darker in effect and has a teal wing which in my estimation improves its effectiveness. While I have taken plenty of trout with both, my sympathies lie with the latter. On more than one occasion the Campbell's Fancy has saved me from defeat both in the east and in the state of Wyoming. Best sizes—6, 10, 12 and 14.

This concludes my list of essential wet flies. That there are many others which are good and no doubt needed for special conditions I do not dispute. But at least you should get the flies in this list which seem most suitable to the waters you intend fishing when you buy your first outfit. Old timers need no introduction to any of them although they will no doubt be interested in what I have to say about them. With the exception of some lakes and wilderness streams the sizes given will be sufficient but in the case of the northern patterns it might be wise to add them in sizes 4 and 2, especially if you expect to fish where the trout run of large size. For instance, the trout in the Oswegatchie River above Cranberry Lake respond very well to these larger flies. However, the times they are needed are rare and in fact since the streamers and bucktails have come into such general use it is hardly necessary to include them. These as well as Steelhead flies will be taken up in following chapters. As a general rule sparsely tied flies are better for heavily fished waters and heavily tied flies are best for the wilderness. However, the reverse is sometimes true so that it always pays to have some of each style.

Wet Fly Leaders

Probably the most generally used length of leader for wet fly fishing is 6 feet. However I believe that one 9 feet long is much more effective. There isn't any doubt that it helps when the water is clear and the trout wary. Despite the fact that nearly all angling writers recommend eyed hook flies there are

PLATE NO. 3
Wet Flies

Darling	Dorset	Dr. Breck	Dr. Burke	Dugmore Fancy	Dusty Miller
Durham Ranger	Edrington	Elliot	Emerald	Emma	Epting
Esmeralda	Ferguson	Fern	Fiery Brown	Feted Green	Fisher
Fish Hawk	Fitzmaurice	Flagger	Flamer	Fletcher	Flight's Fancy
Florence	Forsyth	Fosnot	Francis Fly	General Hooker	Getland
Ginger Palmer	G. R. Hare's Ear	Good Evening	Gold Monkey	Gold Stork	Gordon
Golden Doctor	Golden Duke	Golden Dun	Golden Ibis	Golden Dun Midge	Golden Pheasant
Golden Rod	Golden Spinner	Gosling	Grannom	Gray Marlow	Grouse Spider

Full descriptions of the flies on this plate will be found on pages 413–415.

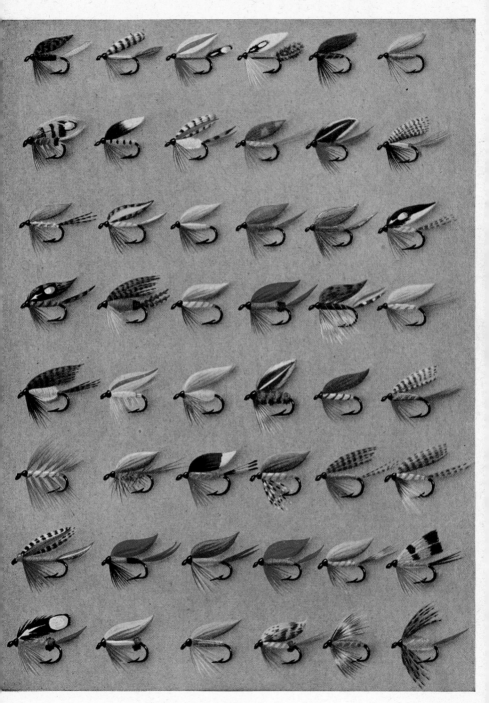

PLATE No. 3

still more snelled flies in use than there are the eyed variety so that the old regulation looped wet fly leader is still a necessity. These leaders should be purchased of a calibration to fit the snelled flies you are able to buy, otherwise the results will be very unsatisfactory. I've seen many a fishing trip marred because of this defect in the tackle. If the snells on the flies calibrate .014 then the leader should calibrate at least that much. Gut as heavy as this is used mostly for northern and western fishing. This weight leader need not be tapered; in fact, because of the heavy tied flies which usually come tied to gut of this calibration I think it is better if they are level. Personally, I can see no need for either the heavy leader or the snelled fly for ordinary trout fishing but because many anglers insist on using them I have given them this mention.

There are some sparse tied snelled flies made which have fine gut. I have some in front of me as I write this and the gut calibrates 1X (.009) on some and 2X (.008) on others. When buying leaders for flies with snells as fine as these it is best to get tapered ones, say from .012 to 1X. The 2X snelled flies will work in nicely at the tail of this leader and those with the 1X snells may be used on the dropper loop. For the heavily fished streams this makes a good combination, both the fine gut and the sparsely tied flies being suitable. But unfortunately fine gut snelled flies are likely to prove very fragile. If they become dried out from age, if they are used a few times and the hook starts to rust at the point where the leader is attached at the head, or if the fly tier when making the flies gets a bit of varnish on the gut near the head of the fly they are likely to snap off at the most inopportune time. You accept a hazard when you use them and it is really quite unnecessary.

Consider the eyed flies and their advantages. First of all they will keep indefinitely, if the moths don't get them. Second, you may carry a flock of them in a miniature container which is

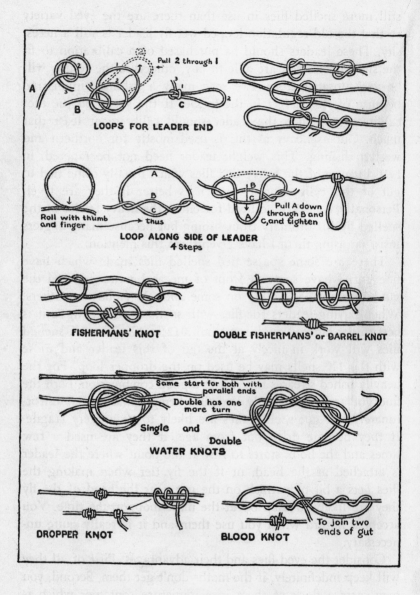

LOOPS FOR LEADER END

Pull 2 through 1

A B C

Roll with thumb and finger → thus

LOOP ALONG SIDE OF LEADER
4 Steps

Pull A down through B and C, and tighten

FISHERMANS' KNOT

DOUBLE FISHERMANS' or BARREL KNOT

Same start for both with parallel ends
Double has one more turn

Single and Double
WATER KNOTS

DROPPER KNOT

BLOOD KNOT

To join two ends of gut

A DISCUSSION ON WET FLY TACKLE

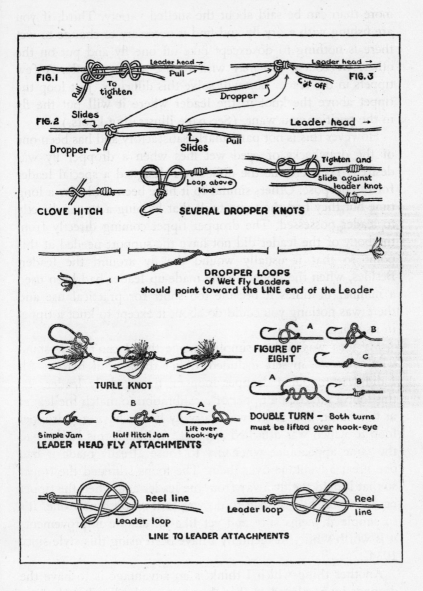

FIG.1 Leader head → Pull To tighten Pull

FIG.3 Leader head → Cut off Dropper

FIG.2 Slides Leader head → Dropper → Slides Pull

CLOVE HITCH

Loop above knot

SEVERAL DROPPER KNOTS Tighten and slide against leader knot

DROPPER LOOPS
of Wet Fly Leaders
should point toward the LINE end of the Leader

TURLE KNOT

FIGURE OF EIGHT A B C

A B

DOUBLE TURN – Both turns must be lifted _over_ hook-eye

Simple Jam Half Hitch Jam B Lift over hook-eye A
LEADER HEAD FLY ATTACHMENTS

Reel line Leader loop

Leader loop Reel line

LINE TO LEADER ATTACHMENTS

more than can be said about the snelled variety. Third, if you are fishing with a dry fly and find it necessary to change to wet there is nothing to do except take off one fly and put on the other. Of course you may wish to use a dropper fly. A few tippets in the leader box will solve this difficulty. Just loop the tippet above the knot in the leader where it will put the fly in the position you want. (See page illustrating knots.)

However this is not particularly satisfactory and has been one of the drawbacks of eyed wet flies when a dropper fly was desired. To overcome the difficulty I designed a special leader for the purpose. Others similar to it have been made for a long time but they had the same fault that looping a tippet directly to leader possessed. The dropper tippet coming directly from the body of the leader did not have the support needed at this point so that it usually wound the fly around the leader. Besides, when the tippet on the made-up leader had been used a number of times it became too short for practical use and there was nothing you could do about it except to knot a tippet in its place.

My idea was such a simple change that I can't understand why someone, myself included, didn't think of it before. All I did was to put a dropper loop on the eyed fly leader. To this loop I attached a tippet of a calibration to match the leader at this point. The result was a dry fly leader having a dropper loop to which was attached a tippet. Although this leader had the same appearance when dry to those already made it had one great advantage over them. The loops stiffened the tippet so that it held the fly away from the leader and when the tippet became short all you had to do was to loop on a new one. It's so simple it seems silly and yet like all simple improvements it is worth while. Incidentally I have been using this style since 1934.

Another thing which I think is an advantage is to have the dropper loops placed so that they are evenly distributed along the leader. For instance, if you prefer a two fly leader the dropper loop should be halfway between the tail end and the line. If you prefer three flies the dropper loops should be spaced three feet apart.

Above all, when buying a tapered leader be sure the dropper loops are tied so that they point toward the line end or at least project out straight from the body of the leader. Otherwise they will hang close to the leader and lose most of their effectiveness. (See pages of knots.) My own favorite eyed wet fly leader is tapered from .014 to 2X in the 9 foot length and .012 to 2X in the shorter lengths. To simplify things for you I herewith give a table of satisfactory leader and gut snell and tippet weights as well as suitable lengths of leaders for the various conditions you might come in contact with.

NORTHERN AND WESTERN TROUT—Large flies—4 to 6—Stout weight level (from .016 to .015)—6 to 9 feet long. Snells or tippets—.016 to .014. Small flies—level medium (.014 to .012)—6 to 9 feet long. Snells or tippets—.012 to .011.

HIGH BUT CLEAR WATER—Broken surface—settled sections. Tapered .014 to 2X in 9 foot and .012 to 2X in 6 to 7½ foot. Dropper snelled fly or tippet to be about the same size as the leader at this point, end fly snell 2X—or if eyed, tie directly to end of leader.

DISCOLORED HIGH WATER—Broken surface—settled sections. Medium level (about .012)—6 to 9 feet long. Snells or tippets—.012 to .011.

LOW AND CLEAR WATER—Broken surface—9 to 12 feet—tapered .017 to 2X.

STILL WATERS—12 to 18 feet. Tapered .017 to 2, 3, or 4X in 12 foot and .019 to 2, 3, and 4X in 15 or 18 foot. It is best to use only one eyed fly for this fishing and as it is the same as nymph fishing you will learn more about this in the next chapter.

TROUT

Wet Fly Rods

Not so many years ago all fly rods were best for wet flies. They were very limber. But when the dry fly came into use it demanded a change in fly rod action. It was found that the false casting necessary to keep the fly dry as well as the power needed to propel the fluffy air-resisting fly against the slightest wind called for a rod with considerable more backbone and stiffness than those which had been made up to that time.

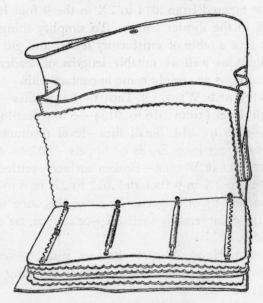

Folding Leather Wet Fly Book for Snelled Flies

Today nearly everyone wants a stiff rod. They've even gone too far and get rods which are too stiff to be satisfactory fishing rods. In my opinion it is unnecessary to have a separate rod for each type of fishing. If a rod is of medium stiffness it will handle either wet or dry fly satisfactorily. An 8 foot rod of the best grade weighing from 3⅝ oz. to 4 oz. works very well. A 9 foot rod of 4⅝ to 5¼ oz. will also perform very nicely. It is impossible to give exact weights because of the great variations in the makes of different rods. For instance I have an 8 foot rod weighing 3⅝ oz. which has the same power and action of one weighing 4 oz. The 4 ounce rod has a locking reel seat which makes up most of the difference. The lightest weights given are for rods without locking reel seats and with very light-weight reel seats.

Aluminum Clip Box for Eyed Wet Flies

For ordinary wet fly fishing a 9 foot rod is as long as anyone will need. For small streams an 8 foot rod is to be recommended. An ideal wet fly rod would weigh from 3⅜ oz. to 3½ oz. in an 8 foot and from 4 to 4¼ oz. in a 9 foot but such rods would not be very useful for dry fly or bucktail fishing. Remember that all these weights are taken from first-grade handmade rods. It should be difficult to give such information about the cheaper rods because there are so many of them.

Fly Books and Boxes

The carrier for your wet flies depends on the type and size. If you insist on snelled wet flies then the fly book is the only satisfactory container. The type with springs to hold the gut straight and a clip to hold the hook of the fly are the most satisfactory. (See illustration.)

For eyed wet flies the small aluminum clip boxes are ideal. One 4¾ inches long by 3½ inches wide is plenty large for most purposes. It will carry 85 flies from size 8 to 14 or smaller. They are inexpensive and light in weight. (See illustration.) For flies larger than 8's, bass size or streamer boxes are best. (See illustration.)

CHAPTER FOUR

Nymphs and Methods of Fishing Them

BECAUSE of the recent widespread publicity given nymph fishing I have decided to devote a short chapter to the different effective styles and methods of using them.

Candidly there is very little difference between nymph fishing and wet fly fishing, especially that type of wet fly fishing wherein you imitate as nearly as possible underwater creepers, not only in pattern but in the way you handle them in the water.

However, artificial nymphs are generally closer imitations to the natural creepers or larvæ found in our streams than the average run of wet flies so that under many conditions they will produce results when the wet flies fail. The very fact that many of the methods of fishing wet flies will not work, when fishing with nymphs proves this. For instance, wet flies will frequently produce best results when they are being moved rapidly, either on the surface or beneath it. In my experience artificial nymphs are never effective to any extent when used in this manner. The inference is clear. Natural nymphs do not move quickly when they are adrift from their rocky homes. They are primarily creepers and not swimmers. Because the artificial looks like the natural the trout are suspicious when it moves with jerks and darts through the water.

Naturally this brings up the question as to what the trout think fast-moving wet flies are? Personally I believe they take them for small minnows or shrimp or some other insect which might dart about. Certainly a drowned fly does not move. It is even likely that fish do not take our wet flies for any specific insect at all but because they look like something to eat and act as if they were trying to escape they strike them out of curiosity. Of course this does not explain why they might prefer certain patterns on some days and not on others. Often the most killing fly is one that to our knowledge does not imitate anything in nature, but then we do not know just how our artificial looks to the fish or how the different degrees of light affect its appearance.

The first nymphs I ever used were made in England. They were nothing more than bodies of flies made a bit thick near the head with a few turns of hackle constituting the feelers. I never did any better with them than I did with a wet fly with the wings cut off so finally discontinued using them. Then Louis Rhead brought out his series which were supposed to be close imitations of the nymphs found in American streams. As far as being even fair copies of the natural they were failures. It would have taken a vivid imagination to see the resemblance, but some of them, especially the pink pattern, were very effective in certain waters.

An outstanding contribution in the way of nymph imitations is Hewitt's Hard Body Nymph. It has a flattened body and is quite realistic although the opaque body does not imitate the translucent body of the natural. My first attempt at a nymph design resulted in a lure which, while not actually imitating the natural, did bring good results in many waters, especially on the Beaverkill, in New York, for which it was originally tied. It was impressionistic rather than imitative and the guinea fowl feelers gave it movement and life which others lacked. Then Herbert Howard and I, in working out a formula for translucent bodies, discovered a combination of materials which made it possible to make a flat body imitation which was also semi-transparent. Also it could be shaped so that it looked like a natural and could be colored in any shade. I made some up in amber, brown olive, dark green and dark orange red and they proved quite successful under certain conditions. However, they require a lot of time to make and unless a way is found to overcome this I doubt if they will ever become widely known. Paul Young as his contribution brought out the Strawman Nymph. Although this looks nothing like a nymph it is one of the most effective lures of this type. It may be that the rough construction closely imitates a cased caddis. Oscar Weber's contribution was an assortment of nymphs in various stages of development. While I haven't had much experience with these nymphs, having procured only one, the Phurea, which was given me by a friend, my success with this pattern was so marked that I felt it deserved a mention here. When I get an opportunity I mean to try out some others in the assortment.

There are probably many more lures of this type which have escaped my attention. While I endeavor to keep up with the various developments no one person can hope to dig out and try the many new patterns which are continually making their appearance. Besides, it would take more money than I can afford, to buy them all. Nevertheless I realize that many of these creations will fill a decided need for certain sections and conditions so that I regret my inability to give them all a trial. Without a doubt I would find many of surpassing merit if I could. Needless to say all the types I have mentioned have their particular place. Often when one of them produces the others will not. So much of this fishing lore is based on personal experience that it is impossible to make hard and fast rules about anything pertaining to it. One man may make a killing with a certain lure while another will never catch a fish with it. This happens more with well-known flies than it does with nymphs so that any conclusion reached is never one hundred percent perfect. The more you learn about fishing, the more experience you get in widely separated sections, the more you will realize the truth and humility in this assertion.

There are a number of methods with which nymphs may be successfully fished. As with wet fly fishing these are hard to describe because so much depends on one's ability to feel and sense both the progress of the lure and the strike of the fish.

I don't pretend to be a good nymph fisherman, in fact I usually feel a bit uncertain when using them. However, I have had some good fishing with them and always use them in apparently hopeless cases when dry and wet flies have failed to produce. Many times this habit of giving them this last chance has resulted in my getting the finest fish of the day, which is a real recommendation when you consider that the other flies get all the best opportunities to prove their worth. Because of these occasional successes under adverse conditions I feel that my descriptions of the methods used will be of some value to the reader.

If I seem to use excessive detail in describing these methods I hope the experienced nymph fisherman will overlook it and realize that many beginners at the game will read these pages so that it is necessary. Even at that I fear that the descriptions may be inadequate. Besides, the intuitive reactions of the angler mean more than the application of advised mechanical operations. Such things cannot be expressed by words. They are too elemental and elusive.

The first method to learn is what I call the " downstream float." Let us take up each move separately. First, if it is one of the type which requires wetting before it does sink, be sure the nymph is well soaked so that it goes down readily. Then make a cast either across stream or slightly down and across stream. As the current carries the lure along follow its progress with the tip of the rod. This allows it to float naturally without drag and is practically the same system with which you would fish a worm. In this method of fishing you really need not see a rise to your nymph. If you do the job correctly you will feel a tug and the tautness of the line will set the hook. If the trout is small then a slight lift of the rod is necessary to set the hook but inasmuch as the natural reaction when feeling a strike is to do this, it will probably be done without the angler being conscious of it. Of course there will be many misses but usually they will be small fish even though you might think differently. I have had large trout take a nymph so hard when fished in this way that the sudden pull made the click of the reel sing and that is music every angler likes.

Another method which I use more frequently than any other is the " upstream float." It is accomplished by casting the nymph either directly upstream or quartering up and across stream. It is practically the same as dry fly fishing except that the lure is under water instead of on the surface. In my estimation this is the most effective way to use nymphs but unfortunately it is also the most difficult method to learn. In the beginning it may be advisable to use a dry fly on the leader as an indicator. In attaching this dobber or float, tie it on as short a tippet as you can manage and attach it to the leader from four to six feet above the nymph. A fly with good floating qualities is necessary, say a heavily tied palmer hackle of a color most visible to you.

The purpose of this dry fly is to give you something to watch for indications of a strike. Sometimes it will disappear quickly, at other times it will simply stop floating with the current, and often it will simply twitch slightly without going under the surface. All these signs signify a strike and you must react quickly by striking back or you will miss the fish. As an example suppose the fly is floating along with the current and suddenly stops or goes a bit slower than the current. At the very instant this happens you should set the hook, otherwise it will be too late. Of course it may be that the nymph touching a rock is what causes the dry fly to act peculiarly but this is a chance you must take. As a matter of fact if the dry fly acts in the slightest degree unnaturally in relation to the flow of the water it usually means that a trout has taken the nymph and sometimes these indications are so slight that it takes a very observant eye to see them. The more you can develop this keenness of observation the better nymph and wet fly fisherman you will become.

Incidentally this sort of fishing demands a thorough knowledge of water currents as well as a keen judgment which tells you when the fly is floating as it should. To develop these talents will give you some invaluable practice in the science of reading a stream. After a time you will be able to discard the dry fly indicator and fish the nymph without its aid. However, I have found that it helps considerably in getting one acquainted with nymph fishing technique and is likely to make it possible for those who have never been able to do anything with these lures really to accomplish something with them.

The " upstream float " method is extremely useful for fishing under banks, log jams or anything else which might afford a hiding place for trout, and which may be reached in this manner. To fish such locations successfully it may be wise first to float a dry fly to it in order to ascertain just how long it will take your nymph to reach the spot, of course allowing a bit for extra time so that the sunken lure will get down into the hole.

After you have figured this out by watching the performance of your dry fly then you may fish your nymph in the same way, being sure that it sinks. When the estimated time has elapsed, pull the line taut and be ready to strike. You are very likely to lose nymphs fishing this way and will also miss many strikes but every once in a while you will take a good trout which otherwise never would have found its way into your creel.

Although I have taken a good many fish with this method of nymph fishing I rarely use it except after I have had a rise and missed it near one of these natural haunts of trout. Invariably a nymph floated down to such fish will bring a ready response and if I am clever or lucky enough I connect, otherwise all I get is the thrill of the second chance. However, I realize that I miss many an opportunity to take fish because I do not fish every one of them with a nymph—rise or no rise to the dry fly.

Fish which are "tailing" in the shallow water fall readily for a nymph fished with the "upstream method." Don't overlook the fact that trout busy at this game of dislodging nymphs from the rocks are quite likely to be cruisers. That is, they sometimes dislodge nymphs from the bottom and then chase after them. I've often had trout follow my artificial from 6 to 8 feet before taking it so do not be in too much of a hurry to lift the nymph from the water to make another cast. If you fish each cast out to the limit it is my humble opinion that you will take more fish than you will if you let it float only a few feet and then lift it. The place for your lure is in the water and not in the air and yet I see many anglers expending more energy in casting than they ever do in actually fishing their fly. I'm inclined to be that way myself and often find it very necessary to curb the impulse.

As an illustration of this let me tell you of an experience which shows how stupid we may be at times. It happened on a stream in northern New York. I had fished a mile of excellent water and hadn't taken a fish although I had frightened many of them as I waded along. The longer I fished the more discouraged I became and the more I flicked my fly here and there instead of fishing it in the water. It got so that the fly barely had time to float a foot before it was lifted and cast to another spot. Finally I caught up with another angler and rather than break in ahead of him I stopped to watch. Within five minutes he had taken two fair fish and I had discovered the reason for my failure. Both the trout he took had struck after his fly had floated at least fifteen feet, in fact they hit so close to him that he was just about ready to lift for another cast

PLATE NO. 4

Wet Flies

Guinea Hen	Governor	Gov. Alvord	Grackle	Gravel Bed	Green Midge
Gray Drake	Gray Midge	Gray Miller	Great Dun	Green Coachman	Green Drake
Green Mantle	Greenwell's Glory	Grizzly King	Gunnison	Harlequin	Hawthorne
Heckham Green	Heckham Red	Hemlock	Henshall	Herman Fly	Hofland's Fancy
Hoskins	Howell	Holberton	Hopatcong	Hudson	Hunt Fly
Ibis & White	Imbrie	Indian Rock	Indian Yellow	Ingersol	Irish Grouse
Irish Turkey	Iron Blue Quill	James	Jay-Blue	Jay-Yellow	Jay-Silver
Jennie Lind	Jock Scott	John Mann	June	June Spinner	Kamaloff

Full descriptions of the flies on this plate will be found on pages 416–418.

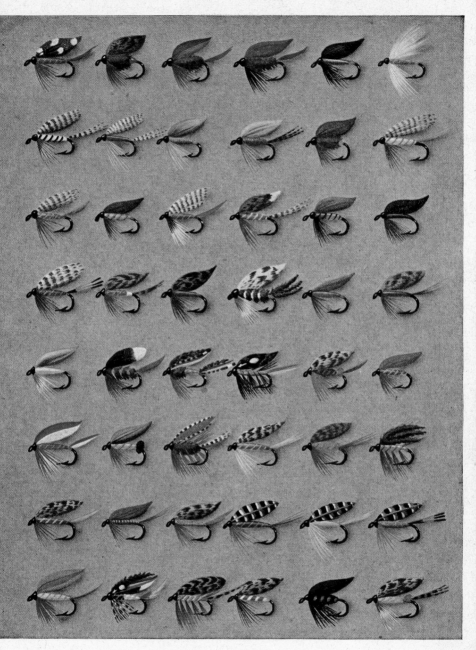

PLATE No. 4

when it happened. Incidentally this fellow was just two trout short of his limit and seventy percent had struck after the fly had made a long float. I turned around, went back to where I had first started and fished the same water again. However, I didn't get very far this time. I kept the fly in the water and was kept busy with rising fish. Practically every one I hooked followed the fly for quite a distance before taking it. A premature lift had been the only cause of my previous failure. While this case is a bit extreme it is applicable to some extent at all times. You never lose anything by keeping the fly in or on the water and you may gain much.

I have a mania for fishing still waters with a nymph. No other fly is better adapted for the work. They sink readily, or should, and are realistic enough to be attractive to the fish. The method of fishing is simple and yet subtle. Of course a long cast is necessary because the trout are able to see you for some distance or otherwise notice disturbing influences which come too close. You should always approach still clear waters with great care. If they are a bit shallow you should keep very low, on your knees if necessary, and make your first cast from some distance below, letting the nymph alight on the water of the tail. If the water below the pool is too fast to make such a cast feasible then work up to the tail with as little disturbance as you can and then wait there for five or ten minutes before you make your first cast.

If you know where the fish usually congregate in any particular still water then make your first cast directly to this spot, otherwise start with a short cast and gradually increase the distance of each cast until you have covered the entire piece of water or find the fish.

On completing the cast, the nymph should immediately sink and it is allowed to descend until it reaches bottom if it does so without being taken. During this period the line should be watched for any movement not in keeping with the normal process of the sinking of the nymph and leader. The line should be well dressed so that it floats. Should it jerk slightly or straighten out after it has started to curve because of the action of the water you should be prepared to strike without the slightest delay. If nothing occurs or if it does and you miss the fish, start retrieving very slowly with the "hand twist" retrieve, about 16 thumb and forefinger movements to the minute being a good speed. Sometimes it is best to let the nymph rest on bottom for several moments before starting the retrieve. When this is done the first movement is a cautious raising of the rod to start the nymph moving after which the retrieve is made as described. This can best be done on a sandy or gravelly bottom. When there are boulders or weeds it sometimes gets you into difficulties though none the less effective if you come clear when the lift from bottom is made.

Once you locate a spot where you get strikes, fish it carefully but not insistently. Retrieve the lure until you can lift it from the water without making a disturbance. A sloppy lift will often spoil your chances of taking any more trout. Always take a few minutes between casts and make each one perfect. If it should land in the wrong spot do not pick it up and make another one. Fish it out just as if it went to the very place you intended it to. Haste in this sort of fishing is very disastrous. If you are deliberate and careful you may nurse a still water for considerable time and take far more fish than you could by racing along the stream trying to fish in as many spots as possible.

Still another method of fishing the nymph I call "dabbling" for want of a better name. Only a very short line is used, in fact often just the leader comes into play. It is not applicable to all conditions but where it can be used frequently brings good results when other methods fail.

It works best in a small deep pool where it is possible to get directly over the deepest part without showing yourself to the fish that may be in it. If the bank is covered with thick vegetation it helps because the trees, bushes or high grass will neutralize your figure and there will be no silhouette. The approach must be exceedingly cautious and under some conditions it is best to keep low down.

By careful maneuvering you may get into a position where you can see the bottom of the hole without alarming the trout and then you are in a good position to fish it by " dabbling." With a roll cast propel the nymph to the head of the pool where the current is sufficient to carry it back into the deepest water. With a bit of practice you will be able to keep the line taut while doing this. The nymph will probably touch bottom before covering the entire pool in which case a slight lift of the rod tip will start it on its way again. During most of this fishing the progress of the lure is guided by the rod and care must be taken not to give it any violent action. An occasional short lift, made deliberately and smoothly and then a drop of the rod tip to allow the nymph to sink to bottom again and thus come taut against the rod, is all that is necessary.

Personally I do not care to fish with a nymph steadily because it is tedious and tiring. Instead I use it as an extra ace for the purpose of getting another chance at a good fish which has missed my dry fly. At least 30 percent of the time I have taken such fish by doing this and on the whole some 60 percent rise to it. To me this constitutes the principal charm of nymph fishing. It so often gives you that additional opportunity to take a good fish.

Tackle for Nymph Fishing

RODS—The same recommendations as for wet flies.

LEADERS—12 foot tapered .017 to 3 or 4X (.007 to .0065) for ordinary conditions although 9 foot will usually turn the trick. The only reason for a long leader in fast or medium fast water is the fact that the longer the leader the more detached the nymph appears and thus the more natural. However, when fishing still waters a leader of 15 to 18 foot tapering from .019 to 3X or 4X will be found a distinct advantage.

NYMPHS—An assortment of those mentioned at the beginning of this chapter in sizes 12 and 14. Don't buy very many to start. A dark colored one will serve for the experimental stage. You may not like the game at all, so it is foolish to get too many patterns to start with. If you like it then go the limit and it will pay you good dividends—at least according to my experiences.

CHAPTER FIVE

Experiences With Wet Fly and Nymph

I N THIS chapter of anecdotes pertaining to sunken fly fishing
I have drawn from some outstanding experiences in different locations. I have refrained from taking any lone
exceptions as examples, because while interesting, they would
not prove of any particular benefit. The incidents I have chosen
have been duplicated in some degree many times and so may be
considered at least logical answers to the problems they solved.
If, at times, my conclusions seem a bit weak or theoretical it
is because they are candid and because the actual results left
me groping. After all, nearly all angling experiences are subject to qualification. No matter how conclusive anything seems
it is always assailable, in fact in many cases it may be torn
apart and completely discredited. It is this very angle to fishing
which makes it the fascinating study it is. We cannot look upon
it as an exact science because the same applications will not
invariably produce the identical results. For instance, perhaps
we find out some method of fishing a certain stream which
proves very successful. For some time we get consistent results
with the method and think we have solved the problem. Perhaps we even get a bit puffed up over it and do some bragging.
Then something happens. We don't get the results we did.
Perhaps the fishing gets so poor that we say the stream is fished
out, and believe it. Just about this time someone else comes
along using a different method and fly. He makes a series of
good catches and so disproves all our conclusions. The follow-

ing account of some experiences on Beaver Brook, New York
State, illustrate how easily this may happen.

For two years I had fished the wet fly on this stream using
the across and downstream " drift " method. It was consistently
effective and produced good catches. When it didn't work I
used a dry fly with fair success. But as time went on the catches
became smaller and finally petered out altogether. Because one
never saw many trout rise on this stream and the water was of
a color which hindered one from seeing the bottom it was hard
to tell whether the trouble was caused by the lack of fish or
not, but because I had previously taken trout and couldn't do
it now I surmised that this was the trouble.

I had about decided to give up fishing the brook for good
when something happened to change my mind. One day on the
way down the brook after a blank morning I spied a man fishing one of my favorite pools. I had fished it that very day
without rising a fish. As I watched this man through the
rhododendron, which bordered the creek, I saw him take three
good trout. He was fishing with bait and I noted that he cast
the worm directly upstream and stripped in line fast enough to
keep the line taut. Each fish he caught seemed to take the bait
at his very feet.

His success gave birth to an idea. I quietly withdrew from
my vantage point and went downstream to another pool which
had formerly been productive. Instead of fishing it in the old
way I now fished it from the lower end, sending the fly to the
head of the pool and then letting it drift with the current.
The movement of the water wasn't strong enough to carry the
fly more than halfway through the pool so when it reached
the slow eddy in the center it wabbled uncertainly and gradually
settled to bottom. During this time I did not see any flash or
movement which could be interpreted as the action of an interested fish. It seemed as if the idea was doomed to failure
but something caused me to fish out the cast completely instead

of impatiently lifting the fly from the water. After it had reached bottom I left it there a moment or two and then lifted the rod tip slightly in order to dislodge it. Then I started pulling it in with the " hand twist " retrieve, doing it very slowly. When it had reached a point some fifteen feet above me I saw a shadow behind it, a shape in the water that hadn't been there before and which moved at the same speed as the fly. Although it was difficult I controlled my feelings and kept the retrieve steady. Just when a few more twists of the wrist would have taken the fly from the surface the trout took it and hooked himself.

I took two more fish from that pool in the same manner and before leaving the stream that day took seven more, all good fish. It was the solution to my problem and proved that the brook was still well populated with trout even though the " downstream drift method " had failed to take them. The new system produced as long as I fished Beaver Brook. I haven't been on it now for some five or six years so do not know if it would still be the best method.

Why the trout in this brook suddenly ceased taking a wet fly when fished in a manner which had formerly proved most effective has always puzzled me. The only solution I can offer is that the larvæ which might have been their favorite food had disappeared and so the old method failed to simulate the action of the larvæ they had been forced to take as a substitute. At any rate the new method proved most effective, not only in this stream but in many others from coast to coast.

However, in order to get any results from this sort of fishing, you must have patience and be very deliberate in anything you do. Haste, unnecessary movements, in fact any movement which is likely to transmit light reflections on the water, may easily ruin any chance of success you might possibly have. It is not easy to keep making perfect casts and to let your fly drift to your feet time after time when you don't get results immediately. You are likely to feel that it isn't any use and so hurry the drift and pick the fly from the water in such a way that it informs every fish in the pool that there is something wrong. Right here we have one of the most common reasons for angling failures—intolerance for things we can't control. Impatience makes us do things carelessly, heedlessly and by so doing we only aggravate the condition which caused our irritation in the first place. No one ever accomplished much by letting impatience upset his judgment. When there are factors present which are likely to make you lose patience, that is just the time when you must exercise rigid self-control so that you do nothing which may impair your chances of success.

Often fish will rise cautiously to the fly when it starts drifting at the head of the pool. They will follow it until it sinks to bottom, when they retire from the vicinity, but not so far that they cannot keep watching this thing which acts and looks a bit strange. When it starts moving again and begins drifting with the slight action given by the " hand twist " retrieve they become interested once more and usually desire and curiosity finally get the best of their judgment so that they take the fly. I have seen this happen in clear water but always any degree of haste, undue motion or a change in the speed of the retrieve would make the fish leave the scene.

Even when the trout seem to be hitting your fly at the head of a riffle or pool it usually pays to take the time necessary for it to sink and get into an eddy or back current from which it is necessary to retrieve it. The " hand twist " method is ideal for this purpose. Some of the best trout I have ever taken have come from the back washes or holes which are caused by the current action of fast water. Consider the following experience which is one of many. I happened to be fishing a long riffle which led into a shallow pool. The fish had been rising steadily in the fast water and I had taken eight 9 to 10 inchers on a six foot maximum drift of the fly. Of course this did not keep up and when the action got slow on one occasion as I lighted a cigarette I let the fly drift past the regular productive section on a slack line. When I tried to lift it from the water I found that it had caught on the bottom. A partial roll cast released it and more from habit than anything else I started to bring it in with the " hand twist " retrieve. I had made about five completed motions with my hand when I got a strike so hard that the reel sang a merry tune as the fish rushed upstream. This trout weighed 3¼ pounds and the incident happened on one of the famous Catskill streams.

Of course locations of this kind are likely to be inconstant, that is, they vary from time to time. Naturally the most logical positions for large fish to choose are those into which the most amount of food drifts because of water action. Large trout prefer to get food which is obtainable at the least effort. But the same force which pulls the food into such places also brings in all the other loose matter stirred up by freshets and so the very spot which might be most productive is also subject to the hazard of being spoiled by the very action which makes it a preferred location for large fish. Often many of the changes in these locations are very slight. A hole may fill up in one place and another may be formed a few feet in some other direction from the original spot. For this reason you should study the stream bottom after each heavy rain or after you have failed to fish some favorite riffle for a long time. Never let your judgment be swayed by past experiences. This is another common failing of fishermen, myself included. Just because one method, fly or location has proved productive in the past does not mean that it will always remain so. Never feel that a pool, riffle or any stretch of water you are familiar with, is no longer any good because it fails to produce when fished in the way you have been accustomed to. Try other places in the stretch besides the spots where you have formerly taken fish; fish it from new angles. You might get surprising results.

As an illustration showing further uses of the " hand twist " retrieve let me give you an account of a rather unusual experience which occurred on a small pond near Lowville, N. Y. It was a somewhat weedy bit of water and because no boats were on it we had to fish from shore. When we got there in the early afternoon no fish were rising within casting distance and although we tried as far out as we could cast, not one rise resulted from the efforts of our party.

I soon tired of casting over apparently fishless water so wandered along the shore looking for favorable cover which trout might like. Coming to a log at the water's edge I sat on it to rest. The water at this point was about knee deep at the shore line so I felt sure the trout would come in there if any place. Besides, about a dozen good fish were rising some two hundred feet out and I thought that they might move in at any time.

About twenty minutes later I spied a succession of rises which always progressed toward shore. They seemed to be made by one fish that had started cruising. Thinking that this trout might come in close enough to be fished for I changed to a dry fly and waited. The rises continued until they reached a distance of some one hundred feet from shore and then stopped. It seemed as if my chance was gone when I saw the rises start again within three feet of shore and some forty feet to the left. Each rise was closer to me so I figured out the speed of the trout's approach and cast the fly so that it alighted in front of his line of movement. Nothing happened. Then I saw the fish, advancing slowly. He suddenly rose to the surface and took something I could not see. I quickly cast the size 18 Blue Dun I happened to be using about three feet in front of him. He started toward the fly when it alighted but soon desisted and went on his way. Directly in front of me he rose again. Although this happened within six feet I could not see what he took, if anything. Then I made a rapid change from dry

fly to nymph and although the fish was now out of my sight
I had seen him rise several times so had a good idea where he
was. I cast the nymph so that it curved slightly over his line of
march and started bringing it back with the " hand twist "
retrieve. About six feet of line had been brought in when the
fish took the lure. The barb took hold and a few minutes later
the fish was in my creel.

The incident gave me a new burst of energy. I first worked
the shore line carefully and then combed the rest of the water
as far as I could reach. Not a single rise was forthcoming.
Again I became discouraged and sat down on the log. As it was
a cloudy day twilight came early and persisted for an amaz-
ingly long time. But the moment this condition arrived one
could notice a difference in the action of the fish. The rises
became more frequent, more splashy, and were definitely moving shoreward.

Soon several trout were within reach, twenty minutes later at
least fifty were within casting range. Because the fish seemed
to be feeding on the surface I had taken off the nymph and had
returned to a dry fly. I lost count of the number of dry flies
I tried but know I tried everything from tiny dark patterns to
large gaudy ones without getting a single indication. By the
time I got through experimenting it was getting so dark that
I could barely see my fly but even at that I took six good fish
with a nymph and the " hand twist " retrieve before it got
black.

As I landed my last fish the clouds broke on the western
horizon and let through a narrow streak of light which colored
the water with the orange and gold of sunset. Then came the
sight which I had never seen before and never expect to see
again. The rises came so close together that the pond took on
the appearance of being pelted by large hailstones. In addition an intense nervousness seemed to have affected all the
fish. When I made a cast it seemed as if all the fish within a

radius of three hundred feet instantly splashed the surface and when they did this it carried through to the fish beyond them and so progressed across the entire lake. It was mysterious, incomprehensible and after it happened the first time I never got another rise.

Then I felt something tugging at the rawhide laces of my shoes. I brought out the flashlight and looked down into the water. Two trout and a score of very small bullheads evidently thought my laces were worms and were trying to make way with them. I have since wondered whether many of the rises that evening hadn't been bullheads. I'm sure they couldn't have been all trout, there weren't that many in the lake. As I think back I remember a great many peculiar little tugs at my nymph which felt like tiny fish, and there were very few trout in the pond under eight inches. I've never had an opportunity to visit this lake since, so do not know if this is a regular occurrence there, but the memory of the experience will always remain vivid. Of course with the rapid-fire changes in fishing these days it is quite likely that the pond now contains nothing but bullheads. I wish I could have taken one with a fly. I know it would have given me a greater thrill than catching trout in this pond.

Here is another incident which shows the value of nymphs and the " hand twist " retrieve. It took place in September in New Brunswick, Canada. I had become a bit tired of catching grilse and salmon and thought I'd like to try some trout fishing. Our guides, Boyd Hovey and Claremont Moon, did not think much of the idea, first because they would rather have us fish for salmon and second because they didn't think there was much chance of taking any trout at that time with conditions the way they were.

This only intensified my desire to catch trout. If they were hard to get then it gave us something to strive for. So we went up what they called a bogan. It was what we would call a flow in the Adirondacks, that is the lower stretches of a small stream into which the waters of the big stream backed. In the south they often call the same type of water a slough. Personally I think " backwater " a good universal name for it. However, in this particular case the water of the Miramichi River was so low that it no longer backed up into the lower stretches of the brook. Instead the overflow from the small stream ran into the river and we had quite a job getting across the shallows with our canoes.

The water in the bogan was as clear as crystal. The bottom was a delight to the lover of trout. It was grassy, mossy, and covered with gravel where the vegetation did not grow. We advanced carefully until we reached a place where Boyd claimed we'd get trout, if anywhere. I started fishing with my regular salmon leader and a number 6 Parmachenie Belle, the approved sort of fly for the region. Nothing happened. I changed patterns and sizes several times and finally put on a regular medium weight 6 foot wet fly trout leader. Still no results. I fished always with the approved northern method bringing the flies rather swiftly through the water with the rod retrieve. After this I tried the " hand twist " retrieve, using the same flies and medium weight leader. Still no response.

The guides did not say anything but in their eyes I saw an " I told you so " look. This put me on my mettle. I must do something to show them that trout could be taken from that bogan. It was noon. The sun was bright and the bottom of the stream showed up clearly without a trout in sight. It looked hopeless and my heart sank. " Perhaps," I thought, " there isn't a trout here anyway."

Then I got an idea. Why not use the methods we did under similar conditions when fishing the hard fished streams near New York City? I started searching through my equipment. I found a few nymphs, two of a salmon red coloration and one with a gold-ribbed gray body and brown back. A little more search uncovered a number of gut strands of various sizes. After a little work I transformed a nine foot light salmon leader into an eighteen foot nymph leader tapering to 4X. Then I looked the situation over while I soaked one of the salmon-colored nymphs so that it would sink readily on touching the water. Over on the far side of the still water a large bush shadowed what appeared to be a hole deeper than the rest of the bogan. It looked like a logical place to concentrate on. All this took time and when I took a side glance at the guides I could see they were getting more impatient every moment. They wanted to get back to the salmon and couldn't see any sense in my killing time fussing with tackle.

But at last everything was ready so I made a cast which dropped the nymph close to the bank under that attractive look-ing bush. I sat motionless while the lure sank to bottom. Guide Hovey looked at me questioningly, in fact a bit disparagingly. For the moment I know my standing with him dropped con-siderably. I didn't blame him but I had hopes that my experi-ment would work. The motion of the line stopped so I knew my nymph had reached bottom. I started retrieving slowly with the " hand twist " system. I had hardly started this when I got a vicious strike and connected with a pound and a half Brook Trout. The bored looks on the faces of the guides disappeared and were replaced by expressions of keen interest.

Outwardly nonchalant but inwardly seething with pride and gratification I proceeded to fish that bogan as if it was the simplest thing in the world. Twice I hooked fish as the lure sank. I saw the line twitch slightly and struck. The rest of the fish took when the nymph was being retrieved. Boyd tried it for a while and so did my wife. But they both retrieved the fly too fast. My retrieve was about eighteen movements to the minute or about nine complete wrist motions. They made about three jerks to my one. Believe me, getting the right speed and timing to this retrieve is very important and it varies with conditions.

During our stay at Jack Russel's camp my wife and I spent many pleasant hours fishing for Brook Trout in this bogan. The best lures were the Impressionistic Nymphs, numbers 1, 2, and 5 as shown on color plate No. 10. The best wet flies were Gold Ribbed Hare's Ear and Greenwell's Glory. Not once did the northern patterns produce, such as Parmachenie Belle, Montreal, Professor and others which are normally good in this territory.

*   *   *   *   *   *

Just the simple process of letting a fly sink to bottom on a slack line sometimes leads to worth-while results. In this connection consider the following incident. Quite a number of years ago, in fact before I knew anything about nymph fishing, I spent considerable time on the western slope of the Adirondacks. Because we occasionally enjoyed a mess of small Brook Trout I sometimes quit fishing for sport and spent a few hours fishing for 8 to 9 inch fontinalis.

One of the best places for these small trout was the Peavine Creek which emptied into the Oswegatchie (River that runs around the Hills) about a mile below the dam of Cranberry Lake. It required a little effort to reach this spot. After reaching the location on the river opposite the entrance to the Peavine one had to pole a raft across the river and then up the creek until the first beaver dam was reached. Here the raft was anchored so that it was possible to stand on it and fish into the pool above the dam.

The surroundings were wild and impressive. Directly bordering the brook were the usual alders. Beyond that on either side, and seen through the openings in the brush, a swamp meadow spread out with all its isolated grandeur and mysteriousness. Beyond the meadow came the rise of land which was densely covered by spruce and other evergreens, lending its touch of the unfathomable to the general outlook. One never went up this meadow stretch of the Peavine without trembling with excitement. It was primeval, elemental. You expected to see bears, deer, almost any wild creature at any moment.

Above the dam, the heights of land on either side closed in on the meadow. Here the forest crowded the brook and the alders limited one's vision to their sky lines.

On this particular morning, dawn was just breaking as I poled the raft across the Oswegatchie. As I moved slowly along, the scarlet and maroon of the eastern horizon gradually spread out until it covered a third of the firmament. It transformed the misty gray atmosphere into a riot of color. The scene changed with every moment and when I reached the beaver dam I stopped a while to enjoy it. The sun suddenly poked over the eastern horizon and the witchery of the scene departed. Its bold rays quickly dispelled the mist and the scene became comparatively commonplace.

Because I had business to attend to I quickly set up my rod and got ready for fishing. In a half hour I expected to have enough trout for our breakfast and dinner.

But something was wrong. The usually agreeable pool was extremely disagreeable. For one hour I worked carefully and hard, changed flies many times, but never got one sign of encouragement. At last I came to the last pattern in my box, a No. 14 Iron Blue Dun. I cast it out and retrieved it several times without results.

It was very discouraging. I began to lose interest and thought more about breakfast. A careless cast to the left side of the pool and close to a thick clump of alders brought a sickly little rise. I was sure that it was a redfin minnow so didn't even bother to strike. Feeling that it was useless I let the fly sink to bottom as I placed the rod partly on the raft and on the dam while I smoked a cigarette.

About five minutes passed. The cigarette was finished and I

knew it was time to leave for camp as breakfast would be ready by the time I got there.

When I took up the rod I received a shock. Instead of the line pointing upstream and to the left it now pointed toward the right. A subtle warning flashed through my brain. It made me cautious. I retrieved the slack line gingerly and as I brought it taut against the rod tip I felt a throbbing. It was the signal to strike and I did. The resulting commotion turned the quiet pool into a cauldron of boiling water. I knew I had something large but didn't know what.

Some ten minutes later I saw the fish clearly for the first time. It almost caused disaster. For the moment I got a bad case of buck fever and froze solidly to the reel. Only the fact that I had a very light rod which absorbed the strain saved me from losing the fish. Before the rod broke I awoke to the precariousness of the situation and released the line which the fish took upstream at record speed.

But he was a fool trout like so many of the big ones we land under bad conditions. Without any effort he could have dashed into the alders where my light tackle would have broken. Instead he simply raced up and down stream and acted like a senseless maniac. Finally he became tired and flopped helplessly on his side. I slipped my long-handled net under him and, although the frame almost collapsed under the strain, succeeded in getting the fish to the raft where I dropped on my hands and knees to keep him from flopping overboard. When weighed on the scales of the general store it proved to weigh 6 pounds 9 ounces, as pretty a specimen of Brown Trout (Salmo fario) as anyone would want to see.

Needless to say I felt quite elated over my success. When I heard the complimentary remarks of those who saw the fish and later experienced the exhilaration which accompanies such local renown I became quite haughty. Fortunately this feeling did not last long. I soon realized that it is on such lucky instances that many reputations are made and that the person reaping the glory from such happenings really does not deserve it insomuch as it applies to his skill and knowledge of fishing. I knew that I did not deserve any credit for my part in this affair. Luck alone had been responsible. The lure had been neglected and the fish already had it in his mouth when I started to bring the fly in. The fish itself did not have brains enough to get away. Of course I used good judgment when I felt the first pull of the fish but if any credit is due anything except luck it should go to the little Iron Blue Dun which was left to shift for itself while I smoked a cigarette.

Everywhere we go we shall find the sunken fly and some form of the " hand twist " retrieve useful. Let me take you now to Pennsylvania, to the upper reaches of the Brodheads Creek. The time of the year was early May, the weather clear—frosty at night and pleasantly warm during the day although when the sun went under a cloud the moderate northwest wind made us wish that it would keep shining.

My companion and I started fishing at the small pond located just a short distance above the lake near Sky-Top Lodge. Because a few fish were rising we first used dry flies but after a half hour without results we changed to wets. I don't know how many times Fred changed his flies but I know that I tried a dozen patterns before I got a rise. It was to a size 14 Orange Fish Hawk which was being manipulated close to the surface by the " hand twist " retrieve. Because occasionally the trout were breaking on the surface we kept fishing our flies near the top but after an hour of hard work we still had only this one fish which had taken the Orange Fish Hawk the first time it was used.

As this fly had given me the only action I decided to keep it on but also felt that I should try sinking it deep before giving it up as a hopeless undertaking. This I did and when some ten completed movements of the " hand twist " retrieve had been made I saw the line twitch and immediately hooked a trout. This combination of depth and retrieve proved to be what was needed and we both took quite a number of fish before tiring of the location.

Of course we thought that we had solved the secret of catching fish for the day so went confidently to the first pool above the dam. But here we struck a snag. The trout would not respond to the Orange Fish Hawk and the "hand twist" retrieve. We fished several more good looking pools in the same manner and with the same fly and still failure dodged our footsteps. Because we had taken fish in the pond with the combination we thought it should work everywhere else and so decided that there were not many fish above the pond. We decided this while we were fruitlessly fishing one of the most enticing pools of the entire stream. But at this very moment the light changed so that it disclosed the bottom to our eyes. What we saw made us gasp. About twenty feet above us the gravel was covered with so many trout that they made a black spot of several square yards on an otherwise light reflecting bottom. Of course we started fishing for them, at first without any idea of what we were doing. But as I let the fly sink to bottom and then retrieved it with the "hand twist" retrieve, the following facts forced themselves into my unwilling brain. First that the fish appeared slightly interested but not enough to strike, and second that the instant the retrieve was started they immediately lost all interest.

It suggested two things—that the fly wasn't just right and that the manipulation was all wrong. Working on this I tied on one of my own nymphs, the No. 2 of salmon coloration. Because the trout seemed to become interested only when the former fly had reached a point a foot or so above them I let this nymph sink before attempting a retrieve. It never reached bottom. Several fish rushed for it before it had sunk three feet and one of them got it. Once again this happened and then the

PLATE NO. 5
Wet Flies

Kate	Katydid	Kendal	Kiffe	Kineo	King of Water
Kingdom	Kingfisher	Kinross	Kitson	Knowle's Fancy	La Belle
Lackey's Grant Lake	Lachene	Lady Gray	Lady Merton	Lady Mills	Lake Edward
Lake George	Lake Green	Langiwin	Laramie	Lanigan	Last Chance
Liberty	Light Blow	Light Fox	Light Polka	Lister's Gold	Lord Baltimore
Logan	Lowery	Loyal Sock	Luzerne	Magalloway	Magpie
Major	Mallard	Mark Lain	Marston's Fancy	March Brown American	March Brown Female
March Brown Male	March Dun	Marlow Buzz	Mascot	Marsters	Martin

Full descriptions of the flies on this plate will be found on pages 419–421.

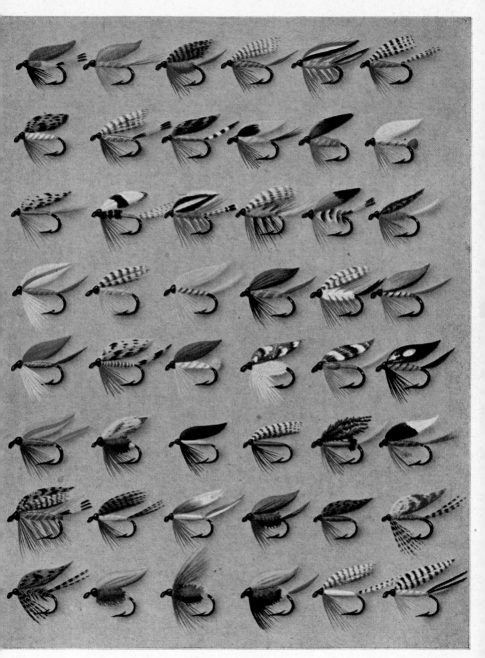

PLATE No. 5

trout refused to bother with the lure when it was sinking. I let it sink until it rested on the gravel, let it stay there perhaps half a minute and then started it moving at the very lowest speed possible. I had hardly started when I got a solid hit and connected.

There was no doubt about the effectiveness of this salmon-colored nymph but we soon found out that we had to fish it just so or else there wasn't any response. The retrieve was effective only when the movements were made so slowly that no jerks were in evidence—about six completed hand movements of the "hand twist" retrieve to the minute being just right provided they were made with slow deliberation. In addition, the retrieve wasn't the least bit effective unless the nymph was allowed to reach bottom before the movement was started.

It may seem odd to some of you that such slight differences in manipulation as changing the speed of retrieve three or four movements a minute or regulating the depth of the sinking fly a foot or so, would make the difference between success and failure, but it is on such trifles that our growth as a fisherman depends, as anyone who has achieved reputation as a successful angler will concede. If I succeed in driving home only a few of these trifles to the reader I shall feel well repaid for the headaches and long hours of work resulting from my efforts to provide positive working knowledge of angling lore for those who wish to improve their style. Generalities entertain but do not teach. As far as worth-while information goes the most important parts of this book are these paragraphs on details of manipulation which are scattered through it.

Even though they may not be aware of it successful anglers all have a certain indescribable something in their fishing which accounts for their personal success. One cannot expect to capture this elusive accomplishment in its entirety. It is a characteristic of the person who wins his success by it. But if one will attempt to analyze these small and apparently insignificant trifles, he will uncover some things which may be isolated and so presented to others that they may grasp the meaning if they are really interested and read to learn as well as for amusement. This is what I am attempting in "Trout." My own experiences and those of many friends are being torn apart, analyzed and reconstructed in some semblance of order for your benefit.

On this very day we had experienced two entirely different conditions which required special methods of attack in order to take fish. Still another was in store for us. In the afternoon we fished the lake above the falls. It was really nothing more than a widening of the stream caused by a dam. Here our nymphs and "hand twist" retrieve were worthless. By mere chance I put on a No. 6 Black Gnat, a regular northern pattern, and began playing with it, jerking it speedily through the water with the regular rod retrieve. A missed rise showed us the possibilities of the combination so we started using it seriously. It resulted in the best fish of the trip besides several others which we lost. But even at that the method was not effective unless the fly sank considerably before the retrieve was started.

The sunken fly and slow retrieve is particularly useful when the streams are so low and clear that it seems useless to fish and when the general consensus of opinion is that small dry flies are the only thing which will possibly produce. As a matter of fact the sunken fly is by far the best bet. When a dry fly alights on water which is clear and still and on which the sun is shining it causes a shadow quite unlike that of a natural insect. You see, the artificial is opaque while the natural is semi-transparent, thus the shadows made by them are quite different. Then too, the leader when used with a dry fly is quite likely to float instead of sink. We know that it is best for it to sink but more often than not it floats despite our efforts to make it do otherwise. This makes shadows which are very disturbing to the fish and does far more harm than most of us realize.

On the other hand a wet fly or nymph, thoroughly soaked before using, will sink the instant it touches the water and it takes a well-soaked leader down with it. The instant the fly and leader go below the surface the telltale shadows almost disappear. All that results is a shadow so slight that its effects are negligible. Also, the instant the fly or lure starts sinking it becomes an object of interest, rather than alarm, thus increasing our chances of success.

The first time I became fully aware of these phenomena I happened to be fishing one of the crystal clear streams of the Catskills. We were using dry flies but although trout were rising we could not take a fish, in fact every time we made a cast, no matter how delicate and perfect, the fish immediately stopped rising and stayed down from periods ranging from forty-five minutes to an hour and a half. If we waited until the fish began rising again it did not do any good because the very first cast put them down once more and this second time they frequently stayed down for good.

It was very discouraging and I would have quit except for a circumstance which led to some enlightening observations. Coming to a long and rather shallow pool I approached as carefully as I could and on reaching an advantageous position made ready to fish it. It was then I noticed that the light was just right for revealing the bottom to my searching gaze. In the deepest part were some thirty fish, most of them apparently inactive on the bottom. A half dozen were working near the surface and rising occasionally when some fly which appealed floated over them. This hole was located in the center of the stream. Some fifteen feet to the right and close to shore was another hole. The bottom here was not distinctly visible, nevertheless I could see that there were trout in it even though none were rising.

Although I was using an eighteen foot leader and directed the cast so that the fly dropped on the water below the fish, instead of over them, the very first false cast caused them to scatter like leaves in a wind. By the time the fly touched the water the entire school was darting and milling around as if greatly agitated. I let the fly lie there for about ten minutes. There was an almost imperceptible eddy current at the location which made it circle slightly. During this time the trout settled back to the bottom of the hole, those which had been rising apparently joining them. Not one fish had shown the slightest bit of interest in the fly floating above them. I began moving the fly slightly. This caused very evident nervousness on the part of the school. Several moments later the line began to belly and sink badly so that it was necessary to retrieve the fly and this action caused the trout to scatter wildly again.

The situation fascinated me. I decided to wait until the fish had recovered from their fright, until some of them started rising again. An hour later a few fish started taking flies from the surface and the rest seemed perfectly at ease, so I made another try. This time, however, I used a No. 14 eyed wet G. R. Hare's Ear. When I made the cast the fish scattered as before but because no false casts were made previous to the drop of the fly it did not cause as much excitement as my first effort with the dry fly. As I let the Hare's Ear sink I noted one great difference in its effect and that of the dry fly on the trout. The dry fly when motionless on the surface did not seem to frighten them but neither did it attract attention, or perhaps I should say interest as it is quite sure that the fish saw it. Not one fish made the slightest move toward it in the spirit of investigation. On the other hand the sinking of the wet fly created quite a bit of interest. Even though the trout had scattered at the cast at least a half dozen came toward the fly before it had reached a depth of three feet.

When it reached bottom I knew that these fish were near

the place. I let it lie there several moments and then lifted the rod tip enough to start the fly from bottom. I did not see any fish take but suddenly felt a tug and reacted quickly enough to set the hook in a fairly decent fish.

Subsequent experiments on this day and many other days and in different localities proved conclusively that trout, after being frightened, resumed feeding on bottom or in midwater before they did on the surface. They also proved that if the leader readily sank a dry fly did not cause as much disturbance as it did when the leader floated and that a sparsely tied translucent body fly caused less suspicion than a heavy-tied fly with a dense body.

The experiments also disclosed the fact that while the trout, after being scared, were soon susceptible to a sinking fly they were rarely interested in a floating one. There is a reasonable answer to this. In deep water trout feel safe. Water is their element just as air is ours and they know that the deeper they get the safer they are from dangers which threaten from outside their world. If you doubt this statement just try the following experiment. First locate some trout in shallow water. Then frighten them. What happens? They immediately go for deep water if it is available or hide under anything which will provide shelter. After this go to a pool of deep water where you can see the fish. Frighten them. They will not leave this hole. If it is filled with rocks which provide shelter they will hide under them but if not they will simply rush frantically around, never leaving the pool unless you get in it and actually push them out. If the bottom is soft or has any muddy portions the trout will hide in such places, burying themselves in the soft substance.

Speaking of mud it brings to mind a small stream in the extreme northern section of New York State. The upper reaches wander through a meadow and here the water ranges from a few inches to a couple of feet in depth. The bottom is soft sand, mud and weeds. Throughout the entire stretch trout are scattered everywhere. Many bends, where the water deepens slightly, contain as many as thirty fish ranging from 4 to 15 inches. If you should walk the banks of this brook every trout will have disappeared by the time you turn around to retrace your steps. However, if you look sharp you will see an occasional tail showing itself in the silt of the bottom. These fish bury themselves in this soft substance and stay there until the threatening danger has passed. Incidentally this is one of the most fascinating streams I've ever fished. I call it Spring Brook and the stream into which it runs River X. Needless to say these are not the real names of the brooks. I withhold them for obvious reasons—one that I do not want them publicized for personal reasons and the other that a friend who loves the place first brought me there and I could not betray his confidence. You'll read more about both of them in this chapter and in subsequent ones.

Here is an incident which illustrates the usefulness of "dabbling" a nymph as described in Chapter Four. The location is the north branch of Callicoon Creek. The fishing was very poor. In the morning we fooled around with nymphs, wet flies and dry flies but didn't get very far. Of course we fished in the orthodox manner and for the time being felt that we were doing the best we could and that the fish were simply off feed. Fortunately for us, finally I got tired of casting and started to think. Years ago I did not have any trouble taking fish under these conditions. I simply went to work gathering live nymphs from the rocks in the stream and then fished them from suitable spots in deep holes. Such methods always brought results. Why wouldn't they do the same now, if I tried them?

When this thought first occurred to me we were in a shallow stretch so that it was unwise to change. For some distance beyond this spot the stream was unsuitable for the idea I had in mind. The water was too fast and there were no deep holes. We fished it without results in various ways and with many different flies. Then we came to a pool which looked just right for the experiment.

On one side it was bounded by a flat and open gravel bar. On the other side the bank was high and well undermined. It was also well covered with brush and trees. The hole itself was normal—fairly shallow at the head where the current ran with fair speed, deep and quiet in the center, and shallow, although smooth and quite fast, at the tail.

It was one of those spots which anyone who has ever had anything to do with fishing would enthuse over. By this time I had become quite subdued by failure so that I did not rush headlong into the project in mind. Instead I looked the situation over carefully and then made a wide circuit of the hole so that I could approach it from the wooded side. When I got within fifteen feet of the pool I dropped to my hands and knees and crawled the balance of the way, stopping some six feet from the edge of the bank to string up my rod and get it ready for the job at hand.

Before starting on the expedition I had tied a nymph to a nine foot 3X leader (.007) and had placed them in a well-soaked leader box. Now I looked at them and because they were not wet enough waited about fifteen minutes more until I knew they would handle properly. I couldn't bring myself to use a live nymph until every other possible experiment with arificials had been tried. The nine foot leader proved too long. It would not straighten out. You see it was simply a proposition of flipping a few feet of line with just the leader dropping on the water. This entailed another wait until a 7½ foot leader tapering from .017 to .007 was soaked and so made ready for use.

I must admit that I was impatient and very nervous by the time this second leader was ready. I wasn't even sure that it would be satisfactory and it took all my will power to resist fishing anyway, even though the tackle wasn't just right.

At last the cast seemed pliable enough to work with. Restraining my impatience a bit more I looked the pool over carefully. Just below me was the deepest part. It was so deep that even though the water was extremely clear I could not see the bottom plainly. However, I could dimly see a score of trout who seemed to be moving slightly here and there in the eddy of the pool so I knew I had something to fish for.

With a flip of the rod I sent the nymph to the lower part of the current leading into the pool. It sank at once and drifted down into the deep water. Here a slight eddy caught it and kept it whirling around some three feet below the surface for a few moments. Then it started to descend rapidly. Soon the slack in the leader was all gone so I lowered the rod tip in order to let it go as deep as possible. Just as the line touched the water I saw a flash deep down and felt a tug. I was a bit slow and missed the hit. A few seconds later I saw another flash and this time struck instinctively and connected with a twelve inch trout. The disturbance caused by landing this fish scared the rest of the trout in the pool so I left it and went searching for another.

The balance of that day was spent in fishing suitable locations in this manner. The net result was seven fish running from 10 inches to 14 inches. Each time one fish was taken it spoiled the pool for further fishing.

Since that time I have frequently used this method when conditions were so contrary that fish could not be taken by ordinary methods. Just to show you how useful it is let me tell you of an experience which took place in 1933—date May 20th, location same stream.

Although it was still early in the season the water was clear and low. In addition there were not many flies hatching and rising trout were few and far between. My companion was a well-known member of the Anglers Club of New York, A. W. Miller—affectionately called Deac—a good fisherman and a student. However, at the time he didn't think much of nymphs, and while he was too much the gentleman to say anything derogatory about them I could see skepticism in his eye every time I mentioned their importance.

When we first started fishing, a trout was rising under the bridge which covered the first hole we selected for our starting point. Although Deac was quite insistent that I fish the water first I refused to do so, because I can never bring myself to fish a good piece of water before my guest has his try at it and because I knew the water, realized the conditions from previous experiences, and was pretty sure that a nymph would be better than a dry fly.

At this time Deac was a dry fly purist. Unless he could get them by this method he preferred to do without any fish. He placed as pretty a fly as anyone could wish to see in just the right position under the bridge. He did it not only once but a score of times. Once he got a half-hearted splash but from where I stood I could see that it wasn't a " business rise " so that he could not be blamed for missing it. As a matter of fact the trout never touched the fly. Some fifteen minutes later he conceded defeat and told me to try my luck.

During this time I had not been wasting my time. I had looked over the situation carefully and had decided that I could move thirty feet closer to the fish than from where Deac had been fishing. Because I did not know this particular bit of water perfectly I used a dry fly dropper on the leader above the nymph. This was to help me in floating the nymph perfectly and at the same time see any action that might occur from the performance of the dry fly.

I selected a position about twenty feet from the fish, off to the left side of the stream. When ready to cast I was almost opposite the trout but because of the broken water where the fish was located felt sure that he did not see me. Nevertheless I waited until he rose again, before casting. The moment he did I cast the lure about four feet above him and in the correct position so that the current would carry it within his vision. This was easy because the cast was short and yet brought into play the required quantity of line to make it accurate. I watched the dry fly closely. For several feet it floated the same speed as the current and then it hesitated—stopped. Immediately I struck and hooked a ten inch Brown.

But this incident did not aid us much. As we went upstream we were discouraged by the absence of rising fish. Coming to an ideal pool for the purpose I decided to do some dabbling." The background was perfectly wooded so that it completely concealed my person. Also the bank was high and the pool small so that I knew I could see everything which transpired as well as handle the nymph correctly.

Although I knew just what I was doing I made a mess of the fishing in this pool. Somehow I could not connect with the fish that hit my lure, even though I saw them take it. I know I had ten good hits from fish ranging from ten to fifteen inches and missed every one even though I felt a decided tug each time one struck.

At the next suitable hole I thought I would try some natural nymphs so upturned a vast number of rocks to get several large enough to use. The net results were two more fairly decent trout. This restored my confidence so that I discontinued using naturals and returned to artificials. The brief interlude of using naturals had effected the desired result. Now I hooked at least 50 percent of the fish which took the artificial. Deac was becoming more interested in nymph fishing every time I got a strike.

By the time evening came I had a nice creel of fish but nothing better than twelve inches and only one of that size. The balance of the day has nothing to do with nymph fishing except to show that when conditions are not right for them they are worthless just as dry flies are when conditions are not right for them. It is a matter of record that as the sun approached the western horizon the nymph became less effective and, as it disappeared behind the hills, became absolutely useless.

At this time Deac and I separated. There were several hundred yards of good fishing water ahead of us and we could both fish good water without disturbing the other. Because the trout no longer took the nymph I changed to a dry fly—a Fan Wing Royal. Instead of fishing all the water I had allotted to myself I decided to head straight for a long pool which I knew contained several good fish. When I got there I saw several trout rising in the fast water at the head. This was good. In water of this sort it did not hurt to hook a fish. The others would not become suspicious unless the hooked one fought directly where hooked—something which was hardly likely to happen because a hooked fish usually immediately leaves the spot where something he thought good to eat turns out to be a stinging, resisting bit which continually forces him to use all his strength to oppose it. (NOTE. In quiet water a struggling fish might make all the other fish within sight of the disturbance suspicious. However, this is not always true because often the rest of the fish in the immediate location will follow the hooked fish—no doubt thinking that it has captured something good to eat that they should have a share of.)

For once in my life I did not get excited. I sat down on the shale rock at the edge of the pool and considered the situation carefully before making the first cast. The flies on the stream were quite large—about number tens—and of a light ginger coloration. Certainly my Royal Coachman did not imitate them in the slightest. By a lucky chance I happened to have a Fan Wing Light Cahill in my fly box—a delicate mixture of light ginger hackle and ginger dyed mallard wings. As far as I could see this imitated the natural better than anything else I had.

Whether it really did remains a debatable question. It is true that the first cast with this dry fly took a twelve inch trout and the second cast a fifteen incher but inasmuch as the Royal Coachman was not used and did not have a chance to prove itself we cannot say that the Light Cahill was necessary. There is a good chance that the fish would have taken any fly which was cast over them in the right way.

As I landed the last fish Deac appeared on the scene. He was very enthusiastic over my good fortune but a bit disgusted with himself. " I muffed my chances," he said. " Had several good rises but the trout are still in the stream." He knew why he had failed to put one of these fish in his creel. He had spent the entire day fishing with a dry fly when the fish refused to take anything on the surface. Being a sportsman of the highest type he repressed his feeling of discouragement and disappointment and so his nerves were on edge by the time his chance came. Because of this he " blew up " when he saw success in his grasp and struck too hard and fast. Need I say more? I've done the same thing many times and shall probably do it many times in the future. On this particular evening I was in good condition for taking advantage of any opportunity which presented itself. I had a fair catch of fish and had had so many strikes at the nymph which I had missed that I had used up all my excess nervous energy, that tension which so often causes faulty striking. When the rise to the surface came I was as cool as a cucumber. Therefore I calculated my chances carefully and fished with deliberation and steady nerves. That was why I had good luck.

The experience was of real benefit to Deac. Although he kidded me about the nymph fishing he was genuinely interested in the game and was soon experimenting with it. Before long he began to get results and so made a step forward in his progress as an all around angler. Besides having a higher percentage of good fishing days when the trout refused to take a surface fly he also became a more efficient dry fly fisherman because the use of the nymph taught him some things which the dry fly fails to do. Incidentally he recently told me that he considered my No. 1 nymph design the best lure of this type for the Beaverkill. As this particular pattern was designed especially for this stream it pleases me to know that an angler of his caliber and standing has placed his seal of approval on the design.

Out at Spring Creek, which was Ollie Deibler's pet project when he was Fish Commissioner of the state of Pennsylvania, I had some interesting experiences with wet flies. For instance, one morning a lightly cast fly was absolutely ineffective. The results were so poor that I finally became careless and slapped the fly on the water so hard that it made a splash. It brought a rise from a good fish which I hooked and landed. I recognized this as a hint and took advantage of it, started slapping the fly on the water as hard as I could. For two hours I had some rare sport and took a lot of fish, all of which were returned to the water after being unhooked carefully.

After lunch this method failed to produce. I fooled around with one thing or another for some time and finally started fishing upstream with a heavy fly which sank deeply. I let it sink as it would and simply kept the line from coming taut against the fly. The first time I did this the fly drifted some fifteen feet and was quite deep when I saw the line twitch slightly. I struck and connected with a nice Brook Trout. Fishing from the same spot and making the same drift each time I took six more good fish on six casts.

Then this method failed. Trying all sorts of things I finally put on a split shot and sunk the fly to bottom before moving it. Then I worked it very slowly indeed with the " hand twist " retrieve. The results were quite pleasing. Three fish larger than any I had caught previously. But toward evening the fish started rising and would not take wet flies or nymphs no matter how they were fished.

Just consider this one day on a stream which probably has more fish to the square yard than any other stream in the country except perhaps those in some private preserves. Four changes in method needed in one day. Do you wonder that I stress the importance of knowing many methods of using flies and lures? One must do so in order to get even fair results, especially in these days of concentrated fishing when the fish are becoming wiser every season.

An interesting angle to the fishing at Spring Creek is provided by the fact that the fish are fed regularly with a reddish conglomeration of ground lights and salt water fish, a combination which they told me at the hatchery had been found very satisfactory. This feeding of the fish in the stream is absolutely necessary because there are far more trout in the water than it could sustain naturally.

When the food is distributed it is thrown on the water with dippers and, being rather soggy in texture, it keeps together well enough to fall on the stream in rather large chunks thus causing an audible smack and some surface disturbance. Because of this I realized that when I cast a large fly so that it slapped the water it was imitating, to some extent, the food which the fish had become accustomed to, and so accounted for my success when fishing a fly in this manner.

But this conclusion did not explain why the fish suddenly refused a fly slapped on the water and preferred one which drifted naturally. Neither did it explain why the fish suddenly refused all artificials except dry flies AND YET TOOK GROUND-UP FOOD AT ANY TIME, EITHER ON OR BELOW THE SURFACE. My first reaction to this thought was to tie a fly of the same color as the food being fed the trout. " They will do the work," I thought as I looked at my creations which resembled the ground-up lights.

But while the idea was sound enough it did not work. The fish took the fly which looked like meat but not any better than they did any other artificial. When my "meat" fly worked so did any other fly. Here another fact showed up. You could fish a stretch of water without a single rise to your credit and then, when food was thrown in, take fish after fish on the same fly which had been refused a moment before. When the food was thrown on the water they seemed to lose all caution and took anything which floated along with it. Why? Was it because the appearance of the food they were accustomed to getting made them feel safe in taking anything which looked edible? Or did the appearance of the food make them excited and piggish so that they dashed at anything which drifted along with the current? Perhaps in such cases each fish tried to get at the food first and selfishly attempted to get more than the rest. According to my personal observations I'd say that the latter reaction was the true one. I feel sure that large quantities of food excite the cupidity of fish. Certainly anyone who has observed at all must know that no individual fish ever gives any other fish any part of what he gets himself. "To the victor belongs the spoils" is a law of nature which cannot be disputed. When one fish gets something he keeps it unless some other fish takes it away from him by force or superior agility. Any fish that has more than he can swallow immediately is followed and harassed by many others and often loses part of what he has secured. No one can possibly deny this.

In the higher organization of humans we often find the same condition, in fact it is always present in some degree. But here we find a difference from wild life. The apparently ruthless human may also be compassionate and everyone is at some time or another. So to relieve a tortured conscience such individuals do deeds of kindness which offset their wrongs and are of great benefit to mankind in general, as well as specifically in some cases. We need this aggressiveness, both in wild and human life. Otherwise we would retrogress to the Stone Age or even further. But we also need those persons who oppose the type so that we will not be controlled by one individual or group of individuals who are more aggressive or more ruthless than the great majority. This balance is what we need for government, and for perpetuating a higher type of civilization. There is no place for a drone. In wild life this condition is very apparent.

Of course the fish in Spring Creek are not usually fed when anglers are on the stream. But for experimental purposes we did have some food thrown out while the section was open to fishing. The results were interesting and thought-provoking. At the time we selected, the fishing was at a low ebb. Not one of the fishermen within our immediate vicinity had had a rise for several hours. It seemed as if there weren't any trout in the water. All true anglers will recognize this feeling. Of course we always know better but we do have our doubts at times.

But the first dipper of prepared food brought at least thirty trout to the surface and several anglers who happened to have flies on or in the water at the time took trout. The next few dippers caused the water to boil and at least seven fishermen connected with good fish. Inasmuch as the flies being used ranged from delicate dry flies to coarse streamers it clearly showed that what they were using had nothing to do with their success. The reason they caught fish was due to the appearance of food the trout were looking for. They expected it and so waited until it appeared unless a particularly appetizing and abundant hatch of natural insects appeared, in which case they started feeding on them and were susceptible to any artificial which imitated them.

To my mind this suggests possibilities for the angler's campaign. I wonder how a concentrated effort on the part of many fishermen would react on such trout? Suppose a group got together and all fished the same water with large flies? Would the fish think that the artificials were real and would they start feeding? I am not in the least sure that they would but there is an idea here which might result in something worth while. After all, heavily stocked waters in which the fish are fed regularly require special thought, and as such streams are becoming more necessary with each advancing season they deserve some consideration.

It is quite likely that the fish would not be fooled by the concentrated attack at all. It is almost certain that the reason they hit the artificials floating down in company with the prepared food was because they knew that in order to get their share of " easy pickings " they had to grab anything they saw quickly and did not wait to investigate its quality or genuineness. I'm puzzled and uncertain about it all, as it pertains to fishing, but I feel that my idea might find root in the mind of some other angler who will delve deeper into the subject.

Writing about this brings back some old memories. Years ago I found out that the sudden appearance of muddy water often started the trout feeding and invariably made them less suspicious. To take advantage of this fact, after the streams had become low and clear, I used to pick out a suitable stretch, go above it and cause a good supply of dirt to muddy the water. Then I would go below and fish the water with a wet fly. Time after time it resulted in good fishing when it was absolutely impossible to get trout by ordinary means. Of course the stream cleared quickly from the results of my work so that the activity was short-lived but it did serve to pep up the blank days of July and August. I haven't used this method for twenty years now, because I feel that it is somewhat unethical, but have included it here because it shows that observation and the application of the knowledge gained by observation invariably lead to successful fishing.

Some fifteen to twenty miles from New York City, in the state of New Jersey, the Hackensack River glides smoothly through meadow and swampy forest land. It doesn't look like a trout stream nor was it one when I was a young man. As far upstream as the Congers-New City Road in New York State this river was populated by pickerel. From this point on one began to take an occasional trout and the brook above the junction at Verdin Brook was one of the best Brook Trout streams one would ever hope to find. But the lower stretches were pickerel water, pure and simple, and although once in a great while someone would pick up a large trout we all knew that it was because the fish was large enough to be immune from the attacks of the pickerel and that no small trout could survive in the water.

When New Jersey became conservation minded and began their program of restocking they decided that the Hackensack near the New Jersey-New York line deserved some attention. Their efforts in its behalf were well worth while. The trout put in here seemed to do very well. Many of them moved upstream and provided trout fishing in the New York part of the stream but most of them stayed in the vicinity of the " Old Tappan " stretch.

However, the type of water at this point does not lend itself to easy fishing and while at first fishermen made wonderful catches without much effort, after a time the fish seemed to get wise and only accomplished anglers could get worth-while results.

While I never happened to fish this particular stretch of the river I have two friends who fish it many times each season. They are Al Argenti and Tony Savoca of Northvale, N. J. Al is a " natural " who instinctively short-cuts through any problem. He seems to know just what to do without fussing or fuming. He does not analyze the problem but he unerringly puts his finger on the things which solve it. Tony, while not possessing Al's intuition, has that analytical sort of a brain which searches for and isolates the reasons for Al's success. Between the two they make a great pair and certainly go places when it comes to taking fish under adverse conditions.

As I worked on this chapter of " Trout " these boys came in to see me. Because I believed that their views on wet fly fishing would be worth while passing on to others I turned the conversation into these channels and we checked up with their experiences on the Hackensack and compared them with mine on waters of similar type.

" The flies must be fished slow," asserted Tony.

" With this retrieve? " I questioned—getting a rod and demonstrating the " hand twist."

" Yes," was the reply. " But sometimes it's best to let them float without any motion except that supplied by the current."

Before we got through we found that the following methods, both of which have been described in previous pages, were the reasons for their success.

" Hand twist retrieve "—SLOW.

" Natural drift "—Both upstream and down and across stream methods.

" Most fellows fish their flies too fast," they insisted. They also stressed the importance of using the pattern and size of fly for the prevailing conditions. This confirmation of my own ideas coming from two fellows who have shown time and again that they know their fishing is very gratifying. Only thoughtful, constructive articles and books are capable of gaining and holding their interest.

Several years ago these two men accompanied me to a pet stream of mine in northern New York. We were out primarily for dry fly fishing and didn't spend any time trying other methods. But one afternoon while we were walking downstream to place ourselves in scattered positions along a favorite

stretch we passed a pool in which we saw the splash of a large
fish.

Of course we stopped to look and presently saw another
wrinkle on the water which looked like a rise. We decided to
investigate.

The boys refused to fish. Said it was up to me. Before starting I looked the situation over carefully. At the head, the riffle
hugged the far shore and was quite narrow. About ten feet
lower down the riffle changed into a smooth glide with fair
speed. This glide also hugged the far shore and the water
looked about twice as deep as the riffle. Below the glide the
stream spread out into a fairly deep and very quiet stretch some
30 feet wide and 70 feet long.

The first rise had been seen about halfway down the glide.
The second rise had occurred at the tail of the riffle. Now as
I got ready I saw a rise at the tail of the glide. At first I thought
that there were several fish feeding but closer observation disclosed that they were all caused by one fish which seemed to
be cruising up and down the stretch. I saw the trout working
up through the glide and saw him take several insects which
seemed to be drifting down at various depths. He then proceeded almost to the top of the riffle where he started " tailing." After several moments at this occupation he came swiftly
back to the tail of the glide and started upstream again.

It didn't take long to see just what he was about. He was
dislodging nymphs from the bottom in the riffle and then working the water below to feed on the food he had uprooted. At
this time the boys were frankly skeptical about nymph fishing.
They had tried it without success. I believed it to be a good
opportunity to present an object lesson on the value of nymph
fishing so proceeded to make what I hoped would be a spectacular demonstration. First I fished with a dry fly. It was my
desire to show the boys that this fish would not take the floating fly. I felt reasonably sure that the dry fly would be ignored

because there were quite a number of duns on the stream and this fish had not taken one while I watched. I gave the dry fly plenty of chance and changed patterns several times but the trout did not take the slightest notice of them. Then I went a bit further and tried the ordinary variety of wet flies. These also were ignored. " So far, so good," I exulted inwardly. " If he'd taken any of these flies it would have spoiled everything."

Now came the ticklish part of my demonstration. I knew that I'd get only one chance and deliberately prepared to make it a good one. Tying on a No. 1 R. B.—size 12LS nymph I waited until the fish had finished his grubbing job in the riffle and was on his way downstream. As he turned to work back upstream my nymph dropped in the riffle and started drifting downstream. It required all my attention to keep the lure located and the slack line at proper length so that I could not see where the fish was but as my fly reached the center of the glide I saw a swirl by it, lifted the rod to take up the slack, and felt that electric thrill caused by the hooking of a good fish.

You should have heard Tony and Al yell. You never saw two more enthusiastic anglers. They were all for nymph fishing now. But strangely enough on this day that one trout was the only one which seemed to be interested in nymphs. The rest all preferred a light ginger fly floating on the surface. Of course I had been lucky in making my demonstration. Everything had worked according to Hoyle and that is quite extraordinary as everyone knows who has tried to illustrate some particular point about fishing to someone he is trying to impress. But the boys stoutly claim that luck had nothing to do with it. I'm glad they feel that way about it because it certainly gives one a moral uplift to know that someone thinks he is a pretty good fisherman.

And here is another incident illustrating the value of nymphs. This took place some 2,000 miles away from New York on a Wyoming stream. Although at this particular time dry flies produced very well, certain sections which contained large fish were so situated that dry flies did not interest the trout which lived in them. You see they were rather deep holes located under banks and undermined tree roots against which the current ran rather swiftly and then turned at an abrupt obtuse angle. Such holes rarely extended more than eight or ten feet below the point where the current gouged out the bank and while the lower portions always yielded some medium sized fish I felt certain that the undercover portions contained larger ones so I determined to experiment a bit.

Picking out one particularly attractive-looking spot I first fished it with a dry fly, making the cast from the tail and placing the fly well up in the riffle. I did this several times until I had impressed on my mind the time required for this fly to float down the riffle and to the alder-covered bank. Once I got this point well established I changed to a nymph which I soaked well and then cast it to the same spot. When I figured that it had reached the bank I allowed some thirty seconds additional time to let it get under the cover and then raised the rod cautiously. I felt a slight pull and instinctively reacted with a strike. Instantly I was playing a fish that felt heavier than any I had previously taken and subsequently landed a three pound Brown Trout, dark and brilliantly colored.

I soon found out that I had been lucky in hooking this fish. Later experiences brought many misses and I could not seem to get the technique of striking down well enough to get a better average than 25 percent. However, strikes I did get, and many of them, so that I considered the experiment of exceeding value.

Incidentally this method is very useful when you get a rise to a dry fly that you miss, especially when they occur a few feet above locations such as described in the above experience. Such rising fish rarely return for another dry fly but will usually take a nymph which is fished so that it drifts under the bank. From observation I find that when a trout rises to a surface fly and misses he usually returns to his normal home and is a bit startled over the occurrence, besides being suspicious of surface food. However, his appetite has not been appeased so when an attractive-looking morsel appears down in his hole he is quite likely to take it. Experiences proving this have happened to me so often that I feel my observations about them are sound and worth while. But you must calculate the drift of the nymph to perfection otherwise you will become discouraged and think it all a lot of worthless talk. The average nymph fishing does not lend itself to careless work or superficial study. You must know what you are doing and do it well, otherwise the results will not encourage you to further trial with them.

One can never tell just what to do nor be sure that because one method works between certain hours that it will continue to do so for the balance of the day. Here is an incident pertinent to this situation. The location is in northern New Jersey. I had never fished the stream and two friends who considered it ideal took me there to show me what a real stream was like.

Of course it was the same old story. " It was never this way before," and " Something is wrong today," were remarks which I heard frequently. At noon not one of us had taken a fish—in fact we hadn't had even a rise.

After lunch things weren't any better. " Let's sit by the stream and watch," I suggested. " Certainly there isn't any use in pounding water the way we've been doing. Either the fish aren't taking at all or else we're using the wrong methods."

The boys were willing so we sat. I happened to take a position directly at the edge of the stream alongside a rather sizeable riffle which contained some good-looking pockets. More to pass the time than anything else I rigged up a cast of three wet flies and when it was finished started whipping it carelessly over the riffle. I got tired of this so let the current take the flies downstream and then amused myself by dancing the two droppers over the water as the tail fly held the leader reasonably taut against the current. It was interesting to see flies skip on the waves of the riffle and I had become quite absorbed in seeing how well I could do the job when a trout rose swiftly to the hand fly which was touching the water only once in a while. He hooked himself securely and I had the pleasure of landing an eleven inch Brook Trout.

Without moving from my comfortable seat I tried the stunt again. This time I skipped the center fly over the water, the hand fly being a foot or two in the air while doing this. A trout grabbed the skipping fly and pulled it under the surface. This brought the hand fly to the top of the water and the instant it arrived there a fish hit it so hard that he broke the fly from the tippet. However the other fish was still on and soon was in the creel.

Of course, this incident woke us up and we went at the fishing with great enthusiasm, using the method which I had stumbled upon while idling. As a matter of fact I had often used it in the past but had somehow forgotten it until I started playing with the flies. Even then I did not expect it to produce but it did and for three hours after we had some good sport.

Then came a change. Suddenly the trout would not take our dancing flies. For an hour I worked diligently without getting a rise. As is usually the case under such circumstances I felt sure that the fish had stopped feeding but on coming to a long glide I saw a good-sized trout breaking at the lower end so knew that the trouble was with my method and not the fish. I first tried the dancing flies over this fish but he ignored them. Then I tried all the other methods of wet fly fishing but it did no good. Although I'm not fond of spinner fishing I decided to try one at this time just to see if the trout would take it. Instead of rigging up a special leader I took off the tail fly and tied the spinner in its place.

The ruse taught me something. The trout did not hit the spinner but he did take the center fly. At first I thought it an accident but when I took another fish on the next cast, also on the first dropper and then caught a half dozen more in other pools, some on the center fly and some on the hand fly, I began to realize that in some way the spinner on the end of the leader had something to do with my success. Not wanting any more fish anyway I did a little experimenting. The cast of flies alone, no matter how fished, would not produce, but the moment a spinner was placed at the end of the leader, action began. Observation showed that the spinner imparted a peculiar action to the flies which seemed to be what the fish desired—AT THIS PARTICULAR TIME. Not one of the fish hit the spinner and I found that when the hooks were taken from it the results were even more satisfying. Incidentally, on subsequent experiments I discovered that sometimes the method worked and at other times it did not. Often the trout would hit nothing but the spinner and sometimes they would not hit either fly or spinner but would take flies manipulated in some other way. The experiences clearly showed the necessity of variation in one's fishing.

Whatever you do, don't overlook the possibilities of very small nymphs and wet flies, that is 14's and 16's and even smaller if obtainable. There is a preponderance of tiny larvæ and flies on most of our streams and while we can't hope to ever imitate the smallest ones we can get some artificials tied as small as possible and so be in a position to take advantage of many rises and feeding periods when the trout refuse our larger flies. Several years ago I tied up two dozen No. 18 translucent nymphs. It took me two days to do it but I've never regretted having spent the time. In ponds and streams from New York to Wyoming they have sometimes turned a day of failure to one of success and would have probably done so in the territories both east and west of those mentioned had it been necessary to use them. To carry these midge wet flies and nymphs in your kit is to be prepared for emergencies. Just remember that one of the toughest times to take trout is when they are feeding on very small insects or larvæ. While having the smallest artificials possible will not take care of all such hatches they will produce results often enough to make having them worth while.

As an illustration let me tell you of an experience which took place late one afternoon in the High Sierras of California. During the last hour before sunset the fish had responded well to a dry fly but after the sun disappeared behind the peaks the trout suddenly refused the floating fly even though they continued to break the surface of the water.

After several changes in sizes and types of dry flies which failed to interest the fish I started experimenting with nymphs. Nothing happened until I tied on one of the tiny 18's. By this time it was getting too dark to fish a nymph well but at that, during the brief period between then and total blackness, I rose twelve fish and hooked two. It is a question what might have happened had I used this midge nymph sooner. Perhaps the fish would have taken it eagerly; perhaps they wouldn't have taken it at all until that last moment when I started using it—perhaps the moment they began to refuse the dry flies was the time they changed their selection of diet. We have no way of absolutely proving things which happen this way as we have no check against them. Nevertheless the small nymphs did the work and took the two best trout of the evening. I missed the others because I could not see what I was doing and so had to strike blindly at swirls which caught the fast fading light in their waves or at slight tugs, which carried through to the tip of the rod.

While the above experience deals with nymphs the same thing holds true with tiny wet flies. As a general rule 14's are the smallest you will need but once in a while a much smaller fly will bring better results. In my experience with these midges I've never found a large variety of patterns necessary, in fact almost any pattern seems to be okay as long as it is small enough. It is also best when tied very sparse with a small body and just a few wisps of hackle. Strangely enough I've found these tiny flies just as effective in fast water as I have in still water. It hasn't been necessary to use them often. The notes of the last four seasons reveal five times when they were necessary to produce fish consistently under the conditions.

Always keep in mind that wet fly fishing is a game in which intuitive reactions are most important. The most infinitesimal happening should be remembered, and analyzed if possible, so that it may be used on future fishing trips. It is the accumulation of such incidents and the absorbing of them so that they become an unconscious part of your angling technique which makes for perfection.

CHAPTER SIX

Bucktails and Streamers

IN FLIES of this type we have a welcome and needed aid for the angler who does not care to use bait under any circumstances and who might otherwise quit without a fish. These flies are excellent for use under conditions when dry flies and ordinary wet flies are ineffective and are also generally useful throughout the season.

I am somewhat surprised to note how many anglers have the idea that flies of this type are adaptable only in the case of high and discolored water or in the early season before good fly fishing starts. As a matter of fact, frequently they produce during low and clear water conditions and there is hardly a day's fishing which can't be made a bit better because of the wise use of such flies in some particularly baffling situation.

By this I do not mean to imply that they are adaptable on all occasions; that you could use them to the exclusion of everything else and benefit thereby. Rather do they serve as an additional artifice with which you may succeed in deceiving some wary specimens or perhaps overcome the difficulties of certain stream conditions not controllable by other methods and flies. At the same time they are quite sporty to use, in many cases the rises to them being as perfectly visible as when made to a floating fly.

In my opinion a large assortment of patterns is not necessary but the assortment should be varied, both in colors and sizes. One type, originally conceived by a Mr. Hobbs in Connecticut and since continued by a reputable New England firm, has always been most satisfactory. It is really nothing more than a regular bucktail fly but has the addition of an enamel head on which is painted an eye. Whether this eye means anything is subject to debate. Some experiences I have had seem to prove that the eye did make a difference. In searching around for a reason for this I noted that some small minnows and other tiny specimens of different species had conspicuous eyes, and that these eyes were visible in the water even when you could not distinguish the rest of the fish. It is possible that an eye painted on the head of an artificial may produce an effect particularly acceptable for some trout and under certain conditions. At any rate, while these flies are not infallible, any more than many other varieties of artificials, I do think the idea has enough merit to be worth considering.

My favorite colors for this particular type are brown and white and black and white. At times I also like a yellow and orange combination. As a rule, when fishing for ordinary stream trout, sizes ranging from 6 to 10 will prove useful and if one size doesn't work do not give up without trying the other sizes. I have run across conditions when a 10 fly took fish when a 6 wouldn't—the same pattern too. On the whole I find the 8's and 10's most useful and if it was necessary to confine my purchases to one size it would be a 10.

Another type of minnow fly is the one made with a combination of feathers and hair (either bucktail or squirrel). While these are not as durable as the straight bucktails due to the frailty of the hackle streamer feathers, which have a tendency to break off, they have additional life and action in the water due to these very feathers and so sometimes excite the trout into striking when the straight bucktails fail. Also, in fashioning these flies one can choose from a variety of feathers to make striped minnow body effects which aids the fly tier to more nearly imitate specific minnows on which the trout may be feeding. Badger comes in several shades and in different densities of black centers. Furnace, Grizzly (barred rock), Red Grizzly and other more rare varieties provide an assortment of natural color combinations which are well worth tying. Besides, you can combine different hairs and feathers or use feathers alone such as " Gootenburg's Jersey Minnow " shown on color plate No. 12. This fly was designed by Dr. Phil Gootenburg of Oakland, N. J., for special use on the Ramapo River and simulates a small minnow prevalent in this stream. It would have been impossible to get this effect with bucktail alone although bucktail or squirrel tail could be added to give a more lifelike effect if required.

Nearly every angler has some ideas along these lines and this is a good thing. It continually creates new interest and provides new topics for discussion. Every once in a while some fellow has an unusually clever idea and produces a fly which is outstanding in performance no matter where used, while patterns for specific localities are continually making their appearance. These patterns for specific places are sometimes necessary but usually some standard pattern will do the same work. This is not intended as a criticism of patterns which have no national standing. It is intended only to show prospective anglers that they need not worry if they haven't got every pattern made. No one could possibly expect to carry all the different flies and be able to find just what he should have at some particular place at the very time he needed it. There is a decided need for simplification and whether you use Tom, Dick or Harry's particular killer it does not matter as long as you have some fly which will work at that particular time. Remember that no one yet has ever devised a fly which always catches fish. It isn't likely that anyone ever will. If someone claims this distinction for a certain pattern just make a bet with him. Go fishing with him day after day and see what happens. As a matter of fact, regardless of all the new flies, I still place my greatest faith in those patterns which have been handed down to us from old time anglers. It's hard to beat them and today's best are mostly variations of these old timers. I know some fellows who carry so many different flies that they spend valuable time trying out their stock when they could get better results if they used only one fly and concentrated on fishing in places where a willing fish might be. From my observations I think most of us spend too much time worrying about our tackle and too little time learning the intimate characteristics of the fish in the streams we fish most. Don't forget that a person who has exceptional knowledge of trout, even though his equipment may be nothing more than a cane pole and a crudely fashioned fly, can take some trout under conditions which might well tax the ingenuity of the most elaborately equipped angler whose knowledge of fish is somewhat above the ordinary. That does not mean that the fellow with nondescript tackle would do poorly with a good outfit. On the contrary he would do much better than with his crude outfit—once he learned how to handle it. But it does mean that no matter how good your outfit, it won't be worth anything to you unless you first assimilate enough fishing sense to make it possible for your outfit to do its part. After all, tackle is not alive. It cannot think. It cannot perform by itself. It needs your directing influence and if that is misdirected the best tackle in the world can't do anything for you.

It is a good rule always to blame yourself if you have poor luck. Be unmerciful in your judgment of YOU; in the way you fish, in the places you fish, in every motion you make. Only in this way can you expect to progress. Each time you discipline yourself you recognize faults which should be corrected and this means advance, for, once you admit a fault, you instinctively try to correct it.

Sometimes extra large and outlandish looking flies are extremely effective, even on small streams. Two such patterns are the Marabou and the Black Ghost. As land-locked salmon and bass patterns these look swell—but for trout? Well, I know I was laughed at several times when I first brought them out in front of conservative anglers but they didn't laugh after they saw the effect they had on trout. The original pattern of the Marabou was described in the book entitled "Just Fishing." It was white and the photographed pattern was tied by A. M. Ballou of North Dighton, Mass. The colored engraving of the one in this book is approximately the same but was tied by myself. Since the advent of this fly other varieties have appeared. One in particular, the Yellow Breeches, a combination originating in the brains of Charlie Fox and Bob McCafferty of Pennsylvania, has proved itself an excellent addition to a family which most likely will grow. In the color plates this is designated by the name Yellow Marabou, simply to avoid confusing the reader and to keep the type classification apart from the regular flies. But Yellow Breeches is the real name and while my pattern as shown on the plate is tied a bit differently from Charlie and Bob's the general effect is the same. I have tried out Blue Gray, Scarlet and Green Marabous but the results obtained with them were not sufficiently outstanding to deserve more than a passing mention. However Bob McCafferty tells me that black is good. It should be. He gave me one he tied and I'm sold on it. I only wonder how I overlooked it in the first place. It should be particularly good in milky water where it certainly would be seen by any trout that was hungry enough to feed.

I don't think it necessary to elaborate further on bucktail and streamer patterns. Most any combination of colors and materials will prove effective and you have quite a number of patterns to select from on the color plates, all being of proven worth. Just be sure you have an assortment of sizes and have them tied both on 3X long and extra long shanked hooks.

While one may fish streamers and bucktails with short and coarse leaders, care in the selection of terminal tackle is just as important for the best success with them as it is when fishing with dry flies or nymphs.

For the smaller sizes, say 12's and 14's, a nine foot leader tapering to 3X is excellent. However, you will often find a 12 foot leader or one even longer is much better when fishing low and clear water. For sizes 8 and 10 I think you will find that a 1 or 2X leader is more satisfactory. In my estimation 2X is tops for size 10LS with 1X being slightly superior for 8LS. The 10LS and the 2X leader are more suitable for average clear water conditions and at the same time will do good work when the streams are very low and clear. The 1X leader and flies from 6LS to 8LS may be used wherever a large fly is necessary and the stream conditions such that the coarser tackle does not make any difference.

Under any conditions where extreme caution is required to keep trout from becoming suspicious 12 to 15 foot leaders will be found more effective than those ranging from 7½ to 9 feet. Regular reasons for this will be found in other chapters of " Trout." Just now I want to call your attention to a special reason. When a fly splashes on the water, something which is likely to happen with bucktails and streamers, it either frightens or attracts. Observation has shown me that in low, clear water when the trout are wary and skittish they will often be frightened by a splash of a fly tied on a 7½ foot leader but will be attracted to the same fly making the same sort of a splash when tied on a 14 foot leader. Of course it does not always work out this way. Sometimes it does not make the slightest difference but it does make a difference often enough to be worth while trying.

As an illustration of the value of both bucktails and long leaders when fishing low, clear water let me relate an experience which took place on Encampment Brook in Wyoming. While ordinarily we considered this an ideal dry fly stream, on this occasion our drys did not produce during the first three days of our stay. For instance, there is one bit of water at the upper end of the canyon stretch which is literally alive with fish. Three days we went there and each day the trout appeared to be rising enthusiastically but unfortunately were taking minute flies impossible to imitate successfully. For at least three hours of this third day Fred Gerken and I worked over these fish with dry flies. We bent pattern after pattern on the leader, tried each one from five to ten minutes and then discarded it. The smallest sizes we had with us were 16's and these looked like giants compared to the microscopic specimens the trout seemed to be taking. However the 16's did do a bit better than the larger flies, getting a few splash rises and accounting for two hooked fish but the results weren't anything to get excited about.

After a time I began to lose interest, so sat myself on a rock in midstream and started flipping the fly haphazardly in an absent sort of manner. As I did this I started speculating and suddenly got an idea. We hadn't tried bucktails or streamers and we were using 9 foot leaders. Perhaps our leaders were too short for the conditions and perhaps a bucktail of some kind would excite the trout into taking what we had to offer. We already knew that our dry flies were too large.

There wasn't anything to lose by trying, so I took a 14 foot leader tapered from .018 to .008 (2X) from my chamois dry leader case and put it in the soak box. I believe I dozed while it softened. At any rate there was a blank period between. Suddenly I was wide awake. I could see Fred a quarter mile downstream and ten feet from the rock on which I sprawled three or four good trout were disporting themselves on the surface of the water. No one ever moved more cautiously than I did in getting the leader and bucktail attached to my line. It was done without disturbing these fish. It was a bit difficult to cast that short distance with such a long leader but somehow it was accomplished and the fly alighted with an audible smack although but a small portion of the leader touched the water. I started it back to me immediately but it didn't move three inches before I was fast to a fourteen inch Brown and the other fish were trying to take the fly away from him. Landing this fish frightened these others but not badly. They went out to the quiet water some thirty feet away and started feeding.

But getting these fish to take the fly required a change in tactics. They boiled to it when I fished it slowly but wouldn't take. This happened so many times that I finally got a bit peeved and slapped the fly over them, bringing it back so fast that it skipped over the water. There were several frantic jumps and then I was fast, this time to a fifteen incher. This seemed to be the answer to the problem. A BUCKTAIL FLY THROWN CARELESSLY—IN FACT A BIT SLOPPILY AND THEN SKITTERED SPEEDILY THROUGH OR OVER THE TOP OF THE WATER. From every part of the eddy section this brought rises and hooked fish. Then I worked the shore on the opposite side of the stream, casting the fly to the very edge of the bank and starting it back almost before it landed. Several very large trout were thus enticed into striking but I hooked only one and this was lost during the resultant fight. From here I worked upstream into the faster water which led into the eddy. Trout appeared from behind every rock and sometimes there were a half dozen trying to get the fly at the same time. Finally I became tired of catching them, so started experimenting simply to see what would happen. It was soon apparent that any bucktail fly in size 8 or 10 produced when fished fast but that large bucktails, streamers, marabous and others of this type were not so good. Regular wet flies proved absolutely useless and what dry flies I tried still failed to bring anything more than a few half-hearted rises.

I then changed back to a 9 foot leader. While using this, even the favored flies of the moment failed to produce very much action. I realized that this might be because of the many trout which had been hooked or nicked in the comparatively limited area so changed back to the 14 footer to check up this point. The results were somewhat amazing and considerably out of the ordinary. In fifteen casts I got fifteen rises and hooked eight fish.

One thing besides the leader was very important. It was the action given the fly. It had to be just right to produce satisfactorily. It was obtained by a combination rod and hand synchronization—the rod being raised by short jerks to the vertical at the same time the hand applied additional speed and erratic jerks by manipulating the line.

Because of the outstanding results of this entire combination one might get the idea that it is an infallible method and that the fly which produced was better than those mentioned which failed to make a good showing. Please don't be so misled. There is no one best method or fly. What may be excellent on one occasion may be useless on another. The lesson this teaches is to try various methods and flies until you get results. Sometimes no matter what you do you won't get anywhere but keep trying anyway. The leader dope is sound. No one ever harmed his chances by using the lightest and longest he can handle but many fishing trips have been failures because the leader was too short or too stout.

Encampment Brook proved to be a grand experimental stream. There were plenty of trout, it was quite small and the water was as clear as crystal. Conditions changed from day to day and what worked well in one stretch didn't always work so well in another.

An experience with the Marabou streamer used over a large gathering of Rainbow Trout is worth recounting. The pool which formed the locale of this incident didn't seem to have any particular advantages—in fact, except for the reason that I saw trout rising there and the fact that my comrade Glenn Jones from Colorado Springs said he had made several large catches in it, I wouldn't have given it a tumble. On both sides, the bottom was mud and silt and the channel ran over a bottom of rather small gravel. The deepest part barely reached the tops of my waders and the only good hiding spot was several rocks at the head where the current from the rocky riffle above broke and skirted both sides. Around this rock and along the entire main stem of the channel we saw a continuous rise of fish and most of them were good ones. We took one side each and fished with dry flies. After a full hour of this we still had to catch our first trout.

I had changed patterns so many times I grew a bit tired. Besides I had gradually increased the length of the leader until it was now about 18 foot and it hadn't helped a bit. It seemed useless. Retiring to the bank I watched Glenn. He finally succeeded in hooking a ten or eleven incher but after that he just cast as we had been doing all the time since arriving there.

A sudden impulse swept over me, a desire to investigate those rising trout, to get as near them as I possibly could. I wanted to see what they were doing. The canyon wall behind me was high and rugged and acted as a perfect neutralizing background for my person so I got within twenty feet of the fish without disturbing them. Feeling that I would ruin any chances of seeing anything if I got any closer I let well enough alone and watched closely. I soon saw that they were not rising directly to the surface but were instead taking something just under it—so close in fact that when taking, first their noses, then their dorsal fins and finally their tails broke through the water in rapid succession. Nearly every time a fish rose it was like three quick rises in a row making it appear that more fish were rising than was actually the case.

This fired my ambition again. A nymph would surely work! But it didn't, either the first one I tried or any other of the dozen or so I tried after. Remembering past experiences when some crazy pattern of fly had produced under trying circum-

PLATE NO. 6

Maurice	Maxwell	Maxwell Blue	McAlpin	McGinty	McKenzie
Mealy Moth	Mershon	Mershon-White	Midge Black	White Miller	Mills No. 1
Mohawk	Moisic	Mole	Montreal	Montreal Silver	Montreal Yellow
Moose	Morrison	Moth-White	Moth-Brown	Munro	Murray
Nameless	Neversink	Neverwas	Nicholson	Nickerson	Nonpareil
Oak	Olive Dun	Olive Quill	Olive Wren	Onondaga	Oquassac
Orange Black	Orange Blue	Orangto	Orange Miller	Orange Sedge	Orvis-Gray
Page	Pale Evening Dun	Pale Sulphur	Pale Watery Quill	Park Fly	Parmachenie Beau

Full descriptions of the flies on this plate will be found on pages 422–424.

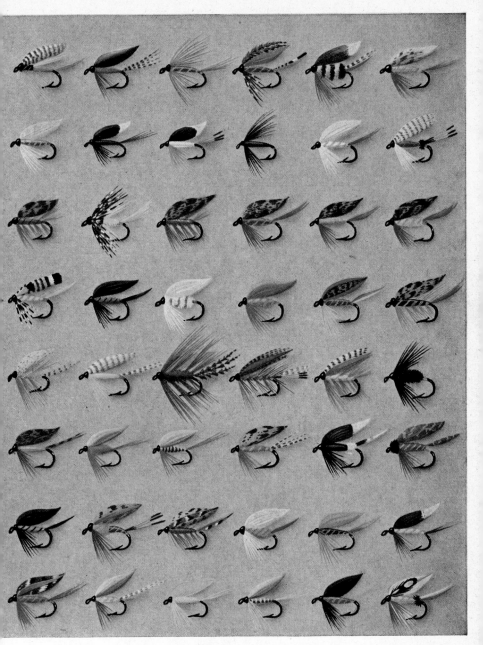

PLATE No. 6

stances I tied on a large white marabou and cast it so that it raked directly through the thickest of the rise when I retrieved. As it darted through the ranks the water boiled, I felt several hard tugs and hooked a ten incher. It looked as if the entire school followed this fish as it was being landed. Then they saw me and disappeared. Once again this happened but this time not so many fish followed and when they scurried for the middle of the stream the rise stopped abruptly nor did it resume even though we waited an hour after. In the meantime we both kept fishing but not another fish followed my marabou while Glenn got only one rise from the far side of the pool on the very edge of the current stem.

In further experiments both the marabou and the black ghost brought queer reactions. They would usually account for two or three good rises in each choice location of every riffle or pool but they also seemed to kill those places for further effort unless you waited for considerable time after disturbing them. These flies were great for the purpose of locating good fish. Many a speculative cast in places where we never got a rise to a dry fly brought a big fellow out of hiding. Occasionally we'd hook one but in the majority of cases it would either be a follow up or a half-hearted hit that we missed. On the other hand they frequently brought good fish to the net which dry flies did not seem to attract so that they were well worth using.

We finally devised a method which seemed to be ideal. First one would fish the water with a dry fly and then the other would follow through either with a bucktail, a marabou or a black ghost. Working it the opposite way was not satisfactory. Dry flying a stretch did not seem to hurt it for the other type of fishing but reversing the procedure seemed to spoil it for the dry fly. From this it might seem that using these excitement makers is not so good for those who might be following close behind you. At any rate that is the conclusion reached from careful observations and notes made during the last two years.

TROUT

As the most effective way of fishing the flies is either slightly up and across, directly across or slightly down and across stream it is possible to work either up or down stream when fishing with them. The main requisite is to keep away from the streams except when you want to fish a particular place and then advance with extreme caution. In many cases where the slope of the shore is such that it rises quickly to a height which might make your figure visible to the fish it is best to remain in the background and let your line lie partially on the shore, if necessary, as you work the retrieve. This is possible if the shore is smooth. In the case of a high bank, keep back far enough and keep low enough so that you are not silhouetted against the sky.

It didn't take long to find out that the black ghost seemed to have a peculiar fascination for big trout. Besides quite a number of really splendid specimens it produced for me it almost got me a record breaker. That it did not was my fault and not the fault of the fly. It happened this way.

Below the road bridge which crosses the river near Wilcox Ranch an island divides the stream. Both sides being good fishing, one may spend a full half day there without any trouble. On this afternoon I had fished both sides with a dry fly and was working back on the right hand side, picking out hidden holes where I had received good rises which had been missed. On reaching the last pool of the stretch I saw a peculiar looking wrinkle in the water near the far bank. It was a long distance to make with a delicate delivery and as the water was almost still at this point I felt that the slightest sloppiness in a cast would ruin my chances so I walked past the scattered bushes until I came to the main riffle leading from it. Although the amount of water coming over this lip was not great, in fact being quite thin, there was a decided drop, so much so that when I kneeled I felt sure I would be hidden from the fish in the pool.

I was soon convinced that this was a large fish. Occasionally his movements sent out waves which a small fish could not have made. I expected that he wouldn't be interested in the dry fly and these expectations were realized. Two dozen perfect floats over him failed to bring the slightest response. Besides, many juicy naturals floated over him, and were neglected just as much as my artificial, so I changed to a bucktail. He made a couple of swirls to this but did not take it. Then I tried the marabou. This brought one splash and then he ignored it. I had only one black ghost left. It was a large one—about three inches long. The first time this fly darted past him he struck and missed but kept following. He came to the very lip of the break from which I was fishing. I could see him plainly, in fact his back was out of water. As I lifted the fly he made a grab at it and then went out a few feet to reach water which covered him and then lay there looking like a miniature submarine. If an inch long he was three feet in length. It was a ticklish situation. The movement of the rod in making the cast might make him suspicious—wise to what was going on. With a supreme effort I controlled my impulse to cast and waited patiently. Finally he seemed to decide that he had lost his opportunity to get that morsel which had disappeared in the air and that it wasn't coming back to give him a second chance. At any rate he turned and started slowly out to deep water.

This was my opportunity. With as little effort and movement of the rod as possible I sent the black ghost out on its mission—directing it so that it would fall within his line of vision but not in front of him where he might possibly see the leader. Of course it was luck, I know that even though I like to imagine it was skill. That fly alighted just in back of his eyes. He turned like a flash and before I knew it he had the fly and was making for midstream with great speed.

Right there I made my mistake or perhaps used faulty judgment. It's not easy to analyze reactions at such an exciting moment. I knew I was using a 3X leader. I knew the slightest untoward strain would break it. Even as he went rushing to deep water I regretted not having changed to a heavier one. Anyway I did not strike and when he got to midstream he came to the surface, gave a sudden flip and my line went slack. The barb of the hook had never penetrated into the hard mouth of this old timer. I imagine he is still there. Because of this book I shall not be trying for him this season but next year will find me haunting his trail.

There is something to be learned from this experience. That is always to take time to change to suitable tackle when you know the quarry is larger than ordinary and is likely to have a mouth which will require a decided strike to set the hook. In the case of a large fly like this was, a really fine leader is not so necessary, especially if you cast so that the leader will not be over the fish. A 1X leader would have turned the trick in this instance, of course, if I should have used the pressure it could stand. But somehow I feel sure that the 3X leader caused my failure. It had instilled in my unconscious reasoning the necessity to be careful in the event of the rise of a large fish. This feeling was so strong that I neglected to strike at all. In this connection remember that the larger and heavier the hook the more pressure you need to send the barb home. 4X gut may set a size 16 short barbed and light wire hook in the mouth of a fish like this but you can't expect it to do so with a size 4 heavy wire hook. It is these things which make it so difficult to prescribe generally when advising what weight leaders to buy. It all depends and there are many ifs. That is why almost any statement regarding fishing and tackle must be qualified. Conditions, size of fish and flies, type of water and other things all have a bearing on what is best to use.

Even the angler's state of mind enters into the problem. Nervous reaction, excitement, overanxiousness, uncertainty, optimism and despondency all have an effect on our fishing and the right tackle combination for the mood would help in making a successful day. When we are in good spirits, sure of ourselves and confident that we can succeed, we can use lighter tackle than when we are out of sorts, nervous and anxious. Far more necessary than perfect casting is the control of emotion and the ability to see and do the right thing at the right time.

In Michigan, bucktails and streamers are of the utmost value. One of their most important uses is for night fishing. Tom Harris, a well-known angler who fishes considerably on the Au Sable near Roscommon, would never take the number of large fish that he does if it wasn't for this type of fly. His favorite, as I recall it, is made with badger streamer feathers, those with a honey cast and with a good dark center. At least this is the impression I have retained since I fished with Tom the last time in a pool a short distance below Charlie Merrill's camp.

Charlie and I were old friends and we both preferred dry fly fishing to anything else, so that Tom's insistence and coaxing that we do some night fishing with large streamers never had an effect when we were together. But Charlie became seriously ill. We had planned to be with him at his camp but, instead, my wife and I visited him at the Ford Hospital in Detroit.

This visit took away all our desire to fish in Michigan that year. As cheerful as Charlie was, in our hearts we knew that probably we would never see him again. But he was so insistent that we go to his camp, made it so apparent that he would be keenly disappointed if we did not, that we could not deny him.

Tom Harris was holding the fort. He was to be our host in place of Charlie. I've never asked what Tom's ancestry was so I may be wrong when I call him the " Lovable Irishman " but if he isn't then my impression of a typical genial, courteous, humorous and gentle Irishman has always been erroneous.

The sight of the cabin made us more gloomy than ever.

Charlie's cabin was Charlie—it breathed his personality; every-thing we looked at brought back visions of him showing it to us. Somber Tom fitted in this background. He had always been with us when we fished with Charlie but now his concern for his friend had put an unaccustomed look on his face—a look which had erased the witty twinkle in his eye and lowered the cheerful wrinkles at the side of his mouth so that they expressed worry and sorrow.

Of course we avoided the topic as much as possible and talked of fishing. Tom took us to the icebox where he dis-played several splendid specimens of Salmo fario. " Night fish-ing," he explained. " You've got to go out with me once, anyway." I wasn't particularly thrilled but acquiesced. " Per-haps," I thought, " it might make me feel better."

About an hour before dark we arrived at the place Tom had selected for the night's operations. It was beautiful water and under different circumstances I would have been thrilled with the prospects. With his innate courtesy Tom let me fish all the choice locations on our way down to the " night pool." He followed behind and fished water I had spoiled. As I remem-ber I rose three fair fish which I missed and took one small Rainbow. Tom thought this was a good sign, that the fish would surely take after dark.

Once at the pool, before we cast a fly, we waited until the shore line had become indistinct and the sky above formed a luminous milky way between picturesque borders of the tops of evergreens. In the meantime Tom had explained the method of fishing so that I would know how to handle my fly. While still light enough to see what we were doing we got into position about a fair cast apart.

It was slow that night. I have no idea how many casts I made but I know I was weary and ready to quit when I got my first hit. It was a vigorous one and caught me off guard so that the line slipped from my fingers. Of course the point of the hook never went home and I lost my only chance. But the incident gave me added enthusiasm which kept me fishing.

Tom was below me. By this time it was so black that I seemed to be enclosed in a vault. But the quiet, which could be felt, intensified individual sounds which were not numerous enough to make noise, so that the swish of Tom's rod and line in casting gave rhythm to my thoughts and told me he was still there. Suddenly the dreamy harmony of the night was shattered by a human shout and a tremendous splash in the water. Tom had hooked a fish and was exultant. Of course I quit casting and listened. Somehow it was too quiet—it didn't seem right. Then I heard again the music of Tom's casting. "What happened?" I called. "Don't know," was the reply. "The hook pulled out. Guess he struck a bit short and was hooked lightly." And that comprised our net catch for the evening.

We left camp the next afternoon. As we said good-bye the old twinkle came into Tom's eyes. "I'll get some fish tonight," said he. "It always happens this way when I want to show someone how good night fishing is." And he did—took two grand specimens. This is not a "fish story." Tom can always prove his catches and I've never known him to say he took a fish if he didn't. If you doubt him he'll take you to the ice-box. But usually he has his best luck when fishing alone. Are you holding something back, Tom? Or are we simply hoodoos?

It was sometime later before we heard more about Charlie. A brief note of thanks and cheerfulness from him which we received in Oregon and then a note from Tom as we were getting ready to make a river float in Missouri. This told us that Charlie had gone West. I hope that Charlie knows my thoughts as I write this. Sportsman, counsellor and true friend. I can't pay any greater tribute to him. Such friends never die in our mentality. Their influence on our lives lasts until we pass over the Great Divide.

I often wonder what his two dogs, Queenie and Ring, think about his absence. To Charlie they were daughter and son. The irony of it all is that, although a bachelor, Charlie's sickness brought him close to a sweetheart of childhood. So optimistic was he, so happy in the wonder of the love which had returned, that even on his deathbed he was planning on the wedding and the companionship to follow. We didn't know the girl but we know she must be a grand person. I hope they both meet on the other side and that they find contentment there.

No matter where I've fished, bucktails and streamers have been effective at some time or another. Often it is necessary to change the pattern and style but their value to the fly assortment cannot be questioned. For instance take the Madison River in Yellowstone Park. At the time we were there this stretch of water was not very productive to dry flies but wets and streamers were excellent. The fish didn't give a darn for any of the patterns in my box but were particularly attracted to a Royal Coachman streamer of fairly large size—about a No. 4. Don Martinez of California tied the ones I used. He didn't think much of them as fish getters himself but finally he had to admit that they did take fish, especially when Vint Johnson and Scotty Chapman of West Yellowstone both proved they did, even when other patterns failed.

But they had to be fished a certain way, otherwise they wouldn't produce. The method used was similar to bait fishing, that is you let the fly drift on a slack line and had to take in that slack when a fish struck. Sometimes you saw the flash of a fish as it took, sometimes you saw the line twitch, and at other times you couldn't see a thing but merely felt a heavy pull as the fish came taut against the rod. In either case you had to strike hard and quick, otherwise you lost out.

This made it necessary to use a rather heavy leader, one that calibrated at least .011 at the fly end. You see, you had to take up all the slack which might be bellied against a strong current, otherwise the hook would not go home and this calls for real "muscle striking." When using a light leader one will occasionally strike too hard for the depth of the fly and the amount of slack and when this happens any leader which cannot stand the strain of that strike will break.

Vint Johnson and Scotty Chapman were artists at this sort of fishing. They knew the currents of the Madison in this section so well that they had no difficulty in gauging the strike when it came. Personally I didn't make out very well. I got strikes from quite a number of fish but failed to set the hook so they got off almost as soon as I felt them. Besides, I wanted to watch what those who knew this stream did when they were really after fish so I spent more time watching than I did fishing. There's no doubt that practice and experience plus a thorough knowledge of the stream are very essential for success in fishing of this sort. However, both Vint and Scotty said that this type of fishing was of limited duration on the Madison, that not long before I arrived normal conditions existed and that as soon as the first snow came, which was expected within a day or so, it would become normal again. This meant that regulation methods of fishing a wet fly or bucktail would once more prevail. Incidentally, we got the snow, but I had become fed up on much bucktail and wet fly fishing before arriving at West Yellowstone, and after this experience had found a stream in the Park which provided dry fly fishing of excellence so that I did not get back to the Madison to check up on the statements of the boys. Now I'm sorry I didn't because it would have made a good climax to the anecdote, whichever way it worked out. My apologies to Vint and Scotty.

For eastern fishing I prefer the smaller bucktails, not too heavily tied, and the combination feather and hair type also tied as sparsely as possible. My notebooks are filled with experiences with such flies on eastern streams but for our purpose here I shall select only those incidents which are particularly outstanding.

First let us go to a stream in northern New York, a stream I shall call River X because it is small, not yet well known and is not capable of withstanding the onslaughts of such concentrated fishing as we have today.

The flow of this stream is controlled by human agencies—a sawmill and a cheese factory. If you wish to fish dry fly when these places are in operation, which is almost every week day, you must watch your chances and do it when the stream is normal.

When first I fished this water I stopped every time the stream became high or discolored. Often, just when fishing was at its best the flood from above would come along and the rise would instantly stop. On some trips I was lucky to get in three hours of fishing a day, especially when I got up late.

On one occasion I was up for a scant two days. Evidently the factories were busy at this time because the first day I barely started out when the water became milky and until late in the afternoon it was unsuitable for a dry fly. As a matter of fact it wasn't normal until 6 P. M. o'clock, Eastern Standard time. It was an hour later before the trout started rising and this left very little time for fishing although it must be admitted that at the last half hour before dark the fish rose well.

The following morning I got up quite early and started up what we called the "High Banks" stretch—a section which was bordered by high cliffs and was heavily wooded. For the first half mile it was ideal. The trout were willing and each pool provided plenty of action when the dry fly floated over them. But just as I got to one of my favorite spots, a place which I knew contained quite a number of large fish, the water started to rise and got very muddy. For the moment I became angry and my language was not all that might be desired. I had to leave that afternoon at four and this meant my fishing was over—unless!—the thought came to me suddenly—I fished with a method that suited the conditions.

There were only two alternatives—bait and sunken flies. I had no bait nor did I care about fishing with it but in my fly box were several bucktails I had put there for emergencies. This was an emergency if there ever was one, so I took one out and tied it on my dry fly leader. By this time the water had come up considerably and looked like weak coffee colored by skim milk—the condition caused by the sawmill. The pool I stood by did not yield anything. The one below was a considerable distance away and as I got there the rise was just beginning. I carelessly dropped the bucktail in the fast water leading into it and woke up with a start when immediately I felt a heavy surging tug and saw the rod bend almost double. The result? A 15 inch Brown, fat and yellow. Two more fish hit here and then the sport stopped. The next pool was close by. It did not produce a strike. The following one was a five minute walk and here again I caught up with the advancing rise. As in the second pool the first cast resulted in a good fish besides two other good hits with which I failed to connect. The net results of this trip proved that if one fished likely water with a bucktail at the start of the discoloration the results were sure and satisfactory but that if one waited until the rise of water had been on for fifteen minutes or more it was almost impossible to take fish no matter what fly was used. Later on, careful observations and experiments along these lines confirmed these first findings. As a matter of record I have notes concerning two consecutive days' fishing which are quite illuminating. FIRST DAY—Followed the rise in water and fished each hole during the first fifteen minutes of discoloration. Results—fourteen holes fished; twelve trout caught; twenty strikes received; three holes unproductive. SECOND DAY—Waited until the rise had been on twenty minutes before starting. Results—fourteen holes fished; five fish caught; seven strikes received;

ten holes unproductive. THE IDENTICAL SECTION OF STREAM WAS FISHED IN BOTH INSTANCES. Each day the rise to dry flies before and after the rise in water was the same. There may be something worth while here for those who fish streams which are subject to the same artificial conditions.

Incidentally, a small spring brook, not subject to these unnatural conditions, which flowed into this stream never reacted favorably to bucktails or to any of the streamer types, even though many of the trout of the main stream made a practice of running up this brook for a considerable distance. Here the dry fly was best most of the time although occasionally, especially on a rise due to rain, artificial caddis and small wet flies were most effective.*

Coming down to southern New York, to a stream approximately 50 miles from New York City and directly at the Jersey line, some experiences with the combination bucktail and feather streamers proved quite interesting.

On the whole this was usually a disappointing dry fly stream even though most of the water looked ideal for the method. Once in a blue moon we'd have a good day with the floaters but mostly our attempts were a joke. On the other hand, regular wet flies and methods were excellent if one knew the stream well enough both as to the lay of the trout and the special tricks necessary to get them to take. This was proved by Ferrier Martin whose uncle owned a farm bordering it. His favorite flies were the Whirling Dun and the Coachman and he seldom failed making a fair catch no matter how poor conditions were.

However, the rest of us, and we were many, did not have such consistent results. We really didn't do so badly but Ferrier did so much better that it piqued us. Then one day Bill Randebrock brought with him some flies which he called Kienbush Streamers. They were those combination flies made with both

* All observations on both these streams were made between July 1st and Aug. 31st.

bucktail and streamer feathers. On the very first pool he rose a half dozen good trout and hooked two. This excited us and we went at the game in earnest with the result that we had a wonderful day. Not only that but they served to bring us results at any time when we couldn't do anything with dry flies. The best method of fishing these flies here seemed to be mostly down and slightly across stream. When the fly pulled taut in the current below you then it was jiggled a bit and finally retrieved jerkily until it was close enough to lift for the next cast. Of course, the stream was quite overgrown so that in most places it was necessary to fish the flies in this way or not at all, so perhaps that had something to do with it. However, in the few locations where a cross stream retrieve could be managed it did not seem to work as well as the other method unless you forgot the retrieve and simply let the fly drift with the current, giving it a slight twitch now and then.

A few miles south of this stream there was another one, a meadow creek called Black Brook. This was in New Jersey. It was sluggish and the banks were muddy and swampy so that it wasn't particularly attractive but in these days it contained quite a number of fairly large Brook Trout so we overlooked the other disadvantages. Most of the trout lay close to or under the banks, which made fly fishing rather difficult especially as these fish didn't care much for a dry fly which could be dapped in the best places after you had crawled to the necessary position to turn the trick, a logical way to fish under such circumstances. Of course a worm worked when fished this way. It was also possible to fish a worm downstream along the bank after you had got placed in a good location and this always produced. But flies were different, the very casting of them seemed to spoil your chances. Several times I gave up in despair and used bait but each time I came back I had a new idea and started fly fishing with great hopes. Finally I found the partial solution, that is, it was partial because it worked only under certain stream formations. This was where the stream made a bend almost or at right angles. If the bends were in duplicate as in Figure 1 you could approach carefully and by keeping low fish successfully the entire stretch from where you crouched or sat to location B. Usually the right bank in this instance was most productive and before casting to the bend at A I

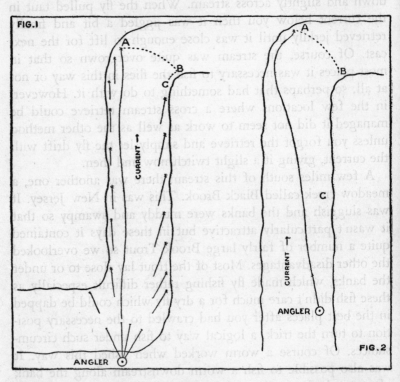

always fished first with a short line to both banks, alternating at each increased length until reaching C on the right bank and A on the left bank. On reaching A the fly was allowed to drift as it would with the current which usually brought it to B. Then it was retrieved slowly and carefully so that it would not catch the grass drooping over the bank between B and C. From C it was brought back slowly and with slight jerks.

When fishing the banks from where I sat to A and C the fly was manipulated on a partially slack line. That is, it was first thrown into the current close to the bank on a slack line. When the line came taut the fly was given a slight jerk and then the rod tip was lowered, more line released if possible, giving more slack. When this straightened out the fly was given another twitch. Usually two of these twitches were all that one could manipulate on a cast. After that the cast was lengthened and the same procedure followed. In this way, with successive casts the water was covered thoroughly and in what seemed the most attractive way as far as the trout were concerned. In most cases the right bank between the angler and C would produce from 1 to 4 rises. The left bank rarely produced more than one and often not that. The drift between A and B produced some of the best fish—on one occasion a three pounder.

When a bend came at the end of a long, straight stretch it complicated matters somewhat. To fish it from either the left or the right bank was awkward and besides it was almost impossible to fish close to the banks of the run leading into the "bend pool." After considerable experimentation I found that by easing myself over the bank into the water, making each movement slowly and with utmost caution, I could get into casting position without spoiling more than ten feet of water below me. However, I did find that to do this it was best to wait from 15 to 20 minutes after getting in the water before casting the fly. From then on the procedure was the same as when fishing the double bends, with the exception that you had to keep your back cast higher than ordinary because of the high banks.

Sometimes, when letting the fly drift from A to B it would snag on the right hand bank. While this was troublesome it was also very killing if you could manage to get it loose by a delicate switch cast and then let it settle a bit before starting the retrieve. More than one fish was taken because of this, even though these same fish had refused the identical fly a number of times when the drift was made without getting the fly snagged.

This releasing a snagged fly by a switch cast is often productive. In one bend hole there was a sunken log, located just where the fly was quite likely to catch when making the drift. I lost at least a dozen flies on this log without getting a fish but finally learned how to handle one so that it didn't get snagged too badly; so that a switch cast, followed by a quick retrieve, both released the fly and brought it away from the danger point. The first time I succeeded in doing this I took a good trout and after that time 50% of my successful manipulations in this particular hole brought results. If I had become discouraged before learning how to do this with a minimum of disastrous snaggings it would have meant one less productive place to fish. As one is always running up against propositions of this kind or some others equally exasperating you can readily see how giving up too easily may reduce your chances of success, while sticking to individual problems until you master them will ultimately increase your catch. As in any other line of endeavor each tough problem you solve makes it easier to solve the next one. Of course this sort of thing is often quite expensive. It frequently means lost or broken leaders as well as flies. But inasmuch as the returns on an angler's investment are computed by the number of fish hooked I believe that it pays to take the chances which might mean a loss of tackle. Even a successful bait fisherman loses plenty of hooks. He knows that many of the fish lie in places where you must take chances with tackle if you expect to get them.

It is always worth the time and effort that you spend in learning how to fish difficult spots without getting hung up.

What if you do spoil your chances a dozen, or even two dozen times and lose tackle while doing it? Trout like such places and the average individual gets hung up while fishing it or else he is too cautious and casts his fly so that it isn't in any danger of getting snagged and so is useless in attracting the fish in that particular spot. Usually after one snagging he quits and doesn't fish the place again. Once you learn how to be fairly consistent in getting the fly in such places without getting snagged you have overcome one of the greatest obstacles to really successful fishing and this advice is well worth storing in the back of your mind for future use.

For your convenience as a reference I am here listing the various methods of bucktail fishing which I personally have had success with. No doubt there are others which I do not know but these are all proven by long and varied experience and so should be of intrinsic value to the reader.

1—Rod Jerk Method. This is accomplished entirely by the rod and the casting arm. No line is held in the retrieving hand. Only enough line should be cast to allow you to handle the fly satisfactorily without the aid of the retrieving hand. This, of course, varies with the length of the rod—the longer it is the further you may cast your fly and yet manipulate it as it should be. To ascertain the limit of the possible satisfactory cast experiment with different distances until you find the furthest distance at which you can work the fly in a satisfactory manner. The cast should never be made beyond that point where the fly cannot be under instant control at the moment you start the retrieve. In other words you should be able to give the fly instant action the moment it touches the water. This does not mean that you should always start it moving just as it strikes the surface. Sometimes it is best that the retrieving action starts BEFORE THE FLY TOUCHES THE SURFACE and at other times it may be best to let it sink slightly before starting the retrieve. Different methods are needed for certain days and conditions and you should ascertain first which method is best for the particular time. But you must always be in command of your line and fly so that you can without effort make it do what you want without excessive slack line.

In manipulating the retrieve after the fly is started, bring the rod upward in short jerks, using the wrist and forearm. When the rod reaches a point just below vertical lift the fly and make a new cast. While this method is particularly effective when used across stream it is also useful and productive when used in any other way. The speed of the retrieve should be varied according to conditions.

2—Sunken Combination Hand and Rod Retrieve. In this method it is not necessary to limit your cast for best results. After making the cast let the fly sink. Sometimes only a few inches is necessary, at others it is advantageous to let it sink to bottom. When the depth desired is reached start retrieving by jerking in the fly with your hand for a few feet or until the rod is in full control of the fly and then finish out with the rod lift and jerk style.

3—Hand Twist Retrieve. This is exactly as described in the chapter on Wet Fly Fishing and is used under identical conditions, being particularly effective in deep still waters and ponds.

4—Natural Drift. This also is described in the chapter on Wet Fly Fishing and is effective when the trout want something large and yet do not wish to rush after it or after anything which is moving contrary to the current. Personally, I believe this method is best for bucktail fishing when the fish are feeding on bottom—on large larvæ which are drifting deep. As a rule the across and downstream cast is best for this method but it is also good when used on upstream casts in which case it is necessary to retrieve slack at the same rate of speed as the current without pulling against it. If you allow the line to get too slack you won't feel the strike if a fish hits and besides the line is quite likely to become entangled with some rocks and cause you real trouble.

Variations of these methods may be indulged in to advantage and frequently you will find a combination of two or more worth trying. These attempts at describing the basic methods of manipulation are in the hope that they will enable the reader not versed in bucktail fishing to get started along the right track. If in some cases I repeat, it is because of the importance of these things. Incidentally, all the methods in the wet fly chapter may be used for bucktail fishing.

Always keep in mind that for this type of fishing, a long rod may be used to advantage. It is always good policy to carry along both an 8 foot rod for dry fly and a 9 foot rod which will also handle a dry fly and yet be better for bucktail than the smaller tool. If you start off dry fly fishing with your 7½ or 8 foot rod and find that the trout won't rise to them but will take a bucktail it will really pay you to go back to the car or the camp for your longer rod. No one ever lost anything by spending the time necessary to be properly prepared. In this particular case there is nothing more true than the fact that struggling along all day with your short rod is a loss in efficiency. Of course I expect I shall be challenged about this contention but all I can say is let those who dispute it compare both the long and short rods honestly and with unbiased judgment when fishing with bucktails. If the long rod doesn't do a better job then I'm having a brain storm and I apologize. And this comes from one who prefers a 7½ rod for dry fly fishing.

CHAPTER SEVEN

Dry Fly Fundamentals and Tackle

I HAVE DECIDED to make this chapter chatty rather than a formal arrangement of technical facts. I thought it might be better if I rambled along as the thoughts came to me, as if we were discussing the subject face to face.

There are two very essential requirements which the angler must master for consistently successful dry fly fishing. These are—delicacy in presenting the fly and the ability to float that fly in a natural manner—the same as a natural fly would float if carried along by the current. Sounds simple, doesn't it? It is, providing you overcome the difficulties which might prevent their fulfilment.

Delicacy is attained through an ability to cast properly, together with a rod, line and leader which work in perfect harmony with the caster. So much has been written about rods, balance, lines, leaders and how to cast that I doubt if I shall be able to add anything to the sum total of knowledge. But it is necessary to say something about these things in order to make this work complete and I offer the following suggestions.

First, for delicacy in casting it is best not to have a rod which is too heavy or stiff. Usually better grade rods ranging from 7½ to 9 feet in length and from 3½ to 5½ ounces in weight will fill the bill but in the matter of weight it is a good idea not to be too particular as some rods of identical length and weight may have actions as different as night and day. For instance I have one 7½ foot rod of 3¾ ounces which is like a poker and as far as I am concerned fit only for spinner or bait fishing but I have several others of the same length and weight which are stiff and powerful without being pokers. It's all in the feel, with power and stiffness being combined with resiliency and suppleness. Some rods have this, others do not. Now this right feel is an elusive thing. It is indescribable, that is to the extent that you can't possibly pick out a rod from the description. The nearest I can come to giving you an impression of it is that you feel a rigid resistance but at the same time feel the rod live and breathe right down to the grip. The action is distributed with a decreasing, even power from the hand grasp to the tip top. If you can understand this at first reading you have super-intelligence. Further than that I shall not go. But if you can't understand it at all then you are a normal person and should feel proud of it.

Very few anglers are able to recognize this quality when they have a new rod in their hands. Only much experience in handling rods can develop one's senses to that point where it is possible to recognize it. For this reason it is best to buy your rods from reliable dealers or makers, from those who have had plenty of experience, either in making or handling rods, from those who know what a good dry fly rod should possess, or from someone who has had contact with so many good fishermen that he has absorbed from them those niceties of judgment which are necessary in order to accurately judge action in a rod.

This is possible, you know. There is one salesman I know well who probably hasn't fished for trout a dozen times in his life and yet he instinctively knows a good dry fly rod the instant he feels it and it is rare indeed to find instances where his judgment is at fault. This skill has come from many years of experience in catering to customers who know rods and who know what they want. No doubt when this salesman was in his learning stage he had a tough time, but it is everlastingly to his credit that he has by this method become the expert he is.

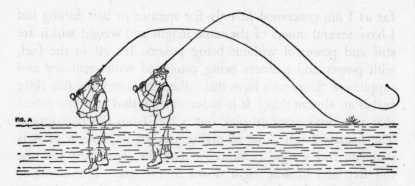

FIG. A

Showing tendency of most anglers to bring rod too far back, thus hitting the water behind. The longer rod aids in preventing the fly from splashing water.

On the other hand when you find a salesman who has had the angling as well as the merchandising experience you will find a certain sympathy and understanding which is hard to beat, as well as someone who really knows what it is all about. So too, rod builders who build both from technical knowledge and from practical experiences on the stream are more likely to produce the rod which has " IT " and which eventually becomes a friend very dear to the owner.

As far as salesmen go, remember these few pertinent facts. The fellow who really knows things will not try to impress you with his knowledge. Only those who have a limited experience are likely to do that. The experience of years and the knowledge gained from it are ingrained in the personality of the possessor. It humbles the ego of a fair-minded person. It makes one realize how little one really knows, how much there is to learn, to discover. For years we might struggle, study, observe and experiment and yet we know, when we look at the results without bias, that we have merely scratched the surface of what could be known if we only had the divine intelligence to be able to take it from what life spreads out before us.

At the time in my angling career when I knew the least I

FIG. B

Showing a short and long rod in action under identical conditions and in hands of good caster. With the short rod the fly will catch on bush. With the long rod it will probably miss it.

thought I knew everything and did not hesitate to let others know that I did. Now that the years of hard work and earnest desire to accomplish something worth while have given me some knowledge I feel that I know nothing, that I am simply floundering upon a sea of uncertainty, always looking for the perfect answer but never finding it. Not that this hurts. On the contrary it is the one thing which keeps me eternally striving, eternally searching for some concrete truth which might be worth while to those who read what I write.

You don't need to be told if a fellow really knows anything about fishing. You sense it after talking to him only a few moments. We who have fished for a good many years can tell, the moment he takes a rod in his hand, if a man is a fly fisherman. The way he handles it immediately tells the story far better than any words.

But also remember that no one ever got to know anything about any subject without experience. If you chance upon an inexperienced salesman who admits frankly his lack of knowledge he deserves your consideration and your help—to the extent that you are able to give it and he is able to take it. Sincerity, desire to learn, willingness to admit lack of knowledge but determination to correct that lack, and brains sufficient to absorb the knowledge which is offered, are traits of character which eventually will make a cub tackle salesman the type of employee which any enterprising firm would be glad to have on their pay roll.

Getting back to rods, many years ago I bought a 7½ footer which proved perfect—as far as I was concerned. In the hands of the average caster it would cast 40 to 50 feet without undue strain and yet was ideal for close work. It was accurate and delicate—good either for a large or small stream. Since then I have purchased three more—had them made to imitate the action of this original. One was the stiff rod previously mentioned and so unsuitable, but the others were positive duplicates. Every angler I have ever let try one has become enthusiastic over their feel and performance, even though not one of them believed in a rod as short as 7½ foot. By actual test I have found that they will do everything that is possible with an 8 foot rod and at the same time give you that additional advantage of less length when on a brushy stream.

I have several objections to short rods for dry fly fishing. They are not satisfactory when it is necessary to wade deep, that is in any water which reaches six inches or more above the knees. Most of us, when fishing, are inclined to drop our backcast and the deeper the water the more this tendency causes trouble. A long rod aids in overcoming this fault which even though it is correctable by casting won't be corrected by the average individual except by mechanical means. (See Fig. A.) Naturally, the longer the cast attempted the greater the possibility of the line dropping. In addition, when the angler has a high background (Fig. B) the longer rod helps in lifting the line high enough to avoid snagging. But even more important than these two things is the advantage you get from using a long rod when standing in deep water, when it comes to lifting the fly from any considerable distance for the next cast.

Regarding the tendency of the average fly fisherman to bring

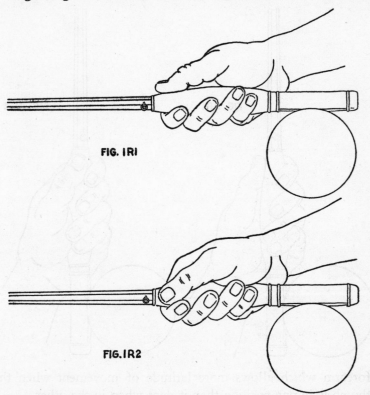

FIG. IRI

FIG. IR2

his rod too far back on the cast here is a simple yet extremely helpful hint to cure the fault. It actually stops it and I am eternally grateful to Dr. Phil Gootenburg of Oakland, N. J., for the information. First, grasp the rod as usual, with the guides underneath and the thumb lined up on the grasp directly above them. (See Figs. 1R1 and 2R1.) Then simply shift the thumb to the side of the grasp, keeping the rest of the hand in the same position. (Figs. 1R2 and 2R2.) (Drawings made of right hand.) You will find that this simple procedure automatically aids in preventing you from bringing the rod too far back. This is due to the construction of the average human

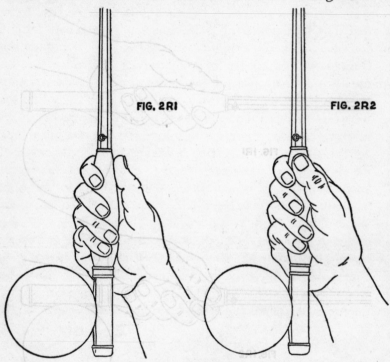

FIG. 2RI   FIG. 2R2

forearm which allows more latitude of movement when the thumb is in one position than it does when in the other.

Even so, the longer rod will prove advantageous when you are standing in deep water, if only for the reason that it allows better handling of the fly when it is floating on the water—(you are able to fish the fly with less line touching the surface), aids in the hooking of the fish because of this, and makes the pickup for the following cast easier. Besides, it makes it possible to drop the fly softer because of better control of the line when making a long cast, usually the very reason for which the angler is standing in deep water, *i. e.,* to get to some spot a considerable distance away.

Of course this is only my opinion but it is based on many years of fishing under all conditions. However, I wish to say that it is the opinion of a fisherman, not an expert caster. I don't belong in this expert caster class so can't apply my conclusions to them. I am just an average individual who can usually put the fly over fish in a way that brings average results. Because I feel that most of us will remain in this class, that we won't ever be able to do what these champions do, I have given you my impressions as they have affected me. But remember this—some of the best fly fishermen I've ever known were merely ordinary casters while some of the best casters I've ever known were poor fishermen. Understand, this does not apply to all those who may be in either class, simply to those with whom I have come in contact and no nationally known characters are included. One positive fact remains. No matter how technically perfect one may be in one branch of the sport, his game could be improved by being perfect in the other branches. In fishing, knowing fish and how to fish for them is more important than knowing how to cast so that you may be classed as an expert. BUT DON'T FORGET THAT IF YOU COMBINE BOTH EXPERT CASTING WITH EXPERT FISHING THEN YOU REALLY GET PLACES. Unfortunately it takes most of us all our lives to get started, let alone getting to the expert class, and delving into the ways of fish is more pleasurable to most of us than perfecting our casting, at least to the extent of being champions or outstanding experts. For this reason what I say here should not be misconstrued as being disparaging to those who take casting more seriously than they do fishing. Neither should it be considered a slur cast on really expert casters. Many such casters may be, and no doubt are, wonderful fishermen. But the average reader of this book will no doubt be just an average caster, with no thought or ambition to be otherwise. He will be more interested in taking fish and this can be done without his being an expert caster. All that is necessary is an ability to cast a fly with reasonable accuracy and to be able to drop it as it should be for a comparatively short distance. But knowledge of fish and how and where to fish is extremely important, whether you are able to cast well or not.

One important point to be considered as far as casting is concerned is the necessity of getting the right line for the rod. In these days the new three diameter or torpedo-headed lines are in great favor. I don't belittle their value. There isn't a doubt that they cast easier and further than the old double taper but as made today they do not seem to be as good for delicate delivery as the old type. I like them for distance and for bucktail and streamer fishing but for dry fly fishing still prefer the double taper. Of course you may achieve delicacy with the use of the right leader, no matter how your lines are tapered, provided they are sufficiently heavy to cast. For instance, even if you use a level " C " line on a 7½ foot 3½ oz. rod you can drop your fly softly with an 18 foot leader and in my experience the torpedo-headed lines react just as favorably to a long leader. Anyway this is just in the way of constructive conversation. Whether right or wrong it will make you think and thought means getting somewhere.

One other point to remember in regards to these three diameter lines. YOU HAVE ONLY ONE END TO CAST WITH. After the taper on the casting end becomes shortened with use it begins to lose its value and when the end is all gone your line is practically useless unless you splice on another piece of line to take its place. One way to do it is to cut your double taper in half and splice a level " G " to it—of course to the heavy part. Dr. Gootenburg who has done good work teaching school kiddies to become fly casters has found this both economical and very satisfactory. At any rate you get the full use of a double taper without changing it from end to end.

A 9 foot leader is long enough for most fly fishing, although I personally prefer a 12 foot whenever conditions permit its use. 3X–.007 is fine enough for most conditions and makes a good general recommendation. However, when using flies smaller than 14 it is often advisable to use 4X–.006 or a trifle heavier. Grading the other way, flies larger than 10 and Fan Wings larger than 14 will usually perform better if the leader is a trifle heavier, either 2X–.008 or 1X–.009. The greater air resistance offered by these flies makes it difficult to straighten out the cast if the leader point is too fine. Large-winged flies are particularly troublesome in this respect and will be found much more satisfactory if slightly heavier gut is used.

For myself I prefer leaders which begin with fairly stout butts. I like the nine footers to start with .017 or .016 and not lighter than .015. 12 footers are satisfactory starting with .017. With 7½ foot .015 to .014 is plenty heavy enough. Of course, the length and weight of the leader you use should be determined by conditions. The direction and velocity of the wind have considerable bearing on your choice. For instance—if the wind is strong and you are casting with it then a long, fine leader will give you a delicate drop of the fly whereas a shorter and stouter leader will tend to spat the water. On the other hand when fishing into the wind a short, stout butt and not too finely tapered leader will enable you to make casts which would be impossible with a very long light one.

When fishing very clear water which in addition is slow moving or absolutely still, a long fine leader is both logical and necessary. In such cases when fishing for wary fish a leader as long as 18 feet tapered from .019 or .018 to 4X will often bring results when shorter leaders fail because they make the trout suspicious or even actually frightened. The more shallow such a piece of water the longer the leader needed. However, sometimes the wind is strong and blowing in such a manner that you cannot cast a long fine leader. In this case it isn't so necessary to do so. If you make your cast only when the water is rippled by the breeze and pick it up under the same circumstances, you will be surprised how well a leader even as short as nine feet will work.

Rough, broken water does not require either long or light weight leaders. As a rule such water is fished with comparatively large flies anyway so that the use of a shorter, heavier leader is advantageous. There are many such stretches of stream where a 7½ foot 1 or 2X leader will work ideally.

As I see it, the leader is used for three purposes, to promote invisibility, to make the fly appear detached from the angler and to drop the line down to a cobweb thickness in keeping with the delicate feathered creations we are using and which we fondly hope imitate the natural insects that trout feed on. Gut seems to be in keeping with the water and it is true that trout are less suspicious of it than they are of a line which appears foreign and out of place in the water.

If you keep these thoughts in mind it will aid you in making your decision as to the right length and weight leader to use for any given condition. After all it is really a matter of common sense. But remember that if a 7½ foot leader is used because of these things and you concede, in fact insist, that a leader is necessary because of them, then it should be logical and consistent for you to admit that the longer the leader, within reason, the more it is likely to make possible the results you are continually striving for.

Of course, as previously pointed out, your choice in this regard is somewhat governed by conditions. Besides strong winds, type of water and so forth, the size of the fly has considerable to do with it. The larger the fly the heavier the gut needed and the smaller the fly the finer the gut needed. For instance, going to extremes for the sake of clarity, you couldn't very well use a 1X point on an 18 fly and it would be correspondingly ridiculous to use a 5X point on a size 8 fan wing. When conditions are such that a combination of large flies and fine gut is needed to produce results then use the finest gut you can and yet make an excellent delivery. You might better make perfect deliveries with gut somewhat heavier than you think will work than make sloppy casts with gut finer than you actually need. Incidentally, length of leader helps out here. The trout seem more fearful of line than leader and you may find it to your advantage to use a 12 foot leader tapering to 1 or 2X rather than a 7½ footer tapering to 4 or 5X.

Fortunately for the angler, it is quite normal for small flies to work best when fine gut is needed so that this problem of large flies and fine gut is not a common occurrence but if you do run across conditions when it is necessary you will find that if you use a leader which is consistent with the size of your fly it will work out better than if you try doing otherwise. But always keep in mind that long leaders will consistently bring more uniform success than short ones and that the finer the gut you use, CONSISTENT WITH THE CONDITIONS AND THE SIZE OF FLY USED, the better chance you have of outwitting wary trout.

This is difficult material to put in usable form for my readers. Even as I write this a kaleidoscopic procession of contradictory experiences flash through my mind so that I find it difficult to segregate the basic elements necessary to form a solid foundation on which to build a working formula. Every incident seems to be related so closely to particular circumstances that to make any rules at all seems superficial. However, I do believe that I have picked out the most important generalities and trust that they will be of benefit to those who desire to learn but who do not have the time or opportunity to make their own decisions from experience.

Before delving into the matter of the natural float, the second requisite of successful dry fly fishing, I wish to call your attention to the artificial fly itself. I purposely left this out of essentials because I'm not so sure that it is positively necessary that the fly be perfection. In other words the crudest, most poorly tied fly in the world may take trout if it is cast and floated properly. At the same time I know that there are certain qualities which an artificial fly might possess which will tend to make it easier to do those things which may bring you successful fishing. Let us consider an artificial fly from various angles and look at the thing sensibly.

To begin with I doubt that close imitations of naturals are essential to success. As a matter of fact I believe that it is impossible to create an artificial DUPLICATE of a natural insect. No matter how cleverly we tie our flies we can never attain that ethereal lightness, delicacy and definite lusciousness which is so apparent in the real thing. The very medium necessary for catching the fish, in other words the hook, immediately presents an unsurmountable handicap. Certainly no natural fly ever possessed an appendage such as every artificial carries from necessity, which is in truth the most necessary part as far as the angler is concerned.

However, there are some qualities which tend to make our manufactured flies more lifelike and so more productive. One is the lightness of wire of which a hook is made. There isn't any doubt that a fly tied on a light wire hook is more advantageous to the angler than one tied on a heavy wire hook. For one thing, the light wire hook enables the fly tier to use less hackle and yet have a fly which will float. Besides, if on a light weight hook you used the amount of hackle needed to properly float a heavy hook you would have a fly that would float higher and so prevent the hook from penetrating as far under the surface, surely an advantage; that is working along the idea that we should imitate a natural as nearly as possible. After all the hook is the one thing we can't do without and also it is the most glaring discrepancy between an artificial and a natural. Therefore, if it can be kept above the surface of the water, that part of the artificial fly which touches the water should appear more like a natural than it would if the entire hook could be seen under the surface.

Comparing, on the water, the appearance of a light wire hook fly to a heavy wire hook fly shows the following. The first alights softly because the hackles offset the weight of the hook sufficiently to prevent a fast and unnatural drop. Also, when it reaches the water it floats well, with the hackle and tail both doing their job as intended. On the other hand a heavy wire fly, unless it is considerably overhackled, will drop like a piece of lead, hitting the water so forcefully that often the tail submerges. This brings the hook under the surface and puts the entire fly out of balance as far as it was originally supposed to float. This does not mean that a fly floating this way will not catch some fish because it will but certainly it does not imitate a natural as well as the light wire hook fly. From my personal experience I find that when it comes to catching fish under difficult conditions the way a fly floats does make a difference and under such circumstances the light wire hook is far superior to the heavy wire hook. This might also account for the success of the spider and variant type flies. When tied properly they float high and lightly. However there are two disturbing contradictions to this reasoning. They are the spider fly tied without a tail and the comparatively new type of fly which can't float any other way except with the hook under water. Both of these flies are very effective at times. On the whole, however, I find those flies on which the hook is somewhat concealed when floating are more consistently effective. Pertinent to this hook concealment I must here mention a new idea in fly construction, a fly which up to the time of this writing has not been made commercially. Marvin K. Hedge and Phil Gootenburg are jointly responsible. Having the same idea as I about the hook being the most disturbing factor of the artificial fly they were clever enough to think of one solution. It was simple enough. They merely tied it in reverse—put the wings on upside down. In order to make it act right they then tied on the hackle crossways and in bunches instead of in the regulation way. They named it the Visa Phledge Fly. It has possibilities. Of course it is not infallible any more than any other fly, and it also presents some complications in making not present in the regular type of fly, but as another welcome aid to bring success to the long-suffering angler it should not be overlooked.

To illustrate these various remarks about flies I had the artist make some sketches. Without explaining the reasons behind my request I asked him to make drawings of the different flies as they actually appeared under two conditions—first on a table as you see them when buying, second as they appeared when looking at them floating on water with the eyes held at water level. These sketches are self-explanatory. First examine them carefully. After that use your imagination and vision a natural fly under the same conditions remembering that the natural fly has no hook in its body and rests on the water with its feet which are exceedingly limited in quantity. Then compare your mental pictures with these sketches and arrive at your own conclusions.

Now to take up that second essential which was sidetracked, the natural float of your fly. If you drop an artificial, which is unattached to anything, on the surface of the water it will follow the current naturally, exactly like a real insect. But the instant you attach this fly to your leader you create the problem which has caused anglers to grit their teeth and curse ever since dry fly fishing first saw the light of day. You have assembled the causes of drag, that bugbear of the dry fly fisherman.

It is easy sailing when the water currents between yourself and where you have cast your fly are of the same speed. In that

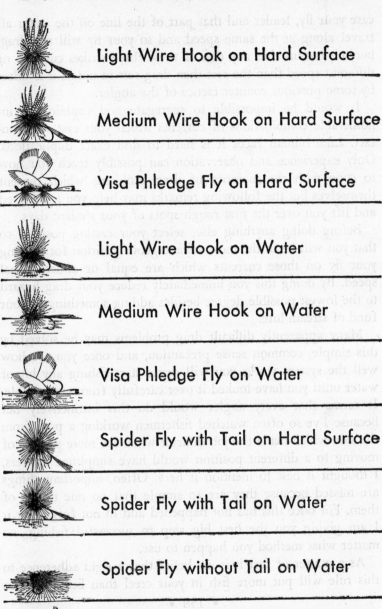

Light Wire Hook on Hard Surface

Medium Wire Hook on Hard Surface

Visa Phledge Fly on Hard Surface

Light Wire Hook on Water

Medium Wire Hook on Water

Visa Phledge Fly on Water

Spider Fly with Tail on Hard Surface

Spider Fly with Tail on Water

Spider Fly without Tail on Water

Sparse Tail Fly on Water

case your fly, leader and that part of the line on the water all travel along at the same speed and so your fly will not drag, but the instant that any one of these three strikes currents of different speed than the rest then drag sets in unless it is offset by some previous counter tactics of the angler.

It would be impossible to segregate and explain the innumerable combinations of currents which your cast will contact. Like human faces it is hard to find exact duplications. Only experience and observation can possibly teach you how to cope with the majority of drag problems which present themselves but the following remarks may help you get started and lift you over the first rough spots of your student days.

Before doing anything else, select your casting position so that you will be in the most advantageous position for floating your fly on those currents which are equal or almost equal speed. By doing this you immediately reduce your drag hazard to the lowest possible degree besides adding something to your fund of stream lore.

Many apparently difficult drag problems may be solved by this simple, common sense precaution, and once you see how well the system works you will never start fishing any bit of water until you have looked it over carefully from every angle. It seems that every angler would do this instinctively but because I've so often watched fishermen working a pool from the side which made the job difficult when the mere process of moving to a different position would have simplified matters, I thought it best to mention it here. Often, important things are missed because they are so simple that no one thinks of them. For once this has not happened and in not forgetting it I am giving you the first big step to successful fishing, no matter what method you happen to use.

As a matter of fact it is my belief that a rigid adherence to this rule will put more fish in your creel than being able to cast excellent curves, loops and whatnots to the extent that you neglect this primary rule of procedure.

You will run into many conditions where it is impossible to find any position from which you can float your fly over a fish without drag when using a straight line. The first thing to learn in overcoming this is the slack line cast. I wish I could so accurately describe this that you could immediately make the cast but I've never seen an accurate description nor can I do better than others. I accomplish it in two ways, sometimes using one and sometimes the other. One way is to check a normal forward cast just before it is completed and then immediately following through to a completion of the forward cast movement. The other way is to make a comparatively sloppy cast, that is lazily and without the power usually used to make a perfectly straight cast. The best thing you can do is to get out your rod and try various timings in your cast until you make your line and leader lay on the water like a snake.

By making such a cast it enables your fly to float naturally until the slack in the line straightens out. Frequently, when fishing small pockets it is necessary to cast only a slight bit of slack in the leader, just enough to get the foot or two float needed to cover the pocket. After the fly gets out of the pocket it won't hurt your chances even if it does start to drag but in this case it is best to let the fly float as it will until it finally comes taut below you, that is if you are fishing across stream. If fishing upstream keep retrieving line as far as the fly floats without pulling against it and make the pick-up when you can do it with a slight flip of the rod, or in other words a few feet in front of you. To lift a fly from the water prematurely, such as the moment it starts to drag or the very second it has passed the spot you think is "hot" will often put fish down quicker than anything else, not only those fish which might be in the particular pocket you are fishing but those below of which you may not even be conscious. Drag is not as likely to put fish down as the rip of the water caused by a premature lift when drag, sunken line or perhaps too much line unite to cause an unnatural disturbance over a considerable area. Many times I have watched anglers put down rising fish and absolutely ruin a pool or glide because of needless haste in lifting the fly for the next cast. If they would only let the fly float, drag or no drag, or retrieve it very slowly once it had passed the objective, the fish would probably keep rising. Besides, often a fly being brought in by a slow retrieve will cause fish to follow and strike, while a fly drifting as it will with the currents and line pulling it in all sorts of crazy ways will sometimes take a fish. We can't possibly check up every inch of the fly's journey. Perhaps there are instances when for a moment or two it passes in a natural manner over a trout. At any rate I know that I have taken many fish on my fly after it had floated perfectly over the rising fish and was dragging badly in water below.

FISH THE CAST OUT is advice which is sound, and which will help to put fish in your creel. Many, many times trout will follow your fly for six or eight feet before taking. Just because the fly has floated over what you think is the lay of the fish without being taken does not mean that the trout has positively refused it. It may be a cagey old fellow. He may wish to investigate it before he takes it. Because no artificial really imitates a natural and the light may be such that he sees the fly clearly, he may be very suspicious so that he follows it instead of rising recklessly. If the fly starts dragging, or even gets sucked under from the pull of the line he is not greatly concerned. He simply refuses to take it and goes back to his feeding spot. Sometimes, if the fly is twitched ever so slightly at the moment it starts to drag he might become momentarily incautious enough to take a chance at it. But if the fly is lifted from the water so that it rips the surface ever so slightly, that fish not only refuses but actually gets frightened and your chances of getting him or any others in the immediate vicinity are gone.

Even where no drag is apparent you must be extremely careful about making a premature lift. When fishing still waters you must use excessive caution in this respect. Suppose the trout are rising in the center of such a pool, say at a point where there is a slight current. Suppose your fly floats over the spot without any trout rising to it. Should you, the moment that fly passes over the hot spot, lift it and make a new cast so that it will immediately float over them again? Decidedly not. On the contrary you should let it ride as it will for several minutes or until the line sinks, if it does so before the several minutes have elapsed.

Then you should start retrieving, but SO SLOWLY THAT THE FLY DOES NOT MAKE A RIPPLE WHICH YOU CAN SEE, EVEN IF YOUR EYES ARE EXTRAORDINARILY SHARP. Often a trout will take the fly before it has been retrieved even a few inches, sometimes they won't take it until it has traveled several yards, and of course there are many times when they won't take it at all.

If no strike is forthcoming as you retrieve, simply continue the slow movement until you are able to take the fly from the water with a slight flip of the wrist. In this way you may keep fishing in such a place for an indefinite period without alarming the rising fish and so put them down.

As a momentary digression from fishing, let me call your attention to the fact that all wild life is extremely susceptible to sudden and quick movement. One may often get very close to wild animals if every movement is made slowly and evenly—practically imperceptibly. With a deer standing a few feet in front of me I have raised my arm from its normal side position to the horizontal in front of me without disturbing the animal but the movement was made so slowly that the animal was not conscious of it. That same deer bounded away when I moved the fingers of that outstretched hand a bare inch but did so quickly.

In the same way, fish are susceptible to movement, but here you have an added susceptibility to unaccustomed forms showing against light-colored backgrounds. Just as soon as your figure comes into relief in line with the trout's vision from beneath the water you have spoiled your chances for the time being of fooling the trout in that area with your artificial fly; in fact it isn't likely they will even take a natural fly until they have recovered from the uneasiness caused by your appearance. With this in mind it must be remembered that even though your body may be out of this line of vision, your rod will be in it and that the movement of casting may apprise the fish of your presence. It is, therefore, well to limit your casts as much as possible to reduce this hazard to a minimum. Fishing out each cast to the last degree aids in this respect as well as giving you a better chance to have the trout rise to your fly. By this time you must know that I believe in keeping the fly on the water rather than in the air and I do hope that you will take this seriously. If you do you will be more likely to say—" I've got a good one," than " Damn, I took that fly right out of his mouth. He rose just as I picked the fly from the water."

Often when fishing up and across stream, the slack line cast will not prove sufficient to stop drag long enough to be effective. In this case one must cast a loop. I have never had much difficulty throwing the right loop. I simply hold the rod off to the right, make the backcast as usual but instead of straightening out the line on the forward cast I leave it incompleted while it is still curved in the air. As a matter of fact the forward cast is made with a decidedly slow motion, adjusted according to the degree of loop desired. The left loop, however, has always been a bugbear. Sometimes I can make it but more often I can't. Therefore I shall not attempt to explain it because I

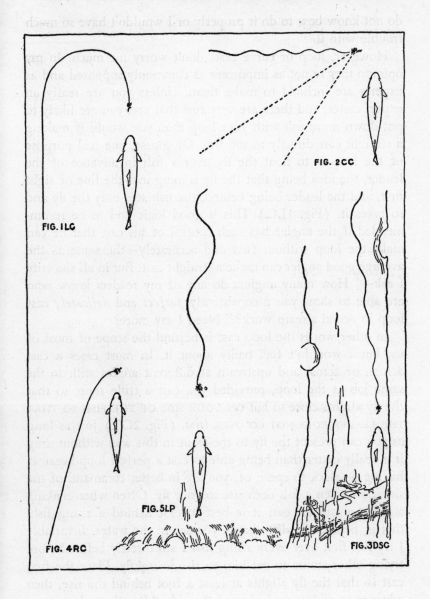

FIG. 2CC

FIG. 1LC

FIG. 5LP

FIG. 4RC

FIG. 3DSC

do not know how to do it properly or I wouldn't have so much trouble with it.

However, loop or curve casts don't worry me much. In my opinion they're not as important as commonly supposed and as experts are inclined to make them. Unless you are really an expert caster, and there are very few that are, you are likely to put down more fish with your loop than you would if making a straight cast directly to the fish. Of course, one real purpose of the loop is to float the fly over a fish in advance of the leader, the idea being that the fly coming into the line of sight first, and the leader being behind, the fish sees only the fly and so takes it. (Fig. 1LC.) This is good logic and to be recommended if the angler has such control of his cast that he can make the loop without fuss and accurately—the same as the average good angler can make a straight cast. But in all sincerity I ask—" How many anglers do any of my readers know who are able to show you a consistently *perfect* and *delicately* cast loop in actual stream work? " Need I say more?

In other words the loop cast is beyond the scope of most of us; but I wouldn't feel badly about it. In most cases a cast across, or across and upstream at different angles will do the same job as the loop, provided you cast a trifle short so that the fly alights close to but ON YOUR SIDE OF THE FISH SO THAT THE LEADER DOES NOT GO OVER HIM. (Fig. 2CC.) Just as long as you can present the fly to the trout in this way without drag it is really better than being able to cast a perfect loop because, having no slack to speak of, you are in better command of the situation when a fish does rise to your fly. Often when making a direct upstream cast it is best to cast behind a rising fish, that is, behind the disturbance you see in the water. Invariably I try this first over every rising fish I am directly below before trying other stunts to get him to rise to my fly. Place the first cast so that the fly alights at least a foot behind the rise, then advance to within six inches of the rise. After that advance no further with a straight upstream cast but follow the other methods of procedure as outlined.

It is also possible and sometimes very advantageous to fish a dry fly downstream. This calls for a slack line cast as your fly must float, without being hindered by the leader or line, far enough to cover the section you wish to fish. (Fig. 3DSC.) This method is particularly useful for casting to fish which are lying close to the upstream side of an obstruction. This might be a log, a mass of debris, a bank, a stand of weeds or a rock. Many such places can't be fished satisfactorily either from the side or from below but can be fished with slack line cast from above. I also use the method frequently when fishing for trout rising at the very lip of the pool. (Fig. 5LP.) These are great places for good Browns to frequent and are very difficult places to fish but the downstream cast with a dry fly does the job better than almost any other known method. One doesn't hear so much about fishing downstream with a dry fly but this doesn't alter the fact that the method is important.

As far as I can see it is only on rare occasions that a real loop cast is necessary. At any rate most of us can make out very well without using it. At the same time a slight curve is often of decided advantage. (Fig. 4RC.) If you find yourself throwing a curve such as this try to develop your skill as it is really good stuff and supplements admirably the cast which puts the fly on your side of the prospective quarry. However, don't worry about it if you can't make the curve consistently. If you do a good job of picking out the right place to cast from and put your fly in the best position for fooling the fish you will have just as good a chance at a rising fish as the fellow who can throw corkscrews or write his name with the line.

So much for fundamentals. Let's go fishing and see what we can do on the stream under tough conditions without using any fancy methods—just using common sense. Here is an incident which happened in the Catskills. It was late in the season. The water was low and the fishing very poor—in fact no fish were being taken, even though rises to natural flies were in evidence every day. On our last afternoon a rise occurred on a long, rocky pool near camp. The deep water of this pool was on the far side of the stream, against a bank covered with heavy undergrowth. The opposite side sloped gently from shore to where the main current swept through, the background was open far enough to make any sort of a backcast possible, and altogether it was an ideal setup for the fellow who wants an easy piece of water to fish.

When we reached the place I first took note of the position of the rises. Eighty percent of them were on the opposite side of the current—close to the heavily wooded bank. When fishing for them from the shallow side one had to throw across the current. Nevertheless, because it was traditionally the thing to do, four of us fished from that side. No matter what sort of loops or slack casts we threw it netted us nothing. I saw some beautiful casts made—flies floated from two to three feet without apparent drag, right over rising fish, but they did not take them. Of course there might have been a drag which wasn't visible to our eyes—that I can't be sure of.

Anyway, at first we all thought that we didn't have the right fly, so we kept changing. I finally quit trying and started thinking, instead. This is how my thoughts formulated. "Every single angler fishing this stretch always fishes it from the same side. Under normal conditions they take trout when casting from this side, which seems to prove that there's nothing wrong with the system, but perhaps there is yet a better way, especially in low water when the fish hang so close to the bank on the other side of the current. Anyhow, trout are always more particular and fussy when the water is low. Perhaps if I fished from the other side——!"

So I waded across, directly to the overhanging bushy bank and started fishing the very water we had been vainly fishing from the opposite side. It was tough going. Here and there it was too deep for my waders and threatened to engulf me while the branches of the trees were so low that the cast had to be made from the side and close to the water in order to avoid snagging.

With a cast barely longer than my rod I proceeded to catch trout, ten of them one after the other, and could no doubt have taken more if I had kept on fishing. However, this bit of success fired me with ambition to try places where the same conditions existed just to see if this was simply a freak occurrence. Results seemed to prove that it was a good idea and worth adding to the book of experience. Out of five pools fished, four had traditional and easy sides to fish from. In each case it was necessary to throw either curves or slack line casts to reach the rising fish behind the current tongue, otherwise the fly dragged so badly that no self-respecting trout would ever think of taking it. Although under normal conditions trout usually rose on the regular casting side of this current, at this time there weren't any there. We made some beautiful casts across this current tongue; we got some beautiful floats over rising fish, but we didn't catch any trout.

The opposite sides of these pools were heavily overgrown and the stream was treacherous wading—but you could make straight casts and have perfect floats of the fly. However, you had to cast so that you did not get snagged in the low-hanging branches. We didn't mind this difficulty because we caught fish readily when fishing from this position.

The one pool which was different couldn't be fished from the opposite side. Beyond the current tongue the water was too deep to wade and the bank too steep and heavily wooded to fish from. Although trout kept rising steadily under this far bank all of our most perfect casts to them failed to bring results.

As far as our experiences in this particular experiment were concerned the loop and slack line casts failed to produce while

PLATE NO. 7

Parmachenie Belle	Parson	Pathfinder	Partridge	Passadunk	Peacock
Pea Jay	Pebble Beach	Pellee Island	Perkin's Ideal	Perkin's Pet	Perry
Peter Ross	Piker	Pink Wickhams	Plath	Plummer	Polka
Poorman	Pope	Post	Portland	Potomac	Potter
Premier	Preston's Fancy	Priest	Prime Gnat	Professor	Prouty
Quack Doctor	Quaker	Queen of Waters	Rainbow	Ray Bergman	Rangeley
Red Ash	Red Fox	Red Quill	Red Spinner	Red Tag	Richardson
Rich Widow	Riley	Rio Grande King	Romaine	Romeyn	Roosevelt

Full descriptions of the flies on this plate will be found on pages 425–427.

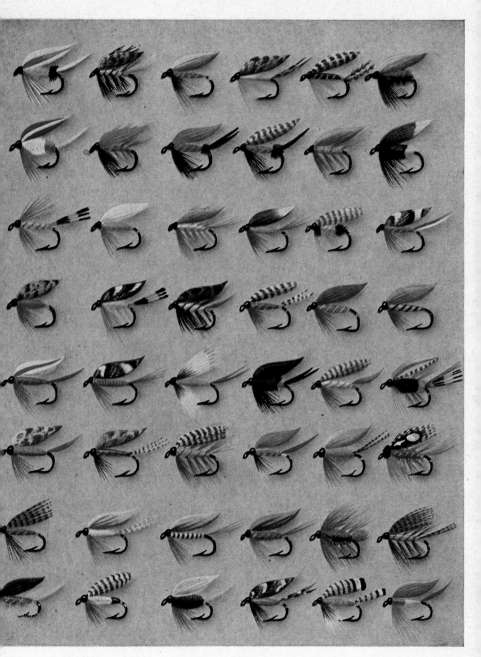

PLATE No. 7

fishing a straight, short line from a more advantageous position produced excellent results. Remember this when you come across conditions which call for fancy casting and look for some way to fish the place with a short, straight cast. If you find it I know you will be agreeably surprised with the results.

Fly patterns probably are more discussed than any other item of tackle. The number of patterns reaches a tremendous total and they will all catch fish at some time or other. The number of patterns we actually need remains a moot question and provides many spirited hours of debate. No matter what any individual decides is the correct assortment there will be many others who disagree with him. This is good medicine. It keeps the subject eternally alive. Candidly I don't believe anyone can be positive about this thing. Even after individuals arrive at definite conclusions they are likely to change their opinions after further experiences bring new flies to their attention, especially when they find that someone else has made a catch at a time when their flies didn't produce. Often new patterns appear, shine like a shooting star for a short time and then are forgotten except by a few to whom the fly has a sentimental interest. Other flies have become bywords among anglers and persist throughout the years no matter how much competition they have. No matter what other flies you may be partial to, no matter what anyone says—put plenty of faith in these non-dying patterns. Remember that they keep living and stay at the top of the heap because they fill a decided need. Just to see how these preferences to patterns work out let us take a candid look at my own experiences and reactions along these lines.

In the beginning I used the old type double-winged style of dry fly. My pet patterns were the Royal Coachman and the Whirling Dun. These two flies gave good results so I clung to them, through good fishing and bad. But there came a time when new flies appearing on the horizon piqued my interest, and besides, others were catching fish with them when I

couldn't take fish with my old favorites. The first different fly
I tried was a Brown Bivisible. It didn't look like much, being
simply a Brown Palmer tied with a white face. But the results
that first day I used it were gratifying, in fact the trout liked it
so well that they wore it out before I had caught all I wanted
and after that they wouldn't take anything else. At the time
this sold me on the Bivisible. It certainly was a marvelous fly.
Today, being somewhat skeptical from the hard knocks of experience I wonder if the trout didn't simply stop rising about
the time that particular Bivisible wore out. In the light of subsequent experiences I'm inclined to think that they did, but as
at the time I had no Bivisible to continue with and the other
flies did not work, the honors must go to the Bivisible. At the
time I was extremely enthusiastic. I gave Bivisible flies complete
and indisputable credit. I believe that I even intimated that they
were the last word—the ultimate in dry flies.

True, they didn't take trout every time I went fishing. In
fact they were refused time after time by rising trout. But I
didn't blame this on the flies or myself. Of course not. The
trout were simply selective, that was all. They were taking a
fly which we could not imitate so that nothing would work.
I was so sold on the Bivisibles for one complete season that if
the trout wouldn't take one I figured they wouldn't take anything and was perfectly satisfied with this decision.

Then one day I watched a man fish a pool I had just left.
As a matter of fact it was the fourth pool I had left that day
without rising a fish with my Bivisibles. This fellow promptly
proceeded to take a half dozen splendid specimens on a Royal
Coachman Fan Wing, a fly I had previously scorned. Not only
that but he quit after this because he had his limit and was
going home. And I didn't have a single fish.

Of course the Fan Wing Royal was added to my collection
and following this came the Light and Dark Cahill, the Quill
Gordon, Pale Evening Dun and many others which gradually

blossomed out with fan wings instead of the ones they were originally born with. They were all swell with the Royal being tops. I really became quite rabid on the subject of fan wings. I even fished them exclusively for two years. " Here is one fly," I stated more than once, " which is infallible. If a fan wing fly won't take trout then nothing else will."

I had the same sort of a crush on the Spider flies. They, also, were the last word for a few months or so. But these infatuations did not last. In rapid succession I fell in love with Quill Gordon, Light Cahill and a score of others. Once I took them on I kept them but continually I also kept adding to my harem. At last it got so extensive that it was a burden to carry them. Every pocket was filled with boxes and every box was jammed to the cover. When I wanted to use any particular fly I was lucky if I found it after fifteen minutes of careful searching. Obviously, something had to be done about it. Many of the patterns were rarely or never used and took up room which could be used to better advantage. Most of them were unnecessary.

This led to an extremist move in the other direction. I felt that one could get along well with not more than 7 patterns and that for most patterns a 12 hook was the best size. This first list I give here.

> Blue Bivisible—12
> Badger Bivisible—12
> Brown Bivisible—12
> Royal Coachman—10 and 12
> Black Gnat—12
> Brown Spider—14 and 16

The Royal 10 was for evening fishing and of course the Spiders were made with the small hooks and wide spread of hackle to give the buoyancy which was the charm of this type.

This assortment seemed just right when I compiled it and until I had given it a thorough workout. Then I discovered that

smaller flies were a positive necessity at times and that the color
range of the assortment was far from complete. The list started
to grow again until it reached the proportions of that shown
in my book, " Just Fishing." I used this list for some five years
without change but since then new experiences have steadily
changed that list to another one. I'm giving you both the " Just
Fishing " list and the new list side by side so that you may
compare them and see how an angler can change his ideas

"JUST FISHING" LIST OF DRY FLIES		"TROUT" LIST OF DRY FLIES	
Fly	*Size of Hooks*	*Fly*	*Size of Hooks*
Badger Bivisible	8–10–12–14–16	Adams	10–12–14–16–18
Basherkill	10–12–14	Badger Bivisible	12–14
Bataviakill	10–12–14	Badger Furnace	
Black Bivisible	12– 16	Spider	14–16
Blue Cahill Spider	14	Black Angel	12–14–16
Bridgeville Olive	10–12	Blue Dun or	
Brown Bivisible	8–10–12–14–16	Coty Light	16–18
Brown Spider	14–16	Blue Fox (R. B.)	10–12–14
Cahill	10–12–14–16	Blue Spider	14–16
Cahill Light	10–12–14–16	Brown Olive	12–14
Campbell's Fancy	12–14	Cahill—Gold	
Hendrickson	10–12–14–16	Body	12–14
Hendrickson Light	10–12–14–16	Cahill—Light	10–12–14–16
Hendrickson—Egg		Coty Light	12–14
Sac	12–14	Flight's Fancy	16–18
Owre	12–14	Fox (R. B.)	10–12–14
Paulinskill	10–12–14	Ginger—Furnace	
Quill Gordon	10–12–14	Spider	14–16
Queen of Waters	12–14	Gray Wulff	8–10
Royal Coachman		Green May Fly	10–12–both LS.
F. W.	8–10–12–14	Hendrickson—	
		Dark	12–14

Also an additional supplementary
list without sizes.

		Hendrickson—	
		Light	12–14
Black Gnat Silk Body		Multi-Color	
Coachman		Variant	12–14
G. R. Hare's Ear		Quill Gordon	10–12–14–16
Grannom		Royal Coachman	
Iron Blue Dun		F. W.	8–10–12–14
Little Marrayatt		Royal Coachman	16–18
March Brown		White Wulff	8–10
Orange Fish Hawk		Yellow May Fly	10–12–both LS.
Pink Lady			
Royal Coachman			
Wickham's Fancy			

about flies as the years pass. But also note that some of the oldest patterns of all still stay in the list. They have stood the acid test of time and of proven use from coast to coast.

While these lists show many differences, some are unimportant, being merely slight changes in the patterns and names. For instance, the Bataviakill was orginally made for an Olive. In subsequent experiments we found that an Olive Brown was better than any other shade so that the Brown Olive took the place of the Bataviakill in this list. The Bridgeville Olive is the original from which I designed the Green May as shown on the color plates. There are slight differences in the body, length of hook and the hackle and the name May Fly is more appropriate than Bridgeville Olive, inasmuch as either pattern is supposed to represent the Natural Green May.

In place of the Brown Spider I now prefer the Ginger-Furnace, the main difference being the black center which seems to give an added effectiveness to the pattern. The Blue Cahill Spider has been replaced by the Blue Spider which has a gold tinsel instead of a gray fur body. This is merely my preference. Others prefer the fur body. The Gold Body Cahill is practically the same as the Campbell's Fancy. The slight difference in make-up is hardly likely to make one pattern better than the other. The reason for the change was merely one of personal preference. In the wet fly I prefer the Campbell's Fancy, in the dry the Gold Body Cahill. The Cahill—now usually referred to as the Dark Cahill—I do not consider sufficiently necessary to be included in a specific list although it would be necessary in a general list.

The Paulinskill also changed a trifle and because the name meant nothing in particular I changed it to Honey Dun to designate a color between Ginger and Cream. Whether you buy a fly tied after the original Paulinskill pattern and called that or buy the new pattern called Honey Dun you will get the color intended provided they are tied according to specifications. The name change was made merely to have it conform somewhat with the color of the fly.

The Coty flies are really offsprings of the Blue Dun and the Iron Blue Dun. Quite a number of years ago Victor Coty, who makes a specialty of taking outdoor movies, was confronted with the problem of finding a fly which would work on the still waters of the Au Sable. His first idea was that something in a light blue-gray would be the ticket. At the time I happened to be a salesman in a New York City tackle shop and we had just brought out a light Blue-Gray Bivisible. Victor tried these, but while they produced better than other flies he tried, they still lacked something. Art Defaa and Victor, both staying at Byron Blanchard's at the time, then got together and produced a light Blue-Gray Bivisible with hackles much shorter than those used in tying a regulation fly. This increased the effectiveness of the pattern but still Coty wasn't satisfied. He felt that the bivisible idea didn't quite fit in with the picture.

After that Victor and I experimented with different shades of blue-gray both in bodies and in hackles. The final result is shown in this book and accurate descriptions of the materials used as well as the color plates will enable any fly tier, professional or otherwise, to duplicate it. It is a good fly, in both patterns. The only objection I have to it is the difficulty of seeing it on the water, in which respect it is as bad as the Quill Gordon. There are two shades, light and dark.

While I list the Hendricksons as well as the Cotys I'm not so positive that you need both. The colors are different, it is true, but the general effect is similar so that if you wish to cut down on the number of patterns for your specific list choose the one which you like best and discard the other. However, I must say that I have had plenty of experiences when the Coty worked and the Hendrickson didn't and vice versa. The Quill Gordon also comes under this general color range. One might well get along with the Blue Dun or Light Coty and the Quill

Gordon, provided the Quill fly is tied dark. Otherwise, either the Dark Hendrickson or the Dark Coty would become absolute necessities. I mention this because the shades of these flies vary considerably, not only when made by different makers but when bought at different times from the same makers. This is the reason I had a color photograph taken of the various hackles. They will give you a guide in selecting flies, regardless of name, so that you get an assortment of necessary color variations to meet the majority of conditions you come in contact with. Simply buy your patterns according to the shade of the hackles and you can't go far wrong in getting a balanced assortment in the more neutral shades. In decided colors, such as scarlet, yellow and so forth, it really doesn't make much difference. The trout which will take them are susceptible to gaudy colors and if your patterns are somewhat near the shade desired they will be all right.

The Wulff flies were designed by Lee Wulff and fill a decided need in large sizes. As the wings and tails are made of bucktail, the flies are very durable and in many cases take the place of fan wings. I consider them necessary to the well-balanced fly box. The Multi-color Variant such as I have listed was born from necessity. A. C. Barrell wrote an article about a Multi-color Variant made from a single hackle which was vari-colored. His story caused such a demand for the fly that a shortage of these hackles resulted. I didn't get any of the originals, and the subject intrigued me, so I made up some multi-colors by combining black, ginger and white hackles. To this I added a black badger tail hackle and a pair of grizzly spent wings. It was a tremendous success, so much so that now I'd feel lost without it.

You will note a few other comparatively recent flies in the list. The Adams, Blue Fox and Fox are all designs wherein two different colors of hackles are intermingled. This mixing of hackles is very effective. It promotes life in the fly and light shining through the combinations gives an iridescent effect to which trout seem to be partial. I've used all three in many states between the Atlantic and Pacific seaboards and they've all proved consistent producers. They also serve to complete a balanced assortment, combining as they do colors which give you a pattern between Blue Dun and Grizzly (Blue Fox), Red and Grizzly (Adams) and between Ginger and Honey (Fox). The Yellow May has been included but is not a necessity. It comes in mighty handy once in a while and gives you a fly with a yellow cast when needed, but you may get along without it.

You will note the addition of some 18's in the new list. There isn't any doubt about the necessity of having these small sizes, only be sure that they are really the size stated and not simply the size hook requested, with hackles large enough for size 14. Not that the 16's and 18's with 14 hackles won't take fish, because they will, but in that case why use anything but a 14?

The real need for the small flies is when midges are on the water and the smaller your 16's and 18's are tied the more chance there is that they will be effective. These tiny flies are difficult to tie nicely, especially when hackles suitable for the size of hook are used. This may account somewhat for the oversized hackles usually found on them. When you buy small flies insist on the right sized hackles but also be willing to pay more for such flies than you do for the ordinary stock variety. Your dealer will be glad to co-operate in this respect.

Not many patterns are needed in these midge flies and I'm not sure that you need to be particular what they are. Remember that the smaller the fly the harder they are to see on the water so that in most cases a pattern easy to see may be best for you to buy. The three most effective patterns as far as I am concerned are—Royal Coachman, Flight's Fancy and Adams.

The Blue Dun is excellent but very hard to see and sometimes a Black Gnat will work wonders.

Speaking of black flies, you will find need for them rather frequently and yet they are not in general use. I'll wager that if you took a census of the flies used on a dozen streams you would be lucky if you found one angler using a black fly. I know thousands of anglers who never use one and I know that I neglect them time after time even though I know from experience that they often produce much better than some other patterns to which we have become attached.

When you compare these two lists I feel sure that you will note the deficiencies in the " Just Fishing " list and the changes in the new list which supplement these deficiencies. The original list was sound but it needed a slight touch here and there to round it out. This I believe has been accomplished in the present list—at least it gives a range of patterns well in the possibility of available hackles and combinations of them. Two new patterns fail to appear because they haven't been tried out sufficiently. Bob Morris of Morrisville, Pa., is responsible. He was complaining because he wanted something different, a cross between a Cahill and a Blue Quill. Together we worked out the patterns which I give here. Incidentally this very day Bob writes me that the Morris Quill proved itself but that as yet he didn't have an opportunity to try out the other.

BOB MORRIS—Hackle, light blue-gray and medium red (Rhode Island) intermingled. Tail—Several wisps each of the two hackles. Body—Blue-gray fur with peacock quill ribbing. Wing—Blue-gray hackle points.

MORRIS QUILL—Hackle, badger and ginger intermingled. Tail—Mandarin breast fibres and ginger hackle mixed. Body—Peacock quill. Wing—Mandarin—same as Cahill.

These new patterns may not live. On the other hand they may fill a long-felt need. At any rate I am passing along the information and the necessary information for making them so that you may try them if you wish.

*   *   *   *   *   *

Much has been said about the way the line and leader should act on the water. Everyone seems to concede that the best combination is a leader which sinks and a line which floats. But it isn't always possible to make these things act as we want. Often the line sinks and the leader floats until the line carries it under, sometimes both sink at once and at times both float.

It is true that in the sunlight a floating leader will cast a tremendous shadow. When in the shade it doesn't matter whether it floats or sinks. When fishing in fast water it is often difficult to know whether the leader is floating or not and I don't believe that it matters much but would concede that the advantage lies in having the leader float under such circumstances. Why? Because a sunken leader in fast water tends to drag the fly under the surface and when floating it does not cause any disturbance, due to the many shadows thrown by the broken water itself which effectually camouflage any disturbance your leader may make.

So let us see what happens on the stream. We come to still water. We want the leader to sink so we rub it thoroughly with mud and some leader soak which is supposed to sink it and start fishing. Sometimes it sinks and sometimes it doesn't. Perhaps we get it sinking just right and at the same time get the line floating just right. Swell! It is ideal! Exactly what we wanted.

But the very next place we fish is quite different. The water is fast, the bottom covered with rocks which project upward close to the surface. The sinking leader pulls the fly under the surface and we have a tough time making it float properly. We lessen the difficulty by putting on a heavy hackled fly. This floats better but the sinking leader catches on the tops of the

• 178 •

rocks and pulls it under anyway and sometimes it gets snagged between the cracks of the rocks and causes us considerable trouble.

After a time we get disgusted. We dry the leader, grease it and start in again. Now it floats and we have a few moments of pleasant fishing. After that we move on and perhaps come to another still water. We forget the leader is greased and have a terrible time. It doesn't sink. Then we remember that we have greased it so rub it thoroughly with mud or sand to get rid of the grease so that it might sink again. We even rub it with a made-up formula which is supposed to make it sink. It might work or it might not. One can never tell until it is tried out, regardless of claims to the contrary.

You have all experienced these difficulties. It is one thing to say that a leader should sink and another to qualify the statement as to what sort of water it should be sunk in or floated on. Besides, you should have the formulas for sinking or floating the leader at will. Otherwise you'll be right only when fishing the water you're fixed for. The solution? It's simple. Just fix your leader each time you change your position or have two boxes of leaders, one fixed for floating and one for sinking and change as needed. Is that what I do? I do not. I've been through it all and now I do nothing but soak my leader so that it is pliable and usable. I've given up worrying whether it floats or sinks and spend the time instead figuring how to put the fly in any particular place to the best advantage. The leader and line might work just right. They may both act abominably. In the first case it gives me the advantage, in the second case my carefulness of approach and selection of delivery location offset the disadvantages of line and leader performance so that it isn't particularly important. Understand, I don't intend to belittle the advantage of having the line float and the leader sink. On the contrary, for certain waters the combination is ideal. But somehow I've never been able to control this sinking and floating proposition so now I neglect it and try to do things to offset it instead. I'm not insisting this is the best thing to do. It simply appeals to me more.

Making a line float satisfactorily is even worse than trying to make a leader sink when it doesn't want to. Usually a line never wants to float when you want it to. I've used about every line made and I'm still looking for one which keeps floating after the first two hours of use—and this length of time is giving them all a break. They usually start out well when we begin the day with the line dry and well greased but after some use, and usually just about the time the trout begin rising, it starts to sink. To dry and redress it takes time out at the very moment that opportunity is knocking and besides, doing this brings only temporary relief. There may be a dressing which can be put directly on a wet and sinking line to make it float but if so I haven't had the good fortune to find it.

There is much talk about the specific gravity of lines. There isn't any doubt that the line which has the least weight for its diameter should float the best, but there is not enough difference in the lines I've used to give any particular consideration to one over the other in this respect. What to do about it? If you insist on the line floating keep drying and greasing it as needed—or dry out one line while using another. Otherwise use the shortest cast possible and fish each cast to completion so that when you lift the fly the entire line will be out of the water. In this way you may avoid drowning the fly, something which is bound to happen every time you make a premature lift with a sunken line and a dry fly. All in all it is an exasperating part of dry fly fishing, one of the seemingly unavoidable evils. Perhaps some day someone will find a real solution. Until then dry your line and grease it when it won't float or let it go as it will and endeavor to do a good job of fishing even if it sinks.

Remember that you can catch trout whether the line or leader sinks or floats. If you become too perturbed about the way these items of tackle "act up" you may easily let it become a big issue and then you forget to see things which are really much more important. Years ago I worried a lot about such things. If the line and leader didn't work according to Hoyle it spoiled my fishing. Today when something goes wrong and I begin to get a bit exasperated I call a halt immediately. I quit fishing, compose myself on a rock overlooking some good water and do some observing. Usually doing this works out in the following manner. Some good fish are spotted rising in places which are hard to get at. I become so interested in the problem of reaching these fish that I forget about the jinx of sinking line and floating leader or whatever happens to be the matter and find myself stalking for a position from which I can make a short cast and a perfect float without alarming the rising trout. All this serves to put me in a pleasantly relaxed state of mind which reacts favorably on my fishing and I manage to make a presentable catch whereas if I had kept fretting through the entire day I'd have been disgruntled and perhaps fishless.

There isn't any doubt that trying too hard, letting trifles upset your temper, and attending to mechanical details rather than to natural problems mitigates against successful fishing. Unconscious rhythm, careful observation of natural stream phenomena and a relaxed state of mind are synonymous with really good fishing. Observation relaxes, relaxation brings rhythm to your movements and so aids your manipulation of the fly. Study the currents, the bottom, the insects on the rocks and in the air. If you concentrate on these you will find the mechanical problems taking care of themselves as long as you possess the rudimentary training and know what should be done.

*　　*　　*　　*　　*　　*

The need of a good floating preparation for your fly is quite important. Something which cleans as well as waterproofs is an advantage. As far as I am concerned two ounces of paraffin dissolved in one pint of gasoline makes a good concoction for the purpose. It not only waterproofs the fly by depositing a film of wax on it but also acts as an efficient cleanser. This last property is especially acceptable after a trout has taken a fly deep and when you take it out of the mouth it is bloody and matted. Simply by dropping the fly in the bottle and giving it a few shakes with your thumb over the top it will come out sprightly and fresh. Of course the fly is left on the leader. This is the best way to use this dope. To put it on with a brush is not so good, you might just as well use some other mixture. For this reason a large neck bottle is necessary. These are easily obtained from any druggist. After the fly has been dipped it should then be whipped in the air a few times. This gets rid of the excess gasoline and starts evaporation of the balance. Then you should dap it on the water of the stream. This congeals the diluted wax film. By the time you make the cast the liquid oil has disappeared and you have a treated fly which does not leave a film on the water. Carbon tetrachloride, ether or benzine may be used in place of gasoline.

There are two objections to using this preparation. One is serious. In dipping the fly the oil gets on the leader and sometimes makes it brittle. However I have never had much trouble in this respect myself, although some others have. The other is that when the temperature gets below 60 the wax congeals. To prevent this I carry it in such a way that the bottle may be slipped under the jacket at times when it is necessary. The warmth from the body then keeps it in good condition.

To make this preparation, shave the wax from the cake and put it in the bottle with the gasoline. If you feel like fussing with something, keep shaking the bottle to dissolve the wax, otherwise place it in the sun and let the heat do it.

There are, of course, many excellent fly-floating preparations on the market and if you do not feel like making your own you may find one that suits your particular desires among them. However, I would advise against mixtures too oily and which are of a consistency which does not evaporate or harden readily. This type is not particularly satisfactory and of course does not clean your fly. Some anglers prefer using a paste grease, rubbing it on with the fingers. This is excellent on a new fly and if done carefully so that the hackles are not matted. It lasts better than the liquid preparations and does not leave the oil ring on the water. However, when using it on a fly which has caught a fish it is first necessary to wash and dry the fly. This not being necessary with the gas-wax combination you can readily see where the latter can save you much time when experiencing a short but spirited rise of trout. Under such circumstances the time spent in drying out a fly may well reduce your chances from fifty to a hundred percent or even more. By actual tests we have shown that under such circumstances an angler using the gas-wax preparation has been able to make as many as five perfect floats of the fly to one made by the fellow using paste grease. When the fish are taking fast anything which will enable you to get your fly in floating condition most quickly is the best preparation to use. When fish are coming slowly then the solid grease is better as it stays on the hackles for a longer time. However, when fish are not rising it doesn't matter much if you must dress it occasionally to make it float, in fact doing so gives you something to do.

The dry fly box has long been a problem. The aluminum individual spring cover compartment types never have been entirely satisfactory. The slightest pressure seems to make dents in the metal. Besides, the springs which manipulate the covers of the compartments get out of order easily and in any of the regulation pocket sizes the compartments are too small to carry such flies as fan wings and spiders which are spoiled by being crushed. There are some metal boxes made which are satisfactory in all these respects but they are mostly too bulky, clumsy and heavy for stream work. They are fine as stock boxes.

In recent years the pyralin, celluloid, or whatever the name

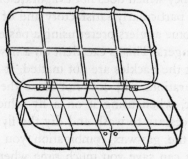

Dry Fly Box

happens to be for this material, boxes have made their appearance in various styles and shapes. The first one I ever remember seeing was a simple round type which originated, as far as I can trace, from the brain of Gene Connett, of the Derrydale Press. He is well known as a writer, publisher and sportsman. I met him first while working for a New York City tackle shop, when at the same time I wrote for various outdoor magazines and was angling editor of one. Connett's idea was a step in the right direction. I fell for the little boxes as soon as they appeared and immediately discarded all my fancy compartment boxes. But these new ones had their faults. To keep flies separate one had to have at least six scattered around in different pockets and usually one had more. I remember one day, because I felt so bulky, I took stock of what I had in my pockets and brought twelve of these Connett boxes to light. Of course if one were careful this could be easily avoided. But they also broke easily and if you got the covers mixed you had a hard time getting them straightened out. If one of the covers fitted too tight it was exceedingly difficult to get it on and when you used the force necessary to get it off it seemed to explode in your hands and spread the flies all over the landscape. A cover too loose was just as bad but it gave you a different sensation. The contents simply disappeared with the bottom of the box and you were left holding the cover. Despite these inconveniences I continued to use them because they were light in weight and inexpensive.

Then came the compartment boxes made from the same materials. They will hold the weight of a heavy man and yet are so light in weight that one is barely conscious of carrying them. Some fishermen object to the ones with the one piece cover, saying that the flies will blow out of the compartments in a heavy wind. I've never had this trouble even when fishing in Wyoming or the High Sierras where day after day the wind blows a gale such as is seldom experienced in the East. However, if you have had trouble with the boxes where every compartment is exposed at the same time there is now obtainable a box of the same material which has individual covers for each separate compartment.

A line carrier of some sort is always in order. It comes in handy for carrying extra lines and also to change your line from end to end so as to get the full use from it. If you don't turn a double tapered line around every two or three weeks the end tied to the spool becomes badly kinked. Of course with the three diameter lines one can't do this. The working end is at one end only, the balance simply being a running line.

The use of two reels is also to be recommended for getting the full value from your double tapered line. By transferring the line from one reel to the other frequently you keep both ends in use and so in good shape. Like rubber tires fly lines deteriorate quicker without use than when being used. I have bought extra lines for emergency and having no need for them have let them lie unused for two or three years. On looking at them after this period I have usually found them gummed together so badly that they were absolutely useless. In this connection let me say that if you find a fly line on any dealer's shelf which has been there over one entire season and it is still dry and in perfect condition it will pay you to buy it if it is of a size suitable for your use. To show how this works I once had three lines of identical make, English, which I had no immediate use for. They lay side by side in a drawer for three years. At the end of that time I had occasion to use one of them. Two were so gummed that they looked as if the coils were glued together. The other was in perfect condition. I've seen this happen more than once. Not being a line manufacturer I don't know the reason. Incidentally, American Line Manufacturers are now making lines which I prefer to the foreign ones. I find that the tapers are more uniform and that they stand up just as well if not better than the others.

One thing is sure. If you store your fly lines in large coils when not in use they will last longer and work better provided you don't put a twist in them when coiling, something which makes them aggravating to use. Take them from the reel directly to the carrier or holder, either by having a handle on the holder so that you can do it as if you were taking the line from one reel to another or by achieving the same effect by the use of your hands.

Care of leaders is a difficult proposition. Despite my years of experience, I am still undecided as to the best way to handle them when in use. The method I've found most satisfactory is to keep the soak box wet all season but keep in it only those leaders which are in actual use. As a rule this box contains the following. 2—7½ foot leaders tapered to 1X, 2—9 foot leaders tapered to 2X, and 2 tapered to 3X, 2—12 foot leaders tapered to 3X, and 1 to 4X. Besides these it contains ½ dozen each 1X, 2X, 3X and 4X points. When the spare leader comes into use and any point sizes get down to three or less they are replenished. Toward the end of the season the box is allowed to run short. (If any wet fly fishing aside from bucktails is intended the box also contains 2—7½ foot leaders with dropper tippet attached and extra tippets of the size necessary.)

These constitute the leaders soaked for ready use. In the car or at camp I always have an emergency case of dry leaders. This is made of chamois. It never contains less than the following when starting on a trip:

$$
\begin{array}{ll}
2- & 7\tfrac{1}{2} \text{ foot—tapered to 1X} \\
2- & 7\tfrac{1}{2} \text{ foot—tapered to 2X} \\
2- & 7\tfrac{1}{2} \text{ foot—tapered to 3X} \\
2- & 9 \ \ \text{ foot—tapered to 3X} \\
2-12 & \text{ foot—tapered to 3X} \\
1-14 & \text{ foot—tapered to 2X} \\
\end{array}
$$

½ doz. each gut points—¼ drawn,
½ drawn, 1X, 2X, 3X and 4X

This is for short trips when the base of supplies is reasonably available. When making trips of three months or more we naturally take along enough to be prepared for all emergencies. For such trips we carry duplicates of all necessities with the stock distributed evenly. Pieces in duplicate are separated and carried in different duffel bags so that if one gets lost or stolen we have another to fall back on. When making a pack or canoe trip only one set of essentials per person is taken along. In case of loss we are inconvenienced only on this particular trip and have the stock at our base to fall back on when moving to the next objective. Incidentally, as an emergency both my wife and I have some flies and leaders scattered around in the pockets of our extra clothes and in other paraphernalia. More than once this has saved the day. I remember once starting off without any dry flies because we didn't expect to need them. As always happens when you figure thus we did need them and we had them—three boxes tucked in various corners of our camping duffel.

As an explanation of the leaders carried in the excess stock, the 7½ footers are useful for small streams or on waters where nothing longer is necessary. By adding the various points you can make well-tapered leaders up to 12 feet in length. Then the 1X may be used for bucktail and streamer fishing or for large dry flies. The 9 and 12 footers are merely extras to take the place of those in use if something happens to them while the 14 footer may be used as it is or lengthened with 3X and 4X points to meet conditions where such precautions are necessary. If you keep up your personal stock of leaders you will never need to fuss about having them when you need them.

The leader soaks on the market certainly seem to preserve gut but after trying them out for considerable time I must say that I don't care about using them. They do not seem to make the gut pliable enough. I have recommended leader soaks and still do so if the main purpose is to preserve the gut and not fish with it. In other words when I take a leader from a box saturated with the leader soak, to make it usable I usually have to soak it some more in plain water. For the last year I have been using nothing except rain-water and find it best. Certainly it is the purest and contains no minerals—if you catch it in glass or pottery. While I haven't made any actual tests I have at times been suspicious that certain waters in a leader box caused a reaction which was unfavorable to gut. While it might not mean a thing the fact remains that during the past year I did not have the least trouble with leaders. Also I'm suspicious of metal boxes which are not enameled or painted on the inside. I may be all wrong, very likely I am, but I do know that I've had far better wear from leaders when using rain water and celluloid soak boxes than I have when using anything else.

When in use the leader should be examined frequently. Often, when casting, a knot becomes tied in one of the strands. This sort of a knot is a danger spot, it makes a weak place in an otherwise good leader which will break easier than the gut at that point. If the knot occurs in the fine points you are quite likely to have the leader break when a fish strikes. Sometimes, if caught in time, these knots may be picked out with a pin or stiletto. If pulled too tight so that you injure the gut in attempting to pick it out, it is best to cut the strand and tie it together again with a blood knot. (See page on knots.) Remember that these knots tied in the leader from casting may well cause you the loss of that prize fish you are always striving for.

Of course, it takes time to do these things. Of course, it is troublesome. But if you wish to make the best of your fishing then you must take care of these details or else suffer the consequences with a smile when things go wrong. It is my frank opinion that more fish are lost by carelessness than by any other reason except perhaps excitability. I'll venture to say that every person who reads this will recall some incident where he would have taken some especially good fish if he'd only taken the time to be careful.

Often we know well enough that our leader is becoming frayed and weak in spots. We know that it has acquired some knots which it shouldn't have. But because we don't want to miss any possible chance, because we keep seeing water ahead we want to get to quickly, because we see some rises ahead that we feel sure mean fish in the creel for us we keep rushing along instead of taking the moment or two it would need to either repair our injured leader or replace it with a new one. The one we are using seems to be holding out all right; we catch several nine or ten inchers with it and nothing goes wrong. Or perhaps fishing is so slow that we feel it isn't worth while to make a change. Probably we won't rise a fish anyway.

And then it happens; the rise of a good fish. Just before it happened we might have been snapping at the rises of small fish; we might have gone partially asleep on our feet because of inaction, casting mechanically and without thought of what we were doing. We may even be in a state of " Blue Funk " caused by our failure to rise some fish which were working but which we put down instead. At any rate we're in a bad state of mind, in no condition to take care of the rise of a really good fish.

Our reaction to the event is violent, all out of reason. Our strike is mighty, almost hard enough to break the tip of our rod if something else didn't give way. The leader parts company with the fly. We have what remains of the leader, the trout has our fly and we have lost the one big chance of the day, even perhaps of the season.

Of course this fiasco can't be completely blamed on a frayed and weakened leader. As a matter of fact under such conditions any leader tapering smaller than 2X is sure to break and even this size may not stand the strain. It depends greatly on which way the fish happened to be moving at the time of the strike. If the fish was moving toward you or if your strike was made before the trout had completed his taking of the fly the strain would be lessened to such an extent that the leader might hold. But if the fish took the fly going away from you or had completed the take and was on the way to bottom with it even a 2X point would be likely to break.

On the other hand, perhaps you don't strike hard enough. Perhaps you gauge the rise accurately and set the hook perfectly and the fish dashes away on its first vigorous run. It is then that you may have occasion to worry about your frayed leader, and if the fish is a real fighter you are almost sure to come to grief and lose him before the fight is over. The slightest rub of a frayed spot against a sharp rock is quite likely to finish the job. When this happens do you blame yourself for having been careless? Or do you blame your tackle and everything else except yourself? Of course you may not have been at fault in any way. If not then you have good reason to feel " sore " about that something which caused your loss. But before blaming that something else first consider your own part in the affair. If you find that you have been negligent make up your mind to avoid a recurrence of the fault. By so doing you build up a resistance against failure and remember, that when your good chances do come, being prepared in every way will be a long step forward to being successful.

Micrometer Calibration Thousandths	Mfgr. 1	Mfgr. 2	Mfgr. 3	Mfgr. 4	Mfgr. 5
.022	0/5	Hebra	Exceptional	—	—
.021	1/5	Strongest	—	—	0/5
.020	2/5	X Strong Salmon	Ex. Stout Salmon	2/5 Heavy Royal	1/5
.019	3/5	Strong Salmon	—	3/5 Hebra	2/5
.018	4/5	Medium Salmon	Stout Salmon	4/5 Heavy Imperial	3/5
.017	5/5	Salmon	—	5/5 Imperial	4/5
.016	6/5	Light Salmon	Medium Salmon	6/5 Salmon	5/5
.015	Padron 1	X Strong	—	Padron 1 Grilse	6/5
.014	Padron 2	Strong	Fine Salmon	Padron 2 Heavy Trout	7/5
.013	Regular	Medium	—	Regular Trout	8/5
.012	¼ Drawn	¼ Drawn Fine	Medium	¼ Drawn	9/5
.011	Strong ½ Drawn	Fine Fine ½ Drawn	—	½ Drawn	0X
.010	X	2X Fine	Fine Trout	¾ Drawn	1X
.009	1X	X Drawn	Finest Undrawn	X	2X
.008	2X	2X Drawn	2X Drawn	2X	3X
.0076	3X	—	—	—	—
.007		3X Drawn	3X Drawn	3X	4X
.0068	4X	—	—	—	—
.006	5X	5X Drawn	4X Drawn	5X	5X
.0055	—	—	—	6X	5X
.005	6X	—	5X Drawn	7X	6X
.0044	8X	—	—	—	—

There is considerable uncertainty about the sizes of gut. Various manufacturers designate the same sizes under different names. There isn't anything new about making up a table showing this. As a matter of fact a complete article about it appears in my column, "Ray's Daybook of Angling," *Outdoor Life,* November, 1936, but because this volume would not be complete without it I have presented it on preceding page. Only 5 leading manufacturers are represented. There are a number of others.

As stated this list is by no means complete. It is simply a list which gives the most used designations for various sizes of gut and the equivalents in thousandths. When a difference as small as that between .0064 and .0060 was encountered it has been ignored and the size given as .006. The only exception was in Mfgr. 1 on size .0068 where this calibration was designated as 4X. This calibration being so close to .007 which seemed equivalent to at least four out of five of the other manufacturers' 3X size it was thought best to show it. As far as I am concerned I think that all sizes should be shown in thousandths. Using that system it would be impossible to have such confusion as exists at the present time. I suppose the reason it isn't done this way is because there is so often a variance in calibration of any specifically designated size. As a matter of fact absolute accuracy in this respect is almost impossible. Anglers should not expect absolute accuracy. After all gut is a comparatively soft substance. Also, it is polished after drawing. It must vary slightly and it does, even though this variation may not be apparent to the human eye. After all there is very little margin to play with when the sizes down as far as 3X vary only a thousandth of an inch and less than that in smaller sizes. There is a tendency to be intolerant in this respect, and it is due to education in the matter of gut sizes without being acquainted with the processes and problems of manufacture.

I believe that as long ago as 1930 a movement was started to make a standard list of gut sizes, so that all British manufacturers would use the same terms for the different sizes. As far as I know this never materialized and everything is just as confusing as ever. Some catalogs even omit the sizes in thousandths, the one medium of designation which really means anything, and recently comparing two 1937 catalogs of British firms well known on this side of the Atlantic I find one thousandth of an inch difference in each of the sizes from 1X to 4X as well as variations in the larger sizes where it might be expected. As far as I can see it all boils down to thousandths. Gut should be bought and sold that way. In sizes up to .012 you should expect reasonable accuracy. Above that size one should not quibble if it varies slightly. The larger it gets in diameter the less one should expect long, round and even strands and the more even, long and round they are the more one should expect to pay, that is if they have been graded for quality and to give you reasonable accuracy. It is this careful selection which makes the price of salmon leaders so high and the price of casts is always based on the selection of gut used.

Not only is this selection made in sizes and calibrations but also in the grade of gut, of which there are three qualities produced for export from Spain. That is the reason why you will find such differences in the prices of made-up casts of the same length. It is a good thing that everyone does not insist on the best grade. If they did the balance of the gut would be wasted and it's hard to tell what we might have to pay for the best.

One word of caution if you wish to calibrate your own gut. Gut bruises easily and when bruised it is really worse than broken because it is deceptive, not noticeable and yet weak.

In tapering leaders it is a good idea to start with the point and work toward the butt. Up to 1X it is unwise to jump more than one size at a time. Beyond that a difference of two one-thousandths is okay and makes a good taper. I find it advantageous to buy 6½ foot leaders tapered from .016 to .011, .010 and .009. These may be made into any size 7½ to 9 foot leader and save one a lot of tying.

The creel situation has never troubled me much since I passed the days when I wanted to bring home fish to show admiring friends. Today I keep very few fish except on occasions when someone who really enjoys eating them puts in a request for a few. For this reason I have abandoned the regulation creel and when I carry anything at all it is the Grass Market Bag type—a flat grass bag which lies flat against the body and which weighs practically nothing.

Flat Grass Creel

These carriers have one objection. They do not wear well. About the best you can get out of one is a season and often you don't get that—you never do if you fish very much. On the other hand they are inexpensive so that even if they must be replaced frequently the cost is not excessive.

The canvas creel is not bad. If kept wet the evaporation keeps the contents cool and helps to save trout from spoiling on a hot day. However, unless you thoroughly scour and wash them after every trip, and every day that you use them on a trip they soon smell to high heaven.

Quite a number of persons I know do not use either a creel or a grass bag. They have a jacket or vest in which is a large pocket with a removable rubber inside. They wrap the fish in cheesecloth and deposit it in this pocket. Some use simply the cheesecloth in a canvas pocket. However this is open to the same objection as the canvas creel. Care must be taken to keep the pocket fresh and sweet. If you insist on a regulation willow creel, get the narrow type for comfort in carrying.

There are numerous wading jackets and vests on the market. Most are good, some are not. Don't pick up the first one you see unless you feel satisfied it meets your requirements as you see them. You might possibly find just what you want somewhere else. If you can't be satisfied why not design your own and have either your tackle dealer or your wife make it up for you? Tastes vary as much in this respect as they do in buying dress clothes, perhaps more, and you might better spend a few extra dollars and be satisfied than to save a few dollars and regret that you ever bought the item in the first place. There isn't a single doubt that the price one spends for an article is forgotten quickly. All that remains after a few months is the satisfaction or dissatisfaction of the thing you bought. Never buy a bargain because of price alone. It is a bargain only if it is just what you want and then it is a bargain at any reasonable price, and this goes for other things besides fishing tackle.

In speaking of wading jackets it brings to mind a fishing kit I bought from the friend who designed it. With this kit you don't need a fishing jacket. The harness is arranged so that the box, a roomy affair, hangs close to the body and in position on the lower part of the chest. With one hand you can open the box and the flies are directly in front of you for easy choosing.

In the lid, also possible to open with one hand, are leader pockets and clips for pencil and thermometer. The leader pockets are too small in diameter to suit me but that is a minor defect. Then on the harness are rings to which are attached a waterproof pouch. This may be detached at will and is easily accessible when worn, by drawing it over the shoulder. In this pouch may be carried many things—spring balance scale, flashlight, insect repellent, bottle of dry fly oil, emergency repair and accident kit and rain jacket.

When you give thought to the fishing hat, it is an important item. It should have a brim wide enough to shield the eyes from the sun and also to protect you from the rain. To do the latter it should be of good quality, otherwise it will leak after a few hours of rain or a very short period of a downpour. And if there is anything more uncomfortable than having cold water trickle down your neck, it is getting soaked to the hide. You can get wet quicker in the places where you feel it most with a hat that lets the rain through than any other way I know of except falling in or not wearing any protection. Remember that a raincoat does not protect if water can trickle down through the margin between the collar and your neck.

Naturally the rain jacket should be of light weight so that it may be rolled into a small package and not be burdensome to carry. The place for this item is on your person. If it is in camp it won't do you any good when a shower comes.

Now for waders, probably the item which hurts the pocket-book as much as any equipment the angler buys. For average streams, use the type which come a trifle above the waist line. Besides these it pays one to have either a pair of hip length wading stockings or a pair of hip length rubber boots soled either with felt or leather and hobnails. For extra deep streams, such as the Steelhead Rivers of the West Coast, it is wise to get waders which fit well up under the arms. There

are some excellent American-made waders of this type manufactured in California.

In this matter of waders I don't believe that it is any longer
necessary to buy a foreign make. American manufacturers are
continually improving their product and today I would just as
soon have them as any of the best made in other countries,
would rather in fact, because the guarantee of perfect merchandise means something to our manufacturers and when a
pair goes wrong the dealer isn't so likely to find making good
is a matter of taking the money out of his own pocket. At
least that is my experience and it applies to some other items
as well as waders.

There are always many discussions on the relative merits of
felts and hobnail shoes. Of course there is need for both. On
well-scoured hard rock bottoms the felts are usually the best.
On mud, slippery moss and slimy rocks I believe that hobnails will give one the best service. However, most hobnails
loosen in the soles as soon as the shoes have been wet and
dried a few times. I've had this happen with the highest priced
shoes. The hobs should really be riveted on the soles. When
having a resole job done I see that the repair man does this.
When having this done one must be sure that the rivets do
not come in contact with the wader foot. The best way is to
have the hobs riveted on the sole before it is sewn to the welt.
If the hobs are simply tacked on, replacing them is a continual and aggravating performance. Screw calks are not bad
for emergency work but those I have used seem to be excessively hard and so do not hold on the rocks as well as the
soft hobs.

Felts are quite satisfactory for comfort but the felt wears
down quickly, especially if you do much walking out of the
stream. Probably the most satisfactory felt sole shoe today is an
American-made canvas shoe. It is low in price and stands up

well. One of the objections to the imported felt sole shoe is its high price, due to duties. The greatest objection to the American canvas shoe is that it does not give adequate foot protection when the foot gets caught between rocks.

From a fishing standpoint I think the felts are the best. One can wade softly and quietly no matter how rocky the bottom. Hobs grit against the rocks and send out vibrations which may frighten the fish or at least make them suspicious. This doesn't mean anything in fast water but it does otherwise. So each style has both good points and bad. Really one should have several pairs if his angling adventures take him to places where the streams vary considerably. If the streams you fish most are of the same type then get the shoe which is most adaptable to those conditions. The same thing applies to the types of boots.

Here is a general rule to follow. For smooth, hard-rocked or sandy streams—the regular soft upper American shoe is very satisfactory. If it is a small or shallow stream where all holes can be reached without wading deep the hip waders or hip length rubber boot will be the best bet. If the stream is very rough with rocks of all sizes cluttering the bottom, with crevices between them for the foot to get jammed in, with water of a dark color which dyes the rocks and hides the bottom from your view, then you need foot protection in the way of a hard reinforcement in the toe of the shoe as well as stiff leather all around the lower part and reinforcement at the heel. Then just remember that mud, slime or anything which needs to be penetrated in order to get a footing on the solid beneath demands hobs for complete satisfaction and that for any other condition felt will no doubt give you the most comfort, and you can't go far wrong.

The average angler has a few streams to which he is partial and which he fishes more than any other. It is for these streams he should buy his equipment, not for some stream which a salesman is thinking of. I find that sometimes salesmen in the stores recommend what some especially good customer uses. If you happen to be fishing under the same conditions as this customer everything is swell but if, as often is the case, you fish under different conditions, what you buy may not be suitable at all. For this reason be wary of a salesman who knows just what you need without asking you pertinent questions.

One must not overlook the service given by the outdoor magazines. They give free advice by letter whenever it is asked for. However, when writing them one should not ask for too much information at one time. Having been an angling editor for ten years or more all told I have had plenty of experience in this respect. While it always gives me great pleasure to answer all the questions I am able to, I must admit that to answer some letters as they should be would require an exhaustive article, which of course is impossible. One thing which will help is to read for enlightenment instead of entertainment; think about what you read instead of rushing through it.

A fishing knife is a great comfort. I have one I wouldn't be without. It is quite small, light in weight, and yet contains a serviceable blade, a pair of scissors, a stiletto, a file, a disgorger and a screw driver. In addition the handle is a three inch rule and all steel parts are magnetized, a handy thing when handling small hooks. If you don't care for a knife of this type, or if you don't care about paying the price for them you may carry a knife separately and get one of the clips which sell for 75 cents. They contain a disgorger, clipper and stiletto and are very satisfactory.

I almost forgot the net and this is natural because I rarely use one. The trouble with them is that you don't need one for the average fish and if you carry one large enough for the fish you do need it for it is rather inconvenient, at least for me. Probably as satisfactory a net as any is the solid wood frame type equipped with a snap catch on the handle. This snap catches on the sling ring or you can have a ring sewed on your wading jacket wherever it is most convenient to you. Some like a ring sewed on a loose bit of tough tape which is attached to the shoulder. With this arrangement you may carry the net over your back and so well out of the way and at the same time reach it easily by taking hold of the tape and pulling it to the front.

There are all sorts of nets to be had. There is one of the telescope variety, which some prefer. The handle telescopes and the net ring folds when not in use. When needed a flip of the arm opens and snaps the net securely in place and the telescope handle lengthens without much effort. This net is also made with the non-telescope handle. One advantage of this type is the leather thong end and the V shape which is generally better for landing fish.

There are also some automatics for those who like that type. One in particular seems to be very satisfactory. It contracts to a reasonably small size and opens with a pressure of the thumb on a trigger. The first models of this type were not satisfactory but the latest improved model seems to work perfectly.

What I like best about any net is the fact that it makes a good photograph of landing a fish. It is also advantageous to use when the trout are taking fast and you want to make every minute count. You may land the fish quicker with a net than without one. For the sake of the small fish the mesh should be small. If too large the gills get caught in the cord and this means an injured and almost always a dead fish even though the angler does put him back. A very small mesh will not cause this damage. Whatever you do don't get a net which you carry by looping an elastic over your shoulder. If you travel through brush such a net may get caught and then release with so much pressure that you get a wicked blow on the side or back.

So much for equipment. Perhaps you will get something from my ramblings. At any rate I hope so.

CHAPTER EIGHT

Dry Fly Experiences in Color and Size

OFTEN ANGLERS ask, "What patterns and sizes of flies would you suggest for the Blank Country?"

One must be careful how this question is answered even though he might know quite well a few streams in the territory concerned. So much depends on weather, time of year, fly hatches or lack of them, and also on the very streams themselves because what may be an excellent fly on one river or brook may not be so good on another stream a few miles away. Besides, conditions change from time to time and one can't possibly keep track of them all.

One thing of which I am positive. No one pattern or size can be used to the best advantage through the entire season in any one place. Neither does it follow that, because one certain pattern and size was exceedingly successful one season, it will be as effective the following, although there are some flies which are consistently good on certain streams year after year. We can make general recommendations which serve very well but unless you follow your own observations to the extent of using flies in conformation with your findings it is quite likely that in many cases your success will be far less outstanding than it would be otherwise.

The real source of angling knowledge is experience. What happens to us on the stream builds up a fund of lore which is far more valuable than volumes of general information. Experiences are real. They actually happen. We live them, not only when they happen but ever after in memory. We apply and contrast one experience with another and so continue to grow.

So it is that narrated experiences of someone else always find ready listeners and by their reality teach more than plain statements of accumulated angling lore. To give you something to think about and perhaps dream over I have in this chapter segregated a number of incidents from my experiences in which patterns and sizes had a definite bearing on the fishing. Being accurate accounts of what transpired they should be of real value to the reader. If they should help you solve some troublesome problem they will have served their main purpose even though they are also supposed to entertain—I hope. After all, experiences take us away from dry technicalities, put action and romance in otherwise dull pages. So let's go fishing together and see what luck we have.

In northern New York, under the shadow of Whiteface Mountain, flows a river which has influenced the piscatorial thoughts of many eastern anglers. Starting somewhere along the northern slope of MacIntyre, it gradually swells in volume as numerous tiny tributaries join it and by the time it comes to an opening where the average fisherman sees it the stream has become quite sizable. It pauses a while after descending the slopes from the really high places and meanders lazily through wilderness meadows, gouging out deep holes close to grassy banks where large trout like to lurk and presenting problems to the angler which tax their utmost skill and ingenuity. Then it gathers together all its strength and with a roar dashes and rages through the Wilmington Notch. It pauses momentarily here and there as obstructions or level spots slow its advance and provide ideal locations for fish, and then tumbles wildly through the flume where once during my time a man lost his life while fishing. Finally it reaches the valley near Wilmington where it becomes more dignified and provides some easier wading. After reaching the Wilmington bridge on the old road en route down river it changes into a stream of expansive riffles and large pools with an odd still water pool here and there to add interest. At Hazleton, it flows at excellent fishing speed and spectacular are the rises I've seen there. After a time it reaches the Sand Country, named as far as I know by Don Bell where again it does some fancy stepping as it batters the tremendous rocks in its bed. Then comes Slant Rock Pool, where many things have happened and of which some tall stories have been told. What stream is this? You who have been there guessed it at the first. It is the west branch of the Au Sable—a river rife with fishing legends, the home of numerous trout; a stream wildly fascinating, capable of giving you both a grand time and a miserable one; a stream possessing a Dr. Jekyll and Mr. Hyde temperament and a character strong enough to spread its fame from one corner of our country to the other. The Au Sable commands your respect. It tests your skill and ingenuity. It is not a stream which will appeal to the timid or the weak. You like it best before you reach the age of forty. After that you wish you had youthful energy so that you could enjoy it as you did before the years of striving for existence had sapped your strength and made you a bit fearful of slippery rocks and powerful currents. But its fascination never dies—it lives forever in your consciousness. Perhaps the stories you tell of your youthful experiences there gain color and magnitude with the years. Perhaps you exaggerate a trifle when you relate some experiences of the earlier days. But this is just because you envy the youth that still can take it and your exaggerations help you to keep a measure of self-esteem.

Fortunately there is another branch of this splendid river— the east branch. This is of different type. It is more like the Catskill streams, being less tumultuous and crystal clear. In most sections it runs through fairly open country and is pleasant and friendly rather than compelling and somewhat terrifying. This branch suffered mightily from droughts some years back but I understand that now, due to restocking, it is recovering from the effects and hope is expressed that it will soon again be the grand stream of former days.

When first I fished this country both branches contained many large trout. Browns and Rainbows were most common but here and there one would find sections where Brook Trout were fairly plentiful although rather small compared to the other species. In these old days we had an unwritten law about the size we kept. Unless a Brown weighed two pounds or more it was returned to the water and usually we never kept Rainbows unless they weighed at least a pound and a half. Of course with the Brookies it was different. It all depended on whether we wished to eat them or not. If we did then we'd keep a few eight or nine inchers because to us they tasted better than the larger ones.

Trout of a pound or a bit more were then really quite common and almost any sort of a day produced enough fish to make a catch which under present-day standards one would rave about. It was a bad day indeed when at least two or three fish of two pounds or more did not come into camp and repose in cold grandeur in Byron Blanchard's icebox. And we all fished with dry flies, too. Exclusively! We disdained using such things as streamers, spinners or bait. It wasn't necessary to do so.

As I delve into the recesses of my memory and read some of the many notes I made in these days I find that the following flies were outstanding in performance—*i. e.,* Brown Spider, Fan Wing Royal Coachman, Light Cahill, Whirling Dun, Badger Bivisible, Brown Bivisible and Gray Bivisible.

I believe that I introduced the first Spiders to the Au Sable, at least I have notes to the effect that I was badgered unmercifully by the fellows at By Blanchard's Adirondack Mountain House when I exhibited them and started expounding on their merits as fish getters. But this badinage changed into an expression of unstinted praise for the Spider when it was demonstrated that Au Sable trout not only would take it but that they also liked it better than many of the other patterns we had come to think perfection. After that it was common to hear the following conversation as a number of enthusiastic anglers looked over an especially good specimen of Brown Trout. " What a beauty! What did you get him on? " " Why, the Brown Spider, of course."

Let me now take you back to an August day in 1926 to show an instance when both color and size were necessary to produce results. It was a normal late summer Adirondack day. The East Branch was low and clear and I arose early to try my luck near camp. On the whole the fishing had been poor for some time due to an extended hot and dry period and I had come to the decision that some " before breakfast " fishing would produce results.

After due consideration I selected a stretch of water between the dam, since washed out, and the bridge at Upper Jay; just about enough water to fish carefully before breakfast. I started in just below the island which divides the stream at this point and stood at the foot of the pool trying to decide which side to fish. One was fairly open and rocky while the opposite side was overgrown and had a sandy bottom. Just as I had decided to fish the brushy side because I figured it hadn't been bothered as much as the other, looking upstream I spotted some fish rising at the extreme left, where a smooth glide flowed glassily between large and showy rocks.

As our best flies up to this time had either been the Brown Spider or the Fan Wing Royal Coachman, with the honors going to the Spider, I started fishing with this fly.

For one hour I worked steadily over these fish. I didn't put them down but neither did I rise one. Then I became sensible and tried something else, first the Fan Wing Royal and then, one after the other, ten patterns as far different from each other as my box could supply. Still no business. Then I happened to tie on a size 12 Badger Bivisible. Evidently it was more to the liking of the trout because it brought five rises from ten consecutive casts but I failed to connect.

I felt I was on the right track but knew something was wrong. Perhaps the color was a bit off. Acting on this thought I changed to a Gray (Grizzly) Bivisible of the same size. This brought seven rises to ten casts but still I hadn't felt a fish. Perhaps a change in size was needed. A size 14 Gray Bivisible was tied on the leader and this did a real good job, rising ten fish on ten consecutive casts and hooking five, an excellent percentage.

Of course I kept using this fly and by the time I had reached the upper end of the island I had hooked and released fifteen good trout and had kept two. I didn't want any more and it was time to go back but because the entire stretch, between the head of the island and the Upper Jay bridge, was dotted with rising fish I kept at it. The fish still coming well, it then occurred to me that it would be a good idea to try various flies to see whether the trout were now taking anything that came along or were still selective. The results proved selectivity. Nothing but Grizzly or Badger would work. A size 14 Badger Bivisible took fish just as readily as a 14 Gray Bivisible but in size 12 the Grizzly Hackle worked best although this really doesn't mean much because it took only one fish. Altogether, it was one of the most outstanding examples of selectivity to a certain color and size that I have ever experienced for while Badger differs considerably from Grizzly, still it has a grayish cast which seemed to be what the trout wanted. The selection of size was definite. When you got to the 14 you took trout consistently as long as the color was right. Brown, Green, Olive, Gingers of several shades, Blue-Gray and the Duns brought no response whatever, no matter what size was used. Unfortunately, I neglected to try flies in sizes smaller than 14's. It may be that they would have shown a better percentage of hooked fish than the fourteens, especially if tied with hackles of Grizzly (Barred Rock) or Badger (Silver Laced Wyandotte)—the two colors which produced in the 14's. Incidentally I got back very late for breakfast and disrupted the planned schedules of some ten people because of that morning's fishing but I have never regretted it because I would have missed the conclusive proof that the fish that morning wouldn't take any other flies except the two mentioned—if I had left the stream in time for breakfast.

The success of this morning led me to try it again the next. Oddly enough neither the Badger nor the Grizzly Bivisible were worth anything. The only trout I took were four Browns and two Rainbows on a Brown Spider and I didn't see a fish rise. Over each place where I knew trout lay I tried from six to ten patterns and sizes. I did get three rises to the Fan Wing Royal size 10 but missed them all. I'm inclined to believe that the general rise of the morning before caused the selectivity. On this second morning there wasn't any rise at all but individual fish here and there reacted favorably to flies which floated high on the water or which were large enough to create a desire to see what they were.

The following season on this same stretch again I had several good days with both the Grizzly and the Badger flies but 90% of the catch were Rainbows. This led me to think that a Gray fly was best for Rainbows—and from the following experience it would seem that some gray in the fly is very acceptable to these fish—even though in this instance they would not take grizzly unless it was mixed with brown.

The locale is Encampment Brook, the headwaters of the North Platte River, and we are situated at the Wilcox Ranch, some five miles from the village of Encampment—a town reminiscent of frontier days.

For as much distance upstream and down from this location as anyone would care to fish on any one day, the stream offers a splendid variety of water, most of it ideal for the dry fly. There are many still pools where the water has just enough movement to carry the fly slowly along and the fast water stretches are mostly slow enough so that the fly may be floated easily.

It is a pleasant stream, companionable and cheery; easy wading and extremely interesting. The high altitude, the perfectly transparent air with its invigorating stimulation, the plains of purple sage stretching away into the horizon, the picturesque rocks etched against the azure sky, the distant peaks reaching heavenward, the verdant fields irrigated by the brook and limited by this water supply, the margin of trees and bushes which so plainly mark the stream's course and are there because of it, creates magic which penetrates deep into your heart and soul and you marvel at the power behind the universe which makes such things possible.

When you wander along by yourself in this country, where the sky is so close that you are ever conscious of its illimitability, where the stars and moon seem to become a vital part of your own little world, where the coyotes sing their yipping wild song at night, you are drawn closer to that something which has made all religion since the beginning of thought, or perhaps I should say, the realization of life.

Our first visit to Encampment was made with Glenn Jones, of Colorado Springs, Colorado. He had been a correspondent of many years' standing so that when we decided to find out something about the Colorado country we asked Glenn about it and he responded not only by arranging the trip but by personally conducting it. He had previously been to Encampment and was so enthusiastic about it that he made it one of the principal objectives of our itinerary, even though it wasn't in his beloved Colorado. Incidentally Jones was not a native of Colorado but if you listened to him extol the virtues of this state you'd think he was. I imagine the reason he tolerates

Encampment Brook is because it is only a figurative stone's throw from Colorado.

At any rate Glenn knew certain parts of this stretch of the Encampment well. He had had exceptional luck on some of the pools and naturally brought me to them first. There was one stretch to which he seemed very partial. It was quite a distance below the ranch, down in the Mica Mine country near the entrance to the canyon. Pool No. 1 was my favorite. Pool No. 2 was small, contained some large rocks which towered above the water and was the home of a few very large trout which were hard to catch because on all sides the water was slow moving and extremely shallow even though the hole itself was deep. Approach was the principal problem there and if you took the time to wade into casting position a slow step at a time and then waited a half hour or more before making the first cast you usually took one fish. Pool No. 3 was really the lower end of a shallow riffle where the formation of the bottom retarded the current and made a glide which spread out from bank to bank before concentrating into a solid volume of water which dashed down a short incline into the pool below. This pool wasn't much to brag about, as far as looks go. The bottom was mostly sand and the only cover was a few rocks at the point where the riffle above deepened and spread out into the basin.

Pool No. 3 was Glenn's pet. He had made some really marvelous catches there. The first day we fished it he took one small Rainbow. I caught nothing. The next day Glenn took two Rainbows. I hooked and lost three. By this time we were in a bad frame of mind. The trout kept rising steadily and in a businesslike manner but we couldn't seem to take them. The third day Glenn ignored the pool and went down into the canyon. Because the pool had aroused my curiosity I stopped at No. 3. As usual the trout were rising continually but I couldn't take any. I tired of it after a while and went down to the fast water below. Here the water was too fast to see many rises but occasionally I saw a dimple in a small eddy close to the opposite shore so knew that fish were working there. For an hour or more I concentrated on these fish, changing flies and sizes of flies until my patience was exhausted. Finally I tied on a No. 14 Adams—why I hadn't used this fly before is inexplainable—and the first time this fly floated over one of the tiny eddies a fish was hooked.

I lost this fish. It was a good one and a hard fighter. He rushed downstream and wound the leader around a rock. He succeeded in snagging it so badly that it was a case of either wading in and take a chance of spoiling the water for more fishing or losing most of it. I selected the latter alternative.

This incident upset my poise. To use a present-day word of expression in such cases I went "haywire." In five minutes I hooked as many fish and lost every one of them because of faulty playing. Everything I did was wrong. I held the fish so hard that they tore out. I forgot I had a reel and played them with loose line held in the hand which caused a break as soon as a fish made a long run. I didn't hold them hard enough and they wound the leader and line around the rocks. I did everything that one shouldn't do.

Fortunately the loss of the sixth fish brought me to my senses. I suddenly realized that I wasn't in any state of mind to land fish that fought like these did. So I quit and waded to shore where I sat and considered the inconsistency of anglers in general and the dumbness of one in particular. I smoked two cigarettes until they burned my fingers and finally I became tranquil.

This exercise of self-restraint did wonders. The first cast resulted in the landing of a 17 inch Rainbow. The next fish was a combination of an aerial acrobat, speedboat and submarine but I landed him. This was because I was coldly calculating and could gauge how much strain the 3X leader would take without breaking, could calmly anticipate the moves of the fish and sometimes forestall them. After I had taken four of these scrappy trout, none of them under two pounds, I bethought me of Pool No. 3. Perhaps this Adams would also take them. So back I went and this time it was like taking candy from a baby. Every cast brought a rise and at least fifty percent of the rises meant a hooked fish, all Rainbows ranging from 10 inches to 2¾ pounds. " These grayish flies are the thing for Rainbows, all right," I exulted.

Then Glenn came along. He also had a good catch although he hadn't had as many rises as I. " What did you get them on? " I asked, fully expecting him to name some gray fly. " The Royal Coachman," was the answer and I was properly subdued. But evidently the trout in the canyon were interested in something different than these in No. 3. Glenn's Royal didn't produce any better than mine had when trying it earlier in the day and he finally put on an Adams which produced. But really it wasn't a fair trial at that. Within ten minutes after Glenn started fishing the pool, the trout stopped rising and you couldn't raise one with anything at all.

On a checkup after the excitement was over we figured that the Adams had taken about three times as many fish as the Royal Coachman. Whether it would have taken as many, if any, in the canyon we do not know as Glenn had not given it a trial there. He had started with a Royal, had taken his first fish on it, so had kept using it all through. However, he was fishing pocket water rather than pools, which may have made the difference.

On the whole the Adams proved most satisfactory on this Wyoming stream, appealing to the Browns as well as the Rainbows. Upstream from the ranch there were a couple of pools which contained mostly Browns, and they were always rising any time between noon and sunset. Before using the Adams I didn't have any luck taking them but with the Adams I always got a rise from any of the moving fish and they usually took it deep. As a rule a size 12 did the work but occasionally a 14 or smaller was needed.

The following year very few Rainbows were in the stream although there seemed to be more Browns than we had seen on our former visit. For the first four days we couldn't make connections with the trout on a dry fly so resorted to bucktails. Only Herb Ogden from St. Louis and New Jersey stuck to the dry fly and by so doing gave us the lead on what our trouble was. Of course he kept changing flies hoping to strike something which would work and finally started taking a few fish on an Adams 14 which had been tied undersize. As I had been using a regular 14 between periods of bucktail fishing, and especially every time I came to a section where there were several trout rising, without having one response I began to wonder if very small flies would work.

Acting on this thought I searched the duffel for a box of 18 and 20 flies I had put in for emergency but had forgotten. I found it but it had no pattern which looked anything like an Adams. However there were some Blue Quills, Flight's Fancys, Pale Evening Duns and Royal Coachman, and they were really small.

Because the Royal Coachman could be seen easiest I tried it first and it wasn't necessary to change. One could fish over any pool or riffle stretch with any other fly and not get an indication, then put on one of the 18 Royals and hook one fish after another. Wherever possible to see them on the water I tried the other three patterns of 18's and they also took fish readily but somehow I missed more rises to them than I did the Royal.

The little fly was especially deadly when fished close to grassy banks, whether you saw a trout rise there or not. It was rare sport to watch the little speck of white bounce along close to the grass and then see it suddenly disappear in a dimple so slight that you weren't even sure you saw it. A slight raise of the rod and you were fast, and usually to a good fish. This type of rise characterized all these rises to the 18 flies. To me it indicated that the trout took them surely, without suspicion, that they really imitated a natural so well that any feeding trout rose to them as long as the cast and the float was perfect. Of course 4 and 5X leaders were necessary and this was a trial because the wind blew a veritable gale most of the time and downstream in most instances. There was only one bad feature to the use of the small hooks. The trout took the flies so deeply that it was impossible to get the hook out of most of them without injuring the gills. For this reason we didn't fish with them as much as we would have otherwise, spending the time instead trying for extra large fish with a wet bucktail.

While flies as small as 18's are not necessary as a general rule, conditions often make them a necessity. As a matter of fact it was the first time I had found a real need for them for at least five years. I was really surprised at their effectiveness and holding power. Of course I do believe that more trout pulled out during the fight than would have been the case with a larger hook but usually they took it so deep that it couldn't pull out no matter what happened.

It so happened that after leaving the Encampment at this time we had no more use for 18 flies but the memory of the need for them in this instance remained and I made it a point to stock up with an assortment for emergency work. I have since had much reason to be thankful that I did.

For instance take our experience on the Firehole River of Yellowstone Park. We fished it the latter part of September. One never saw more beautiful or more accessible dry fly water. The road paralleled it for miles, so that you could watch for rising fish as you drove slowly along and most of the current was just fast enough to get a nice float.

It was filled with a weed growth, dense enough to have done credit to a warm water lake. Wet fly fishing was difficult and in most cases impossible because the sunken fly was continually getting hung up. But most of the weeds were slightly under the surface and between them ran many channels where the water flowed at medium speed and where the trout liked to lurk and feed. Also they seemed to be partial to small weed pockets in the centers of thick beds. As long as you kept your line floating or fished with a short line you could float your fly over the weeds without any trouble but if you made too long a cast and the line sank the slightest you got an infernal drag which ruined the float of your fly and besides sometimes the line tangled up with the weeds.

The first day on this stream I fished with Vint Johnson of West Yellowstone. Being comparatively new in this country, Vint had been on this brook only once so knew very little about it. The only other information we had to go by was that gleaned from a short talk with Ranger Scotty Chapman who knew the stream quite well. But this was sandwiched in during a party at Scotty's home so it didn't register as well as it should have.

Vint and I didn't make out so well this first day on the Firehole. For at least three hours we fished with various flies in sizes 12 and 14, got perhaps a couple of dozen rises each, but never hooked a fish. Vint did have several which he pricked with the hook but as far as I was concerned I never felt one of the rises I had.

Late that afternoon we were still struggling with the problem when some of Scotty's words of the night before penetrated the fog of our own ideas. " Use small flies," he had said. I started searching frantically for my emergency box of midges. It wasn't in my coat. I dashed up to the car which was near by. It wasn't there. Nothing to do but search through the boxes I had on hand in hopes that a stray 16 or 18 would be there. A bit disheartened because I felt sure the box of midges had been lost I went carefully over the stock in the boxes I had on hand. In the last one I found one size 16 Adams.

As soon as I put this over the nearest rising fish I was

fast—solidly. Also I took the next two fish I saw rise, one of them a fairly good specimen. The next fish looked considerably larger and I struck too hard for the 4X gut and lost the fly. By this time it was 4: 30 P. M. and as if arranged by schedule the trout stopped rising so we went back to camp.

That night we told Scotty of our experiences. He smiled as he said, "You need very small flies on the Firehole, at least 16's, and 18's would probably be better yet."

Fortunately I found my box of midges. They were in a duffel bag at camp.

It was two days before I again saw the Firehole. It wasn't my fault. If I'd had my way, the following morning would have found me there long before the fish even thought of rising. Vint Johnson was responsible. Disregarding my feelings he approached my wife and sold her the idea that we should never think of leaving the Yellowstone without having seen Old Faithful, Fishing Bridge, Yellowstone Lake, The Canyon and several other nationally known wonders or whatever you call them. Just as if we couldn't come back another time to see these things which would always be there. When trout are rising, fish for them, are my sentiments. Old Faithful puts on a display every hour or thereabouts, and never fails, but you can never tell about fish.

Of course my wife fell for Johnson's sales talk. Even Ranger Scotty Chapman sided in with them—so what chance did I have? On the second day of this sight-seeing tour we were on our way to see Old Faithful. On the way we skirted the Firehole River. Vint was driving. This had been arranged beforehand. Both Grace and Vint mistrusted that if I did the driving we'd probably stop as soon as I saw a rising fish from the corner of my eye. This left me free to look about to my heart's content but it didn't do me any good. Several times I nearly jumped from the car, but my hard-hearted companions wouldn't stop long enough to even give me an "eyeful."

TROUT

To make matters worse Old Faithful had spouted when we reached her-him-it. Some five minutes previous, so the Rangers told us. This meant a wait of some forty-five minutes before the next show. The time was posted in the Ranger Cabin but I've forgotten just what it was. I thought it would be a good idea to get in some fishing while waiting but Vint said we should see other things instead so again I was dragged hither and yon while we looked at boiling springs of various shapes, sizes and colors and queer formations here and there.

Once in a while I got a glimpse of a stream flowing enticingly along and expressed a wish to stop but it didn't do any good. It wasn't my day—it belonged to Vint and my wife. Finally we came to the Morning Glory Hole—one of Johnson's favorites. This meant that we would stop and look it over. This time I didn't mind. We had been following the course of the Firehole on the way there and I had noted that it wasn't very far away when we stopped.

Pretending that I was enjoying the whole thing immensely I looked into the Morning Glory Hole with the others, made a few very complimentary remarks and while they were losing themselves in the blue depths of the Hole sneaked away to take a look at the Firehole.

What I saw made my temperature rise several degrees. Grace and Vint might have been in raptures over the Morning Glory but I was having an angler's dream of Heaven. The scene had everything: reasonably shallow water, ideal flow of current, rising trout and beautiful surroundings. A couple of casts upstream a fairly pretentious boiling spring diffused its steam in picturesque white billows against a romantic background and as I looked a sudden snow flurry scattered a cluster of large flakes over the landscape and they sparkled gayly in the rays of a mountain sun which momentarily peeked through the clouds. It was spectacular and thrilling but what thrilled me most was the sight of dimples in the water, no matter where

I looked. Trout! Feeding trout. And me without a rod in my hand.

To go back to see Old Faithful was too much. I almost kicked over the traces and told them to go by themselves. But again they won and I meekly got in the car without having cast a single fly. " You'd never forgive yourself," said Vint dramatically, " if you left here without seeing Old Faithful." As if I couldn't see it the next time I went to Yellowstone!

We got back to one of the wonders of the world about five minutes ahead of time. I figured this time should not be wasted so set up my rod. Before I got through I had the satisfaction of watching Vint doing the same. He wasn't as blasé about the fishing as he made out to be. Maybe he planned this whole thing just to devil me.

Then Old Faithful performed and I was glad momentarily that Grace and Vint had been so high-handed in their curtailment of my fishing. But even so, I saw trout rising in Old Faithful's column of steaming white and was ready to leave the moment the force of the eruption had subsided—and Vint didn't do anything to hinder me this time. I suppose he felt that he had fulfilled his duty in bolstering my geographical knowledge first hand and now figured I could play as long as I seemed to be so determined to.

The trout were still rising when we got back to the Morning Glory Hole of the Firehole. This is my own name for this bit of water and is not official. Vint wanted me to have the pool to myself so he went downstream to look things over while I stayed to see what could be done. Of course I went down to the tail. Just as I got there the skies darkened abruptly and a thick wet snow came pulling through the draw on the wings of a gale. In the thick of it I saw trout rising a few feet above the lip of the tail. It was an ideal setup for approach. The tail of the pool was a smooth glide which ended at a jagged natural dam about three feet high. With the gale lashing the smooth water and my position being so much lower I advanced within several feet of the little falls without disturbing the fish. Then I knelt in the wash from the falls and could easily see the water above without being seen myself.

Despite Scotty's admonition about small flies and our experience of two days previous, I started fishing with a 12. I really thought the first experience had been a freak occurrence and that it was unnecessary to keep on using the midges. Some three dozen casts later I changed my mind about this. Although the trout kept rising to naturals they would have nothing of my size 12 Adams which was about the color of the naturals. The stream was covered thickly with these grayish flies but they were so tiny that one could hardly see them.

I had tied a couple of size 16 Adams the night before, so put one on. This brought some three or four half-hearted rises but no hooked fish. So once again I brought out the box of unseeables which I hadn't used for more than a year. Having no Adams in this size I tied on a Blue Dun. I couldn't see this on the water but think I got several rises to it because I felt one when I struck by guess. The Black Gnat I could see quite well but nothing took it. I didn't bother trying any more of these dull patterns. I tied on the old Royal Coachman and on the very first cast took a good trout.

Once again this old-time pattern proved its worth. I could see it better than the others and despite the fact that the naturals on the water were gray they took it better than those artificials which seemed to match the naturals from my point of view. It is quite likely that in this case, due to certain light conditions, the Royal looked more natural than the others but of course this is something we can only guess at. The fact is we know that every rising fish I saw in the tail end of the pool took the Royal Coachman No. 18 and that is conclusive proof it was okay for the time and the conditions no matter what the reason was.

In advancing above the tail I scared a lot of trout from the shallow water at the left. Immediately all the trout for thirty feet upstream stopped rising, only those over at the extreme left under the bank and where the water looked extra deep kept dimpling away. Just about this time the heavy snow squalls which had been pestering us all day suddenly ceased and the sun turned all the drab colors into golden pulsating life. The right bank proved very friendly. Practically every cast brought a rise and about every third rise I hooked a good trout.

Then I came to the log jam and above it I could see a rise which just spelled size. It was a difficult place to fish from below and I didn't want to go too far above because other good fish were rising there. First I tried some loop casts. They seemed to fall well but finally I got caught in the log so quit that. Figuring the fish was worth while trying for I carefully worked upstream until opposite his lie, waited until he rose again and then cast so that the fly dropped on the water about a foot above him. It was perfect. I expected to see the trout rise and take my fly. I expected to see the fly disappear in the little hump this fish made. It disappeared all right but under the log instead of a hump and the trout never rose again—at least not while I was fishing this stretch of water. Fortunately my movements had not disturbed the fish in the water above and here I was successful again. Then came an experience which was new to me. By this time I had reached casting distance of the boiling spring and could see its waters mingling with those of the stream. About a foot from where the wrinkle caused by the meeting of the spring and the stream current projected farthest toward the center I saw a trout rise. It was only a dimple but from the suction I surmised it was a good fish. The conditions couldn't have been better for a good float of the fly. When the little Royal dropped to the water it bobbed along in a lifelike manner until it reached the place where I had seen the dimple and then it disappeared. I raised

the rod and was fast to what felt like the best fish of the day.
Vint came along just as the hook went home and some minutes
later I had the satisfaction of having him take my picture as
I held up the seventeen incher with the steam of the boiling
spring in the background. It wasn't the best fish of the day
but it was the first time I had ever taken a trout where I might
have dropped it into water to cook right where I caught it.

The catching of this fish seemed to be the signal for the rise
to stop. Although both Vint and I fished hard for another half
hour we didn't rise another fish nor did we see one rise. But
after all, it was time for this to happen, being about 4: 30 P. M.

And now I'm going to tell you why I feel that Old Faithful
robbed me of some good fishing. I went back to this pool twice
after this experience and never saw another trout there. If we
hadn't gone to see the geyser I might have had a lot more to
say about the Morning Glory Hole of the Firehole.

Incidentally all through our stay in the Yellowstone the best
fishing seemed to be between 10 A. M. and 4: 30 P. M. with the
last hour slower than the rest of the time. This was no doubt
due to the coldness of the weather. It froze practically every
night and as soon as the sun left the water the air had the feel
of a December day in southern New York. For me it was ideal.
I've become old enough to appreciate the comforts of a warm
camp early in the morning and a good dinner at a reasonable
hour in the evening. But I forgive my wife and Vint. They
were thinking only of me and I must admit that I would have
been embarrassed many times after getting back home if I
hadn't seen the things they insisted I should see. Just imagine
having someone say, " So you've just come back from the
Yellowstone. Wasn't Old Faithful simply gorgeous? What did
you think of the Canyon compared to the Grand Canyon of
the Colorado? "—and so on. Those who ask these things are
never true fishermen and they would have been horrified if I
had to say I hadn't seen them. I wouldn't be surprised if I'd

be considered a dumb-bell or some other equally appalling appellation. So I thank Vint Johnson for saving me from this horrible fate. Nevertheless I still regret those lost hours on the Firehole River and—let me whisper it—I'd rather be called all the belittling names in the dictionary than lose two hours or more of a rise which comes only once in a while. Maybe I'll never find the trout in this hole so willing again. It's a long distance from my home and I can't run out there when things look just right. But the rest of nature's wonders will be there on display no matter when I go: I can always see them and enjoy them, whenever I've got the price and time to visit them. You can't buy rising trout this way. When the gods offer you your chance it should be taken, and the time shouldn't be wasted on things that you can always buy with money. Take heed, fishermen. Never let anything interfere when you have an opportunity to have a real session with the trout. If you do you will regret it to the end of your days—just as now I'm regretting the time I spent looking at national wonders when the trout were really on the rise. Time enough to go sight-seeing when you can't catch fish. At least those are my sentiments.

But to get back to business, it certainly looks as if the midge flies were entitled to plenty of praise. This is further borne out by some experiences in the High Sierras of California although here the small flies suffered a setback when the Spiders showed that they too could give a good account of themselves.

The location now is Arcularius Ranch on the upper reaches of the Owens River. Our cabin is in a swell location. From the bedroom window I can see a sparkling riffle which runs directly toward the house. It is so close that its musical murmur lulls you to sleep at night. From the front of the house you see the stream again after it has curved gracefully around the two bends and is now flowing away from you. In the background stand some of the high peaks of the Sierras, jagged, spectacular,

PLATE NO. 8

Ross	Round Lake	Royal Coachman	Rube Wood	Sabbatus	Sage	Sallie S
Saltoun	Sanctuary	Sand Fly	Saranac	Sassy Cat	Scarlet Gnat	Scarlet
Schaefer	Sheenan	Seth Green	Shad Fly	Shoemaker	Skookum	Silver
Silver Doctor	Silver Fairy	Silver Ghost	Silver-Gold	Silver Jungle	Silver Stork	Silver S
Sir Sam Darling	Soldier Palmer	Something	Soo Nipi	Spencer	Split Ibis	Stebbins
St. Lawrence	St. Patrick	St. Regis	Stone	Secret Pool	Strachan	Stranger
Sturtevant	Sunset	Swiftwater	Teal	Teton	Thistle	Thunder
Tomah Joe	Toodle Bug	Telephone Box	Turkey	Turkey Brown	Turkey Silver	Tuthill
Tycoon						

Full descriptions of the flies on this plate will be found on pages 428-431.

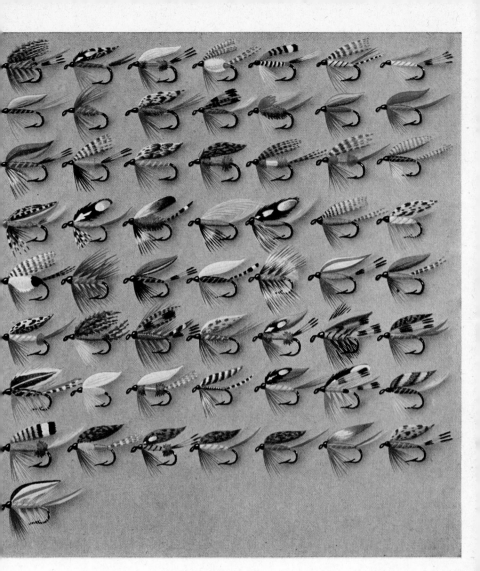

PLATE No. 8

impressive and inspiring except when the storm fogs drop low and give one the sense of being isolated in the clouds.

At this point the stream is small but very fascinating. It is mostly narrow and bordered by grassy banks which have been undermined by the current. This makes ideal resting places for good trout and they are there if you are good enough to catch them. This condition has been the reason for a special method of fishing, locally called "Floating the Bank." Frank Arcularius, son of the ranch owner, is a master at this type of fishing. It is really a form of dapping, except that the fly used is a wet one and is allowed to drift with the current as it will instead of being allowed to merely touch the surface at quick intervals as in true dapping.

I was much interested in the way Frank fished. He prefers a No. 6 wet Coachman with the regular white wings clipped to short stubs. He also uses a heavy leader, one capable of lifting a 2 pounder from the water. When in action he stays as far back from the bank as his rod allows and dangles the fly over the edge, letting the current carry it along as he follows it. It is fast fishing. One must see that the fly is not dragged by restraint from the rod. He works along with the current, always letting the fly seek the hidden cover under the grassy banks. To show how fast it is: while I fished a hundred yards of stream in the regular dry fly style he covered a good half mile, perhaps more.

Of course the method isn't infallible, any more than others nor is it applicable to every stream. Frank claims that even in the headwaters of the Owens if they don't strike right away you might as well quit—or try something else. As a general rule when they don't fall for Frank they don't for anything else although there are exceptions as in everything else.

Watching Frank brought back memories of old days when I used to crawl up to a hole and dap a worm over the edge of the bank. The method was deadly and I often mystified my friends because I sometimes took trout when they failed. There wasn't anything mysterious or skillful about it. The only secret lay in keeping out of sight and dropping a bait or fly as if it had fallen from the bank. It was really fundamental practice and that is what all successful fishing is based on. We might create fancy names for different methods. We might invent fancy casts to overcome some problems, we might even make it appear that we have discovered a way to catch fish that transcends anything yet thought of, but when you really analyze all these things you find that all they do is to arrive at fundamentals from different angles.

I couldn't accept the setup on the Owens. The established methods of fishing were too contradictory. Besides, they didn't completely coincide with the habits of the trout. There were glaring discrepancies between statements and the things that actually happened. But let me tell you about it so that you may formulate your own opinion.

Everyone at the ranch when we were there, both visitors and residents, said that you had to get your fish before 3 P. M. or not at all. This didn't seem to check with the feeding habits of the trout. Every day we were there, between sunset and dark, there was an excellent rise to naturals. On inquiring about this I found it was a fairly regular occurrence but that the fish wouldn't rise very well to artificials at this time. To me this suggested that we didn't fish as we should at this time of the day. Surely feeding trout can be taken if you fish for them in the right way; in other words if you have what they want and present it as they want it you must get action.

It was also emphatically said that any dry fly larger than 16 would not produce and that flies smaller than 16 were the best. As Frank Arcularius made wonderful catches on his size 6 wet Coachman I couldn't quite accept this as gospel. It didn't make sense to my way of thinking. Why should trout go wild about a really large wet fly and yet insist on the tiniest of dry flies?

DRY FLY EXPERIENCES IN COLOR AND SIZE

It wasn't logical. But let me tell you how things worked out.

As usual when visiting any new location I first spent some time watching someone do some fishing who knew the stream. In this case it was Bill Michael of the California Institute of Technology. I find this system is a decided short cut to knowledge. It gives you a grand opportunity to line up the situation from the right perspective and also to get acquainted with any personal peculiarities of the stream.

Bill knew how to handle his dry flies and did a good job. Although fishing was exceedingly poor he managed to make a fair showing. There wasn't any doubt that the small dry flies were most productive. Occasionally I'd try a large fly over some particularly good-looking spot without getting any response while Bill would at least get a rise in the same location and sometimes take a fish. But Bill left for his camp sometime before sunset and I was left to struggle with the alleged poor evening fishing by myself.

As far as I was concerned it certainly was poor. I saw at least a hundred trout rise and took only two and these I caught on a bucktail size 8LS. Finally I had become discouraged over the indifference of the fish to my 16 and 18 dry flies and had resorted to bucktails at the last moment. When I got these two fish I was sorry I hadn't tried them before. The entire day had been poor. Even Frank Arcularius reported the fish inactive and the net catch of all concerned wasn't anything to brag about.

A short distance above our cabin the stream was dammed. Above the dam was a fairly large still water, not positively quiet but with current so slow that you'd think it wasn't moving except for the floating bubbles and the slight disturbance caused when it contacted the banks and other projecting objects.

The following evening Bill decided to stay with me and try this stretch out. At least 200 trout were rising within sight of us as we started out. I selected the lower pool and Bill took the upper. While I fished Lafe Brown of Santa Paula and Frank Arcularius stood by watching me. A few hours previously Lafe had experienced some really good luck there. I worked that stretch for all I was worth and Bill Michael did the same on the stretch above but we never got a fish worth while keeping. I did get a few splashes which looked like good fish but I have since wondered if they weren't really caused by trout that happened to rise to a natural which was floating close to my artificial. At least I must confess that I never felt a tug on any of these occasions, although I tried to set the hook.

The watchers didn't seem the least bit surprised over my poor luck nor did they disparage my fishing technique. I became discouraged after a time and turned around to see Lafe Brown and Frank both smiling at me. " It's always that way here with the evening fishing," said Lafe soothingly. " If you can fish your fly so that it appears to flutter on the water, then you have a chance. Otherwise you can't do anything."

His remark gave me an idea. True to the traditions of the country I had been using very small flies. Perhaps experts can flutter an 18 fly over the surface of the water but I can't. But I can sometimes flutter a Spider or a well-tied Variant, and besides, the very construction of a Spider makes it look as though it were fluttering when being carried along by the current.

When Lafe saw me putting on a fly with a hackle spread of more than an inch he looked at me dubiously. But his expression changed when I got four solid strikes in rapid succession which I missed, because by this time I was a bit upset and excited. I felt each one of these fish but struck too fast in each case and took the fly away from them. But I didn't mind much. Lafe Brown's remark—" I think you've got something there. Gad but I think you're even a worse nut than I am," more than compensated for my failure.

The next evening I tried again, starting with the Ginger-

Furnace Spider which I had been using the previous day. I took several trout with it but had so many refusals that I knew it wasn't right. Then I tried some other patterns—Blue-Gray, Grizzly, Honey and Dark Brown. These were even worse than the Ginger Furnace. I didn't have much hope left when I put the last untried pattern on my leader. It was a Badger Variant, with peacock body and grizzly hackle spent wings. But the first cast changed all that. A trout took it as if it were the very fly it had been waiting for the entire day. It seemed to be the answer for the time being. Resultant experiences while there proved the fly excellent for the evening fishing. Of course the credit belongs to Lafe Brown. His remark about the fluttering fly had been the tip-off. The past experiences with a Spider fly had supplied the necessary connecting link which brought success.

These spider type flies are really remarkable creations. Fluffy and ethereal they fairly dance over the surface of the water. Time after time they have brought me success when nothing else would. Consider the following experience which took place on the north branch of the Callicoon Creek in New York State. It was during that period when I first became acquainted with the effectiveness of the Spiders, as far as I know at the very time when they first made their appearance as dry flies.

These first experiences on the north branch were really wonderful. The stream provided fishing such as I've never seen equaled from coast to coast ever since. You could look into any ordinary hole or bit of water which could be looked into and see any number of trout in each place. One pool near where we camped contained 50 Rainbows by actual count and in size they ranged from 8 inches to 22 inches. I'm sure about them running at least as high as 22 inches because I caught one that size. There may have been even larger.

The first day I fished the stream is unforgettable. I wasn't particularly impressed with it. It was small and in some locations far from attractive. I had been told that the best fishing was directly in the village of North Branch so went to that section.

The first thing I saw was a drowned White Leghorn chicken lying in a shallow riffle. It made me squirm a bit but it was nothing to what I saw when I looked upstream. I saw three more White Leghorns above and two below. Because the first chicken lay near a good-looking pocket I cast the fly there. No one was ever more surprised when the fly suddenly disappeared and I felt the tug of a really good fish that presently made a spectacular jump and showed himself to be a Rainbow of generous proportions. This fish balanced the scales at 2¼ pounds. The resulting day's fishing was something to give any angler dreams for years to come. I can still see the flash of the Rainbows as they rose quickly and dashed wildly away with the fly. I still thrill to the shadowy rise of the golden Brown Trout as with self-satisfied assurance they sucked in the fly.

For three years the fishing on the North Branch was like that. Everyone you saw had a creelful and although I never actually saw it myself it was common gossip that many fellows took two or more limits a day. It could have been accomplished easily enough. The trout were there, they could be caught and I never saw a game warden all the times I fished it. I do know that the toll was greater than the stream could stand. Gradually the fishing became poorer.

It was about this time that I became really interested in the Brown Spider as a fly for interesting wary and much fished over fish. The North Branch had been very discouraging the last two times I had been there and I thought it might be a good idea to try this high-floating Spider even though other patterns had formerly been so good on the stream.

However I fished a half day before trying the Spider. Somehow, I couldn't bring myself to forsake the flies I had used with such success previously. But a half day of inaction except for casting is enough to make you do anything. At the time I had reached the narrow stretch between the village and the next bridge crossing the main stream. I was just about to call it quits and go elsewhere when I thought of the Brown Spiders I had brought along to try but which I had neglected.

At this point, the stream is brushy as well as narrow but there are a few mighty swell holes which had always produced some good fish. Because it was so slow fishing I skipped the lower end of the stretch and went directly to the first big hole which was formed by shale rock. The last two times I had fished it I hadn't got a rise but I felt sure there were still some fish left in it.

So the No. 16 Brown Spider was cast tentatively on the lower end of the pool, where the water ran smooth-topped but quite swiftly. It hadn't floated two feet when a trout took it, rising leisurely and yet quickly and hooking himself against the rod as he went back to bottom with what he thought was a luscious bit of food.

The tough fishing suddenly became incredibly easy. Every trout in every pocket hole, pool and riffle seemed to be waiting for the few wisps of brown hackle tied on a small hook. Action continued until dark.

But as I used this Spider on subsequent fishing trips I found out things about it that weren't so complimentary as this first account. Not always did the trout take it with such avidity. Often they jumped over it, splashed it, looked it over and refused it, did everything but actually take it until one became so exasperated that it would have been a relief to throw one's entire outfit at them.

For some time I wavered between discarding the fly and using it but after stifling impulses and letting calm unprejudiced judgment settle the question I decided that the good features of the fly far outweighed the bad. I found that even the exasperating features had meritorious effects. As an illustration consider the following experience.

The location? A stream in eastern Pennsylvania. The water condition low and clear with very few natural flies in evidence. For five hours the trout teased me almost beyond endurance. The only fly that could bring them to the surface was the Spider, but they wouldn't take it—they simply splashed at it, jumped over it or bulged to it. Not once did they take it. A sudden notion supplied the key to success. It came after fifteen rises to the Spider, in one pool, had resulted in a positive rout. " Perhaps some juicy looking fly would work right now," I thought. " Believe I'll try one of those large Bridgeville Olives."

No idea ever produced more immediate concrete results. The next fifteen casts brought six beautiful trout to net—trout anyone would have been proud to catch. Was the Bridgeville Olive entitled to all the credit? Or did the Spider deserve some recognition? In the light of subsequent experiments I am inclined to give the greatest credit to the Spider because it was the medium which aroused the trout from their lethargy. Exhaustive experiments under such conditions seemed to show that first the fish needed something to get them interested and then something that appealed to their appetite. The Spider seemed to have the power to arouse interest. After that one could never tell what pattern would turn the trick. It might be the Spider itself, and often it was, but in such cases the completed cycle was of short duration. Usually a large and spectacular fly was needed. Any of the Fan Wings were good with the Royal Coachman and the Light Cahill usually taking the honors. Spiders and Variants of different coloration than the one used to create interest also served well as a follow-up fly. For instance, on many occasions I succeeded in getting the trout to start moving with the Brown Spider and then took them with a Badger Spider. There is no absolute rule covering this, nor was there a really logical reason for it as would be the case if it always happened under identical conditions. But the big thing is that it worked, whether it was sensible or not, and for many years I have found that it was a good method to try when the fish were not rising to any particular hatch. Putting your faith in a Spider, when in doubt, is not bad advice—believe it or not.

Here is more proof that color and size had a bearing on success. The location is a northern New York stream. All the gray, brown, badger and other colors brought no response, but light ginger was always productive—although it must be admitted that this was so only during the middle of the day. After exhaustive test we also found that size 12 was most consistently successful. During the period of the day when the sun first made its presence felt to the human body and the first long shadows of evening started to appear a light Cahill size 12 was by far the best bet but before the sun touched the water in the morning and after it had left it at night a Fan Wing Royal Coachman or Dark Cahill size 10 produced most consistent results.

Why this was so is a mystery to me. The fly hatches during the period of this test were of blue-gray cast relieved by an occasional hatch of straw-colored gingers. Of course it may be that the trout were partial to the light ginger naturals and would take them at any time in preference to the blue-gray but what about the evening fishing when they preferred brown— and why should they take the Fan Wing Royal Coachman and the Dark Cahill with equal avidity? It is such things which put your brain in a turmoil of conflicting ideas. No matter what you figure is the right answer it doesn't take much thought to pull it to pieces and prove that your carefully prepared thesis is as full of holes as a piece of chicken wire. Only the fundamentals stand the acid test. The rest of it is simply in your minds and mine but nevertheless it is all fascinating.

Here is another instance where color certainly had plenty to do with getting the fish. I can't vouch for the size being a contributing factor because we had only the one size in the fly which produced results.

This experience took place on the Neversink River at Oakland, N. Y. When we got there a Green May Fly hatch was in progress and although we tried all sorts of patterns including all the colors of natural fowl and some dyed, we couldn't take a trout until we put on a fly made with mottled light green wings, light blue-gray hackles, and a succulent looking whitish colored body.

On the same stretch, seven days later, we had the same experience with a hatch of bluish-gray flies. In this instance, two flies produced and they were quite different in appearance from our standpoint—the Badger Bivisible and the Light Hendrickson. However the Light Hendrickson proved most consistent, taking three fish to every one taken by the Badger. This was logical and consistent, as the fly on the water resembled the Hendrickson and not the Bivisible. Therefore it should have been better.

As I peruse my notes I find many instances of this sort but usually this selectiveness has occurred under specific conditions—such as during a large hatch of flies at any time of or on any sort of a day, at any time the skies were clouded, or in the early morning and evening whether the natural fly hatch was large or not. Under other conditions it didn't seem to matter much what color or size of fly you used as long as it was presented properly.

However, on massing together a lot of similar experiences and comparing the flies used it seems to show that a brown fly of some sort was best on a bright, sunny day and a blue-gray or gray fly was best on a dark day.

It was while I was considering these things that John Hillhouse and I had much correspondence about sunlight and its effect on the trout. John was one of the best fishermen I've ever known. The sum total of our findings in this respect are herewith given.

A rule of physics determines that when white, gray or black are shown against a colored background they appear to have a color complementary to the color of the ground they are shown against. On actual tests it was shown that brown was less changed than gray against a blue sky, therefore could be seen more plainly and as the color it really was. Gray was quite likely to lose its identity when shown against a bright clear sky and thus it may be that it wasn't as easily seen by the trout under these conditions.

On the other hand a gray fly is not complementary to gray sky at all and so a gray fly does not change color in use and so can be readily seen on a gray day. This makes it a good fly for dark days or in the morning or evening if the trout will take gray and are not partial to some special hatch of another color.

Of course we might contend that natural flies are subject to the same changes due to color contrasts but if you will consider the thing carefully you will readily see that they are not so much so if under certain conditions they are subject to the law at all.

The reason? Well, first of all natural flies vary from almost transparent to semi-opaque. When a body held between the eye and the sun transmits light without change it is transparent—it is colorless. If the body is only translucent it appears as white, or if of the right consistency, will show the tints of yellow, red or whatever pigment is intermingled with the body substance. Unless it is transparent or translucent a body is opaque—light does not shine through it and so between a fish and the sun it will appear as purple or black. The artificial fly is practically opaque. Therefore when seen against the light it is nothing but a shadow. For this reason it is a question whether an artificial fly and a natural fly, lying side by side in your hand and appearing duplicates to you, are anything like duplicates to the trout. The fish sees the flies against the light—you see them against a non-luminous background. For this reason alone the matching of your flies means far less than your eyes tell you.

But there is another reason. Most natural flies have what may be called a glazed surface. This acts as a reflector. Your artificial fly does not have this surface and so is not a reflector. Of course we gain a fair effect by using glossy, stiff hackles and gold or silver bodies but these materials do not have the life present in the make-up of the natural. I do believe that fur gives off a certain luminosity when seen against the light and because of this use it in my own flies considerably but aside from the fact that they take fish as any other artificial I have no proof that fur is better than wool or any other substance of which fly bodies are made.

Of one thing I am positive. No artificial really ever looked like a natural to any human, when compared side by side. Even though we could float our product with six points of hackle to simulate six legs of a natural these points would not be placed like the legs of a natural and they certainly wouldn't hold a hook above water—and who ever saw a natural possessing a body which looked like a hook?

No—our artificials do not do a good job of imitation. Even when tied with the extended bodies they fail miserably, in fact I think more so than the regular dry flies which most of us use. They are clumsy, opaque—nothing like a real insect. Personally I'll take my chances normally on high-floating flies— flies with small hooks and plenty of hackle to keep that hook above water. It seems to me that the more you hide the hook the better chance you have of fooling the fish.

Certainly if we give the trout the credit of being able to distinguish the difference between the slightest shades of color (and what dry fly fisherman doesn't have this belief?) we should give them the credit of being able to see the hook and distinguish any artificial from a natural. Figuring along these lines the Spider and Variant flies score as being nearest to perfection. When tied on small hooks and with stiff, rather bushy hackle and tail, the hook will be held high enough so that it does not break through the surface film of the water and besides the hackle points distort the vision of the prospective quarry to the extent that it doesn't see anything above the water. This is logical reasoning and yet it doesn't always work out as we think it should.

For instance, often we find that a fly which floats low in the water is more effective than one which floats high. Despite the fact that the hook of a low-floating fly must be plainly seen by the trout they take it as willingly as they do a natural—as if it were a regular thing to see flies with hooks for bodies. Again, there are times when Spiders tied on short-shanked hooks without a tail will work better than those with tails and yet the very construction of a fly without a tail makes it ride on the water with the hook plainly showing beneath.

The answer to it all? Bless you, but you have me there. Perhaps no one knows, not even the trout. Perhaps they take our artificials because they look good to them, because they look like food of some kind—in fact they must do that, otherwise they wouldn't take them at all. But do they take them because they look like the natural? I doubt it—in fact I can't believe it—and at the same time believe that they can recognize slight variations in color or size. To my way of figuring we've got to accept one of two theories. Either the trout do not see as well as we think they do, in which case they mistake our artificial, hook and all, for a natural; or else they can see exceedingly well, know at once that our artificial is not an imitation of any real natural, but, not being capable of thinking, take it for a different sort of natural and so rise when the color appeals and the fly is presented well enough to simulate the action of a real insect when it alights on the water. Now this theory appeals to me and answers for everything. It explains selectiveness to color and size and yet doesn't outrage the senses by making one believe that our artificial looks like a natural. It gives us the freedom to believe that trout can recognize every little detail in a fly, even to one different degree in color or size without making apologies for the presence of the hook.

That trout have good eyesight for close work I am fully convinced. From observation and study I would say that trout have a perfection of vision that far exceeds that of man and is probably more acute than that of birds, when applied to objects close by. I do not believe that trout have very clear vision for objects more than a few feet away, but for microscopic close-up work no doubt they have sharper vision, or at least as sharp as the vision of any fauna in North America. Certainly this belief is logical, considering the dense medium of water and the necessity for near-sightedness and the lack of need for far-sightedness for the creatures which live in it.

This is the main reason why I can't accept our artificial flies as exact duplicates of naturals. At the same time, I thoroughly recognize the selectiveness of trout to our artificials which plainly shows that they have preferences for one thing or the other under certain conditions. Most of us will agree that trout are selective to our flies. Most of us will insist that they can readily tell the difference between light and dark ginger. Then how in heaven's name can we account for their indifference to the hook in our artificial unless it is by saying they take it for some sort of a fly different from what we know the natural to be? Certainly eyes that see such small details as we insist they do and which most every angler has, to his own satisfaction, proved they do would see that one outstanding thing which sets our artificial apart from anything that nature directly created.

Have you ever put a natural fly and an artificial counterpart on the water and then looked at them from beneath? If you have, you could never credit a trout with good eyesight and selective powers if you still insisted that they couldn't tell the difference between the two flies. The difference is so obvious that unless we consider our artificials as flies which do not imitate nature we must belittle the trout's vision and sagacity, something which would never do. This does not mean that the fish refuse to accept our artificials as something alive and therefore something to be eaten. It merely means that we have created something which they like, even though it doesn't exactly simulate nature, because it excites their appetites. I may be all wrong on this theory—I am not insisting that it really means anything. But I do claim it is much more logical and understandable than the theory which insists that our artificials take trout because they actually imitate naturals. They imitate flies to the extent that they are similar to them in *some ways*— that is true, otherwise the fish wouldn't have anything to do with them. This is a positive statement. But I can't believe that they take our artificial Blue Dun *for* a natural Blue Dun—unless they are so dumb that it doesn't matter much what we use, in which case all this talk is just so much babble. As far as I am concerned, I feel that if a trout can't tell the difference between a natural and an artificial then it can't possibly tell the difference between light and dark gray or any other closely matched colors—in which case all this fuss about patterns means nothing concrete. But the influence of light rays may affect the sight of fish to such an extent that they can't tell the difference between the two—and this gives us another angle on the question. This I shall go into later.

But here is another way to look at it, a way which uses the imagination instead of cold observation. Perhaps it is only occasionally that trout are particular and exceedingly careful. Perhaps when we take them easily with our flies they are careless and reckless. Perhaps when they won't take our flies they are in a careful mood. Even humans have these different moods and some are more susceptible to reckless moods than others. We all have our periods of feeling reckless, when we want to take chances, knowing full well that we have very little chance to win. Again, perhaps it is only the moron trout we catch with our artificials or it may be that the ones we do take are caught off guard. I'm not trying to establish anything here. I'm just giving you some possibilities which might not have occurred to you. If it gets you thinking we might take one or two steps forward in this study of the game of angling.

There is another angle we must consider. As pointed out, our artificials, being of different consistency than naturals, may appear different if identical to our eyes and identical to the trout if different to our eyes. The light shining through a live organism of a certain color may easily create a different effect than when shining through an object of the same color which is not alive. Again, a combination of colors in a lifeless object which does not, to our eyes, even slightly resemble a natural we are trying to imitate, may yet look more real to the trout when seen against the light. Therefore, even when leaving the hook out of our calculations we can't be sure that our carefully tied artificial will look anything like the natural we are trying to imitate as far as the trout are concerned. It is this fact which may in some measure account for the successful careers of some fancy flies which do not imitate anything in nature as far as we can see.

Dr. Phil Gootenburg advances an interesting and quite logical thought in this respect. It is that contrasts in colors and broken body lines create life in a fly through the application of light rays. Also recently he made a step forward in the creation of a fly which eliminated the hook fault. (Visa-Phledge fly, named jointly from Phil and Hedge and the " visa " donated by me—so Gootenburg claims.) He says the night he first tied the fly at my bench so that I could see it, I named it when we floated it on the basin in our bathroom. I don't remember the naming but I do the floating and if Phil says so I must have done it and must say that I feel quite proud to be connected with the fly, even though it is only in the naming. While the fly is too recent an innovation for me to have tried it out exhaustively I would say that it should successfully simulate the large naturals such as May Flies and certainly ought to be an aid in fooling wary trout to whom the fly with a hook showing under water is something to let strictly alone.

The whole thing is a jumble of conflicting ideas. When you really start thinking about it you are left dazed and confused and your pet theories suffer some knockout blows. Perhaps some day we shall know all the answers but I hope we never do. If we eliminate theory, conjecture and imagination from fishing and make it an exact science, we will rob it of the charm which has made it the refuge of minds seeking relief from life's burdens.

Fancy being able to fish by formula as you might mix a drink. Suppose you could pick up a book and find just what was needed, written something like this. " Month—Blank-Blank, day—8th. With wind blowing between steen and twenty miles and 16 clouds per hour passing from horizon to horizon use a whatzis fly size umptyump. If the clouds disappear use formula No. 786 with fly pattern No. 9832 in size 22." Silly? Of course it is but it would be more tragic than silly if fishing could be put on such an exact basis. As it is we never know when we're guessing right and what seems absolutely right today may be all wrong tomorrow. Just when we feel we have everything figured out to our satisfaction something comes along to upset all our calculations and makes us believe we don't know a thing about fishing. When you find someone who answers all the questions you can be sure that he doesn't fish enough to know what it's all about or else—well just or else.

CHAPTER NINE

Sunshine and Shadow

I N THE previous chapter I intimated that under certain conditions trout did not see clearly. What the condition is we shall now investigate. Bear in mind that this is theory although it has been applied to actual fishing and as far as the writer is concerned aids considerably in bringing success. But let us start at the beginning—with a rule first given me by John Hillhouse.

" Trout are selective to color and shape in inverse ratio to the intensity of light." In other words trout are more selective in the early morning and in the evening and on dark days than they are when the sun is shining brightly on the water. For this reason, if the trout will feed at all during the middle of the day then a bright day will be the best sort of a day on which to fool them.

Before you rise up in arms over this paragraph I ask you to go back over your fishing experiences and see if you haven't had the following typical experience many times. The early morning fishing proves disappointing and until the sun hits the water here and there you don't do much better. But the moment the high and low lights, made by reflections from the sun or the sun itself casts its bold rays on the water, you begin to rise trout. While you don't take fish fast or see any spectacular rises, somehow you keep getting a fish here and there and have a really fine day. And then, in the evening, after the sun has set and you expect fishing to be at its best you suddenly find that you have a tough time fooling even a couple of ordinary specimens, if any at all. You change patterns time after time and cast, cast and cast but only occasionally do you strike the right fly and make a really good catch, that is, good compared to the number of fish breaking the water.

To explain how this might happen let us start at the beginning. Under certain circumstances and on clear days trout cannot evaluate either the size, color or shape of objects on the surface of the water. These certain circumstances are caused by bright light. Let me show you what I mean by making a simple experiment. Let us hold a fly directly between the sun and our eye. What happens? Color vanishes; shape is obscured; size becomes an uncertain quantity. About all we are conscious of is a black or purple indefinite shape and an uncontrollable eyestrain. But as we move the fly from the direct line between our eye and the sun we see color and shape become more distinct and eyestrain become less. Further movement of the fly brings it to a position where the fly can be seen fairly well and eyestrain vanishes. In this position we cannot elaborate the little details of our artificial but we get a good general effect. The vision is not so clear that we can tell exactly what the fly is but it is clear enough so that we could make a good guess. Now if we stand with our back between the sun and the fly we will note that we can see it very plainly indeed. We can see each hackle point, the hook and the barb. We can also distinguish the pattern without effort.

In making stream experiments along these lines we find that when the fly is directly between the eye of the trout and the sun we get very few rises but that it makes no difference what fly is used. The fish, if they rise at all, will take a Scarlet Ibis as well as anything else even though the natural on the stream may be gray, black, brown or any other color.

In the area where the fly is somewhat indistinct and yet where the light isn't strong enough to cause bad eyestrain (the second position) we find the trout rise readily and are not particularly selective. This is because in this position they see quite well but not so well that they can distinguish the little departures from the naturals.

In the third position, where the trout looks at the fly away from the sun, we find that we need to exercise excessive caution and use the right fly in order to get results. The fly and the cast must be about perfect. This is in direct contrast with the first position when one doesn't need to worry either about the cast or the fly or the second position where any reasonable care is exercised.

In my opinion we have here the reasons why so often we have good catches during the sunny hours of a bright day, even when there isn't a general rise to naturals and why so often when the tremendous evening rises occur we have such a difficult time to take fish. It is the rises which occur when the light is dull that cause most of our troubles and which make necessary the need for so many fly patterns.

In my estimation fishing on sunny days, when the fish in a stream will rise at all during this time of the day, requires less effort and fewer patterns of flies than fishing on dull days and only in the morning and evening. It is not necessary to fish in direct sunlight to get results. Reflections may easily form that distraction which prevents the trout from seeing too plainly what you are offering them. Understand, I'm not insisting that this theory is unassailable. I know that it is and could tear it apart without too much effort myself. But I do know that experience has consistently upheld my views in this respect so that I consider them worth while passing along to you, to make use of or ridicule as you like.

Remember that on gray days there is no area where the fly is indistinct, and that this applies to any day when the sun does not cast a clearly defined shadow. On bright days, even under the shadow of the trees, the water may catch the reflection from a rock or cliff or the leaves of trees on which the sun is shining brightly and so obscure the vision of the fish when a fly floats by in that area affected by the reflection.

All these things must be taken into consideration when choosing the most advantageous position to fish from and the combinations you run into are many and complicated, in fact the subject is so big that it would take a lifetime of experimentation on this idea alone to definitely arrive at some perfect conclusions. I will say this—If you can ascertain the exact location of a large trout, the depth of water he lies in and then figure out the angles of sunlight so that you can place your fly in that area of sufficient but somewhat indistinct vision, you stand a good chance of taking him, perhaps not the first time you try, but eventually, if you keep at it and make sure you have the thing figured out correctly. At any rate I have given you the thought. Some of you may go further with it, most of you will simply read it, and then forget it, the rest of you will no doubt consider it mere twaddle. All I can say is that the original idea came from the mind of one whom I considered one of the best anglers of my time—a man who could out-think and out-fish any person I know—John Hillhouse. And John is gone, left for the Happy Hunting Grounds some years ago. I only hope I meet him there, that we fish together again and perhaps, in that other world, spend eternity trying to solve unsolvable problems of fishing. To me that would be Heaven indeed.

Just what constitutes a good fishing day? Ask a dozen anglers and you're likely to get a dozen different answers. Of course, each one will insist that his choice is the best. It is, because at these times he has had his best fishing. I have my own choice— right or wrong. It is a bright sunny day with snappy, cool air and a northwest wind. This has been my favorite ever since I've started fishing and I've never had any occasion to change my mind. I don't care if it blows a gale as long as the skies are blue and the air invigorating. This sort of weather makes my blood move faster. I feel vigorous, optimistic, capable of moving mountains. But when I put the cold light of registered facts on experiences, I find that I've had poor fishing on such days, as well as excellent fishing. As a matter of fact no matter what type of day I pick out I find that both good and poor fishing has been experienced on them. Nevertheless I still prefer the snappy day, probably because I feel so good on such days and besides they really do show a positive record of providing more good fishing than poor. But enough of this. Let me tell you of some experiences along these lines.

First the Neversink, at Oakland, N. Y. The time May 30th. Weather cold and squally, sometimes blowing so hard that it was impossible to cast except during a lull. We had been fishing on the Mongaup but hadn't done a thing so on the way home thought we'd go Oakland way and take a look from the bridge. By the time we reached the bridge the day had grown worse. It was much colder and the periods between terrific gusts were shorter. We had no hope of seeing any action but because we had plenty of time we parked by the bridge and leaned over the railing to look at the Ledge Pool which could plainly be seen from this point. A white slash in the center of the hole caught my eye. It was a considerable distance away so that really I couldn't tell what it was but some inner sense told me it was a rise. I didn't say anything to the others at the moment—just kept my eyes glued to the tail of that pool where I had seen that peculiar streak of white. Then I saw another and immediately after that two more. It was enough for me. Without wasting any more time I made a bee line for the car to get my rod. As I went I shouted to the others, "There's something doing down there." They looked at me as if I'd gone crazy. I didn't blame them. Instinct rather than sight had told me that those white streaks were caused by trout.

So we went down to the pool and assembled our rods. While doing so we saw a half dozen of the slashes and now, being so close to the pool, could see that there wasn't any mistake about them being the rises of fish. Then I saw the reason for them. There was a large hatch of green May Flies in evidence. The wind was blowing so hard that it made many of them skate over the surface of the pool so that the trout rising to take them sometimes had to chase them across the surface when the squalls struck. In doing this they made a slash of white spray which the wind caught and accentuated.

The only fly in my box which in any way imitated this May Fly was the Bridgeville Olive, a nondescript fly of the Fan Wing type which I had adopted and named because it had brought me success on the Neversink on the stretch just below Bridgeville. It really should have been called the Green May because it imitated this fly very well indeed. My first cast with it was a failure. A strong gust of wind struck the ledge on the opposite side and backed across the stream with a vengeance, fairly throwing the fly back in my face. This made me cautious so I waited until a momentary lull occurred before making the next cast. The fly alighted perfectly but I had misjudged the currents and got an immediate and bad drag. I tried several more times from the same position but could not get a float which did any business, I presume because of the drag. The fish were feeding in midstream and to get the fly to them required a cast which put the line on three currents of different speeds.

There was only one thing to do. Out in the center of the stream was a flat rock which divided the main current of the deep hole. It was a mean place to get at but I felt sure one could get a perfect float from that position, so I determined to make a try for it. I made it and found that from this location I could not only put the fly over the rising fish but could also fish the extreme right-hand side which had been absolutely unreachable from the first position.

Then, after taking all this time and going to all the trouble I made a fiasco of a splendid opportunity. Although in six casts

I rose six good fish I never had a chance to feel them. In each case I struck too hard and too fast, missed four completely and left a fly in the mouth of each of the other two. This seemed to end any further chances. Either there were only six trout feeding in the pool or else I had put the rest down. At any rate even though the natural May Flies kept floating down with ever increasing numbers they did so without any molestation.

It took fifteen minutes to reach the next place where I could do any fishing. I saw a few rises here and there but the water was very high and I could not wade out far enough to reach them. Coming to a hole where I knew a large fish lived, having had previous experiences with him, I was just about to try for him even though he wasn't rising when from the corner of my eye I saw one of the slash rises some distance out in the swirling current. It could be reached by a long cast from where I stood but feeling sure that it was impossible to make a satisfactory float, I decided to make an attempt to get into better position. This took another ten minutes but it was worth it. There was a shallow spot of small area some twenty feet below and to the left of the rock near which the trout was rising. From this place one had all the control of the short cast, something of distinct advantage any time and of particular advantage on this day with the wind so troublesome and the water currents so contrary.

All during this time the wind buffeted and howled and the trout kept rising. He hit so viciously that several times the wind took the spray from his rise and sent it flying several feet in the air. Watching my chances with the wind I sent the fly out on its mission, confidently expecting to take the fish on the first cast. But I found that a normal cast in line with the side of the rock and slightly above did not float the fly close to the rock where the fish seemed to be rising. While trying to figure out how to make the right float I saw that the trout was not lying at the side of the rock but in front of it and that the occasional slashes were caused when a fly got by him and he rushed after it.

As I made the cast to this point, the wind took the fly, deposited it just above the rock, then skated it alongside. I saw the trout come for it and as the slash was completed I felt the pleasant sensation of a heavy fish fighting.

This entire afternoon was a succession of incidents similar to this. The greatest difficulty was getting in a location where you could reach the rising fish and then waiting your chance to cast it between squalls. The fly hatch was continuous until sunset when they disappeared and the trout stopped moving. I kept three fish which weighed a total of 10¼ pounds and this a distance of about sixty miles from New York City. It wasn't so many years ago either.

According to common belief this shouldn't have been a good fishing day. It was positively wintry. The next week I went back again and it was just the sort of a day the average person would call a perfect fishing day. It was warm, partly cloudy and there was a light breeze. And yet there wasn't a fly hatch to speak of and we didn't see a trout rise, either to a natural or to our own flies.

Of course, the successful day was a memorable one, so much so that the next year I went back at the same time. Conditions were very similar but the trout did not rise. It just goes to show that you can't lay down any positive rules about the weather and your fishing. However, I will say that a careful checkup of notes covering many years shows a preponderance of successful days under such conditions. I find that in many cases the strong wind knocks many flies from the bushes and trees and these start the fish working. This condition is not confined to any one locality or section of the country. Wherever I have fished I have found that it pays to fish when the skies are bright, the air cool and the wind strong. On the whole, dark, muggy days do not show up so well.

Water temperature has a lot to do with the way trout rise but this isn't consistent except when the temperature reaches a mark above 72° Fahrenheit. Sometimes you can get good fishing at this level but it is spotty and when it goes higher it is usually very poor indeed. About your only chance when the water gets really warm is to find where springs cool certain sections or where cold water brooks enter the main stream.

To illustrate this, let us go to the Neversink again, in the middle of summer after a long, hot and dry spell. The water was so warm that you could bathe in it without gasping at the first plunge. We knew that we couldn't possibly catch any fish in the usual haunts so we headed for a small cold brook which I knew, where in fact Fred Everett and I had had some rare sport with Brook Trout at another time under similar conditions.

This brook entered at the shallow part of a very deep and large pool. One never knew if the fish would be there as they didn't use the place regularly, only on certain occasions. To get at them without scaring them, you had to wade out and around and approach from the pool side.

On this day I was lucky. There were about thirty fish in the hole, about twenty-five Brookies and five Browns. You could see them facing the cold water of the little stream. I managed to take five before they took fright and disappeared. On this occasion I waited three hours in the hope that they would return but my wait was in vain. Where they went is a mystery but I imagine that somewhere near by there must have been a deep spring hole in the main river. Certainly they couldn't stay long in the main currents with the water temperature what it was. Incidentally, this same day I saw some fish breaking out in the big pool and finally succeeded in getting them on a salmon dry fly, of which I usually carry two or three for night trout fishing. They were Small Mouth Bass. I caught eight. Two of them were somewhat better than legal size—the others ranged between 8 and 9 inches.

The eastern streams are yearly subjected to these intense heat spells. The miles of open, rocky streams absorb the devitalizing heat of long days and the nights are not cold enough to balance the condition. Low water does not make fishing bad in itself. Trout will rise just the same when the water is excessively low as they will when it is normal if the water temperature doesn't get too high and you use the extra caution and skill needed for fishing under such conditions. If you don't believe this, take a thermometer with you and notice the difference in activity between the streams where the water averages 65 or below and those where it ranges 68 or above. And, let me tell you, it is always possible to catch trout in the upper reaches of the streams where the cold springs and dense shade offset the extreme heat of the sun on long summer days.

It is the effect of this extreme heat which so often, if not always, causes eastern fishing to taper off at the end of June, and why, when the nights of late August become longer, with an occasional cool one, that the fishing sometimes picks up. Of course there is no set rule about it. It all depends on seasonal conditions.

In the trout country, from the Continental Divide westward, the streams are not subjected to these high temperature conditions. In much of this section the summers are too short to cause trouble or else the entire season is moderate enough to equalize things. In all the Rocky Mountain country I've ever fished, you rarely get any dry fly fishing before July 1st. Before then the streams are flooded and filled with snow water. Then, after the fishing does start, the nights stay cool if not positively cold and by the latter part of September you are almost sure to have snow again, and at certain altitudes you will have freezing weather at night. In other words, streams in the mountain country (Continental Divide westward) stay cold in every instance, as far as my personal experience goes, so that your problems are those of finding the right method and lure for successful fishing—solvable problems if we can find the solution and not unsolvable ones as is the case when confronted with excessively high water temperatures.

The only exception to this in my experience is the Firehole River in Yellowstone Park. Here the trout rise well with water temperatures of 74° or higher. Even as I read the proofs of this book I have been fishing this stream, with the water temperature 75°. The trout were active, though wary and full of fight, far more so than most Browns or Loch Levens I have caught elsewhere. There may be other streams like this. As Scotty Chapman says, "Those Firehole trout have become accustomed to warm water and thrive in it. The temperature remains fairly constant and the fish rise quite consistently at all times."

In the season of 1935 we took a trip from Colorado Springs to the southeastern part of Wyoming and back via Trapper's Lake and Independence Pass. It was between the 15th and the 27th of September. During this period we had frost or ice every night except two and ran into a real snowstorm at the Pass which made us trek for home. There was a good twelve or fifteen inches on the ground when we reached Colorado Springs and many of the beauty trees of the city were losing limbs and splitting in half from the terrific weight of the wet snow which clung to everything it touched.

The following year we stayed in the southeastern corner of Wyoming ten days during the latter part of September. Each morning we saw the thermometer hovering between 20 and 25 degrees above zero and then after the sun came out strong a rise to 50 or 60 degrees made you shed everything but the necessities. We never had much luck fishing the few times we tried it early. Usually the trout did not start feeding until the sun had warmed things up a trifle. If we did get out early we had to use a fresh pair of wading sox and shoes unless we brought the wet ones indoors the night before. Otherwise they were frozen as hard as bricks and took considerable time to thaw out.

On this occasion we left just in time. We were working west to Oregon and by way of Ogden, Utah, which we reached the first night. Although the snow blanketed the mountaintops the following morning, it did not descend to the valley we drove through. The wind on this trip was terrific. All across Wyoming we saw countless miniature tornados—or twisters as they call them there. They ranged from a few feet to fifty yards in width at the base (these are guesses) and when we rode through one of them it was all one could do to hold the wheel straight. The ride through the valley west from Ogden was real fun. The mountains were blanketed in a snowstorm but we rode mostly through sunshine. Occasionally the wind would blow some of the storm across our path but it was merely like a squall and soon passed. But one can readily understand why the water in the streams in this country stays cold. The mountain peaks where they originate don't have many weeks without snow. I have noted that the trout in this country will rise to the dry fly when the water is at much lower temperature than in the eastern streams—that is striking an average based on the tabulations of actual experience. Of course, this is logical and understandable. Any living thing becomes acclimated to certain average conditions. These trout of the high altitude streams become accustomed to colder water than do the trout of the eastern streams. It is quite likely that they would also quit rising at a lower water temperature than do the eastern trout which are subject to excessively high water temperatures. All in all the eastern trout has the toughest time of it. The water he lives in touches extremes each year. The trout of the high altitudes suffer some differences in water temperature but it is much more equable than that experienced by the trout in the east.

Incidentally, a friend who was fishing with us in Wyoming stayed over after we left. He was to stay two days longer but when he got up the next morning a regular blizzard was raging so he decided to leave before he got stuck. He wrote us that he had a tough trip getting out and had to go around the long way instead of over the Snowy Range to Laramie.*

In the Yellowstone a year later, we again had snow in September. On one occasion we struck a squall of such intensity and length that anyone in the east would have called it a small blizzard.

To me this is one of the fascinating charms of the mountain country. You might start out on a gorgeous sunny summer morning and by noon or before be tramping through a blizzard as you climb to your fishing objective. It is fascinating, exciting and sometimes a bit terrifying because you're not sure what is going to happen. I love it and thrive on it and so must everyone else who loves nature as she is—not only when she is smiling. When someone tells me of climate where the sun always shines, where the temperature doesn't have much variation, where the wind never reaches high velocity, I can't get particularly enthused, even though it does seem to be what the majority desire and which those who have brag about.

It's nice to stay in such places but too much sameness would bore me, if I had it too long. I'd rather be chased to cover by a sudden shower, see huge black clouds streaked with awesome lightning, witness a blizzard attack with irresistible fury, have a fog isolate me from my surroundings, see the sea rage along a barren stretch of coast, swelter in heat one day and shiver the next—anything where contrasts give one an extra appreciation for that which follows. It is inclement weather which makes you more thoroughly enjoy a perfect day when it comes.

* Snowy Range is shown in the Wyoming scene on the end plate.

SUNSHINE AND SHADOW

It takes hot dry weather and parched soil to make you really appreciate the rain.

But as far as I am concerned this isn't the only reason I like storms. My blood responds hotly to nature when she goes into a temper and for the time I live in the past, in those days when King Arthur, Richard the Lion Hearted and other warriors of history and fable did battle hand to hand; in the way, no doubt, that nature originally intended.

Yes, I can live a lifetime in several hours of raging storm. Have you ever walked in the dense forest when the snow shrouded everything except those objects in your immediate vicinity, when there was no trail to follow, when you knew that only by your woodsmanship and compass you could ever expect to reach camp? If you haven't you have missed one of the greatest thrills that life has to offer to a lover of the outdoors. It is a dangerous thrill unless you know what you're doing or have someone with you who knows. I imagine everyone who has ever traveled the wilderness gets lost temporarily now and then. It is knowing what to do and how to get out of it at such times which is the test of woodsmanship.

But aside from the thrill of this uncertainty, heavy snowstorms bring another which you feel no matter where you are. It muffles all sound, brings the sky to earth and you walk in a world from which all strife seems to have fled. Even cities seem less harsh and forbidding at such times. The swirling clouds of snow envelop the buildings, making them look like mountains and the deserted streets resemble the floors of canyons. I must admit I like them best when nature is buffeting them—those times when everyone is avoiding the streets and going on them only for necessity.

Truly, no one can say that he likes camping until he has been through a siege of really inclement weather and is still eager to go again in spite of it. As a matter of fact, it is the things we consider bad which give us the most pleasurable

PLATE NO. 9

Undertaker	Union	Utah	Vance	Vanity	Victoria Green
Volunteer	Von Patten	Walker	Walker-Hays	Walla-Walla	Wanderer
Warden	Warwick	Wasp	Waters	Watson's Fancy	Webbs
Whirling Blue Dun	Whirling Dun	White Hackle	White Jungle	White King	White Miller
Montreal White Tip	White Water	Whitney	Wickham's Fancy	Widow	Wilderness
Willow	Wilson	Wilson Ant	Winters	Witch Gold	Witch Silver
Witcher	Wood Duck	Wood Ibis	Woppinger	Wren	Yankee
Yellow Coachman	Yellow Drake	Yellow Dun	Yellow Sally	Yellow Spinner	Zulu

Full descriptions of the flies on this plate will be found on pages 432-434.

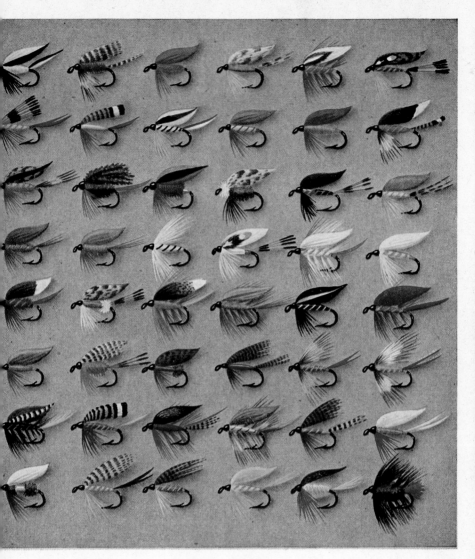

PLATE No. 9

memories. Do we ever keep talking about the trips on which no hardship occurs, when nothing goes wrong? It seems to me that we quickly forget such trips. But how we do gloat over an adventure of some kind—a terrific storm which washed out the roads, getting lost in a big swamp at night, making a dangerous mountain ride through snow or fog, having a blowout and escaping with minor injuries or none at all. It doesn't need to be much but it can be big. Even running short of food on a wilderness canoe trip can provide the chief topic of an entertaining evening. One thing leads to another and the party is a huge success.

But here, I'm getting far away from the actual fishing. What started this anyway? Oh, I know—the vagaries of the mountain country. Well, hats off to you all—you mountains where blizzards swoop down to catch you, you deserts where for days on end the burning sun beats down on barren wastes of sand which can suddenly turn into rivers of raging torrents when the rain does come, where you might easily be stranded on a piece of high ground until the waters subside, to the lake country where a peaceful scene may suddenly be changed to one of whitecapped fury. Regardless of the discomforts, and the perils which such things subject us to, I doubt if we'd be really happy without them. They really reflect our own temperaments with their various moods of sunshine and shadow, happiness and sorrow, elation and despondency.

If anything in nature affects the feeding habits of fish besides food, temperatures, and water conditions it is probably the barometric pressure. It probably affects us too, as we'd find out if we checked it up carefully. Of course, I'm not sure that air pressure has an effect under the surface of the water, although I've read somewhere that it has and one can't check on the barometer when fishing, without taking one along so that our theories are guesses. But I can and will relate some experiences dealing with storms and their effect on trout fishing and these are not guesses but actual happenings.

First let us go back to 1914. I was somewhat afraid of electrical storms at that time and besides, believed absolutely that they ruined the fishing, before and throughout the storm and sometimes for the balance of the day. I really thought that trout were frightened by the thunder and lightning the same as I.

But one day I happened to be fishing with a fellow who didn't believe these things and who had no fear of thunderstorms or anything else for that matter. I heard the first rumble of the shower and wanted to back-track because we were a long distance from shelter, but my friend wouldn't stop fishing.

"They're not rising now," I pointed out, "and they surely won't rise with this storm coming. There's no use in getting soaked for nothing."

"Perhaps the storm might wake them up," was the only satisfaction I got.

Came the dead calm which so often precedes a violent summer storm. The black clouds were towering over our heads and it was getting quite dark. With the crash of a bolt which landed in some near-by timber, the storm suddenly broke and at the very moment it started my friend hooked the first trout of the day. Not only that but he kept getting them one after the other, during the storm and after it had passed. I couldn't do anything while the storm was at its height but after it had dwindled to a light patter, I too started to catch trout.

The storm circled and came back, joining another coming from the northwest. This time there was a deluge. The trout suddenly stopped rising and the stream started to discolor. We dug out some worms from the banks and took several more fish and then even worms wouldn't work. We worked hard until evening when it cleared but we didn't catch another trout, due no doubt to the flooded conditions. Drenched and bedraggled we plodded through the wet brush to our bicycles and then pedaled eleven sodden weary miles home. We worked for our fishing in those days.

A similar experience took place on the north branch of the Callicoon Creek many years later. It was an extremely hot and sultry morning, the sort that only the eastern seaboard states know how to deliver. We left Nyack early and arrived at the stream just as dawn was breaking. The air was so oppressive that I felt quite indifferent about fishing. The water looked lifeless and conditions did not seem right.

My friend, not being as susceptible to climatic conditions as I, came down with his rod all set for action. " Boy, it's hot," he snorted, " but that's just the time you get some good dry fly fishing." With that he cast his Brown Spider over the most productive spot in the pool we were standing by.

But nothing happened. He fished the pool until daylight fully arrived and then moved upstream to the next bit of good water. We went along slowly. My friend fished energetically and perspired freely while I moped along behind, bathing my face and hands frequently but not even bothering to put my rod together although I did carry it along.

Two hours passed, three, four. We stopped in a shady spot to have a bite to eat. "It's queer," said my friend. "I'd say this was a perfect day for dry fly fishing. There are plenty of flies on the water, the stream is in perfect condition and yet I haven't taken a fish nor seen one rise."

"You've got me," I replied, " unless it is that the trout feel this weather as we do and are depressed and indifferent. For a long time I also thought that hot, muggy weather was good fly fishing weather but I've had poor fishing so often under these conditions that I'm beginning to have my doubts. Sometimes I blame the poor fishing on my own indolence but this time we've got real proof because you fished hard and well."

My friend laughed. "You have some queer ideas at times.

As if atmospheric conditions which depress you could have any effect on the fish. It's just a case of coincidence—you just happened on the stream under such conditions when the trout were off feed."

"That may be the reason," I admitted dismally, "but anyway I still know that we won't get any trout today—unless the weather changes."

Until 2:30 that afternoon conditions remained the same. We both fished steadily after lunch but all we saw were a few hungry infants. I was about ready to quit when I sensed a change in the air. A slight gust of wind had drawn through the valley and it smelled of rain; of sodden fields and steaming roads cooling under a deluge.

Instantly my indifference vanished and I began to fish hard. At the moment my friend happened to be resting. He noticed my change in attitude and gave vent to his feelings in the matter.

"What has come over you?" he asked. "One moment you are moping along like a sick cat and the next you act as full of ambition as a robin gathering worms after a rain."

"It's the wind—the wind!" I exclaimed impatiently.

"The wind what?" snorted he in disgust. "Have you gone crazy?"

"Don't be so stupid," I retorted. "Conditions are changing. There has been a rain! The humidity is disappearing if not gone. WE'RE GOING TO HAVE SOME FISHING."

He shook his head in despair as he looked at the still blue heavens.

"The boy's gone mad," he said in mock sadness. "It has rained! The trout are going to rise! Can you imagine that? With the sun getting hotter by the minute?"

But I ignored his ravings. I felt sure that something was going to happen. I could smell it.

Then off in the distance we heard the rumble of thunder and

with it another gust of moisture-laden air swept down the brook.

"Did you say it was going to rain," asked my friend, "or that it had rained?"

I turned to answer him but never did. I heard a splash and missed a good fish.

That started the fun. We took trout after trout during that period when the storm was working toward us. A yellowish darkness settled down on the valley and it became deathly still. Then came a subdued moaning from the distance which quickly gained in volume. After that came a roar which had an ominous sound. Intermittently the thunder grumbled and growled. I heard all this as I rose trout and played them.

With a suddenness that was appalling the storm descended upon us. The wind blew a veritable hurricane, the rain came down in torrents and then changed to hail which pelted us unmercifully. Until the hail came, the trout kept rising, even to our sodden flies.

The deluge lasted twenty minutes or thereabouts. Then it stopped as abruptly as it had come. But the trout had stopped too. We couldn't get another rise. The water began to color and soon became the shade of cream-filled coffee. It was the end as far as we were concerned. A quiet rain then started in and we saw the worm fishers appear as if by magic. This would give them their innings, which come seldom enough in the average summer.

Another incident somewhat similar took place on Forbidden Brook, so called because four fellows who fished together did not wish to advertise it. It was in the latter part of July and between claps of thunder and pelting hailstones as big as marbles we filled our creels until the stream became discolored when they stopped taking our flies. These are just a few of the experiences I have had which seem to prove that thunder showers do not spoil the fishing but on the contrary may even improve it.

On the other hand there have been many other instances where the direct opposite was the case—where the fishing was excellent until the storm broke after which the trout went down and wouldn't start rising again, or when the approach of a storm seemed to stop the rise long before it arrived. I remember one incident in particular. It was a threatening day and when we got to the stream it seemed as if every trout in it was willing to take our fly. We were exultant—it was to be one of those banner days we are always looking for but which come so seldom.

I had just landed my third trout, a plump fourteen incher, when a black cloud poked its head over the edge of a near-by mountain. Three minutes later a squall carrying a mixture of rain and hail assailed us. Immediately the trout stopped rising and although the shower did not make any difference in the water of the stream they did not rise again that day. My notes show many such instances, which of course vary, but which are similar enough to make one feel that the fish should react in a similar manner, which they don't.

Many times before a big storm we have experienced absolutely dead days when conditions seemed perfect. Do the trout feel something which accounts for a cessation of feeding as much as twelve hours before a storm? Or are these things simply coincidence? Because they are so inconsistent I believe they are the result of accident but then there may be some underlying force which causes the reactions, something I know nothing about. At any rate I've never been able to work out any rules concerning the weather and our fishing when such weather did not affect the water itself.

I've had both good and bad fishing in all sorts of weather, cloudy days, muggy days, rainy days, and clear days but when I sum it all up I find that I can still give the most credit to clear, snappy days when it feels good to be alive and there I rest my case. What do you think?

There is one water condition I have found almost infallible for good dry fly fishing. It is just as the stream clears after a storm which has raised and muddied it. Let us examine an actual experience on the Ausable in New York State.

To begin with the water was low and the fishing poor. The storm started with intermittent showers and during this period the trout started rising a bit. Just when we thought we were going to have some good sport a deluge came and we quit because there wasn't any fun fishing in it. It lasted the rest of the day and the next morning the stream had raised several feet, was the color of chocolate malted milk and rain was still coming down.

For three days we killed time by playing cards, looking at the stream every little while to see the progress of the freshet and doing plenty of cussing about the tough break we were having. We got tired of this and began to get quite impatient so Don Bell suggested that we give the girls a picnic and at the same time do a little fishing. He suggested Stiles Brook. "The fish don't amount to much," he said, "but there's a good place to eat and the falls are quite pretty."

This brook runs into the east branch. It was clear and attractive looking. Before lunch I fished up from the river to the camp site and took a half dozen nine to ten inch Rainbows. While lunch was being prepared Don showed me the best spot on the brook—the deep hole under the falls.

The first cast to the foot of the falls produced the rise of a twelve incher and for the next twenty minutes we had quite some sport with fish ranging from eight inches to eleven inches. Then came the call for lunch.

I could see Don getting restless. He finished eating before the rest of us and said he was going down to look at the river —to see if conditions had changed. I knew this small stream fishing was getting his nerve. He was always looking for big fish and there wasn't much chance of taking them in Stiles Brook. But I was a bit intrigued by the Falls Pool so went back there. I rose what looked like a pound and a half Brown three times but did not connect. That ended it. Not another fish would rise.

There didn't seem to be much use of wearing out the casting arm so I went back to chat with the picnic party. I don't know how long we whiled away the time but it was well along in the afternoon when above the chatter and the murmur of the brook I faintly heard what sounded like a hallo. It sounded like Don's booming voice so I left the camp site and started down the road. On the way I heard the call again and knew it was Don.

When I got down to the river I saw Don standing at the edge of a good-looking pocket stretch. I thought the water looked a bit lighter in color. Don's eyes were riveted on the river. He heard me but didn't turn to look at me. "They've started rising," he said. "Look there!" and he pointed to a rock in midstream.

It was the truth. Since starting up Stiles Brook the waters of the river had cleared a trifle and while still quite murky you could now see rocks under the surface which before had been completely invisible. And I had left my rod back at the camp site! You may be sure that I didn't bother to talk about it with Don. I went back to get both Don's rod and my own. Don showed his vast experience by the way he took all this. I was so excited that I puffed and trembled but he took it so calmly that he never changed the speed of the puffs of his pipe.

By the time I got back and we set up the rods, the stream had become almost entirely clear and when I reached a location where I could cast to the first rising fish I could see my feet when wading in two feet of water. The rest of that afternoon had always remained with me as a most delightful memory. Rainbows, Browns and Natives (Brook Trout) all seemed in wonderful humor and took our flies with reckless abandon. As I remember it we each kept four fish and they filled our creels. We kept only the best specimens.

Another incident of this sort occurred on the Beaverkill at Lew Beach, N. Y. There had been a cloudburst in the early morning while we were on the way and when we reached the stream it was over the banks, raging and sullen. To pass the time we fished with wet flies and streamers, sinking them by casting upstream and then letting them float with the current on a slack line. We took several trout this way but it was hard and slow work so we finally quit and passed the time doing other things until the water should clear.

At 6 P. M. it was still dirty and high. We started to eat our dinner leisurely but something happened to make us finish in a hurry. I sat facing a window which provided a plain view of the stream and as I ate I was watching. It seemed to me that the water changed color as I looked. I called Bill's attention to it.

" I believe you're right," he agreed. " Let's get through and see."

It was true. The water had dropped several inches according to our improvised gauge and it was clearing, there wasn't any mistake about that.

Our very first casts brought results. As our flies floated on the still milky water dark shapes came up from the bottom and took them. The trout were definitely on the feed. As we fished, the water cleared rapidly and as it cleared the trout took more readily. By dusk it was so clear that in eighteen inches of water the reflected light from the western sky plainly disclosed the bottom to our view. Before sunset the trout had taken any fly we cast over them. After sunset they became more and more choosy until at the last we couldn't do a thing with them even though it seemed as if every fish in the stream was out to gorge on the large hatch of naturals.

These two experiences have been duplicated in various degrees many times. On the average I find that it is a pretty safe bet to consider such circumstances well worth taking advantage of.

The condition of the water is quite pertinent to the sort of fishing we may expect. In neither of these incidents is there mention of the fishing in the other stages aside from the little wet fly fishing on the Beaverkill. However as a general rule it works out this way. At the very start of the rise we may have a short period of fly fishing. This is very uncertain. In the intermediate stage between the start of discoloration and extreme muddiness we may do good work with streamers, bucktails, large wet flies, worms and minnows. During the height of the rise we are likely to find our best fishing by putting on a sinker and some bait. The thing to do then is to get to bottom, preferably the bottom of deep holes. However there is another alternative, one that has often produced for me. It is to fish the shallow back eddies which are formed by the high water. At times I have even taken trout by fishing a fly well up in the grass which has become flooded. During midsummer rises of water I have found that there always seem to be some venturesome, or foolish, trout who follow the rise wherever it goes. By doing so they find some extra tidbits which evidently tickle their palates. It is a dangerous pastime for them because they sometimes get caught when the waters recede. Quite often I have found them landlocked in puddles, because they delayed departure too long. Most of the fish caught this way speedily become the victims of vermin which is, perhaps, a good thing because otherwise they would die a more lingering death. However, if the muddy water continues for a considerable time it is quite likely that all sporting methods of angling will fail. Under such circumstances I would rather wait for the freshet to subside.

This angling game is so involved that it is almost impossible to segregate any number of incidents dealing with one particular problem without overlapping on some other. Here I have been talking about the weather and suddenly find myself involved in a discussion of water conditions which are a direct result of weather. Having started we might as well delve deeper into the subject and see where it leads. After all that is the charm of fishing and of fishing literature and at this moment I have no more idea where it will take us than you have. What we are doing is making random casts and hoping that they bring a worth-while rise.

Now let us see where we left off. The effects of a summer rise in water. What about the effects of high water in spring? Does it affect the fishing in the same way? Here we have a question which requires some real thought and a journey into memory for experiences which might help us to make a decision. What do I find? First that high water in spring is a normal condition, while in midsummer it is abnormal, therefore the effect can't be the same. Besides, the water is cold and the fish sluggish. Excessive rain at this time will retard the fly fishing because the trout will go to favored deep holes where it requires less effort to fight the current. A worm at this time, sunk so that it drifts in front of them, will usually bring a response. As the waters recede they become a bit more active and take flies but they are not particularly interested in surface food, being more susceptible to minnows or something which imitates them. They will also be interested in worms and grubs. Perhaps the reason for this is that they need bulk in food after the long winter. It is only rarely that I have had any dry fly fishing of any account in the eastern streams before May 15th, no matter what the condition of the water.

This leads to another question. If a person likes fly fishing what is the best time to go? Another brain teaser, because so much depends on the weather and the location. However, I've started this so will lead with my chin, basing my recommendations on the personal experiences I've had.

There are many things to consider. Latitude, longitude and altitude all have their effect, not to mention the sort of season we're having—wet or dry, hot or cold. However, there are a few generalities which are fairly uniform and which will aid us in striking a good average.

For instance—streams located in the southern range of trout will become warmer earlier than those in the northern range. So, too, will the streams in the low altitudes become warmer quicker than those in the high altitudes. You can see how complicated it's getting. Fortunately, the really high altitudes are confined to the west which simplifies it to some extent. Even so we have some altitude differences in the east which make considerable difference in fishing.

About the only way I can get anywhere in this thing is to localize. It's the only way I can possibly give you any worthwhile information and no doubt this will be as full of holes as a woolen shirt after a season with the moths. But at any rate I shall have the satisfaction of knowing that I have at least tried to give some aid in the matter to those who haven't had experience enough to work out their own salvation. It might help them some and the rest probably know more about it than I do anyway so what I say won't matter.

First, let us take a heavily wooded stream in the Catskill Mountain section. In such a stream we are likely to find poor fly fishing during April and May due to the usual *unusual* belated spring rains and cold frosty nights which frequently run through to the first of June. If you do get a break in weather the best fly fishing during this early period will probably come during the warm part of the day when the sun has a chance to get in its work. June is quite likely to be the best month in this territory and if the stream is fairly open and on the east side of the range you may get some fair fly fishing during May although this is absolutely dependent on the weather. Even during June, the best month, you will run into extremes of good and bad fishing according to the influence of the weather and the fly hatches. However, for any of the Catskill territory I would say that the safest time to go would be between May 25th and July 5th. Ordinarily the slope to the Delaware is a trifle later than the slope to the Hudson or the Mohawk with the exception, perhaps, of the upper reaches of the Roundout, the waters of which are exceedingly cold even in August.

During July and the greatest part of August the fishing in this entire section is likely to be poor, except for spurts during or after summer rains as pointed out earlier in this chapter. If the streams do not have any rise in water and the weather is hot then the best chance of getting fish is to confine your operations to the early morning, after the night has lowered the temperature of the water, or at night after the sun has been set long enough so that the cooling rocks and soil exert their influence on the water temperature. Also remember that the night time allows the cooling waters of springs to work their way downstream without being heated by the sun-blasted rocks as is sure to happen in the day. All these things have an effect on the activity of the trout. During the latter part of August conditions may easily change again. The water is likely to remain low and clear but with increasingly shorter and cooler nights the water temperature lowers and thus the daytime fishing is quite likely to improve.

Even as I write numerous exceptions, both in streams and seasons, continually arise in my mind but as far as a general statement of the conditions in the Catskill country is concerned I think you have as accurate a description of the seasons as can be given.

As one moves southward, the setup varies a trifle, on the average about two weeks earlier at the opening and two weeks later at the close. Jersey has had a September open season for several years. With plenty of rain, and weather not too hot, the Jersey fishing will remain good throughout June but it doesn't take much hot weather to ruin it. My notes show excellent dry fly fishing throughout May on Flat Brook, with the early June fishing even better but tapering off quickly with the arrival of hot days. During July, at Flatbrookville, I've registered water temperature at 88 degrees Fahrenheit. I have no record of any higher than that nor have I any complete data covering it. I just mention the fact to show what may be expected of Jersey trout fishing after June 15th. Of course showers will sometimes pep up the streams for a short time but when they get too warm it takes more than one summer rain to bring them back. The wonder to me is that so many fish survive the hot months. Probably if one had the time to do it many spring holes could be found in these Jersey streams where the trout are congregated in quantity. As yet I haven't had an opportunity to check up on the September fishing in New Jersey because I've been somewhere else in the United States and Canada every September since it was opened. However I have had many friends reporting on it and from what I can gather it ranges from poor to good, much like the Adirondack Ausable fishing between August 15th and Labor Day.

Pennsylvania is similar to New Jersey with the exception that in the northern part the streams will coincide with the western slope of the Catskills. Michigan seems to run about the same as the Adirondacks but on the whole I believe that the water stays colder in this state than it does in New York. In the lake sections of Maine and Canada the season opens with the ice going out and it is usually good then. In a few places the fishing is fair all season but as a rule it is best for two to three weeks after the ice goes out, then tapers off gradually during the summer and revives again in the late season. There are sections in the Adirondacks and other New England States which are similar to this.

SUNSHINE AND SHADOW

As a rule the season on the Ausable and streams of similar type in the Adirondacks will run from one to two weeks later than the Catskills with the chance that the fishing will hold far more uniformly throughout the season. Right here, to show how difficult it is to give general information in this respect, I wish to call your attention to the fact that I know some streams in this section where the conditions are different—where the best fishing is between the time the ice goes out and the heat of summer begins—where the July and August fishing is distinctly a matter of spring hole fishing. The whole setup is individual. All through the northern country you will find varying conditions. In some ponds and streams, where the water remains cool, fishing is likely to be consistently good throughout the season but streams which are subject to the direct rays of the summer sun and which do not have enough cold water springs to offset this heat will be devoid of trout except where such springs keep the water suitable for their existence.

In the southern extremity of the range of trout you will find the best fishing in May. While I have never fished in this territory I have frequently contacted anglers who know these waters well and I would place the fishing conditions about two weeks ahead of New Jersey and Pennsylvania which of course means that it gets poor that much sooner.

As far as I can tell from experience and from talks with anglers in the territory I would say that the western trout country, at least in Colorado, Wyoming and Montana, runs from four to six weeks behind that of the Adirondacks. In that country one does not need to worry about streams which get excessively warm. July and August are probably the safest months to plan on for the best fishing and the best weather but you may also get some fine fishing in September as I know from experience. Here again latitude makes a difference. Wyoming may be snowed under while the High Sierras in California may be simply snappy and invigorating. For instance, in the fall of 1937 we fished in the Yellowstone in the latter part of September, just before it closed and had plenty of snow although the fishing was good. Nearly three weeks later we fished the Owens River in the High Sierras of California, at least as high as where we fished in the Yellowstone and I believe somewhat higher and while there was snow on the peaks for several days none reached down into the valley. It was very pleasant fishing, with the temperature almost excessively warm during the middle of the day. By the time we left the country around Bishop it was like midsummer in the Adirondacks.

However, as I have stated before, one can never tell what might happen in the mountain country. Conditions change quickly. In making these observations I trust that the reader will be indulgent and not too critical on fine points. They are merely my reactions according to my experience. My western experiences have been rather recent and I haven't the background of years of fishing there which makes my observations on the eastern streams so comprehensive. One man's life is too short to cover the subject in its entirety, in fact it takes ten consecutive years, from the opening of the season to the end, on one stream alone to even strike an average for that stream. So, how can anyone expect to be accurate in attempting to write about anything of this sort?

After all, the object of this discussion is to show in a general way the approximate conditions you might find in the different sections of the trout country from the Atlantic to the Pacific. In arriving at my conclusions I have relied not only on my own experiences but on the information gleaned from personal contact with fishermen in the localities mentioned. Needless to say there are many exceptions to the general rule. I know I always note them when reading some other author's work. This is natural and expected. But it makes me think of something which would be really great. Suppose we could get a record of the fishing in each lake and stream of the United States—a record covering ten years in each instance and taking in an accurate account of each day—air temperature, water temperature, weather, and a comparison between bait and artificial lure fishing for the day. What an enormous set of records it would make and what a hardship it would be for the anglers who had to confine themselves to one lake or stream all that time, not to mention the enormous labor of compilation. This is rather ridiculous talk but it does show plainly why one cannot be positive about any statement he makes about fishing. And even then there would be many exceptions. Broad experience makes one wonder if anything is certain.

the fishing in each lake and stream of the United States—a record covering ten years in each instance and taking in an accurate account of each day—air temperature, water temperature, weather, and a —— ——— —— bait and artificial lure fishing for the day. What an enormous set of records it would make and publish. — would be — — — — who had to compile themselves to one — — — of all that time, not to mention the enormous labor of compilation. This is

CHAPTER TEN

Water Types and How to Fish Them

PROBABLY every angler has his pet type of water. It is all right to have this preference but it leads to neglect of other types and that is sure to reduce your chances of success. In the old days this didn't matter much. When you went fishing you usually had the stream to yourself, or nearly so and you could skip from one place to another with a surety that all your favorite locations would produce.

Conditions of recent years have changed this. Now the streams are so crowded that you must make the most of whatever bit of water you find unoccupied. Therefore, even though it has always been important that the angler knows how to fish intelligently all types of water, now it becomes vastly more important, if we hope to make our angling days something more than periods of walking and casting.

The most obvious places to fish are the good-looking pools. Being so evident, they are fished by every passer-by and so are less likely to produce under tough conditions than locations which are overlooked by the majority. But even though these attractive looking pools are fished extensively most anglers do not fish them thoroughly. In many cases they fish only the obvious and easy parts and let the rest alone.

One day I stopped fishing with the intention of resting a bit and watching a pool until some good fish started rising. I became so intrigued over the action which passed before my eyes that I spent a half day watching instead of fishing. Fortunately I had selected a cool, comfortable spot on the brushy untrammeled side of the stream so that I wasn't seen, except by one angler.

The first two anglers to fish the water merely worked the main riffle. They did not get a rise. In order that you may follow the different anglers as I tell what they did I have had the artist draw a sketch of the pool, showing the various points and currents.

My position was at X. With one exception the anglers passed up the water in the tail and started fishing at B2, taking their position at E. Some of them made their first cast to B2 and after that fished the intervening water but always when progressing, fishing the far shore first. Others started at B and stuck to the main current straight through to top C. Most of them neglected the backwater, the eddy behind the big rock and the gravel shoal from which they fished as they advanced. But

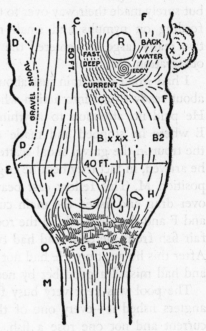

let me describe the procedure of some of the anglers, after I give you some local color.

The first two of the ten fishermen I watched came through within twenty-five minutes of the time I had relaxed on the bank under the heavy foliage. After that at least two hours elapsed without anyone disturbing the water. During that period several things occurred to excite my interest and almost served to end the observation. The first was a rise of a good fish in the eddy behind the rock. This came rather soon and if he had risen a second time this part of " Trout " would never have been written. But former experiences with " one rise " trout curbed my desire to cast over this one. I knew that one seldom took such fish—at least not at the time of the rise. About an hour later something else occurred to whet my appetite for fishing. One after the other eight good-sized fish slowly but surely made their way over to the gravel shoal D and started feeding on nymphs and small minnows. Immediately after, two really large fish entered the backwater directly under my observation post.

I had stood the strain just about as long as I could and was about ready to get into action when angler No. 3 came along. He paid no attention to anything until he reached position E where he stopped and made ready to cast. Of course all the trout in the gravel shoal scattered to deep water as soon as he arrived, in fact they became frightened when he had reached position M. This fellow cast beautifully, had a good control over drag and fished the main current, the shore between B2 and F and the eddy behind the rock R creditably. He took one fair fish from the eddy and had two rises in the main current. After this he went on. He had not bothered with the backwater and had missed a good bet by neglecting the gravel shoal.

The pool was kept very busy for the next two hours. Five anglers fished it—every one of them working only the main current and not one rose a fish. The two large trout in the backwater stayed put and did not seem to be feeding and the passing of the anglers did not cause them any concern because the fishermen all stayed on the opposite shore and never cast a fly beyond the main current.

About a half hour after this string had passed by I saw another fellow approaching. Every one of the others had plowed along to position E before starting to fish but this fellow stopped first at position M and from there to O worked the small falls pockets below the tail of the pool. He took one fair fish from this location.

Then instead of advancing further along the shore he got in the water and waded carefully below the rock at G, stooping here so that his head would not show above the rock. In this position he made a short, rod length cast to the smooth glide at A just a few inches above where the water tumbled down and at the side of the rock. A fish was waiting there. It rose but missed. I almost shouted with admiration. Here was a real angler and no mistake. When the fish rose and missed his fly he didn't react with a fruitless and damaging strike. Instead he let the fly go over the falls and did not attempt lifting it until he could do so with a slight flick of the wrist.

He then deliberately dried out the fly, taking plenty of time in the process and then made another cast to the identical spot where he made the first cast. This time the trout seemed to take it before it had touched the water. As soon as it felt the hook it made a dive over the falls and a few moments later was neatly beached. I was a considerable distance away but from the way it looked the fish was a good one. At any rate the man creeled him.

He then came back to position G and from there to J worked the entire tail carefully. At H he rose another fish and this time I believe he took the fly away from it. At least he attempted to set the hook as the fly went sailing through the air back to him. Then he did a wise thing. Instead of casting the same fly right back he changed it—I suppose to another pattern. I couldn't see plainly enough to be sure of this but I know I couldn't see the second fly on the water and the first was plainly visible. But I saw the splash when the fish rose and saw his rod bend in a perfect arch. This fish fought in the glide but after a time the angler brought him over the little falls and landed him below it.

He then went back to G and fished the gravel shoal D.

Of course he didn't do anything there because the fish were gone but had he happened along before the other men had spoiled the water I'm sure he would have taken at least one of the trout which had been feeding in the shallows.

Not until he had thoroughly exhausted the possibilities of the gravel shoal did he leave position G and then he moved carefully and slowly to K. From there he worked the pool systematically, starting with short casts and gradually lengthening them until he had fished the entire stretch from B to the lower C and from B2 to F. He did not get a rise in this section.

After that he fished the current from C to C. This also failed to produce. I was getting anxious now. I wondered if he'd fish for the trout I could see in the backwater below me. He looked the situation over carefully and started to cross at K but desisted when the water got to the top of his waders and he saw he couldn't make it. I breathed a sigh of relief because I wanted to try for those big fellows myself.

But he had seen the backwater and the eddy behind the rock R as I found out when, instead of going on upstream, he stopped at the head of the pool and started wading across in the rapids above. He finally reached the rock R and found a standing place on the upstream side. From here he fished over the backwater. His fly alighted on the water below me. There wasn't any current to speak of so it simply floated there motionless. I saw one of the big fish start for it and here the angler made his mistake although he didn't know it. Before the fish had gotten fairly started he lifted the fly and the disturbance made the trout scurry for cover. The other trout also took fright and disappeared. Of course the angler knew nothing of this—he was fishing the location because he knew that sometimes that type of water produced good fish. He covered it thoroughly but as no fish were left in it he failed to get any response. The incident made me realize the harmful effects of too quick a lift from the water. If this angler had let his fly rest on the surface for another thirty seconds he would have had a rise even if he didn't hook the fish and the chances are that he would have hooked it.

Now for the first time the angler considered the eddy behind the rock R. Using the rock as a shield he fished it from that position. Not having any crosscurrents to bother him he got a perfect float and I wasn't a bit surprised when he hooked a really good fish. Having accomplished this he seemed satisfied and departed. That coup of the little eddy intrigued me. When fishing the same water from the gravel shoal side one could get only a few inches float without drag at the best. If you got a rise during the time the fly was floating these few inches all well and good but if you didn't your chance was gone and frequently the dragging fly put all the fish in the eddy down. When fishing the eddy from above, you could cover the entire spot with a twenty foot cast and get a perfect round the circle float. If there were any interested fish there at all the ruse was certain to bring results.

It was getting late and I figured that if I wanted a trout to bring home I'd better get busy so I was getting ready to leave when another angler appeared. I waited to watch. But my movement preparatory to leaving had caught his eye and although he whipped a fly over the pool as he passed I could see that my presence bothered him. Of course he did not get a rise.

Then I got busy—went downstream a few hundred yards and started working back over some water that I knew was exceptionally good. Whether the amount of fishing had made the trout quit striking, or whether I did a poor job I can't say. At any rate no evening rise materialized and while I considered the time well spent it did not put any trout in my creel.

Here are some of the important things to be learned from this afternoon of observation, methods of procedure which mean so much but which are ignored by so many.

First—that trout do go into shallow water to feed and unless the angler is mighty careful about approach he will always frighten fish from such locations long before he starts fishing. I have found such places extremely productive and well worth the effort of approaching in such a way that the fish are not conscious of your coming. This takes much thought and time. It is possible to spend a half hour getting into position and then spoil further chances by one poor or misjudged cast or the hooking and playing of one fish.

There are two ways by which success can be attained. One is by wading in the deeper water when you find that a large number of fish are feeding in such locations. By so doing you do not cause as much alarm by your approach as when approaching along the shore and when you hook a fish you stand less chance of disturbing the others feeding there because a hooked fish usually goes to deep water first and you being in it there isn't much fuss after setting the hook until the trout is out in the current where his antics do not bother the rest. The other way is to stand back far enough on the shore so that the fish do not see you and then make your cast so that only the fly and part of the leader alights on the water. A fish hooked in this manner causes a terrific rumpus and many are lost by reason of their frantic acrobatics but it is exciting indeed. This latter method is tough on line and leader. In such fishing the shorter the leader the better and it is also well to have it plenty stout. A 6½ foot tapering to 1X used with a 10 or 12 fan wing fly I have found ideal. Of course the use of the system is subject to the formation of the shore. If the beach is gravel, sand or small round rocks you can manage nicely. If the rocks are rough or there are other things which might catch your line it is hopeless.

There is one thing to watch out for in this shallow gravel bar fishing. DON'T STRIKE TOO QUICKLY. There is a decided tendency to do this because the trout always make a decided wake when coming for the fly. Always wait until the fly disappears before setting the hook. Otherwise, you will simply take the fly away from your quarry and frighten the fish by doing so.

This shallow water fishing has been effective in every stream I've ever fished during the late season provided the trout in such streams were Browns. I've never caught many Brooks or Rainbows in such water. I'm not saying that these last two species can't be taken from such places—I'm simply giving you my personal experiences and the experiences of those I have watched and letting you draw your own conclusions. As far as I can see the Brown is a great forager. He looks for food wherever he can get it. If it isn't plentiful in the deep holes he seeks places where it may be found. The other trout seem to be more confined to tradition, or perhaps I should say habit, and are more likely to be found feeding in places which are favorable to this. In other words, you find Brown Trout anywhere but the others you usually find where they are supposed to be.

It is hard to fish the shallows from the deep water because it is contrary to established fishing methods on the stream. Even though you might know it is the thing to do you find it difficult. You start correctly and then suddenly find yourself wading in the shallows and fishing the deep water. I know that I have fished the shoals this way for many years now and still must force myself to keep in the deep water.

Nor is this problem of disciplining the mind the only one. There remains the problem of wading in treacherous places, of keeping far enough from the possible feeding places so the trout don't become alarmed, of making a good cast when your footing is uncertain. Trout feeding in shallow water are excessively suspicious and wary. They seem to feel that such places are fraught with danger and react accordingly, much like squirrels do when they are adventuring on the ground a considerable distance from the nearest forest cover.

Incidentally, this trick of shallow water fishing learned in the

PLATE NO. 10

Fontinalis Fin	Bergman Fontinalis	Grasshopper	Bob Wilson
Griffen	Gray Squirrel Silver	Red Squirrel Gold	Bell Special

Jess Wood

R. B. Nymph No. 1	R. B. Nymph No. 2	R. B. Nymph No. 5	R. B. Nymph No. 6
R. B. Caddis	Leaf Roller Worm	Hewitt Nymph No. 1	Hewitt Nymph No. 2
Hewitt Nymph No. 3	Water Cricket	Ackle Shrimp	Ed Burke Nymph

R. B. Translucent Amber Nymph	R. B. Translucent Red Nymph	R. B. Translucent Green Nymph	R. B. Translucent Brown Olive	Kol-Ray Caddis	Strawman Nymph

Full descriptions of the flies on this plate will be found on pages 435–437.

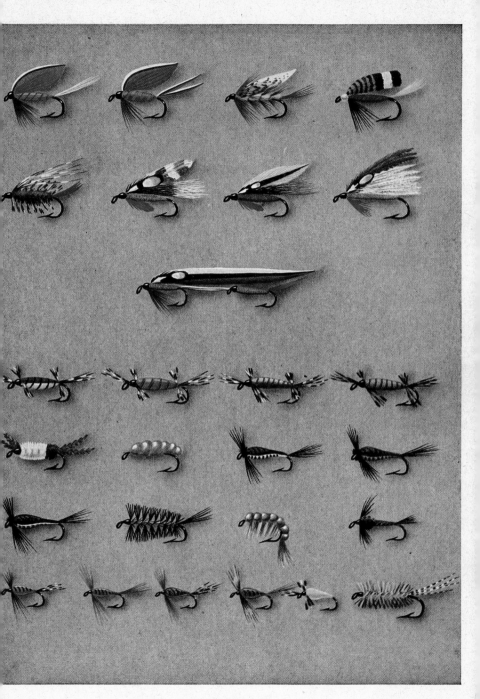

PLATE No. 10

east has served me in good stead in the west, especially in Wyoming. It is something worth trying wherever there are Brown Trout.

Second, the shallow tails of most pools are good locations for feeding trout. It is a natural thing for fish to drop back into this section of the pool when they have a desire for surface food. Often the larger trout in the hole will be found feeding there. To float a fly without drag in such places is difficult. It must be done either with a short cast from below, a long cast from the side if open water, or a short cast from the side if it is possible to remain hidden from the fish while you cast.

Third, that fishing an eddy where you cast across a swift current is not particularly good practice, that you would do better to get into position where the float could be made easier and more naturally.

Fourth, that the backwaters of any pool, or in fact any large pocket, may easily give you a chance at a good fish, provided that you fish it as you should. Never cast a fly into such a location without first considering it from every angle. A little thought often prevents you from doing the wrong thing. It takes a long time to learn the lay of the fish in these backwaters and while experience aids you in fishing them nothing succeeds like knowing the location from personal observation. If you don't get any indication the first time you fish a backwater, try it from a different angle the next time. If you know there are large fish in a stream go a bit further and spend some time investigating and observing such locations. I remember fishing one backwater fifteen times without getting a single hit simply because I always fished it from the wrong angle. One day I fished it from the right position and took one of the finest Browns I've ever caught. It has since yielded me another which anyone would be proud to put in their creel.

I cannot stress too emphatically the importance of this " correct position " detail. Each bit of water in a stream should be fished from the position which will give your fly the most natural float, regardless of how well you may be able to cast. It takes plenty of observation plus experimentation to get to know some types of water. For instance, on the Encampment Brook in Wyoming there was a pool of which I never got the

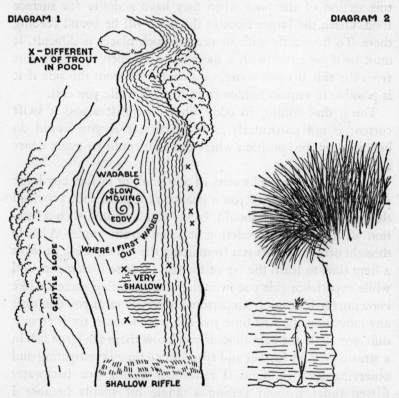

DIAGRAM 1

X — DIFFERENT LAY OF TROUT IN POOL

WADABLE
C
SLOW MOVING EDDY

GENTLE SLOPE

WHERE I FIRST WADED OUT

VERY SHALLOW

SHALLOW RIFFLE

DIAGRAM 2

full benefit until I learned exactly how to fish it. Looking upstream the left bank was a shallow slope with a background of bushes. All this side of the pool was comparatively quiet water. The neck of the pool was narrow and fast. This current first shot over to the right bank at the upper end which was canopied with heavy foliage and then gradually left the bank and ran straight away to the tail of the pool. (See Diagram 1.) This left a rather slow-moving stretch between the current and the right bank which was decidedly grassy and overhanging. (See Diagram 2.) While a few fish lay in the main current the best ones, and most of them, lay in the quieter water close to the bank.

I had no difficulty taking fish rising in the current but I couldn't seem to do anything with those rising against the bank. I did fairly well by fishing from the very shallow water near the tail but could fish only a part of the water from this section due to an abominable downstream drag which came with a long line. The solution was rather simple once I found it. There were two narrow but wadable spots both above and below the deep slow eddy. From the lower one where I first waded out, all but the upper stretch could be fished nicely with a short line and a long rod which enabled you to cast over the current and yet hold the line away from the current. From the upper position C you could fish that part close to the overhanging trees in the same way. Of course I always fished the tail and current first before wading in.

There were, however, two other locations upstream from this pool which I never did succeed in mastering to my satisfaction and I'm waiting until I can get back to Encampment when I'll concentrate on them until I do. One is an exceedingly shallow riffle which is always so filled with trout that the water flies in all directions when you approach carelessly or when you make your first cast if you happen to have approached without alarming them. There isn't much doubt that I have been fishing this place from the wrong angle. Laziness accounts somewhat for not having fished from the opposite side. The only way to get there is by a long circuitous route. So often this is the cause of our not doing well in certain waters. Most of us dislike to exert ourselves any more than is absolutely necessary and frequently keep plugging along the same old way rather than make a really honest attempt to solve the problem.

The other place is a pool on an S bend. Once in a while I take a good fish there but the percentage of rises to the number of rising fish is so small that it really doesn't mean anything. In this place I've tried from all positions except one and this is not only hard to get to but would also be very difficult to cast from. I've determined to try it several times but always gave it up because I got thinking about a nice easy place to fish some distance upstream. At present I am all afire to try from that spot. I simply know it would produce. Whether I feel the same when I get there or once again lose energy when I consider it in actuality only time will tell.

In a previous chapter I wrote of an experience on the Firehole River in Yellowstone Park and mentioned the weeds. These deserve more attention. As a general rule the strips of weeds ran lengthwise with the stream current with open channels in between and small pockets which seemed like eddies in the midst of the beds. The entire stretch was fishing water, that is, there were no barren places here and there where you might sneak up on the next location where the trout lay. Because of this it was very easy to put fish down by alarming others which you were bound to disturb as you made your way to some objective.

By far the most effective way to cover the water was systematically. After getting into the first position at the start I found that if one waited quietly for fifteen minutes without casting a fly, the trout which had been put down would start rising again, usually within easy casting range.

By selecting the starting point carefully and being patient after each change in position it was possible to go from one side of the stream to the other and upstream as long as the rise was on and catch fish. Of course in many cases the weeds served as ideal blinds and one of the most deadly methods was to stalk some rising fish on the opposite side of a particularly heavy weed bed and then dap the fly along the edge of the bed. The trout also used the weeds for hiding places when alarmed. There was one section where the water was very shallow and true to Brown Trout nature they were wallowing through the weeds at this point feeding prodigiously.

When fishing the tails of pools that are shallow and the water clear it is sometimes difficult to approach near enough for a cast without scaring the fish, even if you go to the effort of advancing into position on your knees. Not so many years ago I chanced on the Beaverkill when conditions were abominable. Not a fish had been taken for two weeks and everyone was in the doldrums. Obviously it was a waste of time to fish in the ordinary manner. Better men than I were doing it without getting anywhere so instead I started wandering along the stream looking for something which might give me an inspiration.

I soon noticed that at the tail of every pool at least two or more trout were rising but I also noted that you couldn't get at them without putting them down long before you could make a cast. Once down they didn't start rising again for some time. But here and there was a pool which was grass bordered at the tail. When I came to the first one the experiences of old days came in good stead. I remembered sneaking through the long grass on the banks of a meadow stream and dapping a worm over the edge to a hole where I knew the trout lay. The method was infallible, no matter how low the water or what time of the year it was done. Here was a setup where the same thing could be done with flies.

Before starting I changed my 14 foot 4X leader to a 7½ foot 2X. I wanted something heavy enough to swing a fish out after hooking him, knowing full well that if I didn't the one fish would be all that I'd get. When kneeling, the grass was about six inches higher than my head. I couldn't see the rising trout and I was effectually hidden from them.

Figuring the approximate length of line needed, I made a tentative cast and hoped I'd figured it right for, even though it was nearly a case of dapping, it was necessary to make a flip of the rod and send out enough line to clear the grass and have the fly alight on the water without any more leader than one could help. A few seconds passed. Then I felt a tug and was fast to a fish and had him out so quickly that I surprised myself. It was a ten incher. The next fish resisted more and I had to wait until he got a bit tired before landing him via the air route. This one was 11½ inches. Two more fish came from this pool before I hooked into one which wouldn't lift and when I tried it he tore loose. That was the end as far as this pool was concerned. By looking for such places the rest of the day I managed to have a mighty exciting time of it at a time when fishing was admittedly at a standstill. It was a simple stunt, as old as fishing itself, and yet I see thousands of anglers fishing all the time who never use the idea.

Sometimes the bushes and grasses are too high to fish so simply. In this case you can sometimes stand behind them and cast over the tops with excellent results. In making a cast from such a position it is necessary to use considerably more line than would be used for an unimpeded cast of the same distance. (See diagram.) Saying X is the place where the fly should land you can readily see why an overcast is necessary.

There was a section of the Encampment Brook, Wyoming, which was perfectly adapted to this sort of fishing. The bushes were high, the water clear and shallow. You couldn't get in the stream to wade without scaring trout as far as you could see. Of course in this case the hooking of one fish usually finished the section because it took clever maneuvering first to keep the line from snagging in the bush and then you had to get through it to land your trout. However, the method

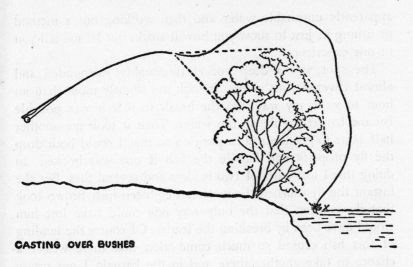

CASTING OVER BUSHES

produced some of the best fish caught by dry fly on the stream so I considered it worth while.

It is the same old story. When streams are fished hard and conditions are tough you might better spend an entire day overcoming the obstacles in the way of one " hard to get at " spot than to fish a couple of miles of open water. No matter how poor the fishing may be in the open you may always be sure of taking trout in the secluded places provided you take the time and study necessary to fish them. Don't marvel at the angler who always seems to have some measure of success no matter how bad fishing is. Instead, cultivate the habit of working the tough places which the average person passes by. Sometimes an entire day's search reveals only two or three such places but if these three places yield one trout each the day will be a success, whereas a day of hard, persistent work over the other waters may result in no fish at all. On more than one occasion this plan has given me a happy day when otherwise it might have been a discouraging one. It wasn't due to any skill on my part. It was because I spent the time looking for apparently unfishable water and then working out a method of fishing it. Just to show you how it works out let me tell you of one experience.

The spot was a deep pocket thoroughly surrounded and almost covered with alders. It took me slightly more than an hour to work my way into the brush so that it was possible for me to get my fly on the water. Then it took me another half hour to get the rod in position so that I could both drop the fly properly and handle the fish if one was hooked. In doing this I lost parts of two leaders and several flies. But the instant the fly touched the water an eighteen inch Brown took that fly so deep that the only way one could have lost him would have been by breaking the leader. Of course the landing of this fish caused so much commotion that there wasn't a chance to take another there and in the bargain I got pretty well soaked because I had to get into the hole to land the fish and the water went over the top of my waist waders, but even so don't you think it was worth it? I did that night, when the net results of the day were compared.

One word of advice about such fishing. You need a heavy leader and a short one. It need never be longer than 7½ foot and shorter is better. 1X is a good size. As a rule a large fly—size 10 will do the trick and in the majority of cases no leader will touch the water anyway. Trout in such locations are not so angler wise as the ones in open water. They are rarely molested and feel secure because of their almost impregnable position. They will take more chances than those fish in open water where everything from fishermen to hawks continually strive to end their existence. Of course 3 and 4X gut may be used if you insist on it but it is almost a sure bet that with gut as fine as this you will lose any fish of decent size. The place for this fine gut is on open water when it is low and clear. It is needed then because the gut is on the water and the finer it is the less noticeable. For the same reason long leaders are of advantage, because gut is less alarming to the fish than the line. Remember that locating fish is more than half

Even in open water there are excellent fishing places which are missed by many anglers. Along the banks many pockets are formed, pockets just large enough to make a suitable resting and feeding place for a single trout. If you proceed carefully and fish every inch of a bank as well as the obvious places you will find that you will see or rise many more fish than if you fish the obvious places alone. I have taken many a good trout from such pockets which could not be recognized as such until experience had brought the location to my attention.

Then there are the shallow riffles. I wager nine-tenths of the anglers skip them, considering them unworthy of notice. Some of them are; no doubt about it. But others have from one to ten pocket holes which contain fish. Are you sure that the riffles you fish do not have such pockets which might produce trout for you? Here again is water that is not molested. It will pay you to investigate their possibilities. Even if you find only one productive spot in a half dozen you try, that place may some day prove valuable to you and the chances are that after a time you will catalog in your mind a number of such locations on every stream you fish and so have an advantage over the other fellow when conditions are bad.

I hope you will understand my reason for devoting so much space to this angle of trout fishing. The reason is because I know it is very important if you wish to make the most of your fishing time in these days of crowded fishing waters. Most of us have so little time to spend at the sport that it defeats our purpose. Having so little time we think we must fish the best-looking spots where everyone else fishes because they must be good or no one else would fish them. This is false reasoning because we are relying on precedents established by easy fishing and in most cases by anglers who have followed the established rather than the dictates of their own minds. It would pay larger dividends if we spent more time at thinking and observing than at fishing. Remember that locating fish is more than half the battle. When you know exactly where they are then you can intelligently fish for them. Otherwise you are simply trusting to luck. I have often observed anglers wading through a shallow stretch, chasing trout out all around them, heard them talk about all the fish they saw and then seen them neglect such a place as far as fishing goes and fish a deep hole near by. The chances are that all the fish in this deep hole were out feeding in the shallows. When scared by the angler they rushed back to deep water or hid under rocks and of course wouldn't feed for some time. The thing to do is to stop short when you start scaring trout in the shallows. Look the situation over, take a half hour or more to do it and then fish the shallows with all the skill and care you can muster.

As an instance of this let me again give an illustration by relating an actual experience. The location was a rocky riffle below a beautiful pool, one that was impossible to pass without fishing. To reach the pool it was necessary to wade to one side of this riffle and frequently one would see good trout dart away from the very shore, in water not over four inches deep. And yet only one out of every thirty anglers fishing this stream ever fished the riffle. They were too anxious to get to the pool which looked so enticing. However, the riffle produced three fish to every one caught in the pool, regardless of the difference in the number of anglers fishing each place. Obviously, the anglers fishing the riffle had an advantage over those fishing the pool. The fish in the fast water pockets had not been bothered very much and so were less angler wise. Of course if the riffle had been fished as hard as the pool it would no doubt be much poorer fishing than the pool because it would not have the capacity of supporting as many fish.

Whenever you find a small stream entering a larger one it will pay to investigate the locality. Sometimes there isn't any hole at the point where it enters but there may be one or more in the immediate vicinity. Usually the best water will be below such streams rather than above.

There are always a certain number of good trout which will run up into these little streams at certain times of the year, as a general rule in the spring when the freshets are on and in the late summer when the waters of the larger streams become cold. Often, at either of these periods, you may profitably fish these small spring brooks. I like best to fish them in the late summer. At this time they are down as low as they ever go. All the water in them comes direct from the springs which keep them cool. It requires the utmost caution; careful and skillful casting and plenty of thinking to get results in these brooks at this time, but if you do it properly you will be surprised at the results.

Speaking of this brings back a memory of one spring brook which I love. Although one could jump across it in most places, it always contained a reasonable number of trout larger than 10 inches and quite a few running up to 18. The amazing thing about this brook was the productiveness of the shallow riffles. If they were more than three inches deep on the average it was a common thing to take twelve inch, or better, fish from them. It had one large hole which would have done credit to a big stream. It was more than eight feet deep on one side, which was thoroughly covered with thick brush, and even on the other side the water was a foot deep at the edge of the bank. At the tail the depth held until the last few feet and at the head, after sliding through what looked like an old sluiceway for running logs which was covered by a farm bridge, it deepened quickly to six or seven feet.

The best fish were taken when a fly was cast directly to the edge of the sluiceway or at the very edge of the heavy brush which was at the right. The tail never produced a fish larger than eleven inches. And pertinent to the subject of pool fishing as related to pockets and unusual places this pool never produced as well as many other sections which didn't look nearly as fishy. For instance, a short distance below it there was a shallow sandy riffle. If I hadn't seen a trout rise there the first time I fished the brook I'd probably never have tried it. But once I did I never passed it up and it never failed to produce although the big pool did.

By far the most intriguing stretches of the brook were the upper reaches which ran through a large cow pasture. The water was slow moving and on the whole very shallow but the banks were considerably undermined, giving plenty of cover, and besides in many places the bottom was covered with moss and silt in which the trout hid when frightened.

The best way to fish this stretch was to crawl along the bank and cast carefully some distance upstream and to the other side. If you fished standing up you not only did not rise a fish but neither did you see any. The moment one fish saw

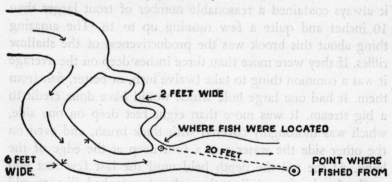

2 FEET WIDE

WHERE FISH WERE LOCATED

20 FEET

6 FEET WIDE

POINT WHERE I FISHED FROM

you it ruined all the water between you and the next upstream curve. This fishing from the bank from a hidden position was a necessity when fishing the still waters or slow-moving stretches but it wasn't so good in the riffles. When fishing them one had to sacrifice the upper stretches and had to do it without sending the frightened fish up through the riffle. In order to accomplish this I would get as near the foot of the riffle as possible hoping that most of the fish in the pool were behind me. Then I would fish that part of the pool with sloppy casts before getting in the water. Usually this resulted in the fish located there going downstream, although it wasn't a sure bet by any means. After that I would ease down to the water; all previous movements, of course, having been made on the knees or lower, and after getting in the stream would wade on my knees until in position to fish the riffle.

It was a lot of effort and perhaps for nothing but at least 50% of the riffles produced, sometimes only one trout but frequently two or three. Often narrow, insignificant looking riffles would net 14 and 15 inch fish and to show what unusual places will produce I must tell you of an experience.

At one point a small channel connected two bends. It was barely twelve inches wide, and looked like nothing more than a surface drain. But as I fished the water into which this led I saw what looked like the wrinkle caused by a fish, so tentatively cast my fly to the place. It no sooner hit the water than a large wake appeared and the next instant I was fast to a trout which gave me a grand tussle. It was 16 inches long. I never expected to get another rise in this place but one usually casts a fly back to a spot which has produced and I did it this time. Again the wake appeared and again I was hooked to a grand fish. This one went 16½ inches. But the climax came when I made still another cast, this time sending the fly as far as I could up the narrow channel. It caught on a blade of over-hanging grass, wabbled there a moment and then dropped when I twitched the rod slightly. I didn't see it hit the water but I did see a splash as a fish struck. In less than ten seconds he had me tangled up in the grass and the bank. I saw him once as he raised himself from the water with a violent shake of his body and then it was over. He had broken the leader.

After, I went over to look at the place. It was just about

deep enough to float the fish that had been in it. I imagine that they had gone in there to take grasshoppers and bugs which fell or jumped in the water from the overhanging grass. Whatever the reason was there were never any fish in it when I tried it again, but the one time had afforded me some thrills which I shall never forget.

It only goes to show that you can't overlook any possibility when fishing. With all one's experience there is always something else to learn. If you fish intelligently, inquiringly, thoroughly and carefully you'll always get plenty of surprises to pay for what you put into the effort. The person who fishes with his head, regardless of whether he is an accomplished caster or not, will get some real joy from the game and it won't all come from catching fish. Most of it will come from ideas and memories which can't be erased.

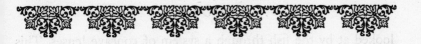

CHAPTER ELEVEN

Vision—Striking—Rise Types—Summary

TROUT CAN see farther under water, if it is clear, than they can see above it. When the angle of sight is obtuse enough the surface of the water acts like a mirror and turns the line of sight back into the water again. The deeper the fish lies in the water the larger his window of sight on the surface.

For this reason when you are wading at any considerable distance from a fish you may forget all of you that is above the water but must watch out for your legs which are under the water. Of course in riffles and broken bottoms this is not so important. Fish cannot see far under such conditions any more than we can through heavy mist.

In still waters that part of you which is in the water is likely to be more disturbing to the fish than the rest of you. For this reason it is best to fish from the shore wherever possible provided your figure is not so high that it is silhouetted against the background, in which case the trout see it and become alarmed. Keeping back, keeping low and selecting backgrounds which absorb your figure are all necessary if you would successfully fish clear still waters.

Trout see objects more clearly under the water than they do those upon its surface or above it. This is easily proved. The surface of the water is never perfectly flat and when it is not flat it acts as a poorly shaped lens and distorts anything above it. Besides, objects on the surface create surface distortions themselves and so provide their own concealment. A fly, for instance, creates depressions where its feet rest on the water and is looked at by the fish through a system of concave lenses. This principle may be applied to glass. Plate glass is perfectly flat— therefore it is perfectly clear. Old-fashioned window glass is not perfectly flat and so causes distorted vision.

From this we may reason that trout cannot distinguish the color, shape and size of flies floating on the surface as they can those beneath the surface. If we use the ideas set forth in the chapter dealing with dry fly construction and have some of our dry flies made so they float high it is less necessary to con- sider color than it is when using low-floating flies in which the body is submerged. In other words, when a low-floating fly is necessary then it is quite likely that the fish will be more selective to color, size and shape than when a high-floating fly can be used. So, too, may we feel that flies fished under the surface, being more visible to the fish, may need to have more color to meet some especial need than any fly floating on the surface. Of course in riffles and broken bottoms this

Size is the most important consideration in a dry fly. Even though trout may not be able to distinguish the colors of a fly which is distorting the vision by its hackles resting on the sur- face they can tell something of its size by the shadow caused by its density. This varies according to the degree of light. As a rule, when fish are rising steadily to a large hatch of flies of the same size, if you imitate the size in any neutral shade it is quite likely to produce. So, too, when you can't seem to imitate the hatch so that the trout will take your artificial, an extra large fly of almost any sensible combination will sometimes turn the trick. In this latter case it is probably a matter of attracting at- tention by means of a large mouthful of food.

But on working toward direct imitations of the natural we are often more prone to match color than size. I've often wit- nessed anglers fishing with size 12 when they should have been using 18, and 14 when they should have been using 10. Rather than carry a large assortment of patterns a small number in all sizes from 18 to 8 especially suitable to the waters you fish, is much more sensible. It is my opinion that you would benefit by an assortment of this kind and you will have plenty of flies in your box if you carry six assorted patterns. Choose them wisely and with an eye to real variety. For instance, don't buy both Whirling Dun and Dark Cahill. If the trout will take one of these patterns it will rise to the other. The fly plates in this book will aid you to make your choice in this respect as you will be able to select a diversified assortment by comparing the colors and selecting only one each of any definite color. The descriptions will give considerable aid in making your choice.

On Striking

As far as I can ascertain the reasons for missing a rising fish come from faulty reactions. When we miss a fish we are either too fast or too slow. I'm inclined to react too fast and a bit too hard and this is a common fault which causes a lot of trouble for trout fishermen in general, especially if they react quickly to emergencies. In all my experience I have fished with only three anglers whose reactions were too slow and who missed rises because of it.

Usually, one's reactions are based on the fishing of the day. If trout rise surely and deliberately, as well as frequently, we have little trouble in hooking them, no matter whether our reactions are fast or slow. If we make a few false moves at the beginning we soon overcome them and once this is done we wonder how it is that we so often miss rises and frequently leave our fly in the mouth of a fish because we strike too hard.

But when we meet with an off day it is different. On such days we get many strikes from small fish. No matter how much we are determined to strike deliberately and without force, a continuation of these rises from small fish gets us into a state of nervousness which causes us to strike with a quickness and verve that are disastrous when a good fish rises. We either take the fly away from him or else leave the fly in his mouth.

In all my experience and years of observation I've never yet found a good sizable fish which wasn't hooked if the strike was deliberate but I've seen countless others lost because of a fast and forceful strike. By a deliberate strike I mean the simple raising of the wrist or forearm to bring the power of the rod taut against the pull of the fish. Naturally the more slack line on the water the greater distance the wrist or arm must move to accomplish this. For this reason it is good practice to have full control of your slack—to fish with as little amount of slack line as you possibly can. If you do this you do not need to worry about striking. When a good trout takes a fly he immediately starts to bottom with it and the speed of this movement is considerable, so fast in fact that a taut line against a reasonably stiff rod will force the barb of the hook through the flesh of the mouth. From the observations of many experiments I have learned that, as long as no pull is exerted against an artificial fly which a trout has taken, he will continue to carry the fly until he has reached his normal and accustomed feeding position. At that time he will eject an artificial unless the line becomes positively taut and is held that way while he is on the way down, in which case the pressure exerted sets the hook. If the angler augments this pressure by a strike which is the least bit excessive he will readily break gut calibrating smaller than .009 (1X) and so lose both fish and fly. In making a decision on which method you wish to select, consider what you would rather have—a large mess of small trout or from one to a few large trout. In view of the fact that almost everyone who fishes is always looking for that big one I fail to see why they don't continually concentrate on control of the strike rather than on anything else.

Keep this fact in mind and try to control your reactions accordingly. Remember that when a good fish takes the fly all you need for a perfect strike is a line handled so well that the downward movement of the taking fish sets the hook. A good fish is a wise one who has survived the onslaughts of anglers and he always takes surely and deeply or not at all so that you always have plenty of time to take in slack and exert the slight pressure necessary to set the hook—if this exertion is necessary which I doubt unless the rod is a very limber one. This holds true with all large fish—either trout or salmon and the larger the fish the more careful you must be about striking.

Types of Rises

There are a number of rises we see which can be identified if we observe closely enough. In this brief discussion of the subject I hope to get others thinking about the possibility of being fully conversant with the most common rise types and so be in a position to take advantage of the conditions they suggest.

DIMPLE, also SUCK and SIP RISE.—Indicative of large fish but looks somewhat like the rise of a minnow. However, if you observe closely you will note a movement to the water which distinguishes it from the rise of a very small fish. These rises often leave a bubble or two and if close enough you can see a slight depression in the center of the ring which has been caused by the process of the fish sucking the fly under the surface without breaking the water. A rise to be careful of and to refrain from striking at too hard. It usually means something worth while if you handle the situation properly. Has the appearance of a small pebble dropping in the water.

SLASH.—Usually occurs during the hatch of large flies, especially the May Flies. Also to flies which run across the surface, of which there are a few. Caused when the trout goes for the fly as it leaves the water especially when the wind affects the movement of these flies. Has the appearance of a stick being slashed through the water.

PLATE NO. 11

Bucktails + Streamers

Black Coachman	Bucktail Coachman	Bucktail McGinty	Carson Royal Coachman
Cummings	Gibson Girl	Golden Demon	Gray Hackle Yellow Body
Kate	March Brown	Parmachenie Belle	Rail Bird
Sawtooth	Surveyor	Umpqua	Well's Special

	Anson Special	Black Bird	Brown and White Bucktail	

	Brown and Scarlet	Edson Tiger Dark	Edson Tiger Light	

	Frances	Jean	MacGregor	

Full descriptions of the flies on this plate will be found on pages 438–439.

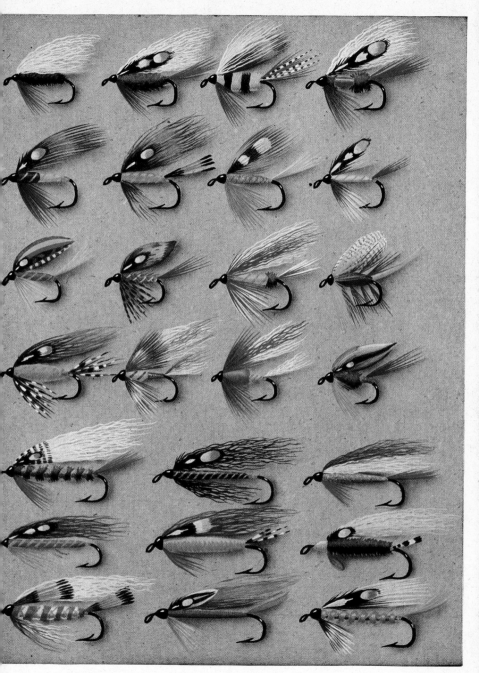

PLATE No. 11

BULGE.—The resulting disturbance caused by a quick turn of the trout after it has made a dash for a nymph or some other underwater prey which happens to be quite close to, but not on the surface. There are some who distinguish this from a mound or hump but it is practically the same thing and for our purpose may be considered as such. There are different degrees of this rise, depending on the way the trout has taken the nymph or other food. At times larvæ may be floating along just under the surface and a trout may be feeding steadily on them but without fuss. In this case the bulge or hump would be barely noticeable. A rise similar to this is caused by a fish taking a minnow but in this case you are quite likely to witness a wake besides the bulge and you surely will if the fish persists in his feeding. Looks like a round mound of gelatine, of course with animation.

TAILING.—Every angler of any experience is acquainted with and knows this one. Of course it isn't a rise at all but is the tail of a trout disturbing the surface as it feeds on the bottom, dislodging and eating nymphs and small crustaceans from the rocks or weeds. When the water is shallow the tail itself may show a trifle now and then. When the water is slightly deeper the tailing may look like a mixture of a ripple and suction. Usually easily identified by the wavering ripple but when the tail is touching the surface only occasionally and slightly it is often mistaken for a genuine dimple rise.

SATISFACTION RISE.—Similar to tailing except that it isn't continuous. Caused by a little wiggle of the tail as the fish drops beneath the surface after the rise. It is a genuine surface rise and is really preceded by an elongated dimple. Often the large selective rises in the Wyoming country are of this type and usually express entire satisfaction with the fly being taken.

SPLASH.—Caused by two entirely opposite reactions—over-eagerness to get the fly or sudden refusal after having decided to take it. In the natural fly it is almost always over-eagerness—

in the artificial it is more likely to be for the other reason. The name is descriptive.

INVESTIGATING REFUSAL.—Purely my own term for a fish that comes directly to the fly, makes a dimple or swirl but does not take it. Mostly to artificials but I have seen it happen with naturals. Needs no other description.

DOUBLE ENDER.—In appearance similar to the Satisfaction but has not any tail wiggle. Sometimes it is combined with the Satisfaction. Is likely to show a very slight wake followed by the tail disturbance. Caused by a trout rising from a position very near the surface instead of perpendicularly.

ROLL.—I'm not sure just what causes this. As a matter of fact I've never been able to take many fish when such a rise was in progress. Sometimes I almost believe that they are playing rather than feeding but this is purely guesswork. On more than one occasion I have fished over fifty trout doing this roll without getting one of them. Looks like a porpoise rolling in the ocean. Of course the back is plainly visible.

Coming back to the Investigating Refusal this is sometimes caused by the effect of sunlight on the vision of the fish. When a trout starts rising to an artificial it may be partially obscured by the rays of the sun, but by the time the fish reaches the fly it may be in the range of total visibility and so he recognizes it for the fraud it is. A change in your position when casting to this fish may result in getting him. Consider the diagrams to get the drift of my thought. The center black spot is the location of total invisibility or at best very poor visibility as shown in a previous chapter. The circle of lighter color around this black center is the section of sufficient visibility where the trout can see fairly well but not too well to recognize discrepancies in our artificial. On the opposite side of the fish he has positively clear sight to the limit of his range of vision. If the sun is directly overhead as in the circular diagram then the point of invisibility would be directly above while both sides would have areas of partial and total visibility. If you give this a little thought in connection with the other remarks on the subject in Chapter Eight, I am sure you will see the advantage of trying to figure out the position of the trout and the sun and if possible cast your fly so that it will float in the range of sufficient visibility without first being in the range of total visibility.

Let us sum up some of the important rules of stream trout fishing, those principles which are so vital to success.

1—Make all approaches to the stream with care and caution. Remember that once you are seen you are at a great disadvantage if not completely defeated.

2—Be prepared for any size fly needed. The box should contain every size between 6 and 18.

3—Develop a gentle delicate cast so that your fly alights softly. This calls for skill as well as suitable tackle to bring about such results.

4—Study the water before fishing it. Select the most advantageous spot to fish from. Remember that the obvious places in the hard-fished streams are less likely to produce than the tough spots which no one fishes.

5—If you fish a place you do not know and fail to take a fish don't leave it until you examine it carefully. It is possible that you didn't fish the right spot or from the right position. A careful investigation is quite likely to reveal the reason why you failed.

6—Use the longest leader you can handle. Usually you can handle one much longer than you imagine. Remember that the purpose of the leader is to conceal artificiality. If you believe a leader is at all necessary then you must admit that the longer the leader the better chances you have for success.

7—The matter of flies, lines and other equipment of the right sort is not absolutely necessary in the rising of fish but they are very important in that they make it easier to do the things which bring success and in some cases are essential to success. Once a person fishes with the best he will never again be satisfied with inferior tackle. If you can't afford the best, get the best you can and be critical when you buy it. Be sure the leaders taper as they should, that your line is the right size for your rod, that your dry flies will float. These are all aids to good fishing and everyone who loves the game will desire tackle which performs smoothly and efficiently.

8—Fish slowly and thoroughly. Haste never paid dividends. Don't worry about the fellow ahead of you. If you start racing to get ahead of him he'll probably try to beat you and from then on it will be nothing but a foot race instead of a contemplative and inspiring recreation. If you like a certain section it may pay you to wait if someone else is fishing it. Wait until he goes and then wait some more and do some observing. When you see fish commence to move then start fishing. Don't whip the stream to a froth. Make fewer casts, make them to places which count and fish each cast out instead of lifting it prematurely.

9—Be courteous even if the other fellow isn't. To lose your own temper and become discourteous because the other fellow started it doesn't help matters. Instead it will lessen your normal angling ability. A calm, peaceful mind and the knowledge that you have been a gentleman will do much to make your fishing successful.

Perhaps some of my viewpoints will be considered radical to those who consider technical skill above anything else. I bow to their skill, admire it, wish I were in the same class with them. But underneath I am still the instinctive, natural fisherman of my boyhood and from this angle the nine rules mentioned seem most important. It seems to me that the fundamentals are the necessities and the other things are accessories which aid in bolstering the fundamentals. Once the fundamentals become instinctive you do the things necessary without thought. Then you can elaborate to good advantage. But to start out with highly technical ideas without the groundwork of lowly experience is to start wrong. It is putting the cart before the horse.

CHAPTER TWELVE

Pond Fishing

CANDIDLY, I do not feel qualified to speak authoritatively on pond and lake fishing even though I have done considerable and really should know a lot about it. However, I don't feel so badly about this because far more eminent anglers than I ever hope to be have also shown by their writings on the subject that little is known aside from the facts which are common knowledge among pond and lake fishermen.

From this you might question why I write this chapter. But "Trout" would be incomplete without it so it is necessary that it be included. If you will consider it a friendly discussion rather than a treatise for study I believe you will derive some enjoyment and perhaps some benefit from reading it. At least the experiences are real and may prove interesting to you.

The first lake I ever fished, aside from those which were merely widened spaces of streams, was Cranberry Lake in the Adirondacks. At that time this was really wild country. The only road which connected the place with the outside country was a miserable affair and tough going for the few automobiles then in use. I know that we found it much more satisfactory to take the railroad, inasmuch as the state roads were still in their infancy and the cars themselves were very different from the smoothly riding auto of today. Even as close to New York City as Nyack and Suffern the main roads were bumpy and full of curves and exceedingly dusty.

The train ride to Cranberry Lake was an experience which always gripped my imagination no matter how many times I made it. As I remember, the train left Harmon, N. Y., around 8 P. M.

On the way up the Hudson to Albany I listened ecstatically to the clickity-clack rhythm of the wheels on the track and the chill-provoking whistle of the locomotive. The sounds of the train on the speeding rails and the whistle brought me a vivid picture of the locomotive itself with driving rods moving at a high rate as we rushed through towns, over bridges, under tunnels and speedily clicked off the miles. Somehow the trip brought back vivid memories of the old eight wheelers like the 999 of the New York Central, and the 499 of the Erie which I knew and loved in my boyhood.

I never slept very much. There were too many sensations to be enjoyed. If I dozed off between Poughkeepsie and Albany I always awoke there and looked out of the window by my berth as the yard engines changed the setup of our train. It gave me a thrill to see the loading and unloading of express and baggage, to hear the chatter of the workers and see the activity of the yard. At Utica this was even more impressive. Here our Pullman was transferred from the main line to the Adirondack division and we lay there for some considerable time. From here we would climb up the southern slope of the mountains.

At Remson I always awoke again, just to get the first breath of the mountain air and at the break of dawn my eyes were glued to the window to see the spruces silhouetted against the eastern sky. As dawn advanced I gloated over the rising mist, the tantalizing odors of dank woods, evergreens and wood smoke, the swamps, ponds and streams. We were in the forest and going deeper into it every minute.

Then, in the early hours of the morning, came the disembarkation at Childwold Station, right in the heart of the wilderness, into a different world which even the locomotive of our train seemed to respect. Its exhaust somehow sounded subdued as it started off after leaving us and our duffel at the deserted station. Then came quietness so intense that you could feel it.

But presently a locomotive whistle shattered the silence and out of the woods came an antique engine dragging a passenger car of ancient vintage and a string of freight and lumber cars. With intent interest we watched the activities of the train crew. There was considerable lazy bustling in the transferring of baggage. Perhaps after a half hour of this we started off and soon came to a little settlement which has always to my mind typified a lumber town—Conifer. Even the name translated one into a world of gleaming axes, singing saws and logs floating down freshet-filled streams. The air was fragrant with pungent wood smoke, with the odor of freshly cut wood and breakfast in the making. Delicate blue tracings of smoke from shanties here and there were etched against the evergreen background and disappeared in the morning mist which still lingered in the treetops. We heard the musical thud of axes against logs. The thin morning mountain air magnified all sound without making it harsh. No one could possibly be in such a place without a feeling of awe.

I have never been able to remember what we had at breakfast although I suppose it was flapjacks, bacon and coffee. I was too excited and enthralled to take much heed of this. No boy making his first trip by train ever got more joy from a trip than I did on this Grasse River Railroad. When the ribbon of concrete from Tupper Lake on the east and Star Lake on the west met to complete a good road through this section, as far as I was concerned the country lost much of its charm.

Our first camp on Cranberry was at the mouth of Brandy Brook Flow and it got a full sweep of wind from the south and west. The first afternoon we reached there the water was like glass. I hurriedly rigged up a rod, put on a worm—(it was early spring and the water was deep) and dropped it over the end of the dock. It never stopped sinking until I checked the reel because a fish had taken it at once and kept running with it—a three pound Brook Trout.

It seemed like Heaven. I had found the place to get them. But it didn't work out that way. It was almost two weeks later before I took the next trout from this spot, and then I took two on minnows. Casting a fly was a heartbreaking job. I spent three solid days fishing the shores of the neighborhood and took one nine incher. This was before I knew anything about the lake. If fishing it now I'd stick to the rock shoals and troll with a spinner.

After a week of rather slow fishing someone told us about Dog Pond. It was quite a trip getting there and on the way we met a party coming out who said they couldn't find it. It was rather late in the afternoon when this happened and it put a damper on our enthusiasm but nevertheless we kept on. The last identification spot was a deserted lumber camp which was supposed to be close to the pond. The party we had met had reached this. Knowledge of the woods solved the difficulty for us. In searching for the pond I came to a small brook, the waters of which were too warm to be spring fed. I followed it and almost immediately came to the pond.

We had no tent but on the pond was a cabin in the last stages of disintegration. About the only place which was usable was the porch, so we gathered a bunch of spruce boughs and large ferns and made our beds there. It was dark before we finished this job and the cooking of our evening meal. I gathered a goodly supply of wood, built up the fire so it would burn for some time and then we all crawled under the blankets.

Once there, I reveled in the wildness of it all. Long after the others were asleep, I lay there watching the flickering light of the dying fire and thrilling to the night song of a bird which sounded like a phœbe. Unfortunately I've never positively identified this song as the phœbe's but last night I heard it here at home and I know we have phœbes here, so perhaps it was.

There's so much one wants to learn and so little time to do it. I've spent the majority of my life learning about fish and I still don't know anything.

Then I fell asleep; for how long I do not know. I was awakened suddenly; startled, just a wee bit terrified. Something was scuffling out there in the black. I grabbed the flashlight and threw its rays out on the clearing. The white light caressed a furry foot, a big furry foot. That was all I saw. The foot disappeared and I heard the sound of quick-moving, heavy steps. Had I seen a bear? Perhaps, and again perhaps not. It might have been a raccoon. But I wanted to believe it a bear, and really it might have been one, so I leaned over to the others and whispered hoarsely—"Did you hear that?" "Yes," came a quavering answer. "What was it?" And what a thrill I got when I answered dramatically—"A bear!—A big bear!" Bear or not I wish I could again experience the thrill of that night. To me that is the only penalty of growing old—the inability to get thrills from little things which experience finally teaches you are nothing at all. I am still imaginative but now the imagination merely takes me on momentary journeys into the realms of fairyland. In those days I really lived what I now imagine. I even wonder now if there was any reality then.

I fell asleep again. Some time later I heard my wife shriek. "What's the matter?" I asked with my heart in my throat. "Something is moving around at my feet," she replied.

Again the flashlight came into use and this time revealed a porcupine who turned when the light shone in his eyes and made for the doorway of the cabin which he entered. This time it wasn't any imagination or guesswork—it was the real thing but only a porky.

And so the night passed. Exhaustion finally overcame excited nerves and we all fell into a sound sleep. We awoke to a cheerful, sparkling world. Close by, the waters of Dog Pond danced in the sunlight and invited us to fish. But I was the only one who responded to the fishing urge. The others were more concerned in making up lost sleep.

On this first attempt, flies would not work. I wasted a good hour trying them, in fact had fished over at least a hundred rises without getting one sign of encouragement. Fortunately I had brought along a can of worms—I did that in those days— but because I had always fished ponds with a dobber when using bait I did so now and used my bait casting rod for the job, because I didn't want to strain even one of my few precious fly rods.

The raft was drifting quietly and slowly so I made a cast off the side and released slack line. The dobber caught the rays of the rising sun and bounced brightly over the tiny waves. Suddenly it started making quick darts. It upended slightly once in a while but didn't go under the surface. I thought—"It must be a tiny fish. He can't even pull that small dobber under." Then I struck and got a surprise. Instead of a small fish I had one which fought against that bait casting rod harder than any large-mouth bass I had ever taken. If you've never taken a trout on a bait casting rod—try it sometime. If he's any size he'll make you step—far more than he ever would on a fly rod which so accommodatingly does most of your fighting for you. It took fast work with the reel, and careful release of the line on the vicious tugs, to bring the trout to the raft and then I lost him when attempting to land him without the net I had left on shore. I won't mention what I thought of his size. I'd probably exaggerate if I did.

At any rate I had a swell morning's sport before getting called to breakfast and then as the weather looked threatening and we had supplies for only one meal we went out.

I fished this pond many times after this and got to know it like a favorite poem. The only consistently successful way to fish it was with worms and the best way to do that was to drag the worm behind the drifting raft. As long as you adjusted your line so that the worm touched bottom occasionally you got trout and as the bottom was singularly free from snags and sharp rocks you rarely had any trouble. But as the years passed by the fishing became different. The drag method became less successful and we had to try different ways. It was during this period I had the best results with bucktails and spinners, casting them to shore close to overhanging or fallen trees or among the boulders which skirted the shore in many places. When you found one trout you always found a half dozen or more and it was a common sight to see three or more fish following the trout you were playing. The use of two flies often brought a double.

There was one spot which was great fishing when the trout came in to it. It was a shallow bay into which ran a tiny spring brook in which some of the trout spawned. The bottom of this bay was thick with weeds which came to within a foot of the surface. Crawfish by the thousands lived in these weeds and at night the trout would often go in to feed on them. We never had any luck getting fish at night but occasionally they would come in early in the evening or stay after daylight in the morning and in that case we could sometimes take them readily, occasionally with flies but always with worms. When fishing this water with worms a tiny dobber was needed to keep the line from tangling in the weeds. I found an ideal one in a medium-sized bottle cork rounded off on a lathe and then fitted with two brass headed tacks for attaching to the leader.

I would not call this pond good for fly fishing. Bait of some sort would always produce but flies were a very uncertain proposition as far as the larger fish were concerned. My biggest from the pond went $2\frac{3}{4}$ pounds but we caught quite a number which went better than a pound. One thing which might be of interest and value to the reader is the fact that the raft itself had plenty to do with the success or failure of the worm dragging system. If the raft was too buoyant and drifted too fast it reduced our catches. If it was low floating and water-logged and drifted slowly our catches increased. We had one opportunity to test this and it was proved beyond a shadow of a doubt. The reason is simple. A bait dragging too fast made the fish suspicious but a bait barely moving over the bottom looked all right.

We once had a narrow escape on a raft. It happened this way. On getting to the pond we couldn't find the old raft in the accustomed place. We started searching for it and while we didn't find it we did find two extremely large logs held together with three cross logs and a few boards. It didn't look any too safe but night was close and we wanted to get our duffel across so took a chance. We got across safely and made camp and then went down on the raft to wash. My comrades, Clyde Post and Fred Geist, went first while I stopped to finish some little job.

Finishing the work and feeling rather exuberant I ran down to the raft and ran out on the board with a hop, skip and a jump. It was too much for it. It parted in the middle and deposited us in the water. Clyde was straddling a log when it happened and came bouncing along it for all the world like a big frog. Fred went in completely and waded to shore like a drowned rat. I had felt the logs go and turned quickly to run back in. I did famously for a few feet then the log turned and in I went. Drenched and shivering we got to the fire and stripped.

It was lucky this accident happened when it did. We fixed the raft after that. It might have happened when all our duffel was on it or while we had been fishing in the middle of the pond. And Fred was the only one who could swim. Incidentally we packed two good paddles to the pond and left them under the tar paper roof of the old boathouse. We haven't been back for years now and I have often wondered who eventually got them and what they thought about it.

In this same country was a series of ponds which provided

good fly fishing. The one I fished most was Cat Mountain Pond, because there was a boat on it. This pond was thick with fish but they ran small, on the average about six to the pound although once in a while a half pounder would show up.

These trout would take almost anything you fished with. While experimenting I tried as many as five flies on a leader and with this string took from three to four fish on a cast. Doubles were a common thing even when using only two flies. I even caught them on a bare hook which was fairly new and shiny. There was only one way to fish and that was with barbless hooks so I always broke the barb off when fishing the pond.

Most of the time we took these trout from the weed beds in comparatively shallow water. Once in a while, however, they couldn't be found in the shallows, in fact I didn't think we could find them anywhere until I happened to sink a worm down in the deepest part of the pond and got an immediate response. It wasn't much sport but a few trout were needed for food so I decided to take enough for that and quit.

It was here that an amusing incident happened. Although from experience I knew the trout in this pond ran small I had a net with me. The boat was leaking badly so after locating the fish I went ashore and got a raft for comfort.

Well, the fish were biting fast, and I was kept busy carefully releasing the small ones and keeping the best ones when I got a peculiar strike. The fish took, I struck and then came a dead weight with a peculiar little wiggle. I happened to be using an 8 foot 2½ ounce rod and it could not lift that fish. When, after some three or four minutes, I did not get anywhere I put the rod down and started pulling the line in hand over hand. The wiggle persisted all the way up and you may imagine my astonishment when I saw a net appear in which was a nine inch trout. The net looked familiar so I turned around to look at mine and it was gone. In some way I had knocked it off without noticing it and a trout had taken my worm and then entered the net. When I brought the net aboard the fish was thoroughly enmeshed—so much so that it took a good ten minutes to unravel the snarl.

While I did not fish Cowhorn or Basshout ponds to the extent that I did Cat, I did fish them enough to find that the catches in Cowhorn might be anything from a 6 incher to a 2 pounder by actual experience and up to a 5 pounder according to old timers; while the Basshout fish ran three to the pound as a general average. Cowhorn was inclined to be very spotty. Sometimes it would produce fish anyone would be proud to catch and at other times the best one could do would be to take 6 to 8 inchers.

Beaver and their dams, in my estimation, are detrimental to trout in most instances. They flood areas which turns the water sour after a time, when the rotting wood gets in its work. To start with, the beaver dams seem beneficial. In them one gets some grand fishing and the trout run of good size. But this condition does not last. Gradually the fishing becomes poorer and finally all one gets is a race of stunted trout. They also ruin many spawning beds, flooding the natural sand and gravel shallows and covering them with a muddy, sour silt. The following quotation from the New York State College of Forestry Bulletin is interesting. (Syracuse University.) Vol. II—No. 1A —Feb., 1929. Subject re Clear Pond. Adirondacks—page 241.

"There were four beaver dams not far apart, counting the one at the foot of the pond, which was the largest and which had flooded a considerable area and killed much small spruce, etc. It had raised the pond about 5 feet above the former level and obliterated the only suitable spawning beds for trout in the pond."

In most cases, the beaver damming streams or small ponds has resulted in just this destruction of trout life. Even if the flooded area does not stop reproduction it eventually creates an inferior race of trout—black, and poorly conditioned. There

PLATE NO. 12
streamers

Scott Special	Summer's Gold	Wesley Special
Gootenburg's Jersey Minnow	Dr. Burke	Black-White Optic Bucktail
Blue Devil	Capra Streamer	Chief Needabeh
Estelle (Gootenburg)	Fraser	Black Ghost
Gray Ghost	Lady Ghost	Nancy
Spencer Bay	Three Rivers	York's Kennebago
	Marabou (White)	
		Marabou (Yellow)

Full descriptions of the flies on this plate will be found on pages 440–442.

PLATE No. 12

may be conditions under which beaver dams would be beneficial but if so I've never come in contact with them. It may be that in the high altitudes where the water remains excessively cold and where the vegetation is not so thick they may be beneficial in raising the water temperature enough to further the growth of some species. It is also possible that the type of soil and vegetation flooded would make a difference in one way or another. In excessively sandy soil, for instance, the creation of a dam might create new spawning beds in place of the old. Study, research and careful observation would be required to learn definitely the good or evil effects of the places I have seen. I am sure the beaver have endangered the trout life. They have made mud puddles out of pretty little natural ponds and of heavily wooded spring brooks. As far as the angler is concerned, the temporary benefits of their work are followed by serious consequences.

Coming back to pond fishing again, there is one thing of which I am convinced. If the pond or lake is fitted in its entirety for the well-being of trout they will cruise all over it in search of food. If only parts of the pond or lake are suitable the fish will settle in such places. Of course certain concentrations of hatching larvæ will cause concentration of the fish even in those ponds which are suitable in their entirety for trout.

Long Island, practically in the shadow of New York's skyscrapers, boasts a number of excellent trout ponds, but as far as I know all are private, or at least club owned. Once I was fortunate enough to be able to fish one of them with Mr. John Gerdes. At the time the fish were located in a narrow arm of the pond and in the midst of the same type of weed-bed which I have always found associated with the northern trout ponds. I had best success on this day, fishing with a salmon-colored nymph which had been successful on some of Pennsylvania's streams. It took the limit quickly, so quickly in fact that the day's fishing was over before lunch time.

TROUT

Once you find the key to any pond it is a simple matter to catch trout. You keep following the same formula and it usually works. The trouble is that ponds and lakes vary so much and you have so little help from the appearance of the surface, which aids so much in the reading of streams, that unless you take the trouble to sound and drag an unknown water you are at a loss to know just what to do, until you see some fish rise. Weed-beds and rock shoals are the two best bets to look for and in the late summer a knowledge of the coldest spots is absolutely essential. No matter where you find trout in ponds, east, west, north or south, the water has certain characteristics not found in ponds which contain only other species, and experience teaches you where in such ponds to first try your luck.

The number of trout in a lake or pond depends upon the food supply and natural spawning conditions. Given plenty of food, sufficient area, and suitable spawning grounds they will prosper and grow to a fair if not large size. If these things are limited the trout will be limited also, sometimes to a large number of small and poorly conditioned fish and at other times ending up in mostly large fish but very few of them. The restocking of any water is not satisfactory unless these things are taken into consideration and often it would be of greater benefit to feed the present population rather than to increase it.

Brown Trout in particular seem to be more inclined toward cannibalistic tendencies under these conditions. In many cases Brook Trout seem to degenerate into an inferior race, small and poor. Browns are more inclined to keep eating each other until the few overcome the balance. Glasby Pond in the Adirondacks illustrates this. It was originally stocked with Browns. Fishing was good for a time with the trout getting larger but more scarce each year. The last record made of any fish being caught in the pond was in 1917 when Richard Jessup caught two which weighed respectively 3 pounds 14 ounces and 4 pounds 4 ounces. From what can be ascertained these were the last two fish left in the pond. This pond was not a natural trout pond and now seems to be devoid of fish life.

The same thing also happens with Brook Trout at times. The late Chan Wescott of Cranberry Lake told me about Curtis Pond. He said that once there was very good fishing there, that the trout grew to large size but that each year they got larger and were scarcer. No small trout seemed to come along as they do in the usual course of events. Finally there came a year when only three very large fish were caught and from that time on no one ever took another one. Whether there were some left I don't know. I did fish the pond several times but never caught anything except some small sunfish which were said to have multiplied greatly during the declining years of the trout fishing. These are things we can only talk about and theorize over. We have no positive facts to prove them as would be the case if the fish could have been watched. All we can go by is the ultimate outcome.

One thing seems to be sure. These complete disappearances of trout from ponds seem to be confined mostly to those ponds which were not natural trout waters. Again let me quote from a bulletin published by Syracuse University—"Hedgehog (Clear Pond on the U. S. Geological Survey Topographic Map) and Glasby ponds were also visited. The steep, absolutely dry bed of the outlet of Hedgehog was followed to the pond. It is said not to have been a natural trout water, but it has been stocked and trout of large size have been caught there. As usual in such instances where suitable spawning beds are lacking, as they appear to be in this pond, the fish taken are or were only grown-up individuals of the original fish planted."

One of the best ponds for fly fishing that I've ever fished is Trapper's Lake, Colorado. This wasn't because the trout ran large but because they rose to flies so well.

It is a beautiful spot, some 9,000 feet above sea level and surrounded by picturesque mountains. No camping is allowed on the lake, although you may camp some distance below, so that the shore line is as nature made it except for a small area on one side where the state has a building and a boat livery. I'm a bit vague about this because we used a boat only once and Glenn Jones got it for us that day.

The afternoon my wife and I first saw the pond was one of those gorgeous mountain days which no pen can describe, but which affect both our physical and mental being like a strong stimulant. Glenn knew the lake well. "The best way to fish it," said he, "is from the shore. Let's stop here a while and I'll show you why."

We were at the edge of the lake on a quiet weedy bay. "There," said Glenn. "Did you see that dimple? I think a fish is working toward us."

I saw the riffle and watched the clear water carefully. Glenn's eyes, being more tuned to the situation than mine, saw the fish before mine did. "There are several of them," he exulted. "Cast your fly in front of them." I saw them and made the cast so the fly alighted right in the range of their course. As soon as the fly touched the water one of the trout started for it and a few moments later I landed my first cutthroat.

We took several trout that night although it wasn't particularly fast going—due to being a bit late, as we found later on. Because I had taken the first fish on a bucktail I stuck to it but Glenn changed to a dry fly and took three times as many fish as I.

It didn't take me long the following day to find out what it was all about. One didn't fish promiscuously. You did more observing than you did casting but when you did cast it was to a rising fish. Walking along slowly or standing in one location by which you knew trout traveled, you watched for rises or for the fish themselves. If you saw a rise you waited until you ascertained the direction the fish was moving and then cast your fly some distance ahead, provided you could do so without putting the leader over the trout. Putting the fly directly over the trout rarely brought a response, in fact it sometimes made the trout move away from you and in some instances put him down. In the case of a fish swimming along but not rising the same procedure was followed.

As a rule it didn't matter what fly was used but occasionally you would discover a fish which was cagey and had to be coaxed. One good specimen fooled around my location for an hour before I got him. He would look over each one of my offerings, coming right up to each one as if he had decided to take it and then go back to his swimming level, with an impudent flip of his tail. One of the most effective flies for me had been a Royal Coachman. The one I had been using was badly chewed up and this fish had refused it. I had tried nearly everything by this time so decided to give him up. I went back to the Royal but selected a new fly instead of the bedraggled specimen. After tying it on I couldn't resist taking one more try at the big fellow, especially as at this time he was lazily swimming by me, so I dropped the fly about two feet in front of his line of progress. To my surprise he rose and took it deeply as if it was just what he wanted. Was the new Royal the reason for his change of mind? I don't know and your guess is as good as mine.

Of course I wanted to try the boat fishing so we spent a half day at it. The dry fly did not work well here because of the movement of the boat which prevented one from handling it correctly. Just when you had made a cast in front of a fish the boat swung or moved and spoiled the entire effect. However, wet fly fishing was better from the boat, although the fish did not average as large as those caught from shore on a dry fly.

This September fishing at Trapper's Lake was best between 10 A. M. and 5 P. M., with a clear sky. The last day there a storm was brewing. Until the sun was swallowed by the clouds there were a goodly number of cruising fish along the shore and fishing was good. After that they seemed to retire to deeper water, the rises stopped and we couldn't do a thing. Whether this means anything I do not know, because we left the following morning to escape bad weather. It was lucky we did. Before we got back to Colorado Springs we had a tough ride through a blinding snowstorm, one bad enough to get pictured in a News Reel. But before long we're going back. No one could ever fish this lake without longing to return—not because of the size of the fish—the average was really quite small—but because of the intensely interesting shore fishing and the delightful atmosphere of the surroundings. The visit there remains one of our cherished memories. And the fish are gorgeous in appearance and fine eating.

Typical of midsummer pond trout fishing in the east is our experience in a little pond of Vermont. At this time I was fishing with George Donovan of East Charleston, Vermont, who has a camp on Echo Lake. Neither George nor I had ever fished the pond so we didn't know where to look for the trout but George had obtained some information and that together with our instincts in the matter took us right to a spot where there were plenty of trout.

We saw rises, had a lot of strikes, but caught only one small trout, the honor of which goes to George. Two anglers never worked harder than we did, we changed flies, methods, and position until we had used up every bit of pond fishing lore we had ever accumulated. Something was wrong. Either we didn't strike the right fly or else we failed to use the right method. But then this is a common experience among anglers. We all have times when we can't catch them and no one knows all the answers.

In all pond fishing the main requisite is to first locate the fish. If they are cruisers one must fish the fly in front of them; if they are concentrated in a few spots one must work these places carefully and thoroughly; if they are in deep water, either a deeply sunken fly, spinner or bait must be used; if they are in shallow water they may respond to either wet or dry fly. First learn your pond is the best advice I can give for pond fishing.

NOTE—Additional pond fishing notes in Wet Fly Nymph Chapter.

CHAPTER THIRTEEN

Steelheads of the Umpqua

B EING born and brought up on the east coast and not being wealthy it took me a great many years to satisfy my desire to fish in Oregon. But now that we have been there twice we'll be going back again—and the prime reason will be Steelheads.

If it had not been for Clarence Gordon perhaps we would not have gone yet. Clarence had a delightful camp at Steamboat on the North Umpqua. We corresponded for considerable time and his letters painted such wonderful pictures of the Steelhead fishing that I finally gave up other projects in the offing and surrendered to the lure of Oregon. I have never regretted it—in fact I feel I owe Clarence a debt of gratitude for having hastened matters.

Our good friend Fred Gerken of Tombstone, Arizona, also had a decided yen to try for Steelheads, so the final result was a meeting at the Wilcox Ranch on the Encampment Brook in Wyoming, where after ten days with the Brown Trout we left for Oregon.

We went by way of the Columbia River highway. When I got the first glimpse of Mount Hood I realized all my dreams of what a real mountain looked like. There were a great many forest fires at the time and by some freak of air currents the smoke obscured the lower part of the mountain entirely leaving the top suspended in mid-air with streaks of snow down its

---

* Some of the material in this chapter was used as a basis for articles in the magazine, *Outdoor Life.*

sides. I had a tough time driving that highway. What with the valley beauties, the impressive river and occasional glimpses of Mount Hood which always made my heart jump into my throat, I had hard work making the curves and keeping off the shoulders.

We had another thrill when we left Roseburg for the trip up the North Umpqua to Steamboat. The first few miles were not so much, but once above Glide it was as picturesque and tortuous a route as one could imagine. You felt sure you were going places and you really were.

The river is wild and beautiful and, at first sight, a bit terrifying. You wonder how you are going to be able to wade it without getting into difficulties. Despite this, it isn't so bad once you learn to read the bottom. On the bottom are narrow strips of gravel which wander here and there and crisscross like downtown city streets, in Boston for example. By walking in these and stepping only on reasonably flat, clean rocks or on other rocks where you can see the mark of previous footsteps you wade with fair comfort and safety. The rocks of the routes between most of the good pools are plainly marked by the tread of many feet and as long as you know what to look for you have no trouble. But do not try to hurry, watch each step closely unless you have the activity and sure-footedness of a mountain goat or Clarence Gordon. When he gets to a hard spot he makes a hop, skip and a jump and lands just where he wants while you gingerly and sometimes painfully make your way after him, arriving a few minutes later. He waits apparently patiently but probably in his heart wishing you would get a move on. He finds it so easy it must seem ridiculous to him for anyone to be so slow and faltering. I once thought I was agile, perhaps I was, from what others tell me, but Clarence—well, just ask those who have fished with him.

Never having fished for Steelheads I decided to watch Gordon a while before trying my luck. From experience I know that you can learn a lot by watching someone who knows the water and the fish in it. This is especially true of Steelheads, at least at the time of the year we were at Steamboat. Then they are found only in certain sections of the main channel. In addition, not all waters containing Steelheads were suitable for fly fishing. If of greater depth than six feet the fish would not take a fly.

Our first try was at the Fighting Hole, so named because it was all very fast water and there was always a good chance of the hooked fish taking advantage of the current and taking you for a ride into the water below. The first thing I noted was the way Clarence handled the fly. He cast quartering across and downstream. The instant the fly touched water his rod tip began to dip and rise rhythmically, approximately every three seconds. At the same time he retrieved a little line with his other hand—about a foot or two all told during the entire drift of the fly. On the first cast the fly did not submerge. Before making the next cast he soaked it thoroughly and from then on it sank readily. He explained that in low clear water, a fly dragging over the surface was likely to spoil your chances. This was good trout fishing lore. Many times I have soaked flies in mud to make them sink quickly because of the same reasons when fishing for wary Browns.

The Fighting Hole did not produce, so we moved down to the Mott Pool. This was a long fast run which terminated in a fairly wide basin. Almost at once Clarence hooked a fish. As it struck he let go the slack line he had been holding. The reel screeched as the fish dashed downstream. He broke some one hundred and fifty feet below and then started a dogged resistance. At this time Clarence gave me a little more information—" Most trout fishermen after Steelheads for the first time make the mistake of stripping line when playing them. They do it with other fish and think they can do it with these, but you have got to play them on the reel: otherwise there is sure to be trouble." As I watched I knew this was true. As with Atlantic salmon it would be certain suicide to your chances to attempt to play them by stripping. Those strong terrifying rushes—some as long as 150 feet, those vicious tugs when, like a bulldog they figuratively shook their heads savagely, would make it well-nigh impossible to handle them in any other way except on the reel. The slightest kink, the slightest undue pressure and something would break.

Watching Clarence fight this fish was too much for my resolve not to fish until I learned something about the game. Besides, I had learned how to manipulate the fly, the rest would be the same as Grilse or Land-Locked Salmon—or at least so I thought.

The lower end of the Mott failed me. Clarence said it was probably because his fish had run into it several times and so disturbed the rest located there. In the next hole—I think it is called the "Bologna" for the reason that when a fish goes over there it is gone and as they usually do go over it is just bologna to fish the hole, but I did not know it at this time. I hooked a Steelhead—there was an irresistible vibrant pull at the strike, the reel screeched a few seconds and then the line was slack. I had lost my first fish.

"You'd have lost the fish when he went over anyway," soothed Clarence. "It is usually over quickly in this hole," and then he told me why. "Going over" on the Umpqua means that a fish leaves the pool it has been hooked in and runs into the white water below. If this stretch of bad water is of any great length a fish that "goes over" is usually lost. When it gets away the fish is said to have "cleaned" the angler.

It seemed as if the Umpqua Steelheads had it in for me—at least I made a poor showing the first three days. I hooked five fish and lost them all. Three pulled out after a short fight and two cleaned me good and proper. I was in the doldrums. The only thing that cheered me at all was the fact that Clarence

Gordon insisted my hard luck was due to bad breaks and not to poor fishing. "Besides," he said, " I have really been giving you the works—bringing you to places that always mean trouble when you hook a fish. Take that hole right here—I've never landed a fish here yet and I have hooked plenty."

On the other hand Fred Gerken seemed to take the game with the greatest nonchalance and was making a record for himself. On the first day he used his $4\frac{1}{2}$ ounce trout rod, 30 yards of line and a 3X leader, went out on the Kitchen Pool and took a five pounder as if he were catching a one pound Rainbow. But he did not tempt fate by continuing the use of the trout outfit. The next day he assembled his $9\frac{1}{2}$ footer and really went after business. Well did he uphold his grand start—a fish the second day and no others were brought into camp. He did the same thing the third day although he wasn't the only one. Phil Edson of Pasadena brought one in about four pounds bigger than Fred's. But still I had nothing to show—it was always excuses—this happened, that happened— well you know how it is. To make it look worse my wife took a $5\frac{1}{4}$ pounder at noon on the fourth day and while she is a crackajack bait caster, she has never done a lot of trout fishing. We started her out with the bait casting rod and she did not like it a bit, but to be a good sport kept using it for three days. Then she rebelled, she wanted to fish with a fly like the rest of us. So I took her out on the Kitchen Pool to give her a little coaching. About a half hour of this and she decided she could go it alone. I had seen a Steelhead jump at the lower part on the pool, so was only too glad to rush ashore for my rod. I had just reached the tackle tent when I heard my wife give a call. I rushed back and found her fast to a fish—I believe the very one I went in to get my rod for. As I say—she had not had much experience fly fishing, but she had turned the trick and handled the hooked fish like a veteran. She was proud of her $5\frac{1}{4}$ pounder, but not as happy about it as I thought she had a right to be. I soon learned why. "It was all luck," she said. "The cast that took him was the sloppiest one I made." I knew exactly how she felt. Said Dr. Phil Edson—"A sloppy cast—in bright sun at midday and a Steelhead in the Kitchen Pool—that's something to make these fellows think. Morning and evening say the experts and drop your fly lightly. I wonder what they will say to this?"

To make Phil's remarks even more pointed, immediately after lunch I slipped down to the Mott Pool and about halfway through hooked a fish. The singing of the reel was music to my ears. Nothing went wrong this time and I had the satisfaction of looking up toward the end of the fight to see Fred, Grace and Phil watching me. Phil was so anxious that I save the fish that he took off his shoes and stockings and with bare feet waded that treacherous water just so he could be on hand to land it in an extremely difficult spot. That's sportsmanship for you. I shall never forget this spontaneous act of his as long as I live. It showed the real soul of the man, his unselfish desire to see that I got my fish. It was all very satisfying. Just one Steelhead a day on the North Umpqua makes you feel like a king.

Now Clarence showed his angling acumen. For several days he had been planning his next move so that it would be most advantageous to me. He explained it now that it was time to carry it through. It seems that when Steelheads are not moving much, they become indifferent to flies fished repeatedly from one side of a pool. Mott Pool had been fished hard from the camp side for some time and was going a bit sour. But it hadn't been fished from the opposite side for at least a week—first because not many would tackle it from that side alone because of the difficulty of wading, and second because Clarence always had an excuse when you mentioned going there. You see he was letting it get hot before bothering it.

There were some bad spots to cross here and there. If it

hadn't been for Clarence probably I'd have floundered the very first thing. Then we reached the upper end of the hole. " Watch yourself," warned Clarence. " There are plenty of big fellows here." Nothing happened until my fly drifted across the very tail of the pool. Here I felt a tug, but did not connect. On the next cast I felt another tug, which was followed by a heavy pull. But there wasn't any run or excitement. He just held steady and heavy and then moved slowly to the center of the pool. Once there he stayed for some five minutes or more and I could not move him. Suddenly he started doing things and I have but a vague idea of what happened. The reel screeched, its handle knocked my knuckles, my fingers burned as the line sped beneath them as I was reeling in frantically to get the best of a forward run. At the end of this exhibition in which were included several jumps, he started a steady and rather slow, but irresistible run which made the backing on my reel melt away. Clarence was by my side looking at my reel drum. " He's gone over," he said. My heart sank. Then for some unaccountable reason, perhaps an unknown ledge below, he stopped running. I started to pump him—work him—he came right along. I reeled as fast as I could and still he kept coming. My spirits revived with this chance of success. By this time he was only 30 feet away. But the fish suddenly decided he had come far enough and started edging off sideways and I could not stop him. He made a short fast run into a shallow riffle at the right and then all I felt was a vibrant weight which seemed like a heavy fish without any pep. " I'm hung up," I groaned. I walked from one side of the ledge to the other—I knocked the rod, gave slack line, did everything I possibly could, but he did not come loose. I could feel the fish so knew we were still connected.

It was partly dark by this time and the water between the fish and me was treacherous. I had never waded it in daylight and could not attempt it in the dark. But Gordon took the chance even though he had never waded the place before. " The leader is caught on a board," he called. "There—he is all yours." I felt a tug, saw and heard a splash and the fish was gone. "About a twelve pounder," said Gordon. "It's a wonder the leader didn't break the instant you snagged." For this is what happened, the leader had finally frayed on the board and parted. The board had floated down from some bridge construction work upstream.

And that night Fred brought in another fish. But fortune treated me better from then on. The very next evening I brought in two fish, one weighing seven and a half pounds and the other ten and three quarters. The latter was the largest fish of the season although a week after we left Phil Edson took one ten and one half pounds. From then on my luck ran better than average, but Fred's held true to form to the last day. At that time his score was seven hooked and seven landed—some record when 50% is an excellent score. Clarence and the rest of us decided something must be done about it. The result of this conference was a trip down to the opposite side of Mott Pool. That night Fred hooked one he couldn't do much with, but even so, he might have upheld the honor of his standing except for an unlucky break. The fish had been hooked lightly and pulled out. Anyway, he came in without his fish—the only day out of eight that this happened.

It is queer the way things sometimes happen. Dr. Dewey of Pasadena arrived at camp a few days before we did, and took his limit of three fish two days hand running and never lost one. But after that it was different. He hooked a number of fish, but something always went wrong. Some "pulled out" and one "went over." He tried to follow the latter, stumbled and fell in. He came in wet, bedraggled and muddy. He hooked a number of other fish on flies from which the points of the hooks had been broken on rocks and of course held these only a second or two. Twice his leader frayed on sharp rocks and broke at a critical moment. But this was good medicine. It

PLATE NO. 13
Dry Flies

Au-Sable	Black Angel	Brown Olive	Gray Translucent	Grizzly Tango
Honey Dun	Light Cahill Translucent	March Brown American	Pink Lady *California* Translucent	Tango Triumphant
Woodruff	Multi-Color Variant	Light Multi-Color Variant	Multi-Color Variant No. 2	Badger Variant
Brown Variant	Furnace Variant	Ginger Variant	Grizzly Variant	Blue Variant
California Adams	Coffin	Spent Blue	Spent Olive	Spent Yellow
Gray Wulff	Royal Wulff	White Wulff	Green May	Yellow May
California Fan Wing Royal Coachman	Fan Wing Silver Coachman	Green Fan Wing Coachman	Ginger or Petrie's Royal Coachman	McSneek

Full descriptions of the flies on this plate will be found on pages 443–445.

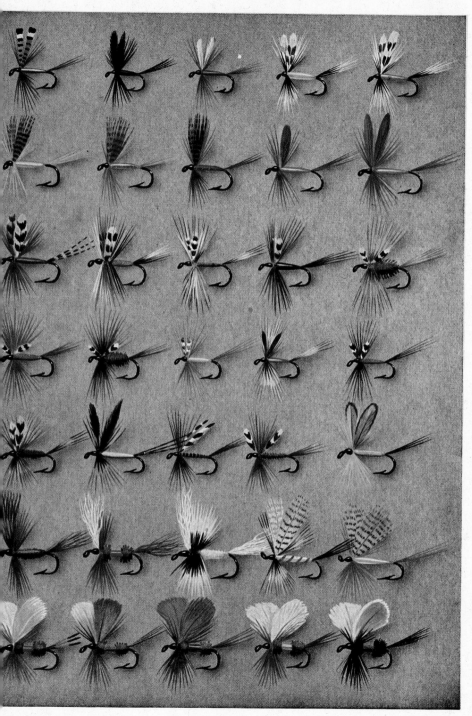

PLATE No. 13

taught him that inspecting tackle frequently is a long step toward success. If I had only changed my leader or if I had only looked at that fly the last time it hit that rock are ifs which should not be.

I experimented considerably with flies. I tried streamers, standard Salmon patterns and all sorts of flies which had brought me success in various sections of North America, but none of them were worth while. The best fly of all was the Umpqua. It had been designed especially for this stream. The Cummings was a close rival and often effective when the Umpqua would not produce.

From my own experience and from many talks with the fellows who fish the North Umpqua every season I gathered that only two sizes were needed—Numbers 4 and 6. I used 4's most but when a fish was missed I would change to a 6. The method did not always work, but it did often enough to be worth while.

My greatest thrill came the day before we left Steamboat. On this day I concentrated on two pools, the Sawtooth and the Surveyor's. The Sawtooth got its name from the sharp rocks which divided the pool. It really was two pools divided by a riffle. If a fish ever ran your leader over the center rock in one particular spot it meant a sure loss of fish and part of that leader.

The first time I had fished this pool both Clarence and Phil Edson were watching me. There was a suspicious smirk on their faces but at the moment I didn't tumble to the reason. When I hooked a fish I could fairly feel their expectant joy in my downfall. I almost played directly in their hands too. I led the fish upstream and only their uncontrolled chuckles put me wise that this might spell disaster because of the sharp rocks. In time I changed my tactics and landed the fish and so spoiled their chance for a horse laugh on me.

On this next occasion I took a six pounder from the Sawtooth with incredible ease but must admit I took him from the smooth glide on the left looking downstream and on my side of the treacherous rocks. But the next fish gave me a taste of what a Sawtooth trout could really do if he started to do it. I hooked him in the center, just across the riffle caused by the rocks. When he struck I almost lost my rod and he never stopped going until he had wrapped the leader around a rock and cut it off like cheese. It all happened so quickly that it left me in a daze.

At the Surveyor's Pool it is not necessary to make a long cast. The first one I made wasn't more than twenty feet and a six pounder took it at the very moment it touched the water. Landing this fish made me feel quite satisfied with myself. Two six pounders in an hour was mighty good fishing no matter how you looked at it.

I rested the pool a half hour and then tried again. This time I had four rises which I missed and then connected with a fish which took slowly but surely. It was the heaviest one I had yet come in contact with. For twenty minutes I just held on. The fish didn't either run or tug, he simply bored to bottom and stayed there. Nothing I could do would budge him, even the taking of the line in my hand and pulling with that. But finally he must have become tired of the continual strain because he suddenly started to kick up a grand rumpus. First, he came direct from the bottom with express train speed and continued into the air until the force of his rush had been expended. When he hit the water he did so broadside making a splash which might have been heard a quarter mile. He then lashed the pool to a froth, made a few more less spectacular jumps and finally came to rest out in midstream and near the surface.

It looked to me as if he had used up his energy so I put on all the pressure the rod would bear thinking he'd come in docilely. Vain hope. I couldn't move him any more than I could when he had been hugging the bottom. He just lay there with a wicked look in his eye and sapped the strength from my arm. Finally I had to release the pressure a bit. I couldn't take it. As I did this he started fanning his tail and his fins. I knew something was going to happen but I didn't know what. I soon found out. Turning quickly he started downstream and this time one could tell he was going places. There was no stopping him. I braked as much as I dared and burnt my fingers as well as knocking my knuckles but the line melted away. When I looked at my reel the end was near. He was in the fast water below the pool and gaining speed each instant so I pointed the rod tip at him and prayed that only the leader would break. Then something snapped and the strain was gone. The leader had broken at the fly and the fish had " cleaned " me. The landing of the 10¾ pounder in the Mott Pool had been thrilling but it did not affect me like this complete rout and now that time has lent perspective to the experiences I know that this particular incident was my most memorable angling adventure. And it is that way all along the line. In every species of fish I've angled for, it is the ones that have got away that thrill me most, the ones who keep fresh in my memory. So I say it is good to lose fish. If we didn't, much of the thrill of angling would be gone.

The following year after this exciting incident found me on the way to the North Umpqua again. This time we went through Yellowstone Park and then took the northern route through Montana, Idaho and Washington. It was remarkably clear the day we drove down the Columbia River valley. Mount Hood stood out so plainly that we decided it was the time to drive around her base. The sight of this mountain did things to me again, put a lump in my throat, a tremble in my nerves. Anyone who is fascinated by towering peaks should never miss the Mount Hood ride. Although the peak is not so very high, being only a bit over eleven thousand feet, the surrounding country is so low that it towers higher than the highest. As much as I love fishing I'd give up a day or two any time just to gaze at this pile, in my estimation the most impressive and fascinating I've ever seen.

But Mount Hood is capricious. After smiling at us for a couple of hours she suddenly veiled her face with a reddish, smoky cloud and with the coming of this cloud our spirits changed from gayety and cheer to gloom and depression. On the west side of the mountain it was dismal and oppressive but as we neared Oregon City the sun broke through the clouds and it was cheery again.

The fishing conditions on the North Umpqua weren't very good. The water was so low that the fish could not get over the racks of the commercial fishermen at the mouth of the river. As a consequence there were comparatively few Steelheads in the water and those that were there had been fished over so much that they had become decidedly wary and particular. It was tough fishing and no one could deny it.

On this occasion I had the good fortune to become acquainted with Jay Garfield of Tucson, Arizona. He and his wife had the cabin room next to ours at Gordon's Camp. He had been fishing the river for about five weeks straight and had been consistently successful with a top fish of some 11½ pounds.

Of course this might have been luck but his success seemed too consistent to be the result of luck so as usual when contacting anything of this sort I proceeded to discover just what there was to Jay's fishing which might account for his good luck.

In this particular case the job was both easy and enjoyable. Jay is the sort of fellow you warm up to as soon as you meet him and he was not only willing but eager to show me everything he knew about Steelhead fishing. So that I might get his idea about it at first hand he asked me to fish with him.

The first place we tried was the Plank Pool. I had always fished it from the opposite side of the river but Jay went to it from the camp side. "I like it best from this side," he said. "I think you have a better chance to fish it right. Besides, I have a special method which works best from this side."

So we waded across the bend just below the junction of the North Umpqua and Steamboat Creek. The spot was both fascinating and fishable, especially where the currents of the two streams united to form the Plank Pool.

Jay did not wade directly to the edge of the hole. He stayed back some distance from the edge so that he wouldn't alarm any fish which might be near his side and perhaps high enough in the water to see him. Then he made a cast up and across stream, dropping the fly so that it floated close to the ledge which skirted our side of the pool. As the fly drifted with the current he followed its progress with the tip of his rod, keeping the line on the verge of being taut and yet not pulling against it or giving the fly any action.

It was the old natural drift method which I had used for Brown Trout for many years. Of course this lent added interest as far as I was concerned because I hadn't expected anything of the sort. He got a follow on the first drift. I saw the flash of the fish but Jay said it did not touch his fly. After that came at least a dozen drifts in the same current which were ignored. But he didn't seem to mind. He just kept working the edge of the ledge on our side of the current.

As usual, when the strike came it was unexpected. I was standing about fifteen feet below Jay and could see the lower part of the drift perfectly. One moment I saw the fly, the next moment it had disappeared and I saw a flash of color. At the same instant came the screech of a reel. Jay had hooked the fish and had proved that his method of fishing the Sawtooth had real merit.

As I watched Jay fish other Steelhead locations around camp I realized why he was a successful angler. He was painstaking, methodical, experimental and extremely patient. He fished every inch of a pool and, if one style of fishing failed to work, he changed methods. He never hurried a cast or a drift, never lifted the fly prematurely. Above all he never seemed to get discouraged, even when all his efforts drew blanks. He would not quit. He used eastern Brown Trout methods on western Steelheads and they worked. At the same time he did not neglect the regulation Steelhead methods. So of course he caught fish.

As I watched him, that old saying kept running through my mind. " The Colonel's lady and Judy O'Grady are sisters under the skin." It struck me that it was much the same with trout. Fundamentals of fishing for them remain the same regardless of the specific details necessary for individual species. And Jay was fundamental and instinctive in his fishing, rather than spectacularly skillful, hence he was a successful fisherman.

Because the Sawtooth Pool had fascinated me from the beginning it was the first place I fished, after watching Jay Garfield do his stuff. At first I fished it from the camp side of the stream. The regular method failing, I then tried the natural drift and a good fish rose when the fly skirted the tail of the left-hand glide, but I failed to connect. No other rises resulting from my further efforts there I decided to go to the opposite side, a good quarter mile walk around. Here again I first tried regulation Steelhead tactics. Because this didn't bring any results I changed to the natural drift method.

Because the day was bright and the water clear and smooth topped where I wished to fish, I knew I was up against a difficult proposition. I had to get closer in order to reach under the ledge with a sunken and naturally drifting fly. So I approached cautiously and crouched low and when in position to do the job stayed down on my knees, knowing that one little glimpse of me by the fish would ruin all chances for success.

The fly drifted along and sank out of sight as the undercurrent pulled it into the hole. I felt a peculiar slow tug and thought the fly had snagged. Instead it was a Steelhead and when I exerted pressure he came out of the water with snap and action. While he was in the air the line went slack and I thought I saw my fly sticking from the side of his mouth. I had seen correctly. My fly was gone. And all because of a faulty knot. I had carelessly tied it to the leader with a simple jam instead of a turle. Because of such things do we anglers so often fail.

I was angry and disgusted with my carelessness and stupidity. I sat down, smoked a cigarette, tied on an Umpqua size 4 and made up my mind to try another natural drift even though I thought my chances were nil.

I misjudged the second cast, dropped the fly a few inches away from where the first started. This changed the drift. Instead of following the current the fly started dragging across current almost at once and headed straight for the fissure in the rocks. I saw the danger of snagging and made an attempt to prevent it but was too late. I succeeded only in jamming it well in the rocks.

It took a half dozen switch casts to release the fly but this was finally accomplished. Then, instead of lifting it from the water to make another cast, I let it settle down in the pocket. What happened immediately after is a question. My thoughts about it are confused and uncertain. All I can really remember is burned finger tips and the sound of a screaming reel. When full realization really returned I was holding the rod tight and the line stretched out in the distance. Some one hundred and twenty-five feet below me the fish had gone under a rock and snagged there.

I thought the fish was gone. Nevertheless, I decided to handle the situation as if he were still there. So I reeled in, kept the line taut and walked toward the place as I reeled. On getting there I tried releasing the line by exerting pressure from all angles. I failed. The feeling of being inextricably snagged remained. I saw Clarence Gordon downstream. He was working toward me. I knew he would be with me shortly to aid me with his valuable counsel. But I became impatient. If the fish was gone I might as well break the line or leader, whichever was caught, and if he was still on I certainly couldn't get any place simply by applying pressure with the rod.

So I laid the rod on the ledge where I stood and took hold of the line itself. At the greater pressure something gave away. I felt a pulsating throbbing and pulled some more. The fish was on and these direct pulls on the line had dragged him from his stronghold. As he came free I dropped the line and grabbed the rod and fortunately made a smooth connection. The fight was still on when Clarence arrived. Some minutes later I had the satisfaction of admiring the fish as he lay in shining splendor on the rock ledge.

Following this practice of careful approach and natural drifts, netted me two more fish when I fished Fred Gerken's Pool, so named because the year previous it had been the one place which made it possible for him to make his record perfect for seven consecutive days. It was the next good hole below the Ledge Pool. The usual way of fishing this pool was to make a long cast from above and across to the KEY ROCK, and then follow through with the regular dip and lift of the rod method of fly manipulation. I had fished it several times in this manner but it hadn't produced for me even though it had for Fred so after the Sawtooth experience I thought I'd try something different.

Instead of starting in from above I went directly opposite the rock, crawled on my knees to a fair sized rock on shore and from its shelter cast toward the KEY ROCK and then let the fly drift downstream, or rather across and toward me. Of course I took in the slack as it did this. About halfway across a fish took, hooked himself solidly and made a rush back into midstream. He didn't fight hard enough to make me get off my knees so I simply held on until he tired and then led him to a little landing harbor near the rock which was shielding me. Although I didn't have any real hope of rising another fish in this water after the disturbance of the fight I thought I'd make a few more casts to make certain about this. In almost the identical spot I hooked the second fish and this time not only did I have to get on my feet but also I had to follow the fish downstream for considerable distance.

There were other incidents which proved the value of the natural drift in Steelhead fishing but this does not mean that it was better or even as good as the regular method. It simply gave you an extra chance at any piece of water; was better for certain locations and certain fish. On various occasions other anglers on the stream took fish with the regulation method after I had failed with the drift method. For instance, consider the following. Late one afternoon both Jay and I fished the Kitchen Pool with the natural drift method. We did not get a rise even though we did see one fish jumping. After we left the pool we met Ed Dewey and told him about the fish we had seen but didn't get. He went back there and took it—or at least he took a fish and we like to think it was the one we saw.

My own fishing for the entire stay on the river was about evenly divided and I believe that adhering exclusively to either method would have reduced my final score. On the whole I think that many Steelhead anglers get so accustomed to fishing far off that they often neglect the " hot spots " near by. The queer thing about this obsession is that whichever side the angler fishes from, the opposite side is the one he feels he must reach to get his fish. This is a natural reaction but it isn't logical or sensible. Although the other side of the stream may look better it doesn't necessarily mean that it is. The side you are on may be where your luck lies. So, approach any bit of water with the utmost caution and keep out of sight until you have exhausted its possibilities under your feet. Not that long casts aren't necessary for a complete coverage of the average pool. They are. But don't neglect the side you are fishing from.

And here is something else to think about. When fishing is good it doesn't matter if you fish far off and neglect the places near by. You'll get all you want no matter where you fish. But when fishing is bad; when you are fortunate to get even one strike in a hard day's fishing, then the man who covers both sides of the pool and fishes them with varied methods is the angler who is most likely to answer " Good," when someone asks him, " What luck? "

RECOMMENDED TACKLE FOR STEELHEADS

ROD—9 to 9½ foot—powerful—weight from 6 to 7 oz. In best grade, weight will probably run from 6 to 6¼ oz. for action desired.

REEL—Substantial with click which can stand the strain of a hard run. Some makes, although supposed to be for Steelheads, cannot take it. Must be large enough to hold 30 to 40 yards of fly line and 300 feet of six thread backing line. The average Steelhead rod will take a G. B. F. three diameter or an H. C. H. double taper line.

LEADERS—9 foot—tapered .019 to .015 heavy—or .019 to .012 light. May also be obtained in sizes .014 and .013 at fly end. Most Steelhead fishermen prefer .014 and I personally prefer .012.

Recommendations on these items cannot be made positively unless one can at least feel the individual rod. However most rods in this category take the lines mentioned. If excessively stiff it may be necessary to go one size larger.

CHAPTER FOURTEEN

CHAPTER FOURTEEN

Lake Trout *

Surface Fishing

SURFACE fishing for lake trout is exciting sport. To cast with a light rod to a rock shoal or to a picturesque shore line and catch fish ranging anywhere from two to twenty pounds is an experience well worth seeking, and returning for, once you've had a taste of it.

The outfit need not be elaborate. It is quite likely you have everything you need in your bass and trout outfits. A 5 to 6 foot bait casting rod, preferably of medium weight, a regulation bait casting reel, and fifty yards of eighteen pound bait casting line covers the casting tackle. In lures, almost any sort of a spoon will do although I would advise a wabbling or darting type of spoon about four inches long.

While shallow water lake trout fishing does not require any particular skill or finesse in casting and anyone who can cast a plug at all will get his share of fish, still there are certain methods of procedure which will tend to increase your catches, especially at times where conditions may be a bit difficult.

Probably the most important thing of all, unless you are depending on a guide who knows his business, is to be able to select good fishing grounds. Usually you will be told of, or will know from observation, some particularly popular location but when the fish are found in such places there are others not so well known, and consequently less fished, which are quite

---

* Some of the incidents in this chapter were used as a basis for articles which appeared in *Outdoor Life* and *Field and Stream*.

likely to provide better fishing if you have any idea what you are looking for. There is also a decided thrill in exploring waters and finding fish in unexpected places and it is quite easy once you become accustomed to reading a lake.

First of all, remember that lake trout are primarily deep water fish and that no matter how suitable a reef or shore may be it will not yield any fishing unless it is in direct contact with the section of the lake where the trout live during their sojourn in deep water. For this reason it is best to confine your operations to those localities which either border or are directly in, the deep sections of the lake.

In searching for possible fishing grounds, in other words reefs or shoals, look for light spots in the water. The lighter they are the more shallow they will be and the larger in extent they are the more fish they will harbor.

The laker seems to prefer boulders to anything else but will be found wherever the rocks form gullies or holes. Flat rock shoals or shore lines where the rocks drop sheer to the deep water are never productive for surface fishing. Islands with boulder-strewn shores are ideal but even around such islands you will find one place which the trout prefer most. It will usually be where a boulder shoal reaches out in the lake.

As a rule the larger trout will stay on the outside of a shoal while the smaller ones will be scattered all over it. As an illustration of this consider an island shoal on Crow Lake, Ontario. It literally swarmed with small to medium size trout. They were so eager to take a spoon that there wasn't any fun catching them. This was when fishing from the outside toward shore. When we reversed the procedure I took two really large ones in a half hour of fishing. On the other hand, when fishing another shoal close by, the outside failed to produce and a deep pocket near shore gave me a really large fish.

A reef surrounded by deep water is something to get enthusiastic about. The outer edges of such a place should be trolled for large trout and the visible portions, that is the apparently shallow parts, should be covered by casting. Look for deep pockets in the shallows. You can easily recognize them because the water will look darker than the surrounding, more shallow parts. These holes are good bets, usually yielding fish even though the rest of the shoal may prove a disappointment. These outside reefs are quite likely to give you the first surface fishing of the fall. They are sometimes productive two or three days before the mainland shoals.

Lakes where the shore lines are not rocky present a real problem. Such a lake is Dog Paw, at least the end which we fished. Not one of our party had ever been there before so Harry Nordine, our guide, throttled the motor low and we stood up looking for possible fishing locations. We both spied one the same instant. It lay some three hundred yards out from an island and to all appearances the water was deep on all sides.

This reef was about one hundred and fifty feet long by eighty feet wide. The shallowest part was about two feet deep and the outer edges about eight feet deep. Then it dropped abruptly to considerable depth. We took two fish from the center and three from the outside, two of these by trolling. They all ran to good size, about sixteen pounds. My wife lost one, just when it was tuckered out, which looked to be about twenty-five pounds.

In my experience it has never paid me to waste any time fishing over shallows having smooth bottoms. The more rough and uneven they have been the better they have produced.

As a rule, lakes having few visible rock shoals are not very adaptable for casting. They are better for trolling and of course during this time of the year trolling may be done with light tackle. However, it is difficult to find the shoals in such cases and to have any success it means plenty of observation, sounding and experiment before you discover where the fish are.

No matter how long it takes, be sure you are in good water

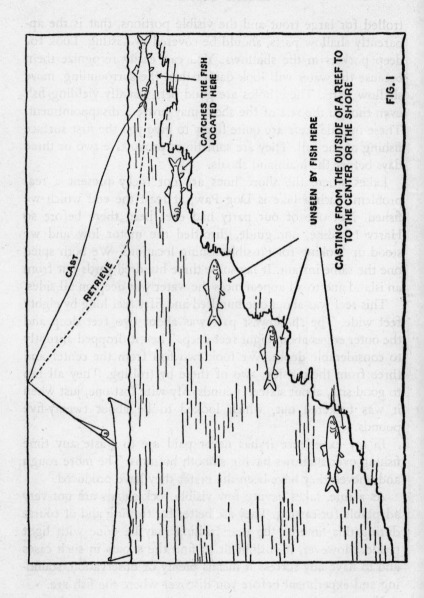

CATCHES THE FISH LOCATED HERE

UNSEEN BY FISH HERE

CASTING FROM THE OUTSIDE OF A REEF TO TO THE CENTER OR THE SHORE

CAST

RETRIEVE

FIG. I

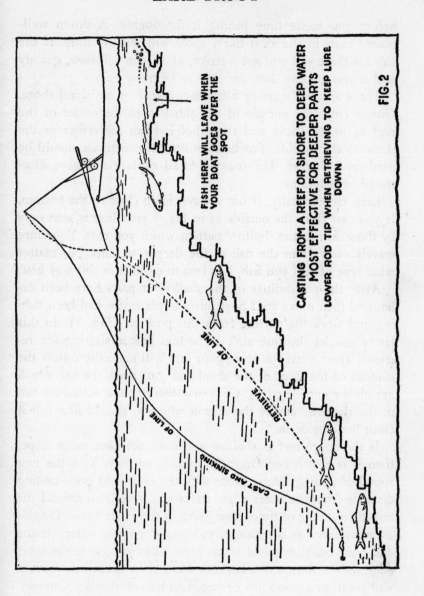

FISH HERE WILL LEAVE WHEN YOUR BOAT GOES OVER THE SPOT

CASTING FROM A REEF OR SHORE TO DEEP WATER MOST EFFECTIVE FOR DEEPER PARTS LOWER ROD TIP WHEN RETRIEVING TO KEEP LURE DOWN

RETRIEVE OF LINE

CAST AND SINKING OF LINE

FIG. 2

before you waste time fishing it thoroughly. A dozen well-placed casts in the most likely spots will tell the story. If the fish are there you will get a strike, or at least a follow, quickly and if you get one there are sure to be more.

There are two ways to fish either a reef or an island shore. One is from the outside of the shoal in to the center of the reef or to the shore and the other is from the center or the shore to the outside. For best results both methods should be used on each reef. The reason I shall explain and have illustrated by diagrams.

Lake trout usually, if not always, hang close to the bottom. If you cast from the outside as in Fig. 1 your lure is seen only by those fish in the shallow part to which you cast. Your lure travels away from the fish in the deeper sections. No matter what type of reef you fish, it is best to cover it in this way first.

After the possibilities of the shallowest parts have been exhausted then move your boat into the place you had been fishing and work the outside from this position (Fig. 2). In this latter you let the lure sink to bottom before starting the retrieve. Then when you start, your lure will naturally follow the contour of the slope of the shoal and thus reach the fish which are on the outside edges. Of course this method scares the fish in the shallows and is the reason why you should first fish it from the outside in.

If the entire reef is shallow and does not have much slope, then it is best fished from the outside entirely, with the first round of casting taking place with the boat held good casting distance from the outer edge. After you have been around the outside a couple of times then move in and circle again. Do this as many times as is necessary to cover the entire water. At the end work out slowly and around and when you get to the outer edge try the deep water beyond. More than once such practice will result in a good fish or two, besides occasionally a musky.

Always fish as deep as you can without getting snagged. But

if you don't get snagged occasionally you're not fishing deep enough. Lake trout are not surface feeders and even when in the shallow water they do not tend to come to the surface for food.

From my experience I would advocate a fast retrieve, provided the spoon travels at proper depth. Some spoons when retrieved fast will rise to the surface. A slow-moving lure tends to bring many follows and hits but not so many hooked fish. This may be due to the fact that they have too much opportunity to examine a slow-moving lure and so recognize it for the fraud it is. On the other hand a trout following a fast-moving lure may be induced to strike by suddenly stopping the retrieve for an instant and then immediately resuming the speed.

During my experience I have many times proved that fast reeling will often produce when slow reeling fails. Here is one graphic instance.

We had gone to shore to warm up and get a bite to eat preparatory to fishing a reef close by. While we sat there toasting our frozen hands and feet, two other boats fished the reef, one about twenty minutes after the first. They worked it thoroughly, cast excellently but did not take a fish. Our guide was downcast. "Not much use fishing there," he said. "And I thought it would be a good bet."

But I had noticed something. Every one of the fellows who had fished the reef had reeled in their lures slowly. "Let's try it anyway," I suggested. "You can never tell what will happen."

It was only a good cast away from where we sat so we were soon fishing. Both my wife and I reeled with great speed. On my very first retrieve I hooked a fish and Mrs. Bergman wasn't far behind. Within a half hour we had our limit and because we were half frozen went in. Incidentally it looked as if the other parties were using the same lure as we, a Jarvinien spoon. The only difference in their fishing and ours was in the speed of the retrieve.

At times, a quick darting movement of the lure, followed by

a pause and then a repetition of the darting, is a very effective method. When in a boat it is accomplished by a quick sideward movement of the rod. At the completion of the movement the slack line must be reeled in very fast at the same time that the rod is being brought forward for the next side movement. Follow the action throughout the entire retrieve. When fishing from the shore, make the movement downward instead of sideways. That is from an approximate forty-five degree angle upward bring it straight down to your feet with a forceful stroke. When bringing the rod back for the next downward stroke you must reel exceedingly fast to take up the slack. It is the same type of lure movement used when fishing for spotted weakfish along the Gulf of Mexico coast. Incidentally, whenever fishing for lakers from the shore while standing up, always reel in with the rod pointing down to keep the lure as deep in the water as possible.

Lake trout are frequently called dirty weather trout and the title is very pertinent. The worse the weather the better they seem to strike, if you can stand the weather long enough to do any fishing. I believe the reason is because bad weather obscures their vision rather than that they feed better because of the inclement weather. Because they can't see the disturbing things above the surface they become a bit reckless and unsuspicious. I am inclined to this belief because experiment has proven that even in the calmest water on a shallow reef you can get good fishing until the disturbance caused by your hooked fish has alarmed the rest of the fish on the shoal. When it is rough, the catching of fish does not disturb the rest nor does your boat drifting over them seem to cause much alarm. As when fishing a quiet pool in a trout stream, you must use extreme care when surface fishing for lakers on a calm, clear day. Naturally, the more shallow the water the more difficult it is to fish without alarming the game under these conditions.

I've fished all day for lakers in a blinding snow and had

them strike so readily that the first cast over any reef brought immediate response and so did the second cast but it was always almost impossible to reel in the second fish because the hands became too numb. I can usually make a cast, no matter how numb my fingers get, but when it comes to hooking or playing the fish it is a different proposition. On one occasion, with the temperature at 20 degrees above zero, I hooked five good trout one after the other and did not have enough power in my fingers to handle them. In each case they took the reel handle out of my fingers on the strike and got away. I then figured it was time to get my fingers thawed out.

Fishing in this type of weather makes you think of ways and means to combat it. After a day or two of misery, we went to shore every hour or so and heated some rocks. One would be put under our feet and the other would be handled after each fish was caught. One rock would usually do for two fish, sometimes three according to how fast they came along. We once spent ten days fishing in snow and with temperatures ranging between 18 and 28 degrees Fahrenheit.

Either in the spring or the fall you will need warm clothing when fishing for lake trout. Anything that will add to your physical comfort will aid you in the catching of fish. No one yet ever made a good job of fishing when he felt miserable.

Once we got to the Lake of Woods country too early. The trout were still in deep water. Our guide, Bill Burke, suggested Height of Land Lake, otherwise Kisskuteena. This meant canoes and an extra guide so we got Oliver Gaudry. Our headquarters were at Ernie Calvert's Cedar Island Camp. The reason for Height of Land was the fact that the trout there were supposed to come up earlier than those in Whitefish Bay. " Of course," said Bill, " they don't run so large there but we've got a better chance than we have here. I know they are still in deep water at Whitefish and certainly won't be up for a week or ten days, if not more."

Badger Bivisible *California*	Black Bivisible	Brown Bivisible	Brown and Gray Bivisible	Blue Bivisible
Gray Bivisible	Pink Lady Bivisible *California*	Black Spider	Blue Spider	Brown Spider
Ginger- Furnace Spider	Orange Fish Hawk	August Dun	Black Gnat *California*	Blue Quill *California*
B. V. Booth	Blue Dun	Bradley	Bronze Quill	Caddis—Light
Campbell's Fancy	Cahill	Cahill Gold Body	Cahill—Light	Cahill Quill
Light Cahill Quill	Coty—Dark	Coty—Light	Coachman	Dark Coachman
Cochy Quill	Ginger Quill *California*	Gordon	Quill Gordon *California*	Gray Drake

Full descriptions of the flies on this plate will be found on pages 446–448.

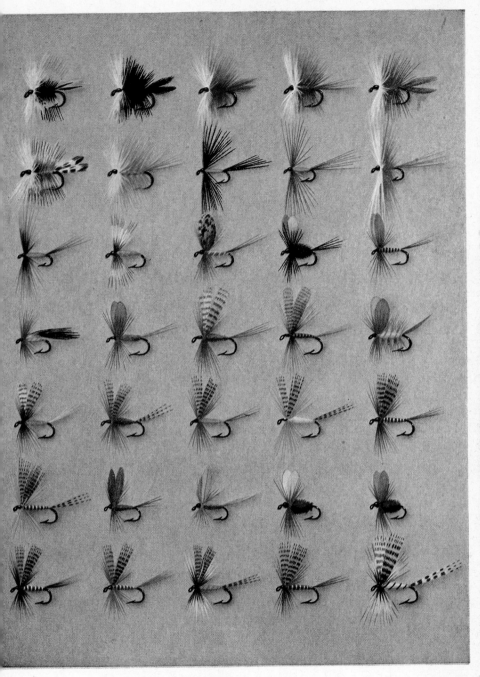

PLATE No. 14

We got to Height of Land Camp in time to get in an hour's fishing while Oliver and Grace fixed up camp. But it didn't look very good here either. We fished a lot of water without getting an indication and then Bill suggested trying for a musky. We picked up one small one and then came to a weedy bay in which was one large rock and a cluster of small ones. On the first cast to the big rock I hooked a fish. " Small musky," said Bill. Then, " No, that don't act like a musky." Meanwhile I was having a grand time. When it tired we saw we had a lake trout. It weighed twelve pounds. " I never saw a trout come from that place before," said Bill. And we didn't catch another from it either, or anywhere else in the lake. According to Burke we were still too early. On the way back to camp we saw a bunch of fish breaking on a reef and he drew in close to shore to look at them. " Now I know what's the matter," he declared. " The trout have just moved into their spawning beds and won't strike for a few days yet."

I wanted this explained and he obliged me. I take no responsibility for the following quotation. All I can say is that it sounds reasonable, is interesting and it may be the truth. At least I've never found out anything to refute it, or prove it either for that matter. Anyway, this is what Bill told me. I questioned him about it again at camp that night and wrote it in my notebook, almost word for word. " The trout usually come up in the shallows about October 1st. The male comes first, cleans off the beds and the female arrives shortly after. During the time when the nests are being prepared, they won't strike. I believe it's because they're too busy to bother about eating. Of course one is picked up now and then but mostly they won't strike at all. Sometimes they start taking the second day after they get through the job but the fishing don't start much until the fourth or fifth day. Once they start taking, they hit fast until spawning really begins. Then they slack off."

As stated, I'm not able to vouch for the authenticity of this statement but Bill was observing, and several others I talked to agreed with him regarding it. And if fishing is any proof then we proved it. We were there six days and the last day had six strikes from lakers. Two were nearly landed but got off when they wound themselves up the leader as they so often do. The reef on which we got these strikes was one we had tried religiously every day because it was one of the best in the lake.

Another guide said the lakers wouldn't take until the leaves were off the birches. Bill's theory had more sense. The most canny guide we ever had in the matter of understanding lakers was Eric Lungrin—I believe that was his last name, anyway it sounded like that. I know after he had told us he grinned and added, " Ay Swedish."

The queer thing about it was that Eric never fished himself. But as he explained—" Ay luk for fish. Ay see wut they do."

There wasn't anything doing the first day but we saw some fish breaking on the outer edge of one shoal. " Bin doin' that four day," said Eric. " Ay tank maybe tomorrow." It made me think of Bill Burke's theory.

The following day we went directly to this reef. We circled it and worked it carefully. The wind was blowing hard and it was tough fishing. All the trout seemed to be congregated in a deep hole of small area. In order to get a strike it was necessary to cast to the shallow water beyond the hole and then reel the lure through it at high speed. By doing this we took four fish and missed five.

The next reef we tried was between two islands and in the wash of the surf. For some reason Eric worked like a trojan to keep the boat directly in this surf. I figured he knew what he was doing so got in all the casts I could. Then it happened. As I was just about to pick the lure from the water for another cast a huge shape swallowed it. It was a long, dogged fight and we drifted a half mile or more before the fish was landed. It was the first and the largest trout of the season which came into this camp. Eric was justly proud and the rest of the guides properly envious, especially as some of them had been poking fun at Eric as a guide.

Flies may also be used for this surface lake trout fishing. In my experience the best patterns have been streamers and bucktails, the same as used for land-locked salmon fishing in the east. (See colored fly plate No. 12.) I've had some very good fishing with marabous and intend experimenting with different color combinations of these flies the next time I go for lakers when they are on the surface. A size 4 long shank hook is about the right size for the flies. For a leader you need something stout, either a regular bass bug leader or something similar. Personally I prefer the steelhead leader, a 9 footer tapering from .019 to .014 or .015. Either the fast jerk method or the hand twist retrieve are quite satisfactory ways of fishing the flies. You may also use fly weight spinners and lures if you choose but for me give me a bait casting rod for a lure of this type. When I use a fly rod I prefer to use a fly with it.

As I mentioned at the start of the chapter I prefer wabbling lures for lakers, those which will not come too much toward the surface when reeled fast. There are a number of such spoons on the market and the same lures may be used either for the surface fishing or trolling.

Deep Trolling

I am going to ignore the trolling done with a line controlled by a winch attached to the stern of a boat. Even though it is necessary, perhaps, in exceedingly deep lakes I could never work up any enthusiasm over the practice and so really know nothing about it. If the water is too deep for me to reach with my light outfit then I willingly give up the fishing.

A regular 6½ to 7 foot trolling or heavy bait rod is excellent for this work and so are light salt water rods. I prefer an ordinary bait casting rod, mostly because when we go fishing we go for months at a time and by using my bass or musky rods I can save that much space. However I would not advise the medium or light weight rods unless they are steel. Dragging from 75 to a hundred yards of copper line or much more of silk weighted with a heavy sinker is considerable strain on any rod. Personally I prefer the steel because the bamboo takes a set from the continual one way strain. The advantage of bamboo lies in its resiliency and casting power and these are not needed for trolling.

In lines we now have some remarkable ones. There is, for instance, one in which the wire strands are twisted very tight. This line is quite small in diameter for its strength and may be had in at least a half dozen sizes and tests. I prefer the No. 18. It tests 27 pounds and is fine enough for me to get 100 yards on a fairly small reel for fishing the average run of lakes where the trout are not too deep. I have another reel on which there is 200 yards of the line, this, of course, being for emergencies, when it is necessary to get deeper. Then there is the monel metal line. From my experience I'd say it is about the best deep trolling line I've ever used. It sinks quicker and stands up remarkably well. You can get enough of the fine size on a level wind bait casting reel to fish in most lake trout waters. However it does not spool as easily as the twisted copper or bronze wire.

There are several important things to remember when picking out a reel. First, be sure it has sufficient capacity for the amount of line you will need. Better have it a trifle large rather than a bit small. Ascertain the length needed for the waters you intend fishing and be governed accordingly. If in doubt get one with a 200 yard capacity. You can use this with 100 yards of line but you can't use a reel which won't take what you need. Often anglers are sold heavy braided wire line for which you would need an excessively large reel in order to get the needed amount. I have one such line. The reel which holds 100 yards of my No. 18 twisted wire line will not take more than forty yards of this. I am calling your attention to these things so that you will not make the mistake of buying a reel and line separately without first trying to see whether they work together. I've witnessed more than one instance where an angler got to his fishing grounds with tackle he supposed was just right to find that only half his line would go on the reel. Such a predicament may easily spoil what would otherwise have been a perfect vacation.

In experimenting with wire, linen and silk line during the past eleven years I have found that wire line takes some fifty percent more fish than the other two lines, when all three are fished in the same water and with the lure at the same depth. Consider this experiment made in 1936. The time spent was eighteen hours scattered over a period of six days. Both silk and wire lines were used equally and were fished at the same depth, this being determined by sounding on the ledges with the lure. During this period the wire line accounted for 24 fish and the silk line 10. This is typical of the other experiences I have had. In cases where the fish were less plentiful than in this particular experiment the wire line took even a larger proportion of the fish caught.

Naturally, with these differences in results, we wondered about the cause. If both lines were bringing the lures down to the same depth why did one catch more fish than the other? This led to another series of experiments and a gathering of statistics. These revealed that a wire line gave us a better control of the strike and a better feel of the fight. They also showed that the silk line produced approximately as many strikes as the wire line but that it hooked fifty percent less fish and also that more were lost in the playing, although this percentage didn't amount to much.

From this it was easy to deduce the reason for the difference. The wire line, being taut and unhindered by any foreign weight, enabled us to sense the very first touch of a striking fish. The silk line, not having any weight, and being sunk with the aid of a sinker, had a decided belly which delayed the feel of the strike and also delayed our response when we attempted to set the hook. When the fish took hard it was all right but when the strike was easy or perhaps to the very end of the lure then this belly caused missed strikes. Another thing which was very noticeable was the better fight of the fish on a wire line after it had been brought up to the surface. After all, as the wire line was reeled in the weight became much less and so the fish had better chance to fight. With the silk line, even when it was reeled in close to the boat, the fish always had the drag of the heavy sinker.

It is a good idea to use a piece of silk or linen line between the wire line and the lure. For one thing it allows more freedom of action for the lure and also saves your wire line if you get hooked on bottom, that is if you don't use a piece of greater breaking strength than your wire line. If you use your lure tied directly to your wire line when you snag and can't get loose you've got to break something and in this case it will always be the weakest spot which may be the hook of the lure, a swivel, or the line itself. The line will break at its weakest point which is where it has kinked the most. If this happens near the lure it's all right but if it happens fifty or a hundred feet above—well, draw your own conclusions. On the other hand, when using a two to three foot piece of silk between, under similar circumstances, only the lure is lost. A short and flexible wire trace with snap swivel is good to tie on the end of your line. It allows you to make quick changes of lures and also prevents the line from becoming frayed by the teeth of a fish which sometimes happens when the lure is taken deep.

Remember that if you want to catch lake trout in summer you must get the lure down to them and when getting it down you are always in danger of losing tackle or wearing it out on the rocks, which cannot be seen when trolling deep. If you haven't the equipment to get down to them or if you are afraid to take a chance on losing lures you might as well call it quits. Many times I have caught my fish simply by taking a chance on losing tackle. In many cases we couldn't get a strike over a ledge unless the spoon bumped bottom occasionally and on one occasion we couldn't get a fish in one particular spot unless the lure snagged and we had to back up to release it. The strike was made always as the bait came free. Of course we lose lures doing these things, but it is better to do that than to fish where there isn't a chance to get anything.

I remember one trying day when I lost every favorite lake trout spoon I had. In addition, we were some four days' travel away from the nearest possible chance of picking up a lure of any kind. It was a situation to call forth every bit of inventive genius in our party of three. It was then that we found various other lures and combinations of lures effective. The large musky plugs were surprisingly good, especially the " float when not in action " type. Because of their buoyancy even a wire line needed a small sinker to keep them down. We tied this sinker on a piece of old silk line and it was good we did. The lure didn't snag because of its buoyancy but the sinker did and if it had been attached with a line stronger than the copper each time it happened we would have lost more than the sinker.

On this occasion I assembled also a combination lure, using an old copper wabbler, a nickel wabbler and on the very end a 1/4 ounce red and white wabbler. This turned out to be a honey and took fish readily. As a matter of fact any string of lures is likely to be attractive for lakers. They are inclined to be voracious feeders and nothing seems to be too large for them to tackle, in fact sometimes it seems that the larger the lure the better it works. If you ever get in the lake trout country without the necessary lures remember this, and while you are about it why not put a reel and wire line in your kit. After all, July and August are frequently poor fishing months for trout and bass and if it's too bad a few hours a day trolling does take the curse off, especially if you happen to land a husky specimen.

There are times when live bait works better than anything else. I have used both worms and minnows with good results. Fishing from a ledge in Partridge Lake, Algonquin Park, I picked up a nice one simply by sinking a worm to bottom. In this instance I didn't even use a sinker. We were killing time preparatory to making a canoe trip and I just tried the worm for the fun of it. As I was using my trout fly rod I had a bit of fun. Phantom minnows, either of the porpoise hide or the celluloid type, are also good if the fish are not in water too excessively deep. I've also had fair success with a bass spinner and fly combination.

* * * * * *

Lake trout locations are usually small in area and somewhat scattered, at least this applies to places where the angler catches fish. If you are not acquainted with the water and have no one to tell you the approximate locations of the hot spots you will have a tough time finding them. You can do it if you go at it systematically but it takes a lot of time and if you have only a week or two vacation this is a serious item.

Once you locate a hole, line it up with objects on shore. (See sketch.) If your memory for such things is excellent you will be able to remember these locations but if it is only ordinary and you fish a number of different places, it is a good idea to make a record of each good hole so that you may readily go there the next time you fish the lake. Put this record in a notebook and put the notebook in your tackle box—then you'll have it when you need it. This is a good idea to follow in all lake fishing and it makes an interesting log as well as a source of information. Speaking of this, prompts another word of advice. Always keep extras of all necessities in your tackle box. By necessities I mean, knife, file, plyers, line, reel, water-proof match box with matches, fly dope and a repair kit. Having these in duplicate will often save you from irritation and loss of temper.

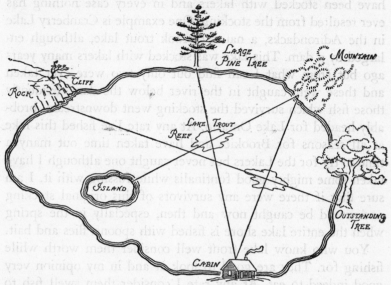

Lake trout are sometimes baited, that is the fishermen put out buoys and then bait the water near them. I don't subscribe to the practice but I will say that you can often get excellent fishing in these baited spots. Only once have I fished near one of these buoys. I had been fishing for wall-eyes with a 9 foot 4¼ ounce fly rod and a minnow and coming to the buoy let the minnow go to bottom. I'm not sure that it reached there for after a short time I felt a tug, set the hook and had a real battle on my hands. The fish went around twenty pounds and the fight became rather tedious and tiring before it ended.

It is rare indeed to find lake trout in discolored water. I don't mean dirty water, either, but simply dark colored. As a matter of fact, in every lake I've ever found them the water has been very clear. Of course you will never find them in lakes that are shallow. They need clear water with depth enough to give them coolness in the heat of summer. I know of several lakes having holes not greater than forty feet which have been stocked with lakers and in every case nothing has ever resulted from the stocking. One example is Cranberry Lake in the Adirondacks, a natural brook trout lake, although enlarged by a dam. This lake was stocked with lakers many years ago but from what I can find out only two were ever taken and these were caught in the river below the dam. Evidently those fish which survived the stocking went downstream, probably headed for Lake Ontario. At any rate I've fished this lake at all seasons for Brookies and have taken time out many a time to try for the Lakers but never caught one although I have taken some mighty good fontinalis while fussing with it. I am sure that if there were any survivors of this original stocking one would be caught now and then, especially in the spring when the entire lake shore is fished with spoons, flies and bait.

You who know lake trout well consider them worth while fishing for. They are good to look at and in my opinion very good indeed to eat. At any rate I consider them swell fish to have on tap when those more widely sought species are off their feed or out of season.

CHAPTER FIFTEEN

Grayling, the Beautiful

A S FAR back as I can remember grayling have fascinated me, and I always looked forward to that day when I might be fortunate enough to fish for them.

There came a time when it looked as though this ambition was to be realized. We were going to Colorado and had been told we could get some grayling in Elk River.

When we got to Colorado Springs, our meeting place with Glenn Jones with whom we were to fish, we immediately inquired about the grayling. "Of course," said Glenn. "The boys were up there a few days ago and took a swell catch on bait. We'll go there in a few days."

So we went to Elk River and caught some of these Colorado grayling; at least Glenn did. I started out with good intentions of trying but spotted some Rainbow Trout and promptly forgot all about the fish we had come there for. But Glenn didn't. When it comes to persistency in fishing he has enough to spare for other anglers and having made up his mind to catch Colorado grayling he proceeded to do so. While I fished a mile of stream and had some grand sport with trout he stayed in one spot and solved his problem.

He proudly displayed his catch when I returned. I looked at the fish and experienced a feeling of keen disappointment. These fish did not have large and colorful dorsal fins as I had expected and besides they had awkward sucker like shapes.

"Had to use size 18 flies," said Glenn, "and they take so

lightly that you hardly know when you get a rise. Lost quite a few. Come on—try it."

I did but made out poorly. For one thing I wasn't particularly interested any more. I should have been warned by this feeling, that something was wrong with the picture. My book knowledge had led me to expect a different fish than what we had caught here. But after all I had never either seen a live grayling or a mounted one so wasn't in a very good position to doubt the statements of fellows who were supposed to know. So I accepted them with reservations and promptly crossed them off my list of preferred game fish. Later on I wrote an article for a sport magazine and mentioned this experience on the Elk. I didn't say very much but what I did say was far from complimentary.

The few sentences were enough to start something and I'm glad they did as it led to my final acquaintance with a grand fish. Shortly after the article appeared I received some letters from men who really knew what grayling were, as well as the fish we had taken in the Elk. The first letter came as a reproof because I had compared grayling with suckers. It was deserved. It also stated that the fish we had caught were Rocky Mountain whitefish. In the letter were drawings which compared the two fish. I knew then why the fish Glenn caught had struck a responsive chord in my memory. Years ago I had fished for Adirondack Mountain whitefish and they had been very similar to these Rocky Mountain whitefish although the latter seemed trimmer built. A little investigation proved conclusively that we had caught whitefish and not grayling. Of course I wrote him at once with apologies. Let me quote from his second letter.

"I was pleased to get yours in answer to my recent outburst concerning grayling. The confusion in the fish seems to be widespread. Last Sunday we had guests who formerly lived in Wyoming. The man is an ardent fisherman and better informed than most. Naturally the conversation turned to fishing so I mentioned our correspondence. I asked him if he had ever caught grayling. He said that he had but when I asked him for a description he described the Rocky Mountain whitefish. I mentioned the difference in the two fishes and asked him if he didn't think that the fish he had caught were grayling. He replied, ' Well, they are the same thing, aren't they? ' This was a new one on me as I had not realized that some considered them the same fish. When I declared they were not the same he did not argue but I think the reason was from politeness and not from any conviction. The next day I received a letter from him which showed he had doubted me. He said he had looked up the fish on getting home and had found illustrations which proved I was correct. The fish he had caught were white-fish."

Another letter stated that almost everyone in the state of Colorado called the Rocky Mountain whitefish a grayling and that there were no grayling in the U. S. A. except in Montana and Yellowstone Park.

All this made me more determined than ever to catch some grayling. About this time I received a letter from Vint Johnson of West Yellowstone. He spoke of grayling and said we should come there for them so we speedily made arrangements to do so.

It was the 19th of September when we arrived at West Yellowstone and by this time some of the grayling waters were closed. I had thought we'd find some in the Madison but was told this was exceedingly uncertain. But Scotty Chapman, park ranger, came to the rescue. He had a pet pond where he said we'd be sure to catch all we wanted. This was Grebe Lake, deep in the forest. After a two mile drive on a lumber road you still had a long two miles and a bit more to walk to get to the fishing.

All that Scotty said about the pond was true. The location was beautiful and wild and there were plenty of grayling in

PLATE NO. 15

Dry Flies

Gray Quill	G. R. Hare's Ear	Dark Hendrickson	Light Hendrickson	Housatonic Quill
Iron Blue Dun	Lady or Female Beaverkill	Mallard Quill	California Mosquito	McGinty
Olive Dun	Olive Quill	Pale Evening Dun	Parson's Dun	Petrie's Egg Sack
Ramapo Special "Gootenburg"	California Royal Coachman	R. B. Fox	R. B. Blue Fox	Red Fox Beaverkill
Red Fox Stoddard	Squirrel Tail	Tup's Indispensable	Turner's Green	Westbrook
Whirling Blue Dun	Will's Spinner	Wortendyke	Yellow Creek	Yellow Mallard
Yellow Spinner	Stillwater No. 1	Stillwater No. 2	Stillwater No. 3	Cooper-Bug

Full descriptions of the flies on this plate will be found on pages 449–451.

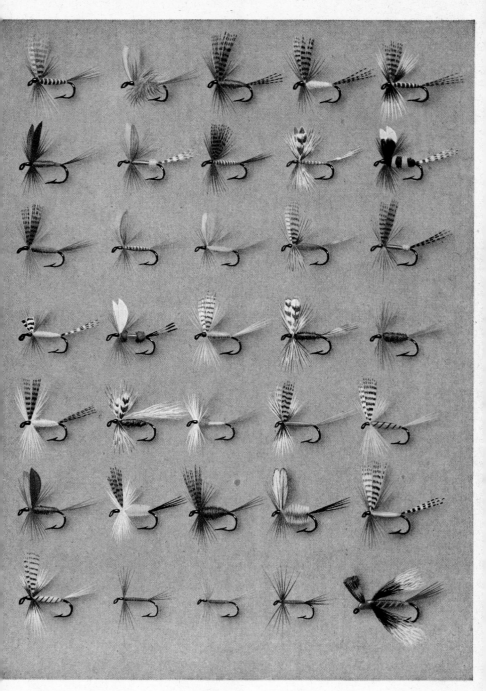

PLATE No. 15

it. When I saw the first one I wondered how I had ever confused them with whitefish. They were graceful, racy and colorful. When you looked at them in the water preparatory to landing them they looked like fish-shaped animated purple flowers.

Fishing for them was similar to spring hole fishing for Brookies in the Adirondacks. It was necessary to let the fly sink until it almost touched the tops of the weeds. Then you used the hand twist retrieve as described on page 35—Chapter Two. In using the method for these fish seventeen thumb movements to the minute seemed most effective although variations were advisable from time to time.

Most of the strikes were touches so light that you were barely conscious of them and if you didn't respond immediately you missed the fish. When missing a hit it was advisable to immediately give a bit of slack and let the fly settle back in the water before continuing the retrieve. If you hadn't used too much force in the strike so that the fly moved too far away from the fish, doing this invariably brought another hit. Often a fish would follow and keep nudging all the way in, until the fly was about ready to be lifted from the water.

Besides doing these things correctly it was also necessary to watch your line closely as the fly sank to bottom preparatory to the retrieve. Often a fish would take the fly as it sank, in which case you did not feel the hit but could see that part of your line which was on the surface make a slight twitch. When this happened you had to act quickly and a bit violently in order to take up slack and set the hook. However, the retrieve was the most important thing. If you got that deliberate and slow jerk timed right you got plenty of touches even if you didn't connect with half of them. A line that sank readily was absolutely necessary. When I tried a new line which would not sink I could not take a fish with it but on going back to the old water-logged one I began to take fish immediately.

One might suppose that a split shot would serve the purpose in the case of the new line but while it did produce it didn't work nearly as well as a water-soaked line and a fly without the shot. The slow descent of an unweighted fly or line seemed to have an appeal which the weighted fly or line lacked.

Certain limited areas were " hot spots " from time to time. Then they would suddenly become dead and another place ten to fifteen feet away would give you action. This appeared to prove that the grayling were moving about in schools.

The best fishing seemed to be in water ranging from 6 to 8 feet in depth and in every case, as far as my experience goes, over a mossy weedy bottom; much the same sort of bottom found in eastern Brook Trout ponds. These weeds were literally swarming with small larvæ, many of which were crustaceans. There is a grayling hatchery on the lake and Scotty told me that the eggs for propagating were taken from the corner of the lake which we found so productive.

Fishing from a boat did not produce nearly as well as fishing from shore. Probably this was due to the reason that you could not manipulate the fly properly when in the boat. It was forever moving one way or the other and spoiling the effect of your retrieve. At any rate experimenting with both mediums seemed to prove this. One evening, with the lake dimpled with rising fish, Scotty and I fished from the boat while Vint fished from shore. Vint took fish readily. The only change he made in daytime methods was that he did not let the flies sink as deeply before starting the retrieve. We got one strike and this came when I had my only opportunity to make a cast and start the retrieve without the boat sheering off in the wrong direction.

In my opinion, grayling are not particularly selective to fly patterns but I must admit that some flies produced better than others. The one that took the most and the largest fish for us was a Royal Coachman streamer. Despite the fact that grayling have small mouths and strike so lightly, a size 4 medium long-shanked hook fly seemed to give perfect satisfaction. Blue Dun, Blue Quill, Olive Dun and Cowdung were all very effective in sizes 10, 12 and 14 and I have no doubt that many other trout patterns would be excellent if tried. It is interesting to note that our most effective patterns here are universally used and are old timers which have stood the test of time and keen competition. The boys who started these patterns knew something and there's no mistake about it.

Sometimes these fish rise best just as the fly touches the water. When they do this it is extremely hard to hook them. On my last trip I kept a record and find that out of seventy bona fide rises I caught ten grayling.

As a morsel of food the grayling is most appetizing, by far the best fresh water fish I've ever eaten. The flesh is firm and sweet and has a really distinctive flavor. In this respect the Rocky Mountain whitefish is a close rival, being in my opinion much better eating than trout.

The wild aspect of Grebe Lake and the forest walk leading to it makes a visit there something to be cherished in the memory. On one trip there we had snow and the evergreen forest was trimmed with a mantle of pure fluffy white. On the lake the wind blew strong and cold. Our lines froze to the guides as we retrieved and finally we had to quit because we could not use our hands. We left in a small blizzard. As far as our feelings went we might well have been trekking the frozen northland hundreds of miles from the nearest habitation instead of being only a couple of miles from our car with its heater and other modern conveniences. And besides this aspect of the Yellowstone, one is always encountering wild life. Never a day went by in our stay there that we didn't see something to make us stop and marvel. Bear, deer, elk and other wild life makes each day an adventure. Even as I write this my wife and I are reserving a little cabin in West Yellowstone. We are going back just as soon as this manuscript is finished.

TROUT

Easterners who love nature should not go through life without seeing this country. Take one vacation to the west, even though you never take any more. Our country has plenty to see and it's not so difficult to see it if you only make up your mind to do so.

CHAPTER SIXTEEN

Grilse and Land-Locked Salmon

New Brunswick's Miramichi

MY SALMON fishing has been very limited, not from choice but from necessity. There have always been some other fish to take my time, fish which were in the thoughts of the great majority of anglers for whom I have always tried to gather information and pertinent facts through experience.

However, because of my extensive fishing, I felt that the experiences I have had with Atlantic salmon would prove of some value to the reader. I believe that the courage to include this chapter was gained from the reaction of the New Brunswick government to an article I wrote just after I had taken a trip there. They were so enthusiastic about it that I felt the article must have had some merit, even though it had been written by one whose salmon fishing had been limited.

It was early September. Conditions were poor. The weather was hot, the water low and clear and most of the fish were in spring holes. When we started out my guide, Boyd Hovey, shook his head dubiously. " It's too hot," he grumbled, " and we need rain and some cold weather to start the salmon moving."

First we tried the Home Pool. It was at the mouth of a still water formed by a cold spring brook. At this point a lookout tower had been erected. When you got up in it you could see down into the pool and locate the fish. My wife and her guide, Claremont Moon, went up in the lookout to see if they could direct us where to cast while Boyd and I anchored within casting distance of the possible locations of the fish.

Claremont told us that the fish were at the very mouth of the still water. The nearest we could get to them without alarming them was about sixty feet. And I had come out from camp with my 7½ foot 3½ ounce rod thinking that I'd have some sport with trout if the salmon wouldn't strike. I had to force the little rod in order to make the necessary distance but finally did so. I retrieved the fly speedily the instant it touched the water. Boyd acted restless and looked distressed, so I asked him what the trouble was.

" You don't handle the fly right," he said.

" Show me," I invited, handing him the rod.

I had cast directly to the fish. Boyd cast to a point a considerable distance above them and to the far side of the current near which they were lying. He let the fly drift without motion until it was just in front of the fish and then started working it with lifts and dips of the rod tip. No line was retrieved; the current was allowed to keep the line taut and action was given at the same time. In this way the fly moved along the entire salmon front.

We heard an exclamation from the lookout. " Two fish started for your fly," came the chorus.

Having been shown what was expected of me I proceeded to do it. But the fish wouldn't take. I changed flies eight times. By this time I had exhausted my assortment of salmon flies. " What next? " I questioned.

" Keep trying," said Boyd.

" What about this fly? " I asked, showing him a size 8 Wickham's Fancy, an ordinary wet trout fly.

" Never saw it used but it looks good," he replied.

The first cast with the Wickham's brought a good swirl but I did not connect. " Don't strike so quick. You pulled before the fish got the fly," cautioned Boyd.

I had been warned that this is a great fault with trout fishermen when after salmon. These fish do not strike like trout. They take quite deliberately and keep hold until they reach bottom or come smack against the taut line. All one needs is a slight upward movement of the rod and usually the taut line does the trick. When you are working right you are never conscious of striking if there is a chance that you do it. You are simply fast to the fish.

I tried again. According to those in the lookout the fish had stayed near the surface after missing my fly and now he came for it as it touched the water. The line was taut and the fish was hooked. It was only a 3½ pound grilse but on the 3½ ounce rod it was an exciting battle. Incidentally I had only 30 yards of line on the reel.

This Wickham's Fancy proved to be just what the fish wanted. I rose three more in rapid succession but missed them all. It was hard to control a taut line with the little rod. Then I made a bad cast and the fish left the place. If I'd been using a rod suitable for the work I'd have probably hooked those other fish and certainly wouldn't have made a mess of the casting, which happened because I was forcing the 3½ ounce rod. Of course I never used it again, depending instead on a 9½ foot, 5¾ ounce rod which worked to perfection. Incidentally, the Wickham's Fancy never worked again on this trip and as you might well imagine I tried it frequently.

That afternoon we again visited the Home Pool. The fish had returned to the same place where they had been seen in the morning. But this time the Wickham's did not interest them and neither did any of the regular salmon patterns in wet and dry flies. Always of an experimental temperament, I then brought out a cork-bodied bass bug, a brown one. Boyd looked at it skeptically but only said, "Never saw anyone use such a thing before but it can't do any worse than the rest of the flies."

Not having any precedent to go by in this case I fished the bug just as anyone would when fishing for bass. First it was allowed to float without movement for a foot or two and then it was given a little twitch. This didn't produce so I gave it a hard twitch, so that it made a slight splash. This did bring results. A grilse of five pounds took it with a smash, coming clear of the water in his eagerness to get it. It clearly showed the possibilities of this type of lure.

That night a heavy rain upriver raised the stream and the fish left the spring hole. It became quite cold and the guides were jubilant. "This will start the salmon moving," they exulted. "Then we'll get some fishing."

I didn't like the high water here any better than I like it on trout or bass streams. The water was too dirty and it all looked the same. You couldn't tell where to cast your fly. We had a hard time locating any fish, at least any that would take. At last Boyd poled the canoe to the very head of the pool. At this point, an island formed a "slick" between two currents. From a point close to the island we got above this slick and centered it. From this position we could fish the current on both sides and finish the drift in the slick. Starting with short casts quartering downstream the entire water was covered carefully. But nothing happened.

We then dropped down in the current, probably a couple of canoe lengths, and anchored opposite the slick. Just to experiment I made a cast directly across the smooth water and drew the fly back with short jerks. As I got no response I changed flies several times and kept trying. "Put on a double hook 1/0 Black Dose," advised Boyd, "and cast to the current on the other side of the canoe."

The change in flies was made but I couldn't resist making another cast over the slick instead of the current as Boyd had directed. Something about it intrigued me. This fly, being heavier, sank quickly and I let it sink deep before starting the retrieve. It caught on bottom, a switch cast released it and just as it did a fish struck, and was hooked. It was a trick method but it did account for several fish during the period of high water.

There was a stretch of still water, called a pond, in front of camp. In this water both salmon and grilse were frequently seen jumping. I always wanted to try for these fish but Boyd would never stop.

" It's no use," he explained. " They won't take in that water this time of the year. Besides, jumping fish won't strike anyway. They are on the move and won't take until they settle in a pool. A rising fish is different. Such a fish can be taken if you keep at him and don't scare him while you're doing it."

But nevertheless those fish in the still water bothered me. I wanted to see what would happen if I fished for them so decided to try it when no one was looking. The opportunity arrived shortly and I tried, not only with wet flies but with dry flies, bugs and all sorts of tricky methods besides the established. I failed to get the slightest recognition. As I gave up and turned back to camp I came face to face with Boyd. He was grinning from ear to ear, but he didn't say anything.

" Well, I just had to try," I said defensively.

By far the most outstanding memory of the Miramichi was the canoe trip we made from Half Moon back to camp at Ludlow, a distance of some fifty-four miles. In the evening we embarked by train—canoes, duffel and ourselves. In the pitch black of a moonless night we got off on the ballast of the railroad track and wondered where in the world we were to stay for the night. Aside from a few flickering lanterns which bobbed along like fox fire with a case of St. Vitus's dance, we could not see a light. Then one lantern came straight toward us and suddenly stopped. " You the ' sports ' from Russel's? " said a voice.

" Yes," we replied.

" Been expectin' ye. Just follow me."

By this time, the guides had unloaded the duffel on the right of way and to give them a hand I grabbed an armful. We stumbled down a steep embankment and then along a dew-drenched path and finally came to a cabin, from which a feeble light diffused through the windows.

We were tired and expected to make an early start the next morning so without much ado my wife and I said good night and went to our room. As we did so we heard a gasp. " Is he going in there with her? " Then we heard Boyd start explaining. In the morning he told us that the old man and his wife had taken me for a guide because I carried in some of the duffel and naturally had been horrified when they saw us going into the bedroom together. Boyd said that when he had explained matters the old fellow had said, " I wondered where the man sport was."

On the way down the river nothing is outstanding in my memory until we reached the stretch at McKeel Brook. This was a sweet piece of water. Here the Miramichi resembles a good-sized trout stream and is full of small pocket holes which may be fished from shore. I rose five fish and hooked three within sight of the campfire we built for lunch. In most cases they took the fly when fished with slight jerks either across or down-stream. But the best-looking hole of all did not react to this method. Because it looked so good I didn't let this discourage me but kept trying different flies and methods, and finally let the fly work directly in the pool on a taut line. This would move it up a foot or two, let it drift back and then I would hold and jiggle. I kept doing this for at least ten minutes. It was finally too much for the occupant. He took the fly so viciously that I nearly lost the rod.

Another place which was very fascinating was Jill Pool just above Push and Be Damned Rapids. I spent most of my time while at the camp there either fishing or watching it. The swift current hugged the far shore and a quiet, deep eddy spread out from this to the shore from which I fished. I felt sure there were large salmon in this eddy, so kept plugging away at it but without any results. I even tried the brown bass bug which had been so good that one afternoon on the Home Pool.

Just as we had left for this trip from Ludlow Jack Russel had handed me a package which had been sent me by one of the tackle manufacturers. It contained some new lures they thought I would like to try out. One of these was a large, bright green bass bug with spreading insect-green wings barred with white. I had taken it with me even though the package was for bass and now I took out that gaudy-looking bug and tied it to my leader.

I must admit it looked out of place on the pool, no matter how good it would have looked on a bass pond, but nevertheless I was determined to give it a good try so jerked it splashily, with several brief pauses, across the water. At the third twitch a fish came to the surface and looked at it. At the next jerk he took it. It was the best salmon of the trip, approximately twelve pounds.

Strangely enough, I wore out this crazy-looking bug in two days. The grilse tore it to pieces. By this time, the water was well down and here and there along the river we found pocket holes and currents where dry flies worked better than anything else. There were a number of different ways in which these dry flies could be used and individual fish called for different tactics. If you were fishing the fast water at the head of a pool it was usually best to cast across the current and bump the fly back. The more you could make the fly jump the better the fish liked it. The only bad feature about the method was that you only hooked one out of every dozen that rose. Twitching the fly steadily for a period of time over a likely place also brought its share of responses. In these methods size 6 and 8 bivisibles in various colors were used.

Several times we ran into selective fish. This called for a special fly and orthodox dry fly methods. The following incident was typical. Just above Clearwater Brook there was a rock cliff. The base of this cliff was washed by a long glassy glide, slow moving and deep. We had been fishing a pool near this place with wet flies and on the way back thought we'd give it a try. Just as we got into correct position for wet flying I saw a fish dimple close to the cliff. On watching closer I saw two more rising below this one.

They took no notice of the wet fly so I changed to a bivisible. This also was refused but as it dragged badly I thought that might be the reason. Boyd recognized the difficulty immediately and soon moved the canoe to a position where a dry fly could be floated without the drag. Six times the bivisible floated over the fish without being noticed. I then changed to a No. 12 Hendrickson, an ordinary trout fly. It resembled the naturals on the water and was just what I would have used if fishing for trout under the circumstances. The fly floated over the grilse rising furthest up the glide first and it never got past him because he took it deep and hard.

As we fished here and there I noted that Boyd rarely let me fish in one place for any length of time. Even if it was good he would move after a matter of fifteen or twenty minutes. One day I protested. We were fishing a small pool which was full of fish. I had missed three and was trying to get them to come back when he moved. "What's the idea?" I asked, a bit crossly I'm afraid.

"We'll come back," he replied calmly. "It's bad to fish a pool too long at a time. The fish get scared and won't rise. The longer you plug over them the longer it'll be before they'll look at your fly again."

It was wise logic. We came back to the pool an hour later and took two fish without any effort whatever. I had reason to respect even further this bit of salmon lore in the light of another experience. While the guides were making camp I went out in the pool, anchored within easy casting distance of eight or nine active fish and proceeded to make a mess of it. I hooked one and then missed three in the first half hour. Right then I should have quit fishing for at least a half hour but instead kept flogging the water. When I persisted, the active fish went down one after the other and before long the pool was as dead as if it never held a fish. What is more they never rose again that afternoon or the next morning. I think Boyd was a bit disgusted about this and I don't blame him. If he hadn't been a guide I'd have got a first class razzing and I wanted him to give it to me but these boys are too well trained for that. It is likely that the heavy line needed to cast with is responsible for alarming the fish. It is all right as long as you happen to be fishing for salmon in front of their line of vision as they then do not see it but when you reach out beyond that and the line goes past them as you retrieve your fly, I believe it does hurt your fishing.

On one occasion I discovered the taking method for the day by accident. We had been trying off and on all day for some rolling fish and couldn't make them rise. As I reeled in slowly to make another change in fly after a particularly long cast I got a strike. Instead of changing the pattern I tried the method again over the very same spot and took the fish. I then tried it over the fish which had been teasing us and had the pleasure of hooking one and missing three.

A threatening storm always seemed to ruin the fishing. As soon as the storm drew near the salmon would start jumping and then they would not look at any fly, either wet or dry. No doubt they sensed a rise in water and became imbued with a desire to move, to the utter exclusion of anything else. At any rate we never could do anything at such times but it may have been a condition peculiar to that particular time of the year. On the other hand, the day after the storm, provided the water did not get excessively dirty, the fishing was usually very good. On the whole, clear days brought the best fishing. Early morning fishing rarely produced, at least for us. It was always 10: 30 A. M. or later before we got any rises. Both of our guides said that this was a normal condition.

In a way, grilse fishing is similar to trout fishing, magnified to the highest degree. Instead of hooking a lot of small fly and occasionally taking a good fish you have a spirited struggle with every one you hook and occasionally take a salmon. Many of the tricks you use for trout will prove effective for grilse and salmon. If they don't, you can always resort to the regular time-tested salmon wet fly fishing. But don't think they are going to jump in your canoe or that you need not be skillful to take them. As with all worth-while fishing you've got to understand it in order to get results.

A Few Notes on Land-Locked Salmon

Some really honest to goodness land-locked salmon fisherman should write these paragraphs. I've fished for them, of course, but sparingly, and do not have the comprehensive background of experience with them which marks my experience with other fishes.

To my mind, in order to write anything which is outstanding on any fishing subject the mind should have a completely rounded and thorough knowledge of it in every detail and under every condition from the beginning of the season to the end, as well as in scattered sections of the range in which the fish is found. This comes only after years of patient endeavor, travel and observation. So far my many years of angling have been filled with numberless experiences with trout, bass, pike, muskies, pickerel and wall-eyes. Even with all my experience with these fish I feel that I am merely well informed on them and that there still remain years of endeavor to glean further secrets from the Book of Nature. But what I write about these

fish really means something. For instance when I think of
trout there immediately passes before my mind's eye countless
streams, experiences, species. To mention the phrase " How can
I catch them " immediately brings to mind the methods used,
the location, the weather conditions, the time of day and year,
the countless exceptions to every general rule. I've been through
them all. They are a part of my very soul. I live them, eat them
and breathe them, have written more than a million words
about them. And measured by the standards of human knowledge I guess I know them. But with land-locked salmon I have
just a casual knowledge. I have caught them, know their characteristics and could bluff a reasonably good chapter. But this
I refuse to do. What I do say comes from my personal experience or from contact with persons with whom I have talked
while fishing for them. When a few more necessary obligations
with some other fish have been taken care of I'm really going
to learn something about these fish and then I shall feel more
qualified to write about them. However, this partial chapter was
deemed necessary.

The first time I fished for land-locked salmon I had fresh
water fish to my credit that weighed up to twenty-five pounds,
including a brown trout of six pounds, ten ounces, a laker of
twenty pounds and a muskallonge of twenty-five pounds. The
first salmon I caught weighed four pounds and he outfought
any of the rest in relation to the tackle used. The brown was
caught on a 2¼ ounce 8 foot fly rod, the laker on a 9 foot
4¾ ounce fly rod and the musky on a 6 ounce bait casting rod.
The salmon was caught on a 9 foot 5 ounce rod. The brown
trout wasn't even in the race. Because of his weight and the
lightness of the rod it was difficult to get him to the net but
the fight consisted of just a few twenty-five foot runs and then
the tough hard work of bringing him close enough to net. The
fight with the laker was a long one, just how long I do not
know but it must have been a half hour or more. Here again

the fight was prolonged mostly by the weight of the fish and not the actual fighting of the fish. After all twenty pounds against the pull of a 4¾ ounce fly rod is considerable and it takes time to tire a fish of that weight and pull him up from the depths when he really does nothing much to tire himself out. The musky provided a real fight for the first five minutes but after that he settled down into a dogged sulky resistance which was tiring and took time but was not in the least bit exciting. But that four pound land-locked salmon—well, it was fireworks from start to finish. He fought so hard that he killed himself and it was all over in five minutes. But short as the fight was, it was the most thrilling I had ever had and has been surpassed only by the sea run steelhead trout in fast water, that is in fish of equal size.

One thing which prevents many of us from fishing for land-locked salmon is the shortness of the fly season in most waters, especially the most accessible ones. A couple of weeks after the ice goes out and then perhaps a couple of weeks at the end of the season, if it lasts long enough, and the rest of the time they are in deep water where it is necessary to troll for them, in just about the same way as you do for lake trout. However, there are some streams where they will rise to a fly throughout the season, of course with a decided slacking off during July and August. During the warm weather and also the late season fishing they seem to become very selective as to what they will take, both as to the pattern and size of fly and some anglers of my acquaintance woo their favor with flies as small as sixteens.

But even though it is said that these fish take flies readily in the spring and that all you must do to take them fast is to be there at the right time I have never succeeded in getting there at that time. I have always had to work to get one or two and everyone fishing at the time had the same trouble so it couldn't have been all my fault. For instance, while fishing in

Vermont some time ago I succeeded as usual in getting to the fishing grounds at the wrong time. They hadn't started to take yet. Once in a while someone was lucky enough to catch one but if two fish came in at the end of the day it was considered a good record.

One day there were quite a number of fish in the shallow water near shore. There were also a dozen or more boats fishing all about the place but no one was doing anything. However, most of the boats kept out in fairly deep water, which I also fished for considerable time without getting a strike. But the sight of an occasional fish rising in the shallow water intrigued me so I finally decided to concentrate there, even though it might not be the thing to do. Carefully I worked this water with the regulation 7½ foot heavy leader and the generally used streamer and bucktail flies. Not a fish was interested in them, in fact they stopped rising.

I figured the trouble was either with the fly or the leader or both. Instead of leaving the place I decided to rest it and in the meantime change my terminal tackle. In place of the 7½ foot .014 calibration leader a 14 foot leader tapered from .019 to .007 (2X) was tied on the line. Instead of a streamer fly of large size the fly tied to the leader was a size 12 Brown Bivisible.

Then curbing my impatience, I waited until I saw the fish start to rise again. This took a half hour. When they started, I cast the fly near where they were rising. Nothing happened. I changed flies, I twitched the dry flies over the surface. I tried everything but to no avail. Then I thought I'd try a small wet fly. Having a few size 12 Silver Grays in my box I tied one on. Instead of fishing it with fast jerks through the water I first let it sink to bottom and then started retrieving with the hand twist method, about eighteen complete movements to the minute. It worked like a charm. In the next hour a half dozen small fish and one really good one came into the boat. This may not be orthodox spring salmon fishing but it did work at this particular time.

Probably the most outstanding day I've ever had with these fish was on the Clyde River in Vermont, directly in the town of Newport. I had been there once before with Vic Coty. On this occasion we both rose several good fish of a possible ten pounds or more but failed to hold them more than a second or two. We got our rises on the Black Ghost and the Edson Tiger and would probably have landed a few except that I had important business at home and dragged Vic away. I doubt if he has ever forgiven me for doing this and I wouldn't blame him if he hasn't. As often since he has grumbled— " There we had the chance of a lifetime and you had to go home."

At any rate, the memory of those fish we had lost bothered me so much that I fairly itched for a chance to get back to the Clyde. The chance came but it was for a very limited time, in fact just time enough to get there, fish five hours and then return. Like the fool fisherman that I am, I decided to make the long trip on the chance that I'd strike it right.

When I reached the river, quite a few fish were rising so I started out with a dry fly. However, although I tried some fifteen different patterns and various sizes, and used long leaders and gut as fine as 4X I couldn't get a rise.

The water being quite clear I didn't think that the streamers and bucktails would work so I tied on a size 12 Silver Doctor wet. This turned the trick. I hooked six fish, lost five of them together with the flies when they got under the overhanging willows and finally landed one, the smallest of the lot. Then it was time to leave for home.

When fishing for rising salmon in a lake it is always best to watch the direction of their movements before casting to them. Once this is ascertained, either a wet fly dragged in front of them or a dry fly floated on the surface several feet ahead of them is quite likely to produce results. Whatever you do don't cast directly to the rise, as the fish are rarely there. Often a slight twitching of a dry fly on the surface will produce results when one merely floating motionless on the surface won't. In doing this be sure to make the twitch very slight indeed—otherwise your attempt may put the fish down instead of taking them.

The average bass bug rod makes a good rod for these fish although I prefer a lighter rod for my own use—a 9 foot 5 ounce being about right. Of course, you need a reel with plenty of capacity, say one which will take the fly casting line needed for your rod and 300 feet of 6 thread backing.

While it is often said that land-locked salmon do not spawn in many places they do reproduce to some extent and it is too bad that more waters are not suitable for them and that their range is not greater. They are a really fine game fish and it would be grand if they were more widely distributed.

In speaking of spawning it brings to mind an incident related to me by Puss Tillotson of Quimby's Camps at Averill, Vermont. He said:

"Salmon don't always go upstream to spawn. Take little Averill, for instance, which has no inlet large enough for spawning. About October 20th the male salmon of this lake started to BACK over the dam. They became cautious as they came to the lip of the falls which made a sheer drop of some fifteen feet. Instead of plunging down head first they let the current carry them backward as they worked with fins and tail to keep from going over too fast. Once in the falls they worked their fins with might and main and so retarded the speed of their drop down to the rocks below. The females followed in about a week and used the same tactics."

If this be true, and with Puss Tillotson's reputation we may believe that it is, then it shows a high order of intelligence among this species of fish, in which case we should use skill and thought in attempting their capture by rod and reel.

A very good average leader for land-locked salmon is a 9 footer tapering from .019 to .013 or .014. I don't believe the calibration on the fly end is as important when it comes to wary fish as the length of the leader. I prefer a twelve to fourteen footer to the nine footer but because the average fisherman won't use a leader of this length they are usually hard to get unless you take the time to tie them yourself. A good idea is to have leaders in the 9 foot length made up tapered from .019 to .014. When the fishing doesn't require a fairly fine leader this will be just right and if you need a finer leader you may add the necessary gut points to make it just the length and weight you desire. As a rule, the conditions which call for a finer leader also demand a longer leader for best results. It is always good policy to carry with you gut points in the following calibrations—.013 or .012, .011, .010, .009, .008, and .007. Then you can easily make a longer and finer leader if needed.

In the color plates I have included a number of land-locked salmon streamer and bucktail patterns. Among them are some of the most popular patterns of recent years. Many of these flies are also used for trout. The patterns referred to are: Anson Special, Black Bird, Brown and White, Brown and Scarlet, Edson Tiger—dark, Edson Tiger—light, Francis, Jean, Mac-Gregor, Scott Special, Summer's Gold, Wesley Special, Dr. Burke, Fraser, Black Ghost, Gray Ghost, Lady Ghost, Nancy, Spencer Bay, Three Rivers, York's Kennebago, White Marabou, Yellow Marabou, Blue Devil, Capra Streamer and Chief Needabeh.

And this is my say on land-locked salmon. Everything else I knew about them was published in my previous book and I didn't want to repeat that. All my other experiences have been ordinary, with nothing of note worth recording. But at any rate, I've told you what I know and nothing more so am at peace with my conscience.

CHAPTER SEVENTEEN

On Tying Flies

I LEARNED how to tie flies by experience, my sole start being an hour's observation of another fly tier at work. After that I procured an outfit and got to work and since that time have tied approximately 100,000 flies. It is with the thought that perhaps what I have learned will aid someone else in fly tying that this chapter is being written. It's not going to be elaborate or exhaustive but I hope to drive home to the person wishing to take up fly tying those essentials which go into the making of a well-tied fly.

One thing I do know. If you want to make good flies you must have both good tools and good material to work with. If you try to save money by buying cheap merchandise it is an easy matter, but the flies you make will reflect just what you have put into them. Once you see and know what goes into the making of well-tied fly you will readily understand why you pay $3.00 a dozen or more for the best grade you can buy.

The tools needed are so few that there isn't any reason why one cannot afford the best. The first item is the vise. Of course, anything of this nature will answer the purpose after a fashion but the best products are made with the special needs of the fly tier in mind and will give you far more satisfaction as well as aid in turning out a workmanlike product in the shortest length of time. Nothing gives you more enjoyment or more assistance in the development of any hobby than good tools to work with and fine material to create with. To see the ideas of your brain materialize in the vise is the prime reward of fly tying. After you have once created, it may become drudgery to keep reproducing that creation. You will find it much more satisfactory to have someone else do this work for you. But the creation is the thing that gets you. It stimulates your imagination and ingenuity and incidentally makes you appreciate the work of a professional who knows his business and who puts workmanship and quality above production. Once having done the job yourself you consider the price he charges very reasonable indeed, because you know just what it means in effort and material to produce a fly which is well built in every detail.

A good vise should facilitate quick changing from one fly to the next and it should also be adjustable to any hook from a large, stout, streamer size to the smallest made. You may start out tying only 10's and 12's but sooner or later you'll be jumping on both sides. Of course, if one is not particular about speed, the thumb screw variety will do the work. However, most of these types have clumsy jaws and they are not placed at a good angle for most efficient work.

Hackle plyers must be good or else they are exasperating indeed. The jaws should be narrow and yet have enough surface to hold and the grip should be tight without being sharp. In other words you want them to hold without slipping or cutting and this means a fine adjustment. There is need for a special pair of plyers which will satisfactorily handle hackles of extremely small size. All those I have ever tried are a bit too clumsy for efficient work with the tiny hackles which should be used on 18 and 20 hook flies. As time passes these small flies are coming into greater use and in my opinion no one can get the most out of his fishing unless he resorts to them at some time or another during any season if one is fishing throughout the season.

The scissors should be small and sharp, especially at the points. Personally I prefer the curved blades. The more narrow the points the better they are for getting in close to the hook without interfering with material already tied on the hook. Scissors get out of adjustment with use and also dull quickly if used for cutting quills, tinsels and other hard materials. As far as I am concerned I find it both economical and efficient to have two pairs on hand at all times; one for the fine work of cutting off hackles, etc.; and the other for cutting off the coarse materials which raise such havoc with a delicately adjusted pair of scissors. If you do a lot of tying it will also pay to have another pair of good ones in reserve.

STILETTO.—This may be easily made by inserting a needle in a cork or a piece of wood. However, you may buy nicely finished ones for about ten cents so it hardly pays to bother making one of your own. It is a simple tool but exceedingly useful. With it you may pull out the hackles which you have inadvertently tied under, finish off the whip knot neatly at the eye, perk up the hackles after they are all wound in and clean out the eyes of the flies which the varnish or lacquer used in finishing has clogged. If magnetized it is also ideal for picking a hook out of the box.

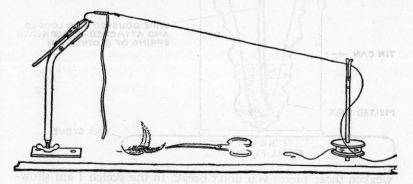

A thread holder, either attached to your vise, to a board on which your vise is attached or on your work bench in the position you find most convient to you is exceedingly helpful when tying flies with long bodies, or in fact any fly of which the body takes considerable winding to make.

As far as fly tying silk is concerned I prefer the finest I can obtain. It makes a much more delicate looking fly, enables you to tie off after each operation without adding noticeable bulk and is less inclined to unwind, thus making a more substantial fly. In my opinion this fine silk should be waxed in bulk before use, using hot melted wax to do the job. If you cut off each piece you wish to use and wax it individually with cold wax you will find that you break many pieces in so doing and also

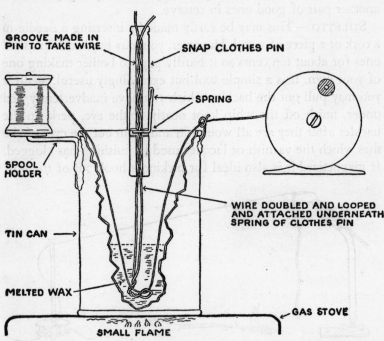

GROOVE MADE IN
PIN TO TAKE WIRE

SNAP CLOTHES PIN

SPRING

SPOOL
HOLDER

WIRE DOUBLED AND LOOPED
AND ATTACHED UNDERNEATH
SPRING OF CLOTHES PIN

TIN CAN →

MELTED WAX

GAS STOVE

SMALL FLAME

weaken those pieces you don't break. In the sketch I am showing you the simple little gadget I use for waxing my thread. All you need is an ordinary tin can fitted as shown, a clip clothespin, and a cheap reel to hold the waxed thread. With this outfit you can wax approximately 500 yards of thread in thirty minutes. The flame for melting the wax should not be too hot.

Once the wax is melted turn the flame up just high enough so that it keeps the wax from congealing. If you use an easy-to-take-apart reel you may put the spool on the base of the thread holder. It will be handy to get at and you will know where it is when you want it. (See illustration of setup on my tying table, showing vise, thread holder and reel full of waxed thread.)

Most tiers use heavier thread for streamers and bucktails than they do for dry flies. Personally I have become so accustomed to the fine stuff that I use it for all flies, even marabous and bucktails. In my opinion every operation in the making of a fly should be finished off with a jam or slip knot. That is, when putting on the tail this should be finished off completely before starting the next step in the making of the fly and so on. Most flies seem to be made with the aid of an extra pair of plyers or a snap clothespin which holds the thread taut between operations. Of course this is necessary when using heavy thread. To tie a knot after each operation with this thickness would make a bulky fly indeed. But with the extra fine silk you may tie all the knots you wish and the fly will still be more delicate than one tied with heavy thread and without any knot except at the head where it is finished off. You don't need to be told which method and thread makes the best fly. The conclusion is obvious.

Before going into any discussion of materials I am going to take up the tying of a fly step by step. I have arranged the photographs in the order that I would naturally proceed to tie a dry fly. The last operation of the whip knot I have purposely shown on an unfinished fly so that it will be easier understood.

Tying a Light Cahill—Dry

The first operation in tying any fly is attaching the thread to the hook. Fig. 1—use either jam or whip knot.

Second—Tie on the tail. Use jam knot—Figs. 2, 3, 4, 5, 6. (See explanations re variations in positions of knot.)

Third—Tie on wings—Figs. 7, 8, 9.

Fourth—Tie in hackles—Fig. 10.

Fifth—Tie in body material—Figs. 11, 12, 13.

Sixth—Wind on body material—Fig. 14.

Seventh—Wind in hackle—Fig. 15.

Eighth—Finish off with whip knot—Figs. 16, 17, 18, 19.

Now let's go back and take up each operation separately. We will assume that the thread has been attached to the hook, and the tail wound on (Fig. 1). We secure it with a jam knot first at the tail. (NOTE—The different operations in the jam knot show different positions on the hook. This was due to the difficulty of holding the positions for a photograph so that several were taken of each position at different times and we picked the best in each instance. As a matter of fact position so that the camera could get what we wanted was considered rather than keeping each step in same relative position. Forget the location of the thread and remember only that the operations in each step are what we are trying to make plain to you. In tying a single jam, naturally the thread would at all times be located at the same spot on the hook.) Now let us tie the jam knot.

First—Take thread in the right hand, pulling it straight toward you. Then put the left forefinger on top of the thread with pressure slightly downward and with the right thumb and forefinger bend the thread upward and back to the hook. Continue this around the hook and bring thread back toward yourself, keeping taut at all times (Fig. 2). This makes a loop held by your left forefinger with the end of the thread held by the right hand. Now with the second finger of the left hand exert pressure downward on the left thread of the loop (Fig. 3), and with the left forefinger pull the thread held by the right hand to the left and toward you, at the same time holding it taut with the right hand. This crosses the threads and makes the jam (Fig. 4). Now keeping the place where the thread

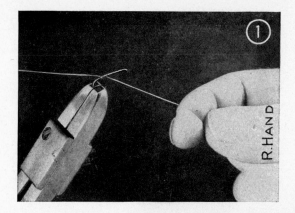

FIRST STEP
IN TYING A
FLY

FIRST STEP IN
MAKING A JAM
KNOT

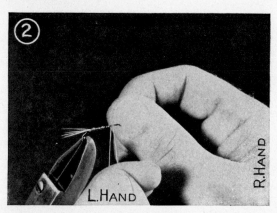

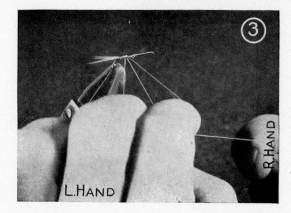

SECOND STEP IN
MAKING A JAM
KNOT

Center thread
being pulled taut
against right hand
thread with left
index finger

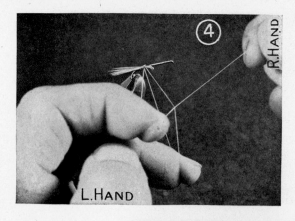

Third Step in Making a Jam Knot

Pull is exerted with the left hand and restraint given by right fingers keeps everything taut

Fourth Step in Making a Jam Knot

Really a continuation of third step, showing tautness kept until reaching the hook where it jams the thread against the hook

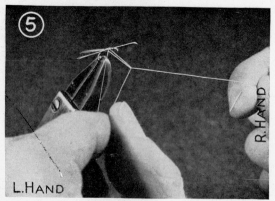

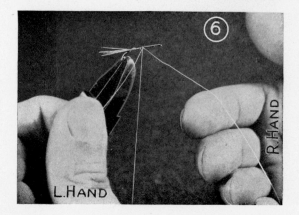

Fifth Step in Making a Jam Knot

Knot completed and thread being pulled through with left hand

FIRST STEP OF
TYING ON WINGS
OF MANDARIN,
MALLARD, TEAL,
ETC.

SECOND STEP OF
TYING ON WINGS
OF MANDARIN,
ETC.

THIRD STEP OF
TYING ON WINGS
OF MANDARIN,
ETC.

TAILS AND WINGS
TIED ON HACKLE

FIRST OPERATION
OF SPINNING
THREAD FOR
BODIES

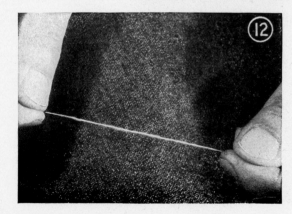

SECOND OPERA-
TION OF SPIN-
NING THREAD
FOR BODIES

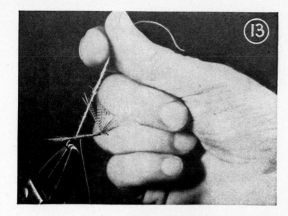

AFTER HACKLE IS
TIED IN, THE
TIER RETURNS
THE TAIL AND
TIES IN THE BODY
WHICH IS WOUND
ON AT THE TIME

BODY WOUND
ON—
The next step
is to wind in the
Hackle

HACKLE ALL
WOUND ON AND
READY TO TIE
OFF

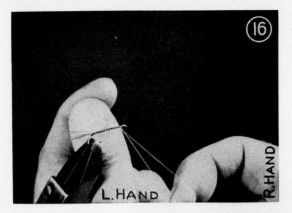

FIRST STEP
OF WHIP KNOT

SECOND STEP
OF WHIP
KNOT
Winding thread

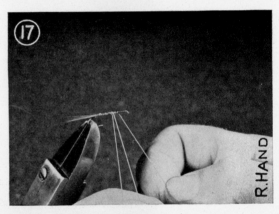

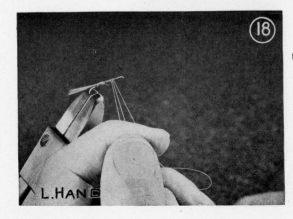

THIRD STEP OF
WHIP KNOT
All threads
taken in fingers

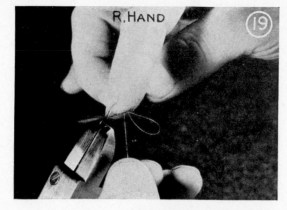

Fourth Step of
Whip Knot
Pulling key
thread and keep-
ing taut with
finger of right
hand

Tying on a Pair
of Fan Wings

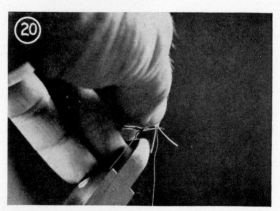

Fan Wings Tied
on—Ready to
Cut Off Stems

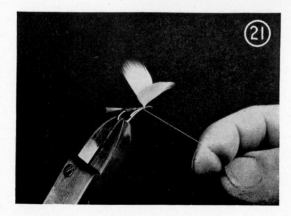

crosses *taut,* pull with the left hand and release thread with the right and at the same time bring the crossed sections of the thread down to the hook. Fig. 5—on way down. Fig. 6 shows the crossed thread jammed against hook with the thread held by the right hand released and the left hand pulling the slack thread through the jam to complete.

We now wind the thread quickly up the shank of the hook into position to tie on the wings. Tie off here with the jam knot. Now take about half of a speckled mandarin feather from the flank of the bird and lay it in the hook (Fig. 7). Tie it fast with either the jam or a single whip knot. Then wind close against the base of the feather IN FRONT enough times to make the feather stand up nearly perpendicular (Fig. 8).

In the next operation we divide this feather exactly in half with our thread and by a few crisscross windings between the divisions, and a knot to hold, we get the wings set permanently (Fig. 9). NOTE—Many tiers cut each side of the wings separately from the mandarin feathers. In my opinion this makes extra work and does not make any better job than the method described here although it does save material.

We now have the tail and wings tied on and completed. The next step is to tie in the hackle. Picking out one or two, according to what you wish, the fibres are spread—(Fig. A—showing hackle as taken from neck and then spread) and tied on hook close to back of wing as shown (Fig. 10). Two hackles are better than one because you can face each one differently 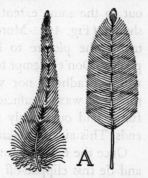 when tying on, making both a better balanced, better looking, and better floating fly. If you desire a sparsely hackled fly make only two winds of each hackle instead of four winds of one hackle. This may run more or less according to how much hackle you wish to have on the fly. This is more expensive than making sparse flies with single hackles but in my opinion the results attained in the finished product are far better as far as floating quality is concerned.

After the hackles are tied in (not wound on) the next step is to put on the body. If the material is wool, silk, tinsel or some other material which may be handled as it is then it is tied directly to the hook. However, in this particular fly we are now tying I am using fur and this must be spun on a thread. The fur used is taken from the soft part between the outside hairs and the skin. To aid you in plucking it from the hide you may clip the long hairs but personally I take the fur off without doing this and pull out any of the long coarse fibres if they come with the downy under fur. This plucked fur is then spread out on the knee as shown (Fig. 11). Now cut off a piece of waxed thread of convenient length to work—say six or seven inches and hold it as shown. Then roll the thread over the fur in somewhat the same way that you would work a rolling pin over dough. Ask your wife or cook. As a rule about half as much fur as shown in the photograph and spread out to the same extent is sufficient for a fly the size of that shown (Fig. 10). More fur than was necessary was used in taking the picture to be sure that the process would show plainly. Don't attempt to spin fur on unwaxed thread. It simply will not adhere, nor will it adhere satisfactorily unless the thread is waxed sufficiently to be slightly sticky. Be sure the fur is laid out evenly and thicker in the middle than at the ends. This aids in making a nicely tapered body (Fig. 12).

Once the fur is spun on the thread clip off close on one end and tie this clipped-off end to the hook close to the tail (Fig. 13). Then wind on, starting small at the tail and gradually making thicker as you get to the finish off point (Fig. 14).

It is now time to make the final operation. Grab the tip of the hackle with the plyers and wind around the hook close to the wing, being careful to keep the hackle fibres standing out vertical to the shank of the hook. (See Fig. B.) If two hackles are being used take the one tied in nearest the tail and wind that in first, tying off, of course, and then do the same with the forward hackle. Manipulate the fibres as you do this so that they do not press over each other and make the last wind or two in front of the wings to tie in there. To make sure everything is set tight against the body after finishing this take your thumb and forefinger and with your fingernails tight against the shank of the hook near the eye push back toward the tail against the wings. This not only sets everything up tight but helps in spreading the hackles a trifle fanwise so that they rest on the water better.

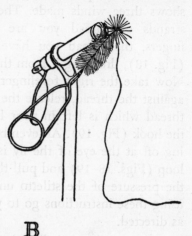

B

The finish-off knot I have shown on a hook without wings or hackle so that it would be easier understood. To start this finish—hold thread in left thumb and forefinger and taut against the hook, of course pulling the thread toward yourself. Place right forefinger against the bottom of the thread and pull taut toward yourself (Fig. 16), keeping tight hold with the thread in left hand. Now bend thread in left hand back to and over the hook, around it and then forward toward yourself. Keeping hold of the thread you have just bent over, grasp that same thread on the lower part of the loop formed by your right forefinger. See Fig. 16 for right thread to take—the lower. If you now release the strand held by the right thumb and forefinger it leaves one strand loose. Fig. 17—right fingers hold thread which is to be wound over hook and if released is slack. Take this strand with the right thumb and forefinger and wind around hook—three times or more for a finish off and once for a simple holding knot between operations. Fig. 17 shows three winds made. Then take, in addition to the two strands of thread you are already holding in your left fingers, the thread you have just wound around the hook (Fig. 18), dropping it from the right fingers and holding taut. Now take the right forefinger and place it on the hook tight against the thread, release the loop and pull the loose end of thread which is left in your left fingers until it jams against the hook (Fig. 19). An even better way to do this when finishing off at the eye of the fly is to put the stiletto through the loop (Figs. 18–19) and pull the free end of the thread against the pressure of the stiletto until it jams against the hook. In using these instructions go to your vise and follow movements as directed.

Figures 20 and 21 show the method of putting on fan wings. First select two feathers from the breast of a mandarin or domestic duck taking care that they have identical shapes and sizes. Strip these of the soft fluffy feathers at the base. Fig. C shows both the feathers as pulled from the skin and as they look after being stripped. Now turn these back to back, match evenly together (Fig. D), and then place as shown in Fig. 20. With the tying thread, bind the two ends of the feathers together ON THE HOOK, then bend them back toward the vise and tie. (See Fig. 21.) If you have done this correctly the wings will set as shown in photograph. If they do not set just as you want, further manipulation of the thread will make them spread either further apart or fit closer together according to the way you make them go with the thread. It is impossible to explain this point—you must gain it from experience. If the wings are not straight when you put them on no matter what you do to straighten them will be to no avail. Either you didn't set them straight to begin with or else the quills of the feathers are flat on the wrong side and so won't set straight, in which case you might better get another set of wings and start over again.

To me the worst task in putting on fan wings is in the selection of the feathers for uniformity in shape for equal size in a pair. As a rule it is best to take two feathers which are together on the bird but even then you will sometimes get two which do not match and unless they do the fly will not look right or cast well. A drop of varnish on the hook between the wings will make them more rigid and durable. Of course the ends of the wings are clipped off after being tied in and a few figure eights between and to both sides of the wings will help to make them rigid and hold their position. I have found that if the wings go on smoothly and straight in the beginning, they stay that way, very seldom getting out of place in use. On the other hand, if they are a bit contrary and I must fuss with them to make them set straight I rarely find that they stay straight in use. For this reason I discard any feathers which do not have stems which tie on straight. If I can get forty-eight pairs of perfectly matched wings from one duck skin for flies ranging from 10 to 14 I feel that I've done very well and while being so particular is costly, at least one has the satisfaction of having a nicely balanced fly when in use. Sometimes a skin is very poor, yielding few if any feathers that will make a really nice fly.

When putting on quill or tinsel the shank of the hook must first be made tapered with the winding silk, otherwise the body will be unsightly. You cannot build up with these materials and make them look like anything so it is necessary to have a base of perfect proportions to wind on. Besides, in the case of tinsels to build up with them even the finest will add extra weight which will make it difficult to float the fly, no matter how stiff the hackles are.

Peacock quills are used for bodies more than any other kind. The best quills come from the eye of the tail feather and they vary in color and density of edging line so that it is possible to get almost any shade of quill you want between light gray and very dark gray. In addition they may be dyed olive, green, red or any other color you desire. Many other birds have usable quills—the condor being one of the best. In this respect, do a bit of experimenting with whatever feathers you can secure. It is all fascinating research when you have time and look on fly tying as a hobby. Of course, the quills when taken from the feather are covered with feathery barbules. These must be scraped off, either with the fingernails or with a dull razor blade. When using a steel edge to do the job lay the quill on a telephone book, celluloid or anything that will give slightly when you scrape. If you try it on a hard surface which does not give you are sure to have considerable trouble with breakage and cutting. My wife uses the thumb and second finger of her hand to do the work and can do it in remarkably quick time. If you do not care about going to the trouble of stripping your own quills they may be bought stripped and ready to use and also dyed any color you wish. These same quills, not stripped, make beautiful bodies. I like nothing better for my Royal Coachman or Coachman flies than the lower quills of a peacock eye although I do use the herl itself when it is thick and of good quality.

Raffia grass also makes an excellent body material. It is tough and makes a fair substitute for quill. However it does not make a good stripe and when dyed does not get so bright nor keep its color as well as quill.

Of all the materials for bodies of dry flies I think silk is the poorest. The only time I use it is when absolutely necessary as when making some special pattern which can't be duplicated with anything else. The Royal Coachman is an example. Of course you may use wool for the center piece of scarlet but it does not have the same appearance as the silk. Most silk changes color as soon as it is wet, becoming much darker. However there are now some colors of silk made especially for flies which are waterproofed. This changes but slightly in color when wet.

One of my favorite body materials is fur. I get all the scraps of fur I can find and use it extensively. Grays of various shades are easily obtainable and make an excellent Dark Cahill and Adams. Red Fox has three distinct shades, all making excellent bodies, bodies that fish like. When fur gets wet it takes on a very juicy look and the edges appear translucent. I believe this is what makes it so effective on a fly. At any rate I have found that fur bodies will take selective trout far more readily than wool bodies. Muskrat, rabbit, squirrel (not American) and other furs will be found a helpful addition to the angler's fly tying kit. You may also dye fur any color you wish, although this sometimes takes considerable experimentation.

WINGS.—For myself I have practically discarded the secondary flight wing feathers for dry flies. Nevertheless in attempting to get some special effect it is sometimes necessary to use them. All sorts of birds may be utilized in this respect and any dealer in millinery feathers will be able to supply you with nearly any color you wish. For wet flies, these wing feathers are indispensable. To make wings from these feathers it is necessary first to have a pair—one wing from each side of the bird. Then from each feather there is cut a piece wide enough for a wing. These pieces are matched together and tied on the hook.

My favorite wings for dry flies are speckled feathers such as mandarin, mallard and teal. (These are all tied on as shown

MATERIALS FOR FLY TYING

1 Peacock Herl
2 Gray Turkey
3 Light Brown Turkey
4 Brown Turkey
5 Peacock Eye
6 Golden Pheasant Tail
7 Prairie Hen
8 Curlew
9 Bustard
10 Mallard Wing
11 Golden Pheasant Tippet
12 Gray Mallard
13 Mandarin Duck
14 Teal
15 Golden Pheasant Crest
16 Jungle Cock Eye
17 Jungle Cock Body Feather
18 Bronze Furnace
19 Badger

20 Dark Ginger Furnace
21 Chinchilla
22 Grizzly Barred Rock
23 Red Grizzly
24 Multi-Color Grizzly
25 Dark Rusty Dun
26 Dyed Dark Blue—(Dark Coty)
27 Dyed Blue Dun—Light Blue or Gray
28 Dyed Chinchilla—Bronze Blue (good for Quill Gordon)
29 Dun
30 Light Honey
31 Light Honey Dun
32 Dark Honey
33 Dark Honey Dun
34 Medium Ginger
35 Medium Light Brown or Light Red
36 Dark Brown or Red

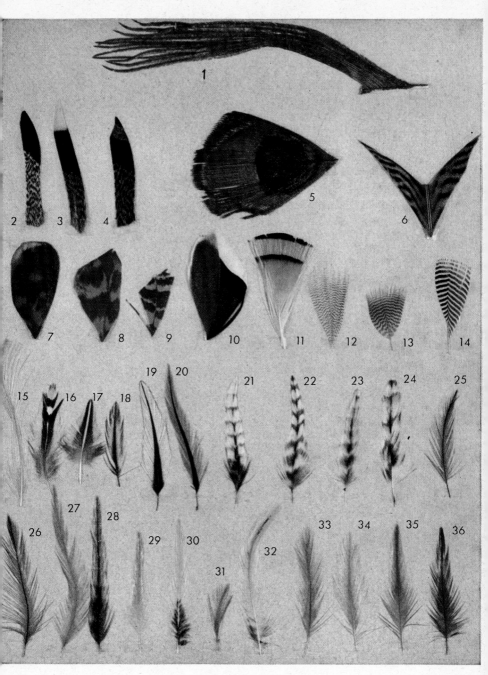

FLY TYING MATERIALS

in Figures 7, 8 and 9.) Such wings are very effective and durable. I also like squirrel tail and bucktail. The wings made from this material are exceedingly durable and while a trifle rough looking make exceedingly effective flies. The Wulff flies are of this construction and several years ago I made one I called simply the " Squirrel tail " which has proved very acceptable for use during low water conditions.

The ends of hackle feathers also make good wings. I much prefer them to the quill wings in general use on foreign-made flies. Of course in spent flies these hackle wings are used exclusively. Spent wings, you know, are tied spreading out flat instead of upright.

Soft hackles are best for wet flies, stiff hackles are best for dry flies. It is the stiff hackles which are difficult to obtain. The old birds yield better feathers than young birds and all roosters produce their best feathers after the advent of cold weather. The pick of the crop is when the new feathers have just reached their prime. Later than that the quills become heavier and stiffer and so make the using of them difficult. The sweetest hackle to use is one with a slender quill and yet with short stiff fibres which hold fairly uniform throughout the length of the feather. There should also be a minimum of denseness in the center. (See Fig. E.) However, some hackles with apparently dense and fibrous centers are very stiff and usable. Naturally, feathers with dark centers are of this type. When you open them up for use (see Fig. E), you can readily tell whether the quality is good. If the hackles keep snapping forward regardless of your  stroking them the other way they are pretty good stuff, even though they may not look it. If they are wishy-washy when stroked they are absolutely useless for dry flies. Another thing, good hackles should be glossy but sometimes mighty poor hackles are glossy also. To be able to select good necks comes only from much experience. These hints will help but won't take care of the many exceptions. And even the most canny expert cannot tell whether a feather will wind on the hook correctly until he tries it. Some of the stiffest hackles I have ever had were useless for tying flies because the hackles twisted as you tied them and there was nothing you could do about it. You don't hear much about these things, of the splendid necks you buy and which turn out useless because of this trouble. All this adds to the cost of tying first-class flies and helps to explain why you can buy some flies for $1.25 a dozen and pay from $3.00 to $3.50 a dozen for others. Aside from the care used in tying, which takes time, first-grade flies are made only with the most select material, chosen from the best obtainable.

In making streamers, bucktails and wet flies the method of construction is necessarily changed somewhat. Of course the tail comes first if there is one on the pattern. Then the body is put on. After that either the hackle or the wings (hackle feathers tied flat or bucktail, etc.) may be tied on, according to the effect desired. I prefer to put the hackle on last. Often instead of a hackle being wound on, a scarlet feather or tip of hackle feather is tied on the shank of the hook underneath the streamer feather or bucktail near the head. (See color plates of streamers and bucktails.) Chenille makes a good body for bucktails, etc., and so does any other bulky material. In putting on tinsel bodies care must be taken to build up the shank of the hook underneath to make the job smooth. As stated in the making of dry flies one cannot build up a body of this sort with the material alone. A very effective body is one tied first with flat tinsel and then ribbed with oval or embossed tinsel.

The more you can catch the light rays with a broken surface the more the body will sparkle and look alive.

Hooks should be purchased according to the need. Dry fly hooks should be light weight and delicate. Wet fly hooks should be heavy so the fly sinks readily. Streamer hooks should have longer shanks according to the length of the fly desired. Some anglers prefer the bend of the hook to be near the end of a streamer fly. From my own experience I prefer it a bit behind the center. Many fish hit from the side rather than from behind and a hook with too long a shank misses such fish. If you have it about two-thirds from the eye of the hook in relation to the fly you stand a good chance of getting the fish whether they are striking from the side or from behind. Of course when fish strike from the front you are out of luck except when using a short-shanked hook.

Spider flies without tails should be tied on short-shanked hooks. In this connection I heartily advise the use of a gold-plated hook. By using this you do not need to wind on any body material and thus you gain in lightness of the fly, hence a better floater. All short-shanked hooks should have upturned eyes for greater effectiveness. Down eyes in smaller sizes cut down the biting surface.

In putting on tinsel bodies they should be lacquered with a clear lacquer to keep from tarnishing. Personally I lacquer the tinsel right on the spools. A thorough dressing will go down into the spool for quite a number of strands and when this is used up the process is repeated. Besides saving the time used in coating each individual fly this takes care of the flies which are only ribbed with tinsel and which cannot be treated after being made.

Dyes are now obtainable for fly tying in any color desired, even to the duns and other delicate shades. This is a great help, as when I first started fly tying I had to mix up the primary colors to get the effect desired.

Moths are the bane of the fly tier's existence but can be controlled if you use sufficient care. If you keep every container well protected with napthalene flakes, inspecting for evaporation frequently, you will find that you can escape the ravages of this pest. However, if you miss one box or container you may be sure the moths will find you out. One year I missed one box which contained three finished flies. When I next went over the boxes I found that in this one only the hooks of the flies were left. When you get new materials look them over carefully and if you are doubtful about them wash them in a mixture of carbolic soap and lysol. Afterward, rinse in pure water and dry.

If you get bucktails direct from the source and uncured be mighty careful about them. Moths simply go crazy about such a feast. First, you should cure them and set the hair. This is done by several washes with the following solution: 2 ounces alum; 1 pint water; ½ pint salt—Boil, let cool and then apply. You may put the tails directly in this solution for a period of 5 to 15 minutes but this leaves a deposit on the hair which must be worked off with the fingers and is not satisfactory. I prefer to rub it on the hide with a rag, giving it from one to four dressings as desired. The final result is a clean whitish looking hide. If you do this after the hair has started to slip from the hide it will not stop it from coming out but if you do it before it starts to slip they will hold tight indefinitely. Once cured and dried out thoroughly, place in a box with a tight cover and sprinkle heavily with napthalene flakes and you won't have any trouble keeping them.

When dyeing necks on the skin the hide gets hard and brittle and difficult to handle. A mixture of half alcohol and glycerine rubbed into the hide softens it and makes it much easier to handle.

The small oriental bucktails are best for the wings of dry flies and small streamers, being fine in fibre and even on the ends. Most of these come in from the east, poorly cured and dirty. They should be first washed in some good soap and then dried. After that treat with the alum solution.

This chapter covers only the most essential details of fly tying and materials. From studying the color plates of flies and the materials you may supplement the deficiencies of these notes on materials. After all, the main thing is the fundamentals and you have them here. From then on you will get your greatest pleasure in adventuring with your hobby.

FULL DESCRIPTIONS OF FLIES SHOWN IN
COLOR PLATES

PLATE 1
WET FLIES

Fly	Body	Ribbing	Tip	Tail	Hackle	Wing
ABBEY	Dark Red Floss	Gold Tinsel	Gold Tinsel	Golden Pheasant Tippet	Red (Light Brown)	Gray Mallard
ACADEMY	Peacock Herl			Crimson	Brown	Claret
ADDER	Brown Floss	Orange Floss	Red Floss		Brown	Brown Turkey
ADIRONDACK	Gray Fur		Orange Floss	Black Hackle Tips	Orange	White
ADMIRAL	Dark Red Floss	Gold Tinsel	Yellow Floss	Scarlet	Scarlet	White
ALDER	Peacock Herl		Gold Tinsel		Black or Brown	Brown Turkey
ALEXANDRIA	Silver Tinsel Flat	Round Silver Tinsel Optional	Dark Red Floss Optional	Peacock Sword	Deep Wine, Dark Claret or Black	Peacock Sword May have dash of scarlet on ea. side.
ALLERTON	Yellow Floss	Gold Tinsel	Gold Tinsel	Teal or Barred Wood Duck	Dark Blue Tied Palmer	Scarlet
APPLE GREEN	Highlander Green Floss	Yellow Silk		Brown	Brown	Slate
ARTHUR HOYT	Bright Green Floss	Yellow Silk	Yellow Silk	Dark Brown	Dark Brown	Brown Turkey
ARTFUL DODGER	Dark Claret Floss	Gold Tinsel	Gold Tinsel		Light Claret	Pheasant
BABCOCK	Crimson Floss	Gold Tinsel	Gold Tinsel	Black and Yellow	Black	Black Stripe over Yellow
BARRINGTON	Peacock Herl	Gold Tinsel	Gold Tinsel		Brown	Gray Mallard
BALDWIN	White Floss		Gold Tinsel	Teal	Claret	Teal
BEAUTY	Dark Gray Floss	Silver Tinsel	Silver Tinsel	Guinea Fowl	Black	Guinea Fowl
BEAMER	Dark Blue Dubbin	Silver Tinsel	Silver Tinsel	Crimson and Dark Blue	Mixed Crimson and Dark Blue	Brown Mallard
BEE	Alternate Yellow & Black Chenille				Dark Brown	Dark Slate
BEAMIS STREAM	Dark Claret Dubbin	Gold Tinsel	Gold Tinsel	Mixed Gray Mallard & Brown	Brown Tied Palmer	Brown
BEATRICE	Yellow Floss		Green Floss	Scarlet	Yel'w Tied Palmer Gray Tied Palmer or Crimson	Barred Mandarin
BEEMAN	Light Green Chenille				Brown	Gray Turkey

• 408 •

PLATE 1 (Continued)

Fly	Body	Ribbing	Tip	Tail		
BELGRADE	Yellow Wool or Dubbin	Gold Tinsel	Black Chenille	Crimson and White		
BIG MEADOW	Peacock Herl		Gold Tinsel	Crimson		
BISHOP	White Floss					
BISSET	Peacock Herl		Yellow Silk			
BLACK DOSE	Black Silk Floss	Silver Tinsel	Yellow Floss and Silver Tinsel	Golden Pheasant Crest		
BLACK GNAT	Black Chenille				Black	Slate
BLACK GNAT SILVER	Silver Tinsel					Slate
BLACK PALMER RED TAG	Peacock Herl		Scarlet Tag—Wool			
BLACK JUNE	Peacock Herl	Silver Tinsel	Silver Tinsel	Green	Black	
BLACK MOOSE	Black Silk Floss		Silver Tinsel		Black	
BLACK PRINCE	Black Silk Floss	Gold Tinsel	Gold Tinsel	Crimson	Black	
BLACK QUILL	Black or Dark Gray Quill			Black Hackle Fibres	Black	
BLOCK HOUSE	Yellow Silk Floss	Gold Tinsel	Gold Tinsel		Scarlet	Sca...
BLUE BLOW	Blue Silk Floss		Gold Tinsel		Black Tied Palmer	Slate
BLUE BOTTLE	Blue Silk Floss	Silver Tinsel Optional		Black Hackle Fibres	Black	Slate
BLUE DUN	Blue Gray Fur Dubbin			Blue Gray Hackle Fibres	Blue Gray Hackle	Blue Gray
BLUE JAY	Orange Floss Silk	Gold Tinsel	Gold Tinsel	Gln Ph. Tippet	Orange	Blue Gray
BLUE PROFESSOR	Blue Silk Floss	Gold Tinsel		Crimson	Brown	Gray Mallard
BLUE QUILL	Blue Gray Quill			Blue Gray	Blue Gray	Light Slate
BOB LAWRENCE	Cinnamon Dubbin	Silver Tinsel	Silver Tinsel	Scarlet	Guinea Fowl	Scarlet Jungle Cock Eye
BOG POND	Black Chenille			Golden Pheasant Tippet	Grizzly	Brown Pheasant
BOSTWICK	Silver Tinsel			Barred Mandarin	Mixed Brown & Griz. Tied Palmer	

PLATE 2
WET FLIES

Fly	Body	Ribbing	Tip	Tail	Hackle	Wing
BOUNCER	Black Floss	Gold Tinsel	Orange Tag		Orange	Yellow
BONNIE VIEW	Brown Wool	Gold Tinsel	Gold Tinsel	Gray Mallard	Brown	Gray
BOOTES BLACK	Maroon Wool or Fur	Gold Tinsel	Gold Tinsel	Black	Black	Very Dark Slate
BOTTLE IMP	Blue Gray Wool or Fur			Scarlet	Black	
BRANDRETH	Yellow Wool	Gold Tinsel	Gold Tinsel	Scarlet	Scarlet and Yellow	Gray Mallard
BRIGHT FOX	Yellow Floss			Brown Hackle	Brown	White
BROWN HEN	Peacock Herl		Gold Tinsel		Brown	Brown Turkey
BROWN MALLARD	Brown Wool	Gold Tinsel	Gold Tinsel	Brown Mallard	Brown	Brown Mallard
BROWN SEDGE	Dun Fur				Brown Tied Palmer	Light Slate
BROWN TURKEY	Brown Floss			Brown Hackle	Brown Tied Palmer	Brown Turkey
BRUNTON'S FANCY	Peacock Herl			Scarlet	Badger Tied Palmer	
BUNTING	Black Floss		Silver Tinsel		Black	White
BUTCHER	Scarlet Floss	Yellow Silk		Scarlet	Badger	
CAHILL	Blue Gray Fur Dubbin		Gold Tinsel if desired	Mandarin or Dyed Mallard on low price flies.	Brown	Mandarin or Dyed Mallard on low price flies.
CALDER	Orange Floss	Gold Tinsel	Peacock Herl Tag	Barred Mandarin	Brown	Peacock Sword over Light Brown Turkey
CALDWELL	Brown Floss	Yellow Silk		Brown Mallard	Brown	Light Brown Turkey
CANADA	Red Floss	Gold Tinsel	Scarlet Tag		Red	Gray Turkey or any mottled Black & White
CAPTAIN	White Floss		Peacock Tag	Scarlet and Yellow	Brown	Slate

PLATE 2 (Continued)

Fly	Body	Ribbing	Tip	Tail	Hackle	Wing
CAPERER	Red Brown Wool				Scarlet	Copper Pheasant
CARDINAL	White Chenille				White	Cardinal
CARTER HARRISON	Black Seal Fur	Gold Tinsel	Gold Tinsel	Scarlet	Brown	Brown Mallard
CASSARD	Scarlet Floss	Gold Tinsel	Gold Tinsel	Scarlet Yellow Insect Green Barred Mandarin	Yellow Tied Palmer	In order Scarlet Yellow Insect Green Barred Mandarin
CASSIN	Yellow Floss	Gold Tinsel	Gold Tinsel	Peacock Sword and Scarlet	Brown	Yellow
CATSKILL	Orange Floss			Mandarin or Dyed Mallard	Brown Palmer	Dyed Mallard or Mandarin
CAUGHLAN	Dark Claret Chenille or Wool			Gray Turkey	Dark Claret Palmer Tied	Gray Turkey
CHAMBERLAIN	Orange Wool	Gold Tinsel	Gold Tinsel	Golden Pheasant Crest	Brown	Gray Turkey
CHANTRY	Peacock Herl		Gold Tinsel		Black	Dark Slate
CHATEAUGAY	Pale Yellow Floss			Brown Mallard	Brown	Gray Mallard
CHENEY	Yellow Floss	Scarlet or Red Silk			Yellow	Slate
CINNAMON	Dark Brown Floss	Gold Tinsel	Gold Tinsel		Brown	Cinnamon
CLARET GNAT	Dark Claret Wool or Chenille				Dark Claret	Slate
COACHMAN	Peacock Herl Green		Gold Tinsel if desired		Dark Red or Brown	White
COACHMAN LEADWING	Peacock Herl Green		Gold Tinsel if desired		Dark Red or Brown	Dark Slate
COBLER	Brown Wool	Gold Tinsel	Gold Tinsel	Mandarin	Brown	Barred Mandarin
COLONEL FULLER	Yellow Floss	Gold Tinsel	Gold Tinsel	Black	Yellow	Yellow with Scarlet Stripe
CONCHER	Insect Green Floss			Scarlet	Insect Green Floss	Insect Green Floss
COOPER	Orange Floss				Black	Brown Turkey

PLATE 2 (Continued)

Fly	Body	Ribbing	Tip	Tail	Hackle	Wing
CORNELL	Black Floss	Gold Tinsel		Black	Black	Black
COWDUNG	Olive Green Wool				Brown	Cinnamon (Orpington Cock)
CRITCHLEY FANCY — Peacock Herl Head	Yellow Floss or Wool	Gold Tinsel			Yellow Tied Palmer and faced with Gray Mallard	Narrow Strip of Scarlet over Gray Mallard
CRITCHLEY HACKLE	Yellow	Gold Tinsel	Gold Tinsel	Yellow	Pale Yellow mixed with Grizzly	
CUPSUPTIC	Silver Tinsel			Yellow Hackle	Crimson Tied Palmer	Narrow Guinea over Brown Turkey
DARK SPINNER	Dark Claret Floss	Purple Silk		Purple Hackle	Purple	Dark Slate
DOWN LOOKER	Brown Floss		Orange Floss	Brown Mallard	Brown Tied Palmer	Brown Mallard
DEACON	Yellow				Scarlet at Shoulder and Yellow Tied Palmer	Gray Mallard
DEER FLY	Blue Gray Floss				Blue Gray	Blue Gray
DENISON	Orange Floss		Green Floss Tag and Gold Tinsel Tip	Barred Mandarin on Crimson, Yellow and Green	Yellow Tied Palmer	Crimson, Yellow & Green Topping Barred Mandarin
DOLLY VARDEN	White Floss	Gold Tinsel	Gold Tinsel	Cinnamon	Brown	Cinnamon (Orpington Cock)

NOTE—Many of these patterns shown in the wet plates make excellent dry flies. Because any pattern shown in color is designated as wet or dry does not mean that they may be tied in either manner.

PLATE 3
WET FLIES

Fly	Body	Ribbing	Tip	Tail	Hackle	Wing
DARLING	Black Dubbing		Orange Floss	Golden Pheasant Crest	Furnace Brown	Brown Turkey
DORSET	Green Floss			Furnace Hackle	Light Brown Furnace	Teal
DR. BRECK	Silver Tinsel			Jungle Cock Eye	Crimson	White with Crimson Stripe
DR. BURKE	Flat Silver Tinsel	Silver Tinsel		Peacock Sword	Yellow	White—also Jungle Cock Eye
DUGMORE FANCY	Black Floss	Silver Tinsel			Black	Bronze Black
DUSTY MILLER TROUT	Gray Wool				Blue Gray	Blue Gray
DURHAM RANGER	Crimson and Orange Floss	Silver Tinsel	Black Chenille Tag—Yellow Silk and Silver Tinsel Tip	Golden Pheasant Crest	Dark Blue Face Deep Wine Tied Palmer	Jungle Eye G.P. Crest-Top—G.P. Tippet Blue Shoulder
EDRINGTON	Orange Chenille	Black Floss			Brown	Black with White Tip Turkey
ELLIOT	White Chenille			Pheasant and Scarlet	Green	Gray Mallard Scarlet Stripes
EMERALD	Light Green	Gold Tinsel		Light Brown	Light Brown	Pale Brown Mottled
EMMA	Dark Red Floss	Gold Tinsel	Gold Tinsel	Light Claret	Light Claret	Jungle Body Feather
EPTING	Yellow Floss		Red Floss	Orange	Black	Gray Mallard
ESMERALDA	Light Green Floss	Yellow Silk Rib		Brown Mallard	Brown	Light Slate
FERGUSON	Yellow Floss	Gold Tinsel	Gold Tinsel	Yellow and Crimson	Green Hackle	Brown Turkey Yellow Stripe
FERN—As Shown	Pale Pink Floss— Gold Tip—				Brown	Light Slate
FERN—As Also Tied— (MARBURY)	White Floss	Silver Tinsel	Silver Tinsel		Gray	Slate

PLATE 3 (Continued)

Fly	Body	Ribbing	Tip	Tail	Hackle	Wing
FIERY BROWN	Fiery Brown Wool		Gold Tinsel	Crimson Tail	Brown Hackle	Brown
FETED GREEN	Medium Dark Green Floss		Crimson Floss	Green same color as wing	Green same as wing	Medium Dark Green
FISHER	Yellow Wool	Gold Tinsel		Wood Duck or Mandarin	Claret	½ Black, ½ White Married Jungle Eye
FISH HAWK	Gold Tinsel	Brown Silk		Brown Turkey	Brown	Brown Turkey and Jungle Eye
FITZMAURICE	Crimson Chenille		Black Chenille	Peacock Sword	Yellow Hackle	Brown Mallard
FLAGGER	Pale Yellow Floss	Gold Tinsel	Gold Tinsel		Blue Gray	Slate
FLAMER	Gold Tinsel		Black Chenille	Crimson	Brown	Crimson
FLETCHER	Black Floss		Silver Tinsel	Scarlet Yellow Guinea	Gray Tied Palmer	Light Brown Turkey
FLIGHT'S FANCY	Pale Yellow Floss	Gold Tinsel	Gold Tinsel	Brown Tail	Brown	Light Slate
FLORENCE	Pink Chenille		Silver Tinsel	Brown Mallard	Black	Brown Mallard
FORSYTH	Yellow Wool		Light Blue Floss		Yellow Tied Palmer	Yellow with Brown Stripe
FOSNOT	Yellow Wool or Chenille				Light Blue	Light Slate
FRANCIS FLY	Peacock Herl	Dark Red Floss			Gray (Dark Grizzly)	Jungle Body Feather
GENERAL HOOKER	Yellow Floss	Green Silk			Brown	Dark Slate
GETLAND	Green Floss	Gold Tinsel	Gold Tinsel	Brown	Brown	Gray Mallard
GINGER PALMER	Pale Yellow Floss	Gold Tinsel	Gold Tinsel		Ginger Tied Palmer	
G. R. HARE'S EAR Wet	Rabbit Fur—Not Plucked	Gold Tinsel		Brown	Formed by the long fibres of unplucked Rabbit Fur as it is wound on.	Slate

PLATE 3 (Continued)

Fly	Body	Ribbing	Tip	Tail	Hackle	Wing
GOOD EVENING	Scarlet Floss or Wool	Gold Tinsel		Golden Pheasant Tippet	Brown	Dark Blue—White Tip
GOLD MONKEY	Pale Yellow	Gold Tinsel	Gold Tinsel		Guinea (Black and White)	Slate (Gray)
GOLD STORK	Gold Tinsel			Gray Mallard	Brown	Brown Mallard
GORDON	Yellow Floss	Gold Tinsel	Gold Tinsel	Brown Mallard or Mandarin	Badger	Brown Mallard or Mandarin
GOLDEN DOCTOR	Gold Tinsel			Scarlet Yellow Green	Claret	Gray Mallard Blue, Red
GOLDEN DUKE		(Front)—Gold Tinsel—2/3rds (Back)—Black Floss—1/3rd		Crimson	Black	Crimson
GOLDEN DUN	Orange Floss or Wool			Gray	Gray	Gray (Slate)
GOLDEN IBIS	Gold Tinsel			Scarlet	Scarlet	Scarlet
GOLDEN DUN MIDGE	Pale Green Floss	Gold Tinsel		Gray	Gray	Light Slate
GOLDEN PHEASANT	Orange Floss	Gold Tinsel	Gold Tinsel	Black	Orange	Golden Pheasant Tippet
GOLDEN ROD	Orange Floss	Gold Tinsel	Peacock Tag	Crimson	Orange	Jungle Eye
GOLDEN SPINNER	Pale Yellow Floss		Peacock Tag		Brown	Light Slate
GOSLING	Green Floss			Gray	Gray	Slate
GRANNOM	Pale Yellow Wool	Gold Tinsel	Peacock Tag		Brown	Light Brown Turkey
GRAY MARLOW	Red Floss or Wool	Gold Tinsel	Gold Tinsel		Grizzly Barred Rock	
GROUSE SPIDER	Orange Floss or Chenille	Gold Tinsel	Gold Tinsel	Scarlet	Grouse	

PLATE 4
WET FLIES

Fly	Body	Ribbing	Tip	Tail	Hackle	Wing
GUINEA HEN	Crimson Fur or Wool	Gold Tinsel	Gold Tinsel	Crimson	Claret Light	Guinea
GOVERNOR	Peacock Herl				Brown	Brown Turkey
GOV. ALVORD	Peacock Herl		Scarlet Floss	Dark Scarlet	Brown	Slate Married to Cinnamon
GRACKLE	Peacock Herl			Dark Scarlet	Black	Dark Scarlet
GRAVEL BED	Dark Slate Floss		Gold Tinsel		Black	Black
GREEN MIDGE	Green Floss	Gold Tinsel	Gold Tinsel		Light Blue Dun	
GRAY DRAKE	White Floss	Black Floss		Gray Mallard	Gray	Gray Mallard
GRAY MIDGE	Crimson Floss			Gray Mallard	Light Gray	Gray Mallard
GRAY MILLER	Blue Gray Wool or Fur		Silver		Light Gray	Slate
GREAT DUN	Brown Cast Fur or Wool			Brown Mallard	Blue Gray	Slate
GREEN COACHMAN	Peacock Herl		Gold Tinsel		Green	Slate
GREEN DRAKE	Pale Yellow Floss	Brown Silk		Green	Green	Gray Mallard Dyed Yellow Green
GREEN MANTLE	Green Wool	Gold Tinsel	Gold Tinsel	Green	Green	Gray Mallard
GREENWELL'S GLORY	Olive Floss	Gold Tinsel	Gold Tinsel		Dark Brown Furnace	Very Dark Slate
GRIZZLY KING	Green Floss	Gold Tinsel		Scarlet	Badger Gray	Gray Mallard
GUNNISON	Green Floss	White Floss		Gray Mallard	Brown	White Tipped Turkey
HARLEQUIN	½ Blue Floss ½ Orange Floss	Black Silk			Black	Dark Slate
HAWTHORNE	Black Floss				Black Mixed with Light Claret	Black
HECKHAM GREEN	Green Floss	Gold Tinsel	Gold Tinsel	Golden Pheasant Tippet	Brown	Teal

PLATE 4 (Continued)

Fly	Body	Ribbing	Tip	Tail	Hackle	Wing
HECKHAM RED	Scarlet Floss	Gold Tinsel	White Floss	Turkey Brown	Light Red	Bittern or Light Turkey Brown Mottled
HEMLOCK	Dark Gray Floss				Brown	Dark Brown Turkey
HENSHALL	Peacock Herl	White Floss	Gold Tinsel	Peacock Sword	Grizzly "Barred Rock"	Light Gray Turkey
HERMAN FLY	Crimson Floss		Gold Tinsel		Brown	Slate
HOFLAND'S FANCY	Dark Claret Floss			Brown	Brown	Bittern Light or Light Turkey
HOSKINS	Yellow Floss				Gray	Light Slate
HOWELL	Peacock Herl	Gold Tinsel	Gold Tinsel	Light Claret	Deep Wine	White Tipped Turkey
HOLBERTON	½ Peacock Herl ½ Orange Floss	Gold Tinsel	Gold Tinsel	Barred Mandarin, Crimson, Yellow, Peacock Sword	Crimson	Peacock Sword, Crimson, Yellow—Barred Mandarin
HOPATCONG	Silver Tinsel			Scarlet and Yellow	Black Tied Palmer	Brown Turkey Jungle Over
HUDSON	Dark Brown—Almost Black Wool	Gold Tinsel	Orange Floss Tag	Green	Orange	Light Brown Turkey
HUNT FLY	Green Floss	Yellow Silk			Brown Hackle	Cinnamon Orpington Cock
IBIS & WHITE	Crimson Floss	Gold Tinsel	Gold Tinsel	Red and White	Red and White Mixed	Red and White
IMBRIE	Yellow Floss	Gold Tinsel	Black Chenille Tag		Brown	Slate
INDIAN ROCK	Peacock Herl			Crimson over Gray Mallard	Crimson Palmer	Gray Mallard and Crimson
INDIAN YELLOW	Very Light Brown Floss	Pale Yellow Silk		Very Pale Ginger or Dark Honey	Very Pale Ginger or Dark Honey	Grouse

PLATE 4 (Continued)

Fly	Body	Ribbing	Tip	Tail	Hackle	Wing
INGERSOL	Orange Chenille	Gold Tinsel		Pheasant	Brown	Turkey
IRISH GROUSE	Orange Floss	Gold Tinsel			Furnace Tied Palmer	Peacock Herl
IRISH TURKEY	Green Floss	Yellow Silk		Yellow	Brown	Light Brown Turkey or Bittern
IRON BLUE QUILL	Dark Blue Quill			Dark Iron Blue	Dark Iron Blue	Dark Slate
JAMES	Silver Tinsel			Scarlet	Light Claret	Brown Turkey or Bittern
JAY-BLUE	Light Blue Floss	Gold Tinsel		Light Blue	Light Blue	Blue Jay
JAY-YELLOW	Yellow Floss			Yellow	Yellow	Blue Jay
JAY-SILVER	Silver Tinsel	Oval Silver Tinsel if desired		Golden Pheasant Tippet	Ginger	Blue Jay
JENNIE LIND	Yellow Floss	Gold Tinsel		Light Purple	Scarlet	Light Purple, Scarlet Stripe
JOCK SCOTT	Black Floss at head Yellow Floss at tail	Silver Tinsel		Golden Pheasant Crest and Scarlet Tuff	Guinea Fowl—Black and White	Peacock Sword Blue—Yellow, Scarlet & White Tipped Turkey—Married—Jungle Cock Eye
JOHN MANN	Yellow Floss	Gold Tinsel	Scarlet Tag	Brown Turkey	Brown Tied Palmer	Dark Brown Turkey or Bittern
JUNE	Alternate Scarlet and White Floss				Black	Light Brown Turkey
JUNE SPINNER	Black Chenille	Broad Silver Tinsel			Black	Black
KAMALOFF	Yellow Wool	Gold Tinsel	Red Floss Tag	Brown Mallard	Grizzly " Barred Rock "	Light Brown Turkey or Bittern

PLATE 5
WET FLIES

Fly	Body	Ribbing	Tip	Tail	Hackle	Wing
KATE	Scarlet and Yellow Floss	Gold Tinsel		Golden Pheasant Tippet	Black	Cinnamon "Orpington"
KATYDID	Green Floss "Highlander"	Gold Tinsel		Green	Green	Bright Green
KENDAL	Deep Wine Chenille			Scarlet	Scarlet	Brown Mallard
KIFFE	Dark Green Floss Silk	Gold Tinsel		Scarlet	Scarlet	Gray Mallard Dyed Yellow
KINEO	Scarlet Wool	Silver Tinsel		Black, White Scarlet—Married	Scarlet Tied Palmer	Scarlet, White, Black—Married
KING OF WATER	Crimson Floss	Gold Tinsel		Gray Mallard	Brown	Gray Mallard
KINGDOM	White Floss	Bluish Green Floss	Gold Tinsel		Brown—sometimes Scarlet	Brown Turkey or Gray
KINGFISHER	Crimson Floss	Gold Tinsel	Gold Tinsel	Golden Pheasant Tippet	Brown	Gray Mallard
KINROSS	Olive Green Floss	Silver Tinsel		Barred Wood Duck or Mandarin	Olive Green	Dark Brown Turkey Wing
KITSON	Yellow Floss or Wool	Gold Tinsel	Gold Tinsel	Black	Light Claret	Yellow-Black Cheeks
KNOWLE'S FANCY	Light Brown Wool	Silver Tinsel			Brown	From Black Cock's Tail Feather
LA BELLE	Light Blue Floss	Silver Tinsel		Scarlet Wool Tag	Light Blue	White
LACKEY'S GRANT LAKE	Olive Green Floss		Gold Tinsel	Light Brown	Light Brown	Light Brown Turkey
LACHENE	Shoulder—Black Chenille—Tail End Embossed Silver Tinsel	Silver Tinsel		Gray Mallard Dyed Pale Yellow	Dark Claret	Amherst Pheasant
LADY GRAY	Blue-Gray Rabbit Fur	Silver Tinsel		Barred Mandarin	Scarlet Tied Palmer	Jungle Body Feather

PLATE 5 (Continued)

Fly	Body	Ribbing	Tip	Tail	Hackle	Wing
LADY MERTON	Blue-Gray Rabbit Fur	Silver Tinsel		Golden Pheasant Crest	Black Tied Palmer Scarlet Shoulder	Gray Mallard
LADY MILLS	White Ostrich	Silver Tinsel & Black Ostrich		Golden Pheasant Tippet	Blue Gray	Cinnamon with Black Tip
LAKE EDWARD	Light Brown Wool or Fur	Gold Tinsel	Gold Tinsel	Yellow	Scarlet	Yellow, Dark-Blue, Brown Turkey
LAKE GEORGE	Scarlet Floss	Gold Tinsel	Gold Tinsel	Scarlet	White	White with Scarlet Stripe
LAKE GREEN	Yellow	Insect Green Silk			Light Ginger	Teal
LANGIWIN	Yellow Floss			Bright Yellow	Bright Yellow	Bright Yellow
LARAMIE	Deep Wine Wool	Silver Tinsel	Silver Tinsel	Deep Wine	Black	Dark Gray or Speckled Dark Gray
LANIGAN	White Chenille			Black	Light Claret Tied Palmer	Gray Mallard
LAST CHANCE	Yellow Floss	Black Silk	Gold Tinsel	Crimson	Light Brown	Light Slate
LIBERTY	Pale Blue Floss	Gold Tinsel		Dark Blue	White	Scarlet
LIGHT BLOW	Quill—Pronounced Stripe			Light Brown Turkey	Crimson	Light Brown Turkey
LIGHT FOX	White Wool	Gold Tinsel	Gold Tinsel	Yellow Wool Tag	Yellow	Slate
LIGHT POLKA	White Chenille				White	Guinea
LISTER'S GOLD	Dark Claret Wool at Shoulder—Gold Tinsel Rear	Gold Tinsel		Yellow	Orange	Guinea
LORD BALTIMORE	Orange Floss	Black Silk		Black	Black	Black—Jungle Eye
LOGAN	Brown Floss	Gold Tinsel	Gold Tinsel	Crimson, Orange Married	Dark Brown	Orange, Crimson Stripe
LOWERY	Peacock Herl		Yellow Floss		Brown	Mixed Gray or Cinnamon

PLATE 5 (Continued)

Fly	Body	Ribbing	Tip	Tail	Hackle	Wing
LOYAL SOCK	Pale Yellow Floss				Black	Black
LUZERNE	Dark Claret Floss				Black	Gray Mallard
MAGALLOWAY	Light Brown Wool		Black Chenille Tag—Gold Tinsel Tip	Yellow	Brown Furnace	Peacock Sword
MAGPIE	Brown Floss	Gold Tinsel		Brown	Brown	Magpie or Black Turkey, White Tip
MAJOR	Purple Wool	Gold Tinsel	Blue Floss Tag—Also Gold Tinsel Tip	Golden Pheasant Tippet.	Scarlet Palmer Blue at Shoulder	Brown Turkey Gray Mallard
MALLARD	Yellow Wool	Gold Tinsel		Brown Mallard	Brown	Brown Mallard
MARK LAIN	Yellow Floss or Wool		Gold Tip	Scarlet and White	Scarlet	Cinnamon—White Tip
MARSTON'S FANCY	Peacock Herl			Dark Gray		Dark Gray
MARCH BROWN American	Brown	Gold Tinsel	Gold Tinsel		Brown	Brown Turkey
MARCH BROWN Female	Gray-Brown	Gold Tinsel		Partridge	Partridge	Pheasant (Light)
MARCH BROWN Male	Gray-Brown	Gold Tinsel	Gold Tinsel	Partridge Dark	Partridge Dark	Pheasant (Dark)
MARCH DUN	Medium Green Wool		Gold Tinsel			Light Slate
MARLOW BUZZ	Peacock Herl		Gold Tinsel		Brown Furnace	
MASCOT	Peacock Herl		Yellow Floss Tag	Scarlet	Black	Slate
MARSTERS	White Floss or Wool		Gold Tinsel	Gray Mallard	Scarlet	Widgeon or Gray Mallard
MARTIN	Yellow Floss	Gold Tinsel		Yellow and Black Alternate	Deep Yellow	Widgeon or Gray Mallard

PLATE 6
WET FLIES

Fly	Body	Ribbing	Tip	Tail	Hackle	Wing
MAURICE	1/3 Black Floss 2/3 Scarlet Floss			Scarlet	Yellow Tied Palmer over Black Floss	Teal
MAXWELL	Copper Tinsel			Teal	Brown	Iridescent, Green, Wood-Duck
MAXWELL BLUE	Medium Dark Blue-Gray Floss	Silver Tinsel	Silver	Light Blue	Light Blue	Wood-Duck
McALPIN	Claret Wool	Gold Tinsel	Gold Tinsel	Wood-Duck (Barred) Topping Scarlet	Guinea	Peacock Herl Topping Scarlet
McGINTY	Alternate Black & Yellow Chenille			Gray Mallard Topping Scarlet	Brown	Black-White Tip Turkey
McKENZIE	Light Olive-Green Wool	Gold Tinsel	Gold Tinsel	Brown	Brown	Mottled Slate and Brown
MEALY MOTH	Lightest Gray Wool	Silver Tinsel			White	White
MERSHON	Black Silk Floss			Black	Black	Dark Blue, White Tip
MERSHON-WHITE	White Silk			Golden Pheasant Tippet	Light Brown	Dark Blue, White Tip
MIDGE BLACK	Black Floss				Black	
WHITE MILLER	White Silk Floss	Gold Tinsel	Gold Tinsel	Scarlet	White	White
MILLS NO. 1	Crimson Floss	Gold Tinsel	Black Tag, Gold Tinsel Tip	Golden Pheasant Tippet	White	Mallard Dyed Yellow
MOHAWK	Light Claret Floss			Brown	Brown Tied Palmer	Brown Turkey
MOISIC	Black Wool Shoulder, Yellow Wool End		Gold Tinsel	Golden Pheasant Crest	Guinea Face Yellow in Back	
MOLE	Gray Wool				Brown Tied Palmer	Brown Turkey

PLATE 6 (Continued)

Fly	Body	Ribbing	Tip	Tail	Hackle	Wing
MONTREAL	Claret Floss Silk	Gold Tinsel	Gold Tinsel	Scarlet	Claret	Brown Turkey
MONTREAL SILVER	Silver Tinsel (Flat)			Scarlet	Claret	Brown Turkey
MONTREAL YELLOW	Yellow Wool	Gold Tinsel	Gold Tinsel	Scarlet	Claret	Brown Turkey
MOOSE	Yellow Floss Silk	Gold Tinsel	Gold Tinsel	Yellow	Guinea and Yellow Intermingled	Barred Wood-Duck—Golden Pheasant Tippet Eye
MORRISON	Claret Wool	Black Silk		Black	Black	Black
MOTH-WHITE	White Chenille	Silver Tinsel	Silver Tinsel		White	White
MOTH-BROWN	Cinnamon Wool	Gold Tinsel	Gold Tinsel		Brown	Cinnamon Dark Orpington Cock
MUNRO	Green Floss	Gold Tinsel	Gold Tinsel	Scarlet and Yellow	Yellow	Scarlet with Brown Turkey Stripe
MURRAY	Black Floss	Silver Tinsel		Scarlet	Orange Tied Palmer	Brown Turkey or Pheasant
NAMELESS	Embossed Silver Tinsel			Mallard Dyed Yellow	Scarlet Tied Palmer Half Way	Light Pheasant Light Brown Mottled
NEVERSINK	Pale Yellow Floss			Gray Mallard	Yellow	Gray Mallard
NEVERWAS	Peacock Herl			Peacock Sword	Dark Green Tied Palmer	Orange
NICHOLSON	Claret Wool	Gold Tinsel		Gray Mallard Golden Pheasant Tippet	Light Blue and Claret Mixed Tied Palmer	Brown Mallard Blue Stripe
NICKERSON	Yellow Wool				Brown Tied Palmer	Gray Mallard or Teal—Scarlet and Brown
NONPAREIL	Black Chenille		Gold Tinsel		Black	
OAK	Orange Floss			Brown Turkey	Brown	Brown Turkey
OLIVE DUN	Olive Wool			Olive	Olive	Slate
OLIVE QUILL	Quill Dyed Olive			Olive	Olive	Slate

PLATE 6 (Continued)

Fly	Body	Ribbing	Tip	Tail	Hackle	Wing
OLIVE WREN	Olive Brown Wool	Silver Tinsel	Silver Tinsel	Gray Mallard	Brown Furnace Preferred	Light Brown Turkey or Pheasant
ONONDAGA	Black Silk Floss		White Chenille	Black and White Turkey Tip	Black	Black and White Turkey Tip
OQUASSAC	Claret Wool	Pink Silk	Yellow Silk Floss	Pheasant Tail	Claret—Black Chenille Collar	Pheasant Tail
ORANGE BLACK	Orange Floss	Black Silk		Black	Black	Black
ORANGE BLUE	Orange Chenille and Blue Floss	Gold Tinsel	Gold Tinsel	Golden Pheasant Tippet	Claret	Light Brown Turkey or Pheasant—Orange Stripe
ORANGTO	Gray Wool		Gold Tinsel	Scarlet and Guinea	Yellow Face and Brown Tied Palmer	Pheasant—Guinea Stripe
ORANGE MILLER	Orange Wool or Chenille	Gold Tinsel	Gold Tinsel	Scarlet	White	White
ORANGE SEDGE	Black or Dark Gray Wool	Gold Tinsel	Gold Tinsel	Orange		Orange
ORVIS-GRAY	Olive Yellow Wool	Gold Tinsel	Gold Tinsel	Blue-Gray	Blue-Gray	Black Turkey with White Tip
PAGE	Crimson or Scarlet Floss	Gold Tinsel	Gold Tinsel	Scarlet	Scarlet	Guinea with Scarlet Stripes
PALE EVENING DUN	Pale Yellow	Gold Tinsel	Gold Tinsel	Gray Mallard	Blue-Gray	Light Slate
PALE SULPHUR	Pale Yellow Wool			Pale Yellow	Pale Yellow	Yellow or Pale Yellow
PALE WATERY QUILL	Peacock Quill			Greenish Yellow (Pale)	Greenish Yellow (Pale)	Light Slate
PARK FLY	Crimson Floss	Gold Tinsel	Gold Tinsel		Black	Black
PARMACHENIE BEAU	Pale Yellow Floss	Silver Tinsel	Black Ostrich Herl	White and Scarlet	Mixed Scarlet and White	White with Scarlet Stripe Jungle Eye

PLATE 7
WET FLIES

Fly	Body	Ribbing	Tip	Tail	Hackle	Wing
PARMACHENIE BELLE	Yellow Wool	Silver Tinsel	Black Ostrich	White and Scarlet	White and Scarlet	White with Scarlet Stripe
PARSON	Gray Wool	Silver Tinsel	Orange Floss	Golden Pheasant Crest	Black Tied Palmer	Light Brown Turkey
PATHFINDER	Scarlet Wool	Gold Tinsel	Gold Tinsel		Brown Furnace	Light Slate
PARTRIDGE	½ Pale Yellow Floss ½ Silver Tinsel			Gray Partridge	Honey	Partridge Tail (Gray)
PASSADUNK	Black Floss	Green Silk Floss	Green Silk Floss	Peacock Sword	Olive Yellow Hackle	Teal
PEACOCK	Peacock Herl				Black	Slate
PEA JAY	White Chenille		Red Chenille Tag	Yellow	Orange	Scarlet with White Stripe
PEBBLE BEACH	Dark Claret Floss or Wool	Silver Tinsel	Silver Tinsel		Black Shoulder Brown Tied Palmer	Orange
PELLEE ISLAND	Scarlet Floss	Gold Tinsel	Black Chenille Tag	Black	Black	Scarlet
PERKIN'S IDEAL	Scarlet Floss	Gold Tinsel	Black Ostrich Herl	Black	Black	Gray Mallard
PERKIN'S PET	Silver Tinsel				Brown Tied Palmer	Slate
PERRY	Black Chenille		Pink Chenille Tag		Black	Black Turkey with White Tip
PETER ROSS	Yellow Floss	Gold Tinsel	Gold Tinsel	Golden Pheasant Tippet	Light Ginger	
PIKER	Orange Wool		Gold Tinsel		Brown	White
PINK WICKHAMS	Pink Floss		Gold Tinsel	Light Brown	Light Brown Tied Palmer	Dark Slate
PLATH	Bright Green Wool		Gold Tinsel	Crimson	Crimson	Gray Turkey— White Tip

· 425 ·

PLATE 7 (Continued)

Fly	Body	Ribbing	Tip	Tail	Hackle	Wing
PLUMMER	Black Ostrich Herl—Butt Yellow Floss	Gold Tinsel	Black Ostrich Herl		Yellow	Teal
POLKA	Scarlet Floss	Gold Tinsel	Gold Tinsel	Brown and White	Scarlet	Guinea
POORMAN	Brown Olive Wool		Gold Tinsel		Brown	Tan Mottled Turkey
POPE	Yellow Floss (Pale) Silk		Gold Tinsel	Golden Pheasant Tippet	Green Shoulder and Yellow Tied Palmer	Guinea
POST	Pink Floss	Gold Tinsel	Gold Tinsel	Crimson	Black Tied Palmer	Dark Brown Turkey
PORTLAND	Scarlet Floss	Gold Tinsel	Gold Tinsel	Teal	Crimson	Teal
POTOMAC	Bright Green Floss	Yellow Silk Floss			Brown	Cinnamon
POTTER	Blue Green Floss	Black Silk	Black Silk		Dark Brown	Slate
PREMIER	Scarlet Floss	Gold Tinsel	Gold Tip	Scarlet	Scarlet	White with Scarlet Stripe
PRESTON'S FANCY	Gold Tinsel			Brown	Brown	Guinea Fowl
PRIEST	Silver Tinsel			Scarlet	Gray Badger	
PRIME GNAT	Black Ostrich Herl		Orange Floss or Wool	Black	Black	Black
PROFESSOR	Yellow Floss	Gold Tinsel	Gold Tinsel	Scarlet	Brown	Gray Mallard or Teal
PROUTY	Black Chenille		Orange Chenille	Blue and Golden Pheasant Tippet	Yellow Shoulder and Brown Tied Palmer	Married Slate, Scarlet and Yellow and Gray Mallard
QUACK DOCTOR	Flat Silver Tinsel			Scarlet	Scarlet	Light Brown Turkey
QUAKER	Gray Silk Floss	Gold Tinsel	Gold Tinsel	Gray Mallard	Grizzly	Gray Turkey
QUEEN OF WATERS	Orange Silk Floss				Brown Tied Palmer	Teal or Gray Mallard

PLATE 7 (Continued)

Fly	Body	Ribbing	Tip	Tail	Hackle	Wing
RAINBOW	Light Blue Silk Floss	Gold Tinsel	White Floss	Scarlet	Grizzly	Cinnamon
RAY BERGMAN	Rusty Orange Wool			Brown Mallard	Brown	Slate
RANGELEY	Light Claret Dubbin	Gold Tinsel	Gold Tinsel	Orange	Orange Shoulder Light Claret Tied Palmer	Gray Mallard Jungle Eye
RED ASH	Red Floss	Gold Tinsel	Gold Tinsel		Blue Dun	Brown Mallard
RED FOX	Light Red Fox Under Fur		Gold	Gray Mallard	Brown	Slate
RED QUILL	Tawny Quill sometimes Red			Brown	Brown	Slate
RED SPINNER	Dark Claret Wool	Gold Tinsel	Gold Tinsel	Brown	Brown	Dark Gray
RED TAG	Peacock Herl			Scarlet Tag (Wool)	Brown Tied Palmer	
RICHARDSON	Light Blue Floss		Gold Tinsel	Brown Mallard	Black Tied Palmer	Brown Mallard
RICH WIDOW	Light Blue Floss	Gold Tinsel	Gold Tinsel	Yellow	Yellow Tied Palmer	Black
RILEY	White Wool		Black Floss Silk and Gold Tag		Brown	Teal or Gray Mallard
RIO GRANDE KING	Black Chenille		Gold Tinsel	Yellow	Brown	White
ROMAINE	Green Wool		Gold Tinsel	Guinea	Black	Guinea
ROMEYN	Green Floss Silk		Scarlet Silk Floss Tag—Gold Tinsel Tip	Barred Wood-Duck or Mandarin	Grizzly	Barred Wood-Duck or Mandarin
ROOSEVELT	½ Claret Wool ½ Yellow Wool			Brown	Orange (Dark)	Slate

PLATE 8
WET FLIES

Fly	Body	Ribbing	Tip	Tail	Hackle	Wing
ROSS	Brown Silk Floss	Gold Tinsel	Gold	Green, Golden Pheasant Tippet	Brown Furnace Tied Palmer	Peacock Herl over Brown Mallard
ROUND LAKE	Claret Wool	Gold Tinsel	Orange Chenille or Wool Tag	Blue	Orange	Brown Turkey Jungle Eye
ROYAL COACHMAN	Peacock Herl with Scarlet Floss Center		Gold if desired	Golden Pheasant Tippet	Brown	White
RUBE WOOD	White Chenille		Scarlet Floss	Teal	Brown	Gray Mallard
SABBATUS	Alternate Black and White Floss Ribbing		Scarlet Silk Floss	White and Black	Yellow	Barred Wood-Duck, Kingfisher Cheeks
SAGE	Yellow Wool	Black Silk Thread	Silver Tinsel	Scarlet, Insect Green, Gray Mallard	Orange	Dark Gray Mallard
SALLIE SCOTT	Palest Gray Floss	Orange Floss		Pheasant Tippet	Pale Yellow	Light Blue Parrot
SALTOUN	Black Silk	Gold Tinsel	Gold Tinsel	Ginger Hackle	Ginger	Slate
SANCTUARY	Dark Hares' Ear Fur	Gold Tinsel	Gold Tinsel		Brown	
SAND FLY	Gray Fur			Blue-Gray	Brown	Lt. Brown Turkey
SARANAC	Claret Floss	Gold Tinsel	Gold Tinsel	Golden Pheasant Crest	Claret	Golden Pheasant Tippet
SASSY CAT	Peacock Herl			Scarlet	Yellow	Yellow with Scarlet Cheek
SCARLET GNAT	Scarlet Wool		Gold Tinsel		Scarlet	Slate
SCARLET IBIS	Scarlet Floss	Gold Tinsel	Gold Tinsel	Scarlet	Scarlet	Scarlet
SCHAEFER	Reddish Brown Wool	Gold Tinsel	Gold Tinsel	Golden Pheasant Tippet	Grizzly	Scarlet, Dk. Blue, Bright Green
SHEENAN	Yellow Silk Floss		Pink Chenille Tag	Golden Pheasant Tippet	Black	Gray Mallard
SETH GREEN	Green Silk Floss	Yellow Silk Floss			Brown	Lt. Brown Turkey

PLATE 8 (Continued)

Fly	Body	Ribbing	Tip	Tail	Hackle	Wing
SHAD FLY	Peacock Herl—Gold Tinsel Center				Brown	Brown Turkey
SHOEMAKER	Gray Ostrich—White Silk Floss Center			Brown Mandarin Speckled	Brown	Brown Mandarin Speckled
SKOOKUM	Scarlet Chenille—Silver or Gold Center			Scarlet	Mixed Bright Green and Scarlet or Claret	Teal
SILVER BLACK	Black Floss	Silver Tinsel	Silver Tinsel	Gray Mallard	Grizzly	Light Widgeon
SILVER DOCTOR	Flat Silver Tinsel	Oval Silver Tinsel	Scarlet Floss and Gold Tinsel	Golden Pheasant Crest—Dash of Blue	Blue and Guinea	Brown Turkey, Teal, Blue, Yellow
SILVER FAIRY	Silver Tinsel			Scarlet	Guinea	Jungle Cock Eye
SILVER GHOST	Peacock Herl	Silver Tinsel if desired		Barred Mandarin	Grizzly	Silver Condor, Black Tip
SILVER-GOLD	Silver Tinsel			Golden Pheasant Crest	Badger	Golden Pheasant Crest
SILVER JUNGLE	Orange Silk Floss Shoulder—Silver Tinsel Back			Golden Pheasant Crest	Grizzly—Palmer over Orange Section	Jungle Cock Eye
SILVER STORK	Silver Tinsel			Gray Mallard	Brown	Gray Mallard
SILVER SEDGE	White Wool	Silver Tinsel	Silver Tinsel		Light Ginger Tied Palmer	Light Brown Turkey
SIR SAM DARLING	White Chenille		Black Chenille	Brown Mallard	Brown	Gray Mallard
SOLDIER PALMER	Scarlet Wool	Gold Tinsel	Gold Tinsel		Brown Tied Palmer	
SOMETHING	Black Silk Floss	Gold Tinsel	Gold Tinsel	Golden Pheasant Tippet	Black	Green, Scarlet, Purple, Yellow Married
SOO NIPI	Black Silk Floss	Gold Tinsel	Gold Tinsel	Barred Mandarin	Light Blue	White
SPENCER	Gray Fur	Gold Tinsel	Gold Tinsel, Yellow Wool Tag		Gray Badger Tied Palmer	

PLATE 8 (Continued)

Fly	Body	Ribbing	Tip	Tail	Hackle	Wing
SPLIT IBIS	Silver Tinsel			Golden Pheasant Tippet	Brown	White Scarlet, White Scarlet Married
STEBBINS	Green Wool		Gold Tinsel	Widgeon	Brown Furnace	Dk. Gray Turkey
ST. LAWRENCE	Yellow Floss	Gold Tinsel	Scarlet Tag Chenille	Scarlet	Scarlet	Light Gray Turkey—Top Brown Turkey
ST. PATRICK	Silver Tinsel			Peacock Herl	Light Blue-Gray Dun	Peacock Herl
ST. REGIS	Very Dark Gray Fur			Guinea and Golden Pheasant Tippet	Brown Tied Palmer	Brown Mallard Golden Pheasant Tippet over
STONE	Blue-Gray Fur	Yellow Silk		Blue-Gray	Blue-Gray	Very Light Gray Turkey
SECRET-POOL NO. 1 (Dr. Burke Pattern)	Peacock Herl—Gold Tinsel Center			Golden Pheasant Tippet	Claret	Slate, Jungle Eye
STRACHAN	Cinnamon Fur	Gold Tinsel	Yellow Wool Gold Tinsel	Golden Pheasant Tippet	Light Blue at Shoulder—Black Tied Palmer	Yellow, Dk. Blue Golden Pheasant Tippet
STRANGER	Dark Brown Wool	Gold Tinsel	Gold Tinsel	Brown	Brown	Brown Turkey Golden Pheasant Tippet
STURTEVANT	Black Wool	Gold or Silver Tinsel	Gold or Silver Tinsel	Scarlet, Gray Mallard	Blue-Green Tied Palmer	Jungle Body
SUNSET	Yellow Wool				Yellow	White
SWIFTWATER	Peacock Herl Orange Center			Gray Mallard	Brown	White
TEAL	White Floss Silk	Black Silk		Teal	Grizzly	Teal
TETON	Yellow Silk Floss	Gold Tinsel	Gold Tinsel	Brown	Brown	Slate, Jungle Eye

PLATE 8 (Continued)

Fly	Body	Ribbing	Tip	Tail	Hackle	Wing
THISTLE	Green Silk Floss	Gold Tinsel	Gold Tinsel	Golden Pheasant Crest, Scarlet—Golden Pheasant Tippet	Mixed Yellow and Scarlet Tied Palmer	Jungle Eye Golden Pheasant Tippet
THUNDER	Black Silk Floss	Orange Silk		Golden Pheasant Crest	Yellow	Guinea
TOMAH JOE	Gold Tinsel or Silver Tinsel		Peacock	Yellow	Mixed Scarlet and Yellow	Barred Wood-Duck or Mandarin
TOODLE BUG	1/2 Yellow Wool 1/2 Blue Silk Floss		Gold Tinsel	Gray Mallard	Brown	Brown Turkey
TELEPHONE BOX (Dr. Burke Pattern)	Orange Silk Floss or Wool	Black Silk	Peacock Herl Tag	Golden Pheasant Tippet	Brown	Brown Turkey Jungle Eye
TURKEY	Yellow Wool	Gold Tinsel	Gold Tinsel	Scarlet	Brown	Brown Turkey
TURKEY BROWN	Brown Floss	Scarlet Silk	Gold Tinsel	Scarlet	Brown	Brown Turkey
TURKEY SILVER	Scarlet Floss	Silver Tinsel	Silver Tinsel	Scarlet and Yellow	Green	Gray Turkey
TUTHILL	Purple Floss Silk	Orange Silk		Golden Pheasant Tippet	Brown	Light Brown Turkey
TYCOON	Orange Floss	Gold Tinsel	Scarlet Floss	Scarlet and Yellow	Claret Shoulder Yellow Tied Palmer	Black White, Scarlet White Married

PLATE 9
WET FLIES

Fly	Body	Ribbing	Tip	Tail	Hackle	Wing
UNDERTAKER	White Wool			Black and White	Black	White and Black
UNION	Unstripped Brown Condor			Teal	Grizzly	Teal
UTAH	Cinnamon Wool	Gold Tinsel			Ginger	Cinnamon
VANCE	Gold Tinsel			Light Mottled Turkey	Yellow	Light Mottled Turkey
VANITY	Orange Floss	Gold Tinsel			Brown Tied Palmer	White—Jungle Body Feather
VICTORIA GREEN VICTORIA REGULAR	Green Floss Blue Floss	Gold or Silver Tinsel	Gold or Silver Tinsel	Golden Pheasant Tippet	Yellow	Brown Turkey Jungle Eye
VOLUNTEER	Yellow Silk Floss	Gold Tinsel	Gold Tinsel	Scarlet	Green	Golden Pheasant Tippet
VON PATTEN	Yellow Floss			Scarlet	Brown	Barred Mandarin
WALKER	White Floss	Black Silk		Scarlet and White	Yellow	White with Gray Turkey Stripe
WALKER-HAYS	Yellow Floss Silk	Scarlet Silk Floss	Scarlet Silk Floss		Brown	Slate
WALLA-WALLA	Yellow Mohair or Wool		Gold Tinsel		Brown	Cinnamon
WANDERER	Amber Wool	Gold or Silver Tinsel	Gold or Silver Tinsel	Barred Mandarin	Badger Gray	Blue-Jay with White Tip
WARDEN	Tan Wool	Silver or Gold Tinsel	Silver or Gold Tinsel	Guinea Dyed Yellow	Ginger	Light Brown Turkey—Black Stripe
WARWICK	Peacock Herl	Gold Tinsel		Orange	Orange	Black—Peacock Herl over
WASP	Alternate Black and Brown Ostrich Herl		Orange Floss		Brown	Tan—Black, Tan

PLATE 9 (Continued)

Fly	Body	Ribbing	Tip	Tail	Hackle	Wing
WATERS (White at Head)	Peacock Herl				Black	Light Gray Turkey
WATSON'S FANCY	½ Scarlet Silk Floss—½ Black Silk Floss	Gold Tinsel		Golden Pheasant Tippet	Black	Black
WEBBS	Very Pale Green Wool	Gold Tinsel	Gold Tinsel	Grouse	Pale Yellow	Green Parrot
WHIRLING BLUE DUN	Blue-Gray Fur	Gold Tinsel	Gold Tinsel	Blue-Gray	Blue-Gray	Dark Slate
WHIRLING DUN	Blue-Gray Fur			Brown	Brown	Slate
WHITE HACKLE	White Floss Silk	Black Silk or Silver Tinsel Optional			White	
WHITE JUNGLE	White Wool		Scarlet Tip	Amherst Pheasant Tippet	White	White Jungle
WHITE KING	White Silk Floss	Gold Tinsel	Gold Tinsel	Orange	Orange Shoulder White Tied Palmer	White
WHITE MILLER	White Silk Floss	Silver Tinsel	Silver Tinsel		White	White
MONTREAL WHITE TIP	Claret Wool	Gold Tinsel	Gold Tinsel	Scarlet	Claret	Black Turkey White Tip
WHITE WATER	White Ostrich Herl—Green Silk Center			Amherst Pheasant Tippet	Light Blue Gray	Grouse
WHITNEY	Tan Fur	Gold Tinsel	Gold Tinsel	Yellow	Orange at Shoulder—Brown Tied Palmer	Turkey—White Tip
WICKHAM'S FANCY	Gold Tinsel			Brown Hackle Tips	Brown Tied Palmer	Slate
WIDOW	Black Silk Floss	White Silk			Black	Black with White Stripe
WILDERNESS	Green Wool	Gold Tinsel	Silver or Gold Tinsel		Brown Tied Palmer	Dark Red over Brown
WILLOW	Olive-Gray Silk Floss		Gold Tinsel		Brown	Dark Slate

PLATE 9 (Continued)

Fly	Body	Ribbing	Tip	Tail	Hackle	Wing
WILSON	Orange Wool		Gold Tinsel	Golden Pheasant Tippet	Orange	Gray Mallard
WILSON ANT	Medium Brown Floss		Peacock Herl Tag		Brown	Pheasant Wing
WINTERS	Claret Floss Silk			Brown Mallard or Light Gray Mallard	Brown Furnace or Dun	Brown Mallard
WITCH GOLD	Light Gray Silk Floss	Gold Tinsel or Yellow Floss Silk	Gold Tinsel	Scarlet	Honey Badger	
WITCH SILVER	Gray Silk Floss	Silver Tinsel	Silver Tinsel	Scarlet	Gray Badger	
WITCHER	Black Wool	Gold or Silver Tinsel	Yellow Tag or Gold Tinsel	Golden Pheasant Crest	Black Tied Palmer	Gray Mallard Stripe over Slate
WOOD DUCK	Bright Green Wool	Gold Tinsel	Gold Tinsel	Yellow	Bright Green	Barred Wood-Duck
WOOD IBIS	Dark Claret Wool			Orange-Brown Mallard	Orange Tied Palmer	Iridescent Black
WOPPINGER	Gray Silk Floss			Blue-Gray	Dark Grizzly Tied Palmer	Slate
WREN	Light Gray Floss	Yellow Silk	Yellow Silk	Gray Mallard	Brown	Brown Mallard
YANKEE	Light Blue Floss Silk	Gold or Silver Tinsel	Gold or Silver Tinsel	White	Scarlet	White
YELLOW COACHMAN	Peacock Herl Yellow Center		Gold Tinsel		Brown	White
YELLOW DRAKE	Yellow Floss Silk	Gold Tinsel	Gold Tinsel	Black	Yellow	Gray Mallard Dyed Yellow
YELLOW DUN	Gray Fur	Yellow Silk			Yellow	
YELLOW SALLY	Yellow Floss Silk	Gold Tinsel	Gold Tinsel	Yellow	Yellow	Brown Mallard
YELLOW SPINNER	Yellow Chenille		Gold Tinsel	Yellow	Scarlet	Yellow
ZULU	Peacock Herl		Scarlet Wool Tag		Black Tied Palmer	Black

PLATE 10

WET FLIES—STREAMERS AND NYMPHS

Fly	Body	Ribbing	Tip	Tail	Hackle	Wing
FONTINALIS FIN "Phil Armstrong"	Orange Wool	Gold Tinsel		White Hackle Wisps	Furnace	White and Gray Stripe Married to and Topping Orange
BERGMAN FONTINALIS "Phil Armstrong"	Alternate Ribs of Gray and Orange Wool			White, Gray and Orange Married 2 Sections	Dark Blue-Gray	White and Gray Stripe Married to and Topping Orange
GRASSHOPPER	Yellow Wool Tied to Overhang Hook			Scarlet Hackle Wisps	Brown Sparse Palmer	Light Brown Turkey
BOB WILSON (Yellow Head)	Copper Tinsel			Golden Pheasant Crest	Black	Barred Mandarin
GRIFFEN	Peacock Herl			Scarlet Hackle Wisps	Clipped Grizzly Tied Palmer and Clipped	A Few Long Wisps of Grizzly Hackle
GRAY SQUIRREL SILVER R.B.	Silver Tinsel	Silver Tinsel if desired			Scarlet Tied in Whole—Not Wound Around Hook	Gray Squirrel Hair—Grizzly Hackle—Jungle Cock Eye
RED SQUIRREL GOLD R.B.	Gold Tinsel	Gold Tinsel if desired			Scarlet Tied in Whole—Not Wound Around Hook	Fox Squirrel Hair Honey Badger Hackle—Jungle Cock Eye
BELL SPECIAL	Silver Tinsel				Scarlet Tied in Whole—Not Wound Around Hook	Brown Ostrich White Ostrich Jungle Eye
JESS WOOD May be tied on single hook	Silver Tinsel			Scarlet	Furnace	Yanosh Tied Streamer Jungle Eye
R.B. NYMPH No. 1	Buff Wool, Brown Enamel on Back	Black Linen Ribbing		Guinea Fowl Also Feelers from Body Feathers	Guinea Fowl Legs from Wing Feather	

PLATE 10 (Continued)

Fly	Body	Ribbing	Tip	Tail	Hackle	Wing
R.B. NYMPH No. 2	Rust Wool	Gold Tinsel		Guinea Fowl Also Feelers from Body Feathers	Guinea Fowl Legs from Wing Feather	
R.B. NYMPH No. 5	Gray Wool	Gold Tinsel		Guinea Fowl Also Feelers from Body Feathers	Guinea Fowl Legs from Wing Feather	
R.B. NYMPH No. 6	Dark Olive Wool	Gold Tinsel		Guinea Fowl Dyed Olive from Body Feathers	Guinea Fowl Legs from Wing Feather	
R.B. CADDIS	White or Light Gray Chenille		Black Chenille or Ostrich Tag	Peacock Herl Also Peacock Herl Feelers		
LEAF ROLLER WORM	Cork Painted Insect Green					
HEWITT NYMPH No. 1	White, Brown Back	Black		Black	Black	
HEWITT NYMPH No. 2	Deep Yellow Brown Back	Black		Black	Black	
HEWITT NYMPH No. 3	Gray, Brown Back	Black		Black	Black	
WATER CRICKET	Pink Silk Floss			Black Hackle Wisps	Black Tied Palmer and Clipped	
ACKLE SHRIMP	Tan Colored Rubber	Segmented by Bucktail		Bucktail		
ED BURKE NYMPH	Black Wool Heavy at Head	Gold Tinsel Back End of Body	Gold Tinsel	Black Hackle Wisps	Black	Turkey Tied Down to Cover Wool Bunch on Top
R.B. TRANSLUCENT AMBER NYMPH	Amber Composition Flattened	Black Silk		Guinea Fowl Body Feather Wisps	Badger	
R.B. TRANSLUCENT RED NYMPH	Tango Composition Flattened, Amber Under	Black Silk		Brown Hackle Wisps	Brown	

PLATE 10 (Continued)

Fly	Body	Ribbing	Tip	Tail	Hackle	Wing
R.B. TRANSLUCENT GREEN NYMPH	Dark Green Composition, Amber Under	Black Silk		Olive Dyed Guinea Body Wisps	Brown Olive	
R.B. TRANSLUCENT BROWN OLIVE	Brown Olive Composition, Amber Under	Black Silk		Unstripped Brown Quills from Mandarin Duck	Grizzly	
KOL-RAY CADDIS	Very Pale Yellow Cellophane or Composition Tapered				Guinea Body Feather Wisps	
STRAWMAN NYMPH	Deer Body, hair tied to stick out from book and clipped	Yellow Floss Silk		Gray Mallard		

PLATE 11
STEEL HEAD AND LAND LOCKED SALMON

Fly	Head	Body	Ribbing	Hackle	Tail	Wing
BLACK COACHMAN	Black	Black Chenille		Brown		White Bucktail
BUCKTAIL COACH-MAN	Black	Peacock Herl		Brown	Crimson or Scarlet	White Bucktail Jungle Eye
BUCKTAIL McGINTY	Black	Alternate Black and Yellow Chenille		Brown	Mixed Scarlet and Gray Mallard	White and Brown Bucktail
CARSON ROYAL COACHMAN	Black	Peacock Herl with Scarlet Floss Center		Brown	Crimson	White Bucktail Jungle Eye
CUMMINGS	Black	Shoulder Claret Wool—End Yellow Wool or Floss	Gold Tinsel	Claret or Deep Wine		Brown Bucktail Jungle Eye
GIBSON GIRL	Black	Orange Wool	Gold Tinsel Also Tip	Dark Brown Bucktail	Golden Pheasant Tippet	Brown Bucktail Jungle Eye
GOLDEN DEMON	Black	Gold Tinsel Flat	Round Gold Tinsel	Orange	Yellow	Brown Bucktail Jungle Eye
GRAY HACKLE YELLOW BODY	Black	Yellow Floss	Gold Tinsel and Tip	Grizzly	Crimson	Jungle Eye
KATE	Black	Scarlet Wool	Gold Tinsel Also Tip	Yellow	Golden Pheasant Crest	Married Red, Yellow and Blue Brown Turkey Gray Mallard Jungle Eye
MARCH BROWN	Black	Rabbit Fur	Yellow Silk	Brown Partridge	Crimson	Light Brown Turkey Jungle Cock Eye
PARMACHENIE BELLE	Black	Yellow Wool Peacock Herl Tag	Gold Tinsel	Scarlet and White	Scarlet and White	Scarlet and White Bucktail
RAIL BIRD	Black	Dark Claret Wool		Yellow Throat Claret Tied Palmer	Yellow	Gray Mallard
SAWTOOTH R.B.	Black	Orange Chenille	Gold Tinsel	Guinea Fowl	Guinea Fowl	Fox Squirrel Jungle Eye

PLATE 11 (Continued)

Fly	Head	Body	Ribbing	Hackle	Tail	Wing
SURVEYOR R.B.	Black	½ Yellow Chenille ½ Red Tinsel	Red Tinsel Continued Through Chenille	Grizzly and Brown	White and Brown Bucktail	
UMPQUA	Black	2/3 Scarlet Chenille—1/3 Yellow Wool	Silver Tinsel Continued Through Chenille	Brown	White Bucktail	White and Scarlet Bucktail
WELL'S SPECIAL	Black	Peacock Herl with Gold Tinsel Tip		Greenish Yellow	Dark Claret	Slate—Black Pelee Stripe—Blue, Yellow & Scarlet Strips on Top Jungle
ANSON SPECIAL	Black	Silver Tinsel	Peacock Herl	Scarlet	Scarlet	White Bucktail Teal Cheek Jungle Cock Eye
BLACK BIRD	Black	Black Silk or Wool	Gold Tinsel and Gold Tip	Black Bucktail		Black Bucktail Jungle Eye
BROWN AND WHITE BUCKTAIL	Black	Silver Tinsel		Crimson	Crimson	Brown Bucktail Topping White Bucktail
BROWN AND SCARLET BUCKTAIL	Black	Scarlet Floss	Gold Tinsel	Yellow		Brown Bucktail Jungle Eye
EDSON TIGER DARK	Black	Yellow Chenille		Scarlet	Guinea or Barred Mandarin	Brown Bucktail Jungle Eye
EDSON TIGER LIGHT	Yellow	Peacock Herl		Scarlet Gill Feather	Barred Mandarin	Honey Bucktail Jungle Eye
FRANCES	Black	Alternate Scarlet and White Chenille	Gold Tinsel Crossed	Brown and White Bucktail Intermingled	Golden Pheasant Tippet	Sparse White Bucktail, Golden Pheasant Tippet Cheeks
JEAN	Black	Copper Tinsel Flat		Yellow	Orange	Blue-Gray Bucktail—Orange Bucktail Stripe Jungle Body Feather and Eye
MacGREGOR	Black	Orange Chenille	Silver Tinsel Also Tip	Grizzly	Golden Pheasant Crest	Gray Squirrel Jungle Eye

PLATE 12

ADDITIONAL STREAMERS AND BUCKTAILS

Fly	Body	Ribbing	Wing	Tip	Hackle	Tail
SCOTT SPECIAL	Light Brown Wool	Silver Tinsel	Yellow Bucktail Jungle Eye	Silver Tinsel	Yellow	Scarlet
SUMMER'S GOLD	Gold Tinsel		Brown Bucktail Topping White Bucktail		Scarlet	Golden Pheasant Tippet
WESLEY SPECIAL	Silver Tinsel	Round Silver Tinsel	Slate Bucktail Topping White Bucktail Jungle Eye		Black	Golden Pheasant Tippet
GOOTENBURG'S JERSEY MINNOW (Peacock Herl Head)	Gold Tinsel		Dark Honey Badger Hackle Feather		Ginger or Brown Mixed with Pink	Golden Pheasant Tippet
DR. BURKE	Silver Tinsel	Round Silver Tinsel	White Hackle Feather Jungle Eye	Gold Tinsel	Yellow	Peacock Sword
OPTIC BUCKTAIL (Painted Eye Head)	Silver Tinsel (Flat)	Round Silver Tinsel	Brown or Black Bucktail over White Bucktail Jungle Eye			Scarlet
BLUE DEVIL	Gold Tinsel		Grizzly Hackle Feather with Blue Peacock & Kingfisher Cheek		Grizzly, Golden Pheasant Crest Added Underneath	Golden Pheasant Breast
CAPRA STREAMER	Silver Tinsel Scarlet Sac About 2/3 from Front	Round Silver Ribbing	Light Slate Capra Topping Yellow Capra Jungle Eye		White Capra Tied Same Length as Wing	
CHIEF NEEDABEH	Scarlet Floss	Silver Tinsel	Orange over Yellow, Hackles Tied Streamer Jungle Eye	Silver Tinsel	Yellow and Scarlet Mixed	
ESTELLE (Gootenburg)	Alternate Scarlet and White Chenille	Gold Tinsel Wound Opposite to Chenille Stripes	White Hackle Tied Streamer Scarlet Cheek	Gold Tinsel	White	Scarlet

PLATE 12 (Continued)

Fly	Body	Ribbing	Wing	Tip	Hackle	Tail
FRASER	Green Wool	Silver Tinsel	White Hackle Streamer with Short Yellow over Jungle Eye	Orange Chenille Tag		
BLACK GHOST	Black Wool or Floss	Silver Tinsel	White Hackle Tied Streamer Jungle Eye		Golden Pheasant Crest	Golden Pheasant Crest
GRAY GHOST	Orange Floss	Silver Tinsel	Blue-Gray Hackles Tied Streamer Silver Pheasant Cheek, Long Golden Pheasant Crest, Jungle Eye		Peacock Herl White Bucktail Tied Streamer	
LADY GHOST	Silver Tinsel		Honey Badger Hackle Tied Streamer, Brown Pheasant Cheek Golden Pheasant Tied Streamer and Low Jungle Eye		Peacock Herl and White Bucktail Tied Streamer	
NANCY	Copper Tinsel	Silver Tinsel	Green Hackle Long, Orange Short, Both Streamers Light Brown, Mottled Cheek	Silver Tinsel	Yellow Tied Under Only	
SPENCER BAY	Silver Tinsel	Silver Tinsel (Round)	Honey Badger Streamer, Brown Pheasant Cheek, Jungle Eye		Mixed Light Blue and Yellow	Golden Pheasant Tippet
THREE RIVERS	Claret Wool Body	Wide Silver Tinsel	Grizzly Streamer Jungle Eye	Wide Silver Tinsel	Scarlet	Teal
YORK'S KENNEBAGO	Silver Tinsel	Round Silver Tinsel	Honey Badger Jungle Eye	Scarlet Floss Tag 2/3 from Eye	Scarlet	

PLATE 12 (Continued)

Fly	Body	Ribbing	Wing	Tip	Hackle	Tail
MARABOU (White)	Silver Tinsel	Silver Tinsel (Round)	White Marabou Peacock Herl on Top (5 Strands) Jungle Eye		Scarlet Under Only	
MARABOU (Yellow)	Silver Tinsel	Silver Tinsel (Round)	Yellow Marabou Brown Ostrich Herl on Top Jungle Eye		Scarlet	

PLATE 13
SOME SPECIAL DRY FLIES

Fly	Body	Ribbing	Tip	Tail	Hackle	Wing
AU-SABLE	Blue-Gray Hard Body			Light Blue-Gray	Light Blue-Gray	Barred Mandarin or White Tipped Starling
BLACK ANGEL	Black Hard Body			Black Hackle Wisps	Black	Black Hackle Tips
BROWN OLIVE	Brown Olive Hard Body			Brown Olive Dyed	Brown Olive Dyed	Blue-Gray Hackle Tips
GRAY TRANSLUCENT	Yellow Cellophane or Composition			Grizzly (Barred Rock)	Grizzly	Grizzly Hackle Tips
GRIZZLY-TANGO	Tango Cellophane or Composition			Grizzly Hackle Wisps	Grizzly	Grizzly Hackle Tips
HONEY DUN	Cream Cellophane, Composition, Wool or Fur			Honey Hackle Wisps	Honey	Mandarin Speckled
LIGHT CAHILL TRANSLUCENT	Deep Yellow Body, Cellophane or Composition			Ginger	Ginger	Mandarin Speckled
MARCH BROWN AMERICAN	Brown Cellophane or Composition	Gold Tinsel		Brown Hackle Wisps	Brown	Brown Mallard
PINK LADY TRANSLUCENT	Pink Translucent Composition			Brown Hackle Wisps	Brown	Dark Slate Hackle Tips
TANGO TRIUMPHANT	Tango Cellophane or Composition Body			Brown	Brown	Ginger
WOODRUFF (Usually Tied Spent)	Green Cellophane or Wool			Gray Mallard	Brown	Grizzly Hackle Tips
MULTI-COLOR VARIANT R.B.	Gold Tinsel			Dark Badger or Black, Ginger & White Mixed	White at Eye Dk. Ginger Center, Black Rear	Grizzly Hackle Tips

Calif.

PLATE 13 (Continued) Dry

Fly	Body	Ribbing	Tip	Tail	Hackle	Wing
LIGHT MULTI-COLOR VARIANT	Silver Tinsel			Red Mixed Grizzly Natural	Red Mixed Grizzly Natural	Grizzly Hackle Tips
MULTI-COLOR VARIANT—No. 2	Black Silk			Blue-Gray, Red & Black Intermingled	Blue-Gray, Red and Black Intermingled	Grizzly Hackle Tips
BADGER VARIANT	Peacock Herl			Badger	Badger	Grizzly Hackle Tips
BROWN VARIANT	Gold Tinsel			Brown Hackle Wisps	Brown	Grizzly Hackle Tips
FURNACE VARIANT	Blue-Gray Ostrich Herl			Furnace Brown Hackle Wisps	Furnace	Grizzly Hackle Tips
GINGER VARIANT	Cream Silk Floss, Wool or Cellophane			Ginger Hackle Wisps	Ginger	Grizzly Hackle Tips
GRIZZLY VARIANT	Tango Cellophane or Light Claret Silk Floss			Grizzly Hackle Wisps	Grizzly	Brown Hackle Tips
BLUE VARIANT	Gold Tinsel			Grizzly Hackle Wisps Dyed Blue-Gray	Grizzly Hackle Wisps Dyed Blue-Gray	Grizzly Hackle Tips
ADAMS	Blue-Gray Fur			Grizzly	Mixed Grizzly and Rhode Island Red	Grizzly Tied Either Spent or Upright
COFFIN	White Silk Floss			Pheasant or Black	Badger—Very dark & speckly if possible	Black Hackle Tips
SPENT BLUE	Quill Body			Blue-Gray Hackle Wisps	Blue-Gray	Grizzly Hackle Tips Spent
SPENT OLIVE	Unstripped Condor Dyed Olive			Olive Hackle Wisps	Olive	Grizzly Dyed Blue-Gray Tied Spent
SPENT YELLOW	Pale Yellow Wool Body			Black Hackle Wisps	Pale Yellow	Badger Hackle Tips, Dyed Yellow Tied Spent

Calif—

PLATE 13 (Continued) Dry

Fly	Body	Ribbing	Tip	Tail	Hackle	Wing
GRAY WULFF	Blue-Gray Fur			Brown Bucktail	Blue-Gray	Brown Bucktail
ROYAL WULFF	Peacock Herl Scarlet Silk Floss Center			Brown Bucktail	Brown	White Bucktail
WHITE WULFF	Cream Color Fur, Wool or Something of that Nature			White Bucktail	Light Badger	White Bucktail
GREEN MAY	Cream Body of Cellophane, Composition or Silk Floss	Gold Tinsel	Gold Tinsel	Dark Blue-Gray	Grizzly Dyed Light Blue-Gray	Gray Mallard Dyed Pale Green
YELLOW MAY	Cream Cast Cellophane or Composition or Cream Floss Silk			Ginger Hackle Wisps	Mixed Ginger and Grizzly	Gray Mallard Dyed Yellow
FAN WING ROYAL COACHMAN	Peacock Herl Scarlet Silk Floss Center			Golden Pheasant Tippet	Brown	White Mandarin or Domestic Duck
FAN WING SILVER COACHMAN	Peacock Herl, Silver Tinsel Center			Blue-Gray Hackle Wisps	Blue-Gray	Light Blue-Gray Dyed Mandarin Fan Wings
GREEN FAN WING COACHMAN	Peacock Herl Green Silk Floss Center			Green Hackle Wisps	Green	Dyed Green Mandarin Fan Wings
GINGER or PETRIE'S ROYAL COACHMAN	Peacock Herl Pale Yellow Silk Floss Center			Ginger Hackle Wisps	Ginger	White Mandarin or Domestic Duck
McSNEEK	Black Dyed Peacock Herl, Silver Tinsel Center			Black Hackle Wisps	Black	White Fan Wings

Calif.

PLATE 14
DRY FLIES

Calif —

Fly	Body	Ribbing	Tip	Tail	Hackle	Wing
BADGER BIVISIBLE				Badger Hackle Tips	Badger Tied Palmer, White Hackle at Eye	
BLACK BIVISIBLE				Black Hackle Tips	Black Tied Palmer White Hackle at Eye	
BROWN BIVISIBLE				Brown Hackle Tips	Brown Hackle Tied Palmer, White Hackle at Eye	
BROWN AND GRAY BIVISIBLE				Mixed Brown and Blue-Gray Hackle Wisps	Mixed Brown and Blue-Gray Tied Palmer, White at Eye	
BLUE BIVISIBLE				Blue-Gray Hackle Tips	Blue-Gray Hackle Tied Palmer White at Eye	
GRAY BIVISIBLE				Grizzly Hackle Tips	Grizzly Hackle Tied Palmer White at Eye	
PINK LADY BIVISIBLE	Gold Tinsel			Ginger Hackle Wisps	Ginger Hackle Tied Palmer Pale Yellow or Pale Green Hackle at Eye	
BLACK SPIDER	Gold Tinsel			Black Hackle Wisps	Black	
BLUE SPIDER	Gold Tinsel			Blue-Gray Hackle Wisps	Blue-Gray	
BROWN SPIDER				Brown Hackle Wisps	Brown Tied Palmer, White at Eye	
GINGER FURNACE SPIDER	Gold Tinsel			Ginger Furnace Hackle Wisps	Ginger Furnace	

Calif —

PLATE 14 (Continued) Dry

Fly	Body	Ribbing	Tip	Tail	Hackle	Wing
ORANGE FISH HAWK	Orange Floss	Gold Tinsel	Gold Tinsel		Badger Light	
AUGUST DUN	Light Brown Floss	Yellow Silk	Yellow Silk	Dark Brown	Dark Brown	Pheasant or Light Brown Turkey
BLACK GNAT	Black Chenille			Black Hackle Wisps—Some Prefer Without Tail	Black	Slate
BLUE QUILL	Gray Peacock Quill			Blue-Gray Hackle Wisps	Blue-Gray	Slate or Blue-Gray
B.V. BOOTH	Olive Wool	Gold Tinsel			Brown	Dark Woodchuck Tied Flat Along Hook
BLUE DUN	Blue-Gray Fur			Blue-Gray Hackle Wisps	Blue-Gray	Blue-Gray or Slate
BRADLEY	Blue-Gray Fur			Brown Hackle Wisps	Brown	Gray Mallard
BRONZE QUILL	Dark Quill			Dark Flame Hackle Wisps	Dark Flame (Bronze)	Gray Speckled
CADDIS, LIGHT	Olive-Yellow Wool or Mohair			Brown	Brown Tied Palmer	Slate or Blue-Gray
CAMPBELL'S FANCY	Gold Tinsel			Golden Pheasant Crest	Furnace	Gray Mallard
CAHILL	Blue-Gray Fur		Gold Tinsel if desired	Mandarin Speckled	Brown	Mandarin (Speckled)
CAHILL, GOLD BODY	Gold Tinsel			Brown Hackle Wisps	Brown	Mandarin Speckled
CAHILL, LIGHT	Creamy White Fur			Mandarin Speckled Light Shade if possible	Ginger	Mandarin Speckled Light Shade If Possible—Not Important
CAHILL QUILL	Peacock Quill			Brown	Brown	Mandarin Speckled
LIGHT CAHILL QUILL	Light Colored Imported Condor Quills or Peacock if desired			Mandarin Speckled	Ginger	Mandarin Speckled

PLATE 14 (Continued)

Fly	Body	Ribbing	Tip	Tail	Hackle	Wing
COTY, DARK	Blue-Gray Fur Mixed with a Mite of Scarlet Wool			Dark Blue-Gray Hackle Wisps	Dark Blue-Gray	Dark Blue-Gray Hackle Tips
COTY, LIGHT	Blue-Gray Fur Mixed with a Mite of Scarlet Wool			Light Blue-Gray Hackle Wisps	Light Blue-Gray	Light Blue-Gray Hackle Tips
COACHMAN	Peacock Herl			Brown Hackle Wisps if desired	Brown	White
DARK COACHMAN LEAD WING	Peacock Herl			Brown Hackle Wisps if desired	Brown	Dark Slate
COCHY QUILL	Peacock or Condor Quill			Cochy-Gondhu	Cochy-Gondhu	Mandarin Speckled
GINGER QUILL	Light Colored Imported Condor Quill			Ginger	Ginger	Mandarin Speckled or Blue-Gray Last my choice
GORDON	Golden Floss Silk	Gold Tinsel		Mandarin Speckled	Badger	Mandarin Speckled
QUILL GORDON	Peacock Quill			Bronze Blue-Gray	Bronze Blue-Gray	Mandarin Speckled
GRAY DRAKE	White Silk Floss	Black Silk		Teal	Light Grizzly	Teal

Calif

Calif —

(Page 400 #28)

PLATE 15

DRY FLIES

Fly	Body	Ribbing	Tip	Tail	Hackle	Wing
GRAY QUILL	Peacock Quill			Dark Grizzly Hackle Wisps	Dark Grizzly or Blue-Gray	Gray Mallard or Teal
G. R. HARE'S EAR	Fur from Hare's Ear	Gold Tinsel	Gold Tinsel	Brown Hackle Wisps		Slate
DARK HENDRICKSON	Dark Blue-Gray Fur			Speckled Mandarin Wisps	Dark Blue-Gray	Speckled Mandarin
LIGHT HENDRICKSON	Cream Colored Fur			Speckled Mandarin	Light Gray	Speckled Mandarin
HOUSATONIC QUILL	Quill			Speckled Mandarin	Gray Badger	Speckled Mandarin
IRON BLUE DUN	Blue-Gray Fur		Scarlet Floss Silk	Furnace Hackle Wisps	Furnace	Dark Blue Slate
LADY or FEMALE BEAVERKILL	Gray Silk Floss		Yellow Chenille Tag or Egg Sack	Gray Mallard	Brown	Slate
MALLARD QUILL	Peacock Quill			Dark Brown Hackle Wisps	Dark Brown	Brown Mallard
MOSQUITO	Dark Peacock Quill			Dark Grizzly	Dark Grizzly	Dark Grizzly Hackle Tips
McGINTY	Alternate Stripes Yellow & Black Chenille			Gray Mallard or Teal	Brown	Black Turkey with White Tip
OLIVE DUN	Fur or Unstripped Condor Quill Dyed Dark Olive			Olive Hackle Wisps	Olive	Speckled Mandarin or Slate
OLIVE QUILL	Peacock Quill			Olive Hackle Wisps	Olive	Slate
PALE EVENING DUN	Greenish Yellow Wool			Pale Blue-Gray	Pale Blue-Gray	Slate or Blue-Gray
PARSON'S DUN	Brown Olive Wool Body			Honey Grizzly Tail	Honey Grizzly	Gray Mallard
PETRIE'S EGG SACK	Gray Wool or Fur Body		Pale Green Chenille Egg Sack	Speckled Mandarin	Medium Blue-Gray	Speckled Mandarin

Calif—

PLATE 15 (Continued)

Fly	Body	Ribbing	Tip	Tail	Hackle	Wing
RAMAPO SPECIAL "Gootenburg"	Red Fox Fur Cream			Gray Mallard	Mixed Ginger and Blue-Gray	Gray Mallard Clipped Short
ROYAL COACHMAN	Green Peacock Herl, Scarlet Floss Center		Gold Tinsel if desired	Golden Pheasant Tippets	Brown	White
R.B. FOX	Gray Fox Fur			Honey Hackle Wisps	Mixed Honey and Ginger	Gray Mallard
R.B. BLUE FOX	Blue-Gray Fur			Grizzly Hackle Wisps	Mixed Grizzly and Blue-Gray	Grizzly Hackle Tips
RED FOX BEAVER-KILL	Blue-Gray Fur from Red Fox	Gold Tinsel	Gold Tinsel	Ginger	Ginger Faced with Pale Blue-Gray	
RED FOX STODDARD	Cream Fur from Red Fox			Speckled Mandarin	Honey	Speckled Mandarin
SQUIRREL TAIL	Blue-Gray Fur	Gold Tinsel	Gold Tinsel		Grizzly	Squirrel Tail Tied Flat Along Hook
TUP'S INDIS-PENSABLE	Yellow Floss Silk with Pink Wool Tuft at Shoulder			Ginger	Ginger Faced with White	
TURNER'S GREEN	Pale Green Wool			Dark Honey	Grizzly Dyed Blue Dun or Badger	Gray Mallard Dyed Light Green
WESTBROOK	Pink Wool	Black Silk		Dark Honey	Dark Honey	Gray Mallard
WHIRLING BLUE DUN	Blue-Gray Fur or Wool			Brown Hackle Wisps	Brown	Dark Slate
WILL'S SPINNER	Unstripped Condor Dyed Yellow			Black Hackle Wisps	Cream White	Gray Mallard or Speckled Wood Duck
WORTENDYKE	Smoky Gray-Brown Fur			Black Hackle Wisps	Black	Gray Mallard or Speckled Mandarin
YELLOW CREEK	Light Gray Ostrich Herl			Black Hackle Wisps	Light Blue-Gray	Badger Hackle Tips
YELLOW MALLARD	Yellow Wool or Fur			Gray Mallard	Ginger	Gray Mallard

Calif

PLATE 15 (Continued)

	Body	Ribbing	Tip	Tail	Hackle	Wing
	Yellow Floss	Black Silk		Yellow	Honey Badger	Gray Mallard Dyed Yellow
...ER—No. 1	Copper or Silver			Sparse Blue-Gray	Sparse Blue-Gray	
...LWATER—No. 2	Copper			Sparse Light Ginger	Sparse Light Ginger	
STILLWATER—No. 3	Copper or Gold			Sparse Furnace or Black	Sparse Furnace or Black	
COOPER-BUG	Green Wool or Floss Silk	Gold Tinsel	Gold Tinsel	Scarlet Hackle Wisps	Gray Squirrel Tuft at Head	Gray Squirrel Tied Spent

A NOTE ON THE TYPE IN
WHICH THIS BOOK IS SET

This book is set in Garamond, a modern rendering of the type first cut in the sixteenth century by Claude Garamond (1510–1561). He was a pupil of Geofroy Tory and is believed to have based his letters on the Venetian models, although he introduced a number of important differences, and it is to him that we owe the letter which we know as Old Style. He gave to his letters a certain elegance and a feeling of movement which won for their creator an immediate reputation and the patronage of the French King, Francis I.

This book was printed and bound
by the Kingsport Press, Inc.,
Kingsport, Tennessee

Fly

YELLOW SPINNER

STILLWAT

STII